JAN CHRISTIAN SMUTS

The Conscience of a
South African

JAN CHRISTIAN SMUTS
The Conscience of a
South African

Kenneth Ingham

St. Martin's Press · New York

First published in the United States of America in 1986

Printed in Great Britain

Library of Congress Cataloging-in-Publication Data

Ingham, Kenneth.
    Jan Christian Smuts, the conscience of a South
African.

    Bibliography: p.
    Includes index.
    1. Smuts, Jan Christian, 1870–1950.   2. Statesman—
South Africa—Biography.   3. South Africa—Politics
and government—1909–1948.   I. Title.
DT779.8.S6I54   1986   968.05'092'4   86-6507
ISBN 0-312-43997-0

To Elizabeth

Contents

Illustrations

Smuts as State Attorney of the South African Republic, 1898 (BBC Hulton Picture Library)

Smuts on commando in Cape Colony during the Anglo-Boer War, 1902 (Central Archives Depot, Pretoria)

Smuts with his wife and daughter, 1904 (United Party Archives, UNISA, Pretoria)

J. X. Merriman (Sibbert Collection, University of Cape Town Libraries)

Louis Botha (Sibbert Collection, University of Cape Town Libraries)

Smuts with his cabinet, 1921 (BBC Hulton Picture Library)

J. B. M. Hertzog (BBC Hulton Picture Library)

Sir Patrick Duncan (Foster Scrapbook, University of Cape Town Libraries)

Jan and Isie Smuts at the laying of the foundation stone of the Voortrekker Monument, Pretoria, 1938 (*Sunday Times* Library Prints)

Houses of Parliament, Cape Town (BBC Hulton Picture Library)

D. F. Malan (BBC Hulton Picture Library)

Smuts with Winston Churchill, Mrs Churchill and his son, 1943 (Trustees of the Imperial War Museum)

Smuts as Chancellor of Cambridge University, 1949 (*Sunday Times* Library Prints)

The unveiling of a memorial to Smuts in Parliament Square, London, 1956 (BBC Hulton Picture Library)

Statue of Smuts, Botanical Gardens, Cape Town (*The Star*, 26 May 1964)

Acknowledgements

My thanks are especially due to the British Academy which provided generous financial assistance for a research visit to South Africa and to the University of Bristol which also contributed financially to the visit. In South Africa itself the staff of the National Archives in Pretoria were at all times courteous and helpful and I am indebted to them for their efforts on my behalf while I consulted the magnificent collection of Smuts's correspondence housed in the archives. In the archives section of the University of Cape Town Library I also received unstinting help, in particular from Miss E. Eberhard whose suggestions about possible source material were invaluable. In a very real sense my book owes its origins to Mrs Raemonde Simkins of the University of Cape Town Library, who sought out the newspaper comments about Smuts's statue in the Botanical Gardens in Cape Town which confirmed me in my opinion that a reappraisal of Smuts was needed. Many others in South Africa were helpful to me and in singling out Mr and Mrs J. C. (Jannie) Smuts, Miss Mell Hendry and Mr Ralph Hardingham, member of the Union parliament, I do so because their kindness and hospitality was most generous. They cannot, however, be held responsible for any of the views expressed in this book. To my students in the History Department of Bristol I am also grateful, because with them I have discussed the career of Smuts almost endlessly it seems and their views have opened new avenues of enquiry for me. Finally, my greatest debt is to my wife who, as research assistant in South Africa and as typist and critic throughout, has sustained me constantly.

Introduction

In the Western world today to speak of South Africa is to speak about apartheid, the policy of separate development for people of different races. It is a policy which requires non-Whites to accept a subordinate role and which permits Africans to enjoy the rights of citizenship only in restricted areas designated as homelands. African complaints about this situation have met with an increasingly sympathetic hearing in the West and the indignation expressed by those sympathisers has, in its turn, encouraged African political leaders in South Africa to make increasing, and in some cases increasingly violent demands for equality with the white population. At the same time, majority white opinion in South Africa, while possibly conceding the need for minor reforms, has reacted to outside pressure by reaffirming its rejection of any surrender of the political kingdom to the African majority.

Apartheid did not always occupy this central position in western thinking about South Africa. It is only since the 1960s that the issue has aroused serious attention outside the Republic. Even within South Africa it became a subject of controversy only after the Second World War. Then, the National Party adopted apartheid as an essential part of the constitution, giving it a quasi-religious sanction instead of treating it as an expedient to protect white interests. In so doing they gave formal status to a bastard version of the tribal exclusivism long advocated by a minority of conservative Afrikaners. Larger numbers had also accepted it from time to time, but only in moments of crisis when the identity of the Afrikaner people seemed threatened. The new version of exclusivism differed from the old, however, because it embraced all people of European descent and it won increasing approval as the white population began to appreciate the material benefits and protection which it conferred upon them.

Although the doctrine of apartheid became prominent only recently the problem of race relations is much older in origin. The subject of this book, Jan Smuts, died in 1950, but he could not escape the problems to which the issue of race relations gave rise. Since his political career spanned more than half a century and for a quarter of that time he was prime minister of South Africa this is not surprising. As early as

1892 he predicted that the most important issue South Africa would face would be that of ordering the relations between the white minority and the numerically overwhelming black majority. But he did not see the problem in the form in which it appears today and that is why it would be wrong to overemphasise the racial question when writing about Jan Smuts.

Throughout his life Smuts's main concern was to defend Western European civilisation which he saw as representing the highest form of human achievement. At first his concern was with South Africa but later he saw his task as being related to the problems of the whole world. In South Africa he saw western civilisation confronted by black barbarism and for him barbarism and blackness appeared synonymous. He neither believed that Africans could be induced to adopt European standards of behaviour, though Christian missionaries were demonstrating that they might, nor could he foresee any salvation for them through the evolution of their own traditional customs. Thus his attitude towards Africans – and towards the coloured population also – was, even at its best, no more than humanely paternal. His only answer was to permit Africans to pursue their traditional way of life in segregated areas so long as they were prepared to serve the material needs of the Whites.

Because of this outlook, the 'native question' found only intermittent expression in Smuts's words and actions. Instead he focused attention upon the importance of white unity in South Africa in order to promote western civilisation. Later in his life he strove for western unity in face of the new barbarism of powerful nations like Nazi Germany and 'Bolshevik' Russia. It is only right, therefore, that any study of Smuts should reflect this emphasis in Smuts's thinking. Nevertheless, so versatile were his ideas and so all-embracing his actions and interests that the underlying consistency in his outlook was not always apparent. In his early life it was further obscured by his willingness to attempt a variety of differing and sometimes apparently conflicting tactics to achieve his end.

It is important to remember, however, that Smuts's attitude was far from reactionary in his day. Though humanitarians had long pleaded the cause of non-Whites in South Africa and elsewhere, theirs was a minority voice. To the members of a technologically advanced society such as existed in Western Europe it seemed inconceivable that Africans could, in the foreseeable future, deserve parity of esteem or equal rights with Europeans. The French, it is true, were wise enough to avoid generalisations. They recognised that some, if only a few, Africans would be able to escape from their own background and become 'black Europeans'. Such people they were prepared to accept as equals. But the British generally, together with the people of Dutch descent in South Africa, could not believe that such a transformation was possible, even when it was occurring before their very eyes. So they were deaf to the appeals for recognition which came from Africans educated in the European tradition. At the same time, as competition for African labour increased among farmers, mine-owners and industrialists, they became deaf, too, to the appeal of uneducated Africans for a reasonable standard of life.

To his credit Smuts was not as deaf as many others to the cries of uneducated Africans. But his concern for white unity was so great that he was reluctant to endanger it by apparently responding to African needs. Faced with the white refusal to acknowledge the justice of their complaints Africans experienced a growing sense of despair and resentment which united hitherto disparate elements in a demand for redress of their grievances. Seeing themselves officially condemned to permanent exclusion from citizenship in the country of their birth by the formal adoption of apartheid, African protests grew more violent. The seeds of that violence were already germinating in Smuts's lifetime but it was only in his closing years that he began to realise the form which this growth would take and he had no idea as to how it might be changed. It would be unfair, however, to judge Smuts in a modern context. This book has been written not so much with an eye to what Smuts could not have foreseen, though we may see it now, but with placing Smuts within the context of his own time. His career spanned the first half of the twentieth century but one must not forget that his formative years were in the nineteenth.

1

The Student

On 29 May 1964 a statue of Jan Christian Smuts was unveiled in the Botanical Gardens in Cape Town and at once aroused considerable controversy. Some people liked it. One observer described it as 'fearlessly conceived, courageously chosen and executed'.[1] He was in a minority. The editorial writer of the *Cape Times* spoke with the cautious optimism of one who, though treading on unfamiliar ground, feels he must demonstrate his ability to give a lead to society. He remarked that the sculptor had provided a stimulating outline which the beholder could fill in according to his views and emotions.[2] More typical was the comment that the figure looked like a mass of candlewax which had melted in the sun.[3] There was some sympathy, too, for the bewildered onlooker who said he was grateful that Smuts's name had been engraved on the plinth to provide a means of identification.[4]

Creative art has often met with a hostile response from the general public. In this case the sculptor, Sydney Harpley, an Englishman, explained that he had never intended to create a mere physical likeness. He had hoped, he said, to arouse an emotional response in those who saw the statue which would give them a deep and intimate awareness of Smuts's real greatness. For most observers he had clearly failed to achieve his aim. Yet for both Harpley and his critics there is some excuse. The artist had had a difficult task. Even a more realistic approach would have met with difficulties in attempting to portray a man whose career had spanned so many years and who had been seen by so many people in widely varying circumstances. Smuts's qualities could not be adequately conveyed in monolithic fashion even on a three-dimensional scale. Looking back on his early career, he seems like an actor trying out a succession of roles and creating innumerable strong but often evanescent impressions. In those days he might have been a subject for a Renoir but certainly not for a Rembrandt. In his later years he could have posed for Bellini as inscrutably as any Venetian Doge. Though by that time opinions about him had grown firmer, they were as divergent as they had ever been.

For Smuts himself personality was an enthralling concept. To reconcile human personality with the whole of nature was a captivating pursuit.

1

In that pursuit Smuts's own personality took shape only slowly. His early life seems to have been governed more by intellectual experiment than by conviction. He aspired to truth but it frequently eluded him. Thus he earned the reputation for being 'slim' – untrustworthy. It was an unjust description. He possessed a devouring hunger for knowledge and an unusually retentive memory. His mind sifted information with computer-like efficiency and produced a variety of not always consistent answers at an astonishing speed. That inconsistency, though springing from a search for accuracy, became for less subtle minds a vindication of that same charge of 'slimness'.

The experiences which Smuts enjoyed from the age of thirty-five to forty-nine established the persona which for the last thirty years of his life won him the admiration and loyalty of many and the abiding hostility of others. Throughout his life he remained a man of ideas who from force of circumstances frequently appeared as a man of action. The latter role was one he could not always sustain. He was at his best when producing plans. Their implementation often posed problems for him. He was, too, a preacher rather than a teacher. Those who followed him did so from faith rather than from a full understanding of what he was trying to do. His ability to stir deep emotions by his oratory was matched by his failure to explain his intentions to those around him. By the end of a career which spanned almost two generations the younger men who worked with him revered him but were stifled by him. He had become an institution about which fantasies could be woven but which only his wife and a small group of loyal women friends ever understood.

This complex character was the product of both heredity and environment, touched with divine gifts. Jan Smuts was born in 1870, so that he came to manhood as a new century began to reject the beliefs and standards of its predecessor. The place of his birth, South Africa, confronted him with a range of problems, political and moral, with which the civilised world was only just beginning to wrestle. The circumstances of his birth, to devout Cape-Dutch parents – his father a comfortably off farmer who became a member of his country's legislature – left him with the legacy of a Christian faith which he questioned but could never wholly reject and with prejudices which he might seek to shed but which lingered, obscurely and insistently, in his innermost being. The divine gifts of which he was the beneficiary included an acute intellect, boundless curiosity and an inescapable, fundamentally religious sense of purpose.

Jan Smuts's boyhood on a farm near Riebeeck West, in western Cape Colony, provided the stability and the mild adventures which enable a boy to develop whatever potential there is in him. Cape Colony, though it numbered more people of Dutch than of British descent among its population – and more non-Whites than British and Dutch together – was for all practical purposes a loyal, largely self-governing member of the British Empire. Far to the east, the profoundly British crown colony of Natal cherished its separate existence while keeping a watchful and sometimes fearful eye upon the powerful Zulu kingdom to the north and the overwhelming numbers of Africans within its own borders. Further north the two Boer republics, the Orange Free State and the South African Republic – the latter soon to be renamed the Transvaal – had been largely populated, as far as their white inhabitants were concerned, from Cape Colony and Natal. Now they pursued their separate ways in accordance with the wishes of their white citizens. Between those white settlements there still remained a number of African states, the presence of which gave their European neighbours occasional *frissons* of uncertainty. But Riebeeck West was far removed from the tensions which sometimes led to war between the white settlers and black pastoralists along the eastern Cape frontier. Far removed, too, from the turbulent life of the South African Republic beyond the Vaal River, where a white minority dominated a black majority inside the boundaries of the Republic and kept defiant but confident watch upon their Zulu and Swazi neighbours.

Minor tremors may have been felt on the Smuts's farm when Britain annexed the South African Republic in 1877, and there may have been some fraternal satisfaction when the Boers of the Republic rose and defeated the British forces at Majuba Hill in 1881. But there was little sympathy in the Smuts family for the Afrikaner Bond movement which had its origins in Paarl in 1877 and which preached Boer exclusivism. More to their taste was the reorganised Bond, crafted by the veteran Cape-Dutch politician, Jan Hofmeyr. Hofmeyr wanted to promote the interests of the Cape farmers through co-operation with the colonial authorities and by drawing together in common cause people of both British and Dutch descent. Hitherto the farmers had prospered by supporting that policy and they saw no reason for abandoning it in favour of Boer separatism.

His untroubled rural childhood bred in Jan Smuts an enduring love of nature which, as his botanical knowledge grew, became an engrossing scientific rather than aesthetic hobby. In later life it provided a valuable distraction when momentous events crowded in upon him too closely. Still more significant was Smuts's introduction to Christianity. His family was not of that narrow religious persuasion which animated the Boer trekkers who had sought refuge from a materialistic world beyond the Vaal River. Nevertheless, Smuts's parents revered the Christian faith

3

in the manner of most of the Cape Dutch of their day. The spiritual education given by his mother, Catharina Petronella Smuts (formerly de Vries), a sister of the local minister and herself an educated woman, made a deep and lasting impression upon him.[5]

When Smuts was twelve years old his elder brother, Michael, died. It had been their parents' intention that Michael should be ordained into the ministry of the Dutch Reformed Church. That mantle now fell upon Jan. Hitherto he had had no formal education. At the age of twelve he was now sent to school for the first time. He was equipped with a vocation imposed upon him by others but by no means unacceptable to a serious-minded, sensitive boy of Smuts's background. His moral outlook was unquestioningly based upon the religious teaching he had received from his mother. The story of his academic success was to become legendary. At school in Riebeeck West he leaped ahead of his fellow-students who had begun their education at a much earlier age. Before he moved to Victoria College, in Stellenbosch, at the age of sixteen he took the precaution of writing a letter to Professor Charles Murray. He was anxious, he said, to avoid the Babylonian temptations which might lie in wait for a teenage student. Professor Murray hastened to reassure him.

Smuts's devotion to his studies in Stellenbosch was as wholehearted as it had been at Riebeeck West and his achievements were even more noteworthy. He was a solitary youth, finding his physical enjoyment as he was to do throughout his life in walking on the veld rather than in games with his fellow-students. He studied both science and the humanities and was introduced to poetry. The works of Shelley made an instant and permanent impression on him and he later read Keats, Wordsworth and Shakespeare. He learned German and read the works of Goethe among those of other German writers. Greek was a basic requirement of the curriculum and he seized upon it gladly because it enabled him to read the New Testament in its original language. In this way he was able, he maintained, to understand as he could not otherwise have done what the early Christian communities were striving to apprehend.[6]

After some years in Victoria College, Smuts began the exploration of the nature of man. At the age of nineteen he wrote and had published an essay entitled *Homo Sum* which set out to investigate human personality. It was the beginning of a quest which was to occupy him for the rest of his life. Another essay, written in 1890, developed the theme of the universality of knowledge and of the centrality of man to it. It looked more specifically at an issue which was to impose a heavy claim upon his political attention in future years. He had been reflecting upon the prospects for a South African customs union. Forcefully it dawned upon him that, though it consisted at that time of several parts, South Africa was in reality a commercial and moral unit. It was a conclusion which seemed borne out by his developing belief in the wholeness of the universe. It was also in close accord with the ideas of another man who reached his conclusions by pragmatic methods rather than as a result of intellectual enquiry. Cecil Rhodes, the one-time sickly youth who, by his flair for buying and selling diamond mines, had become the most powerful figure of South African finance and politics, was soon to be condemned for dividing South Africa irrevocably. In the late 1880s, however, in alliance with Jan Hofmeyr, he was still regarded as the leading protagonist of South African unity. He saw Cape Colony as the foundation stone upon which he would build a federation expanding beyond the Limpopo River as trade and opportunity offered.

The opinion of the British government about such a scheme, had they known of it, would have been ambivalent. Most British colonial secretaries in the latter half of the nineteenth century would have been glad to see the white settlers gaining in confidence and strength. This would have enabled Britain to shed responsibility for their protection. But they would have been wary of possible clashes with foreign powers who might also be interested in African trade. It was Rhodes's fate that the climax of his project coincided with the term of office of a colonial secretary, Joseph Chamberlain, who wished to strengthen rather than reduce Britain's involvement in South Africa and who did not welcome Rhodes's idea of a colony largely independent of Britain save for its defence against external powers.

In the year in which the youthful Smuts wrote his essay on the customs union, Rhodes became prime minister of Cape Colony. Simultaneously, in his other capacity as managing director of his recently chartered British South Africa Company, he launched an expedition into the territory beyond the South African Republic. His aim was to investigate the mineral potential of the land that was to become Southern Rhodesia, now Zimbabwe. When Rhodes visited Victoria College, Smuts seemed the obvious person to deliver a speech of welcome on behalf of the students. He did so, happy to address the man he believed to be promoting in practical terms his own developing political ideas.

In 1891, Smuts wrote his final examinations in Stellenbosch, gaining honours in both science and literature and being awarded the Ebden Scholarship for overseas study. He decided to go to Cambridge, not to study divinity or even philosophy, but law. The reason for his change of direction is not clear. It may possibly have been linked with his hopes of a future marriage to a fellow-student at Stellenbosch, Sybella

5

Margaretha (Isie) Krige, for whom he had developed a deep affection. Isie was a young woman of strong views and a lively humour, but she was less confident than Smuts of her religious faith.[7] More probably he feared the study of divinity would channel him irrevocably into the Dutch Reformed Church whose teachings already seemed constricting. His introduction to science had led him to question some of the Church's dogma and, although he had probably not yet rejected the idea of ordination, he needed a period of more diversified study before his future was finally determined. It was in Cambridge that this problem would be sorted out.

The decision not to be ordained was taken gradually, almost imperceptibly, but it was not taken easily. The process had a profound effect upon the development of Smuts's philosophy of life, and filled him with a sense of obligation to humanity to which he felt he must respond if the course he had chosen to follow was to be justified. J. I. Marais, professor of Theology in Stellenbosch, a friend and benefactor, contributed to that process by challenging the wisdom of Smuts's decision to study law. Law, he wrote firmly, was classified humbug and, from a theoretic, philosophical standpoint, utterly useless.[8] Smuts could not ignore the challenge, and the correspondence which followed embraced a wide range of topics and gave both stimulus and pleasure to both participants. Marais was prepared to admit that legal studies could pave the way to a useful career. As a qualified lawyer, Smuts might serve his country in parliament, at the bar or on the bench. But Marais still maintained that legal studies contracted one's outlook. In an attempt to resolve what was for him a deeply rooted problem of conscience and not simply an intellectual conundrum, Smuts wrote an article entitled 'Law a Liberal Study' which was published in *Christ's College Magazine* in 1893. In it he argued that from Moses onward lawyers had been the great lights and ornaments of the Church. He then rehearsed the concept he was beginning to develop of the interdependence of all creation and went on to demonstrate how law had expanded to encompass the rights of personality at one extreme and the interrelationship of nations at the other. No other academic discipline could have met those demands, he wrote. While literature confused the permanent with the temporary, history, economics, ethics and theology were too concerned with the individual or the supernatural. Legal studies alone offered an understanding of the wider forces which governed the environment wherein the individual personality flourished.[9] It was neither a convincing nor a particularly lucid argument. But Smuts was only twenty-three and he was pleading a case to which he knew he had not found a conclusive answer.

While still attending divine service regularly in the presbyterian church in Cambridge, Smuts gradually expanded his new ideas in a series of articles. For the time being these were to culminate in a lengthy study of the American poet, Walt Whitman, whom he took as an exemplar of his theory of the development of personality. The choice of Whitman was not fortuitous. Smuts was still seeking to explain and to justify both to himself as well as to others his drift away from the religious vocation towards which his parents had directed him. He believed that Whitman's writings helped him to achieve an understanding of natural man and by so doing freed him from the domination of some of the theological concepts he had absorbed through his conventionally pious upbringing. In retrospect he was to claim that it was at this point that sin ceased to dominate his view of life. He compared that experience with the release of St Paul from the dominion of the law by the revelation of the power of grace. Later in life, when his achievements had dispelled his earlier feelings of guilt at having abandoned the idea of ordination, he felt confident enough to admit that a reversion to natural man could not be the true way to achieve full human stature. By that time he justified the course his life had taken by affirming that a deeper understanding of the nature of humanity can only be reached through the experience of one's limitations and weaknesses.[10]

It was only after half a century of experience that Smuts could make such a claim with a clear conscience. But in Cambridge Whitman's poetry was enough to encourage him to look upon life in a way which made it possible to combine his tentative scientific and philosophical theories and, in so doing, to transcend, in a manner which satisfied his own conscience, the limitations imposed by the formal theology in which he had been grounded. His philosophy, which he called holism, freed him to pursue the life of intellect and action for which he craved. Though he believed he saw in it parallels with the writings of classical Greece, holism bore a closer resemblance to the electicism of Hindu philosophy. To justify his philosophy in action, Smuts was henceforward to don the formal dress of the statesman or the uniform of a soldier as a substitute for the robe of a *predikant*. In time he came to identify his own conscience as the conscience of mankind. It was an onerous burden, but in later life he bore it more easily because of a deep-seated conviction of his own rectitude. In this lively but fluctuating state of mind it was not surprising that Smuts came to enjoy the friendship of a Cambridge don, H. J. Wolstenholme, whom Sir Keith Hancock has described as a 'lapsed Christian who retained his Christian conscience'.[11] Smuts himself did not fall far from that description.

Another issue which was to plague Smuts throughout his life attracted only fleeting attention while he was in Cambridge, though it already seemed that his views on the subject had been rigidly formed. 'It must never be forgotten', he wrote in an article in 1892, 'that the race struggle is destined to assume a magnitude on the African continent such as the world has never seen and the Imagination shrinks from contemplating; and in that appalling struggle for existence the unity of the white camp . . . will not be the least necessary condition . . . of warding off annihilation.'[12] Up to that point in his life, Smuts had had virtually no contact with the African population of South Africa. Few Africans, as distinct from coloured people, had made their way to the Western Cape by the 1890s. But Smuts had acquired the instinctive aversion from mixing with Africans in any relationship save that of master and servant which was already common to most Whites in South Africa. At that time his feelings sprang from the fear that one day the Africans might rise up and overthrow white domination if the Whites did not remain unified, strong and vigilant. In 1892 that attitude was already something of an anachronism. The last frontier war against the Xhosa along the Eastern Cape frontier had been fought in 1878 and the last of the Transkeian territories was on the point of being annexed to Cape Colony. The power of the Zulus had been undermined by the Zulu War of 1879 and their destruction as a nation completed by the subsequent division of their country. The lesser threats from the Pedi in the South African Republic and the Tswana to the north and west of the colonies and republics had also been overcome. In Cape Colony itself a non-racial constitutional tradition could be traced back to 1828. Since 1853 every male citizen over the age of twenty-one who possessed the necessary property or salary qualifications could claim the right to vote, regardless of colour. Since 1860 African voters had played a significant part in returning representatives from some of the Eastern Cape constituencies to the legislature. In the economic field, too, many Africans had abandoned their former customs to seek a share in the wealth-producing activities introduced by Europeans on farms and in the diamond and gold mines. Only in the social sphere were there minimal signs of integration.

None of this affected Smuts's attitude. Old prejudices die slowly, especially in districts far removed, as was the Western Cape, from the reality of racial contact. The barely concealed fear of the overwhelming hordes of apparently barbarous people, born of years of conflict along the Cape's eastern frontier and further north in the republics, had produced a state of mind in which apprehension sought reassurance in a feeling of cultural superiority. In doing so it blinded the majority of Whites to the realities of the problem which faced them. Only later did Smuts grow to appreciate that it was not physical conflict that was to be feared, but rather the penetration and possible alteration of the European ethic by people of a different culture. Even that assessment failed to embrace the full complexity of African reactions to white domination, yet Smuts never seriously attempted to analyse the facts of the situation. For him there must be no suggestion of integration. Africans and Europeans must be forever separate. Even the coloured population, the descendants of racial intermixture, were for Smuts a distinct species. The question of relations between the black and white races was not a problem to be resolved but a threat to be averted. In his later life Smuts favoured a greater generosity in material things as the means of attaining that objective. But always he believed in segregation.

While he was in Cambridge, Smuts's life was as solitary as it had been in Stellenbosch. He still took his exercise mainly on unaccompanied walks. Shortage of money contributed something to his avoidance of the university's social life. An extreme seriousness of purpose contributed more. In spite of the spiritual problems which tormented him, he did not neglect his legal studies. Having adopted the unusual course of reading the two parts of the Law Tripos concurrently, he gained first class honours in both. That success resulted in the extension of his scholarship for a further year. In December 1894 he passed, first in his year, the honours examination of the Inns of Court. Simultaneously he completed his study of Whitman, but was unable to find a publisher for it. With the prospect of a distinguished academic or legal career opening before him, Smuts might well have been tempted to stay in England. But to have done so would have been at odds with his sense of obligation to his own country. After completing his additional year of study, he sailed for South Africa.

2

The young lawyer

The country to which Smuts returned in 1895 was superficially at peace, but a plot was being hatched which would shatter that condition. The man behind the plot was Cecil Rhodes. During Smuts's absence in England, Rhodes's hopes of a united South Africa had received a serious set-back. The gold discoveries of the 1880s in the South African Republic, which had shifted the economic focus of South Africa from Cape Colony to Johannesburg, could no longer be regarded as a transient phenomenon like the gold rushes of the Yukon or Colorado. Rich, new seams were being opened up at a deeper level and processes were being evolved to make the mining of them both possible and economically profitable. This meant that the South African Republic might dominate the South African economy indefinitely and this did not accord with Rhodes's plan to build a union on foundations laid at the Cape. To add to his problems, the hope of mineral discoveries north of the Limpopo River to counter-balance the wealth of the Rand had proved evanescent. Furthermore, Rhodes knew that, although Paul Kruger, President of the South African Republic and an avowed opponent of Rhodes's plan, was an old man and might soon be succeeded by younger men of a more co-operative frame of mind, his own health was too uncertain to permit him to be patient.

These considerations led Rhodes to contemplate achieving federation by force. It was a terrifying plan. For the prime minister of a British colony to plot the overthrow of a neighbouring government by unprovoked violence was to court disaster. So provocation – or the semblance of it – must be provided. From October 1894 Rhodes began to foment an uprising in Johannesburg on the pretext that British citizens living there were being persecuted by a reactionary and repressive government. Grievances – some real but not crippling, others imaginary – were mustered to stir up discontent while Rhodes secretly provided arms to would-be rebels.

A rising of the sort Rhodes contemplated was still unlikely to succeed without outside help. So Rhodes schemed to acquire Bechuanaland, the territory to the west of the South African Republic, ostensibly to establish a link between Cape Colony and his company's sphere of activity in

Rhodesia. There he planned to station a force of armed men to ride to the assistance of the rebels. To make his plan foolproof, he hoped to arrange for the British High Commissioner to hasten from Cape Town to the scene of action when the rebellion broke out. The High Commissioner would then call upon the two sides to desist from further conflict and would replace the existing, inefficient government by one which would co-operate in Rhodes's plan for federation. The position seemed hopeful because the new British secretary of state for the colonies, Joseph Chamberlain, though he did not like Rhodes and did not want a South African federation dominated by him, was prepared, for his own ends, to give limited assistance provided his involvement remained secret. Chamberlain's intention was to amend the plan without Rhodes's knowledge so as to ensure that any federation which emerged would be controlled by Britain.

All these developments were unknown to Smuts, for whom Rhodes was still a heroic and noble figure. Though he had established a legal practice in Cape Town, briefs did not shower upon him. With time on his hands he was attracted to politics. He attended debates in the legislative assembly in Cape Town and wrote articles on political subjects for both English- and Dutch-language newspapers. He had a lively mind and a fluent pen, as he had already demonstrated during his time in Cambridge. A crisis in the relations between Cape Colony and the South African Republic in October 1895 gave him an early opportunity to show his paces. The dispute had arisen over the tariffs charged on the railways serving Johannesburg. For several years the Cape had had a monopoly of rail transport to the Rand, but in 1894 a new and shorter line had been opened from Lourenço Marques. Kruger had taken advantage of the situation and the reduced rates offered by the new line to switch traffic away from the Cape railway. A price war had followed, to put an end to which Kruger closed the customs houses through which goods from the Cape entered the Republic. He backed down when his action was shown to be in contravention of the terms of the London Convention of 1884 which governed Britain's relations with the Republic, but not before war had appeared a lively possibility.

Smuts was naïvely unaware of the nuances of the situation. To him it seemed tragic that divisions should arise between people of the same blood. He therefore wrote an article for the press reminding his readers that the Republic had been peopled by men from the Cape and that in every respect the two countries were inseparable. He was prepared to recognise that Kruger might be genuinely afraid that the pastoral, God-fearing nation he had helped to found was being threatened by the steadily increasing number of immigrants. These latter were mainly

11

connected with the gold-mines and their standards of behaviour certainly differed from the Old Testament morality of the Boers. But, Smuts insisted, the President was unduly prejudiced against them because of the malign advice of Dutchmen who only sought office in the Republic for their own ends and whose policies were clearly divisive for South Africa. It was an idealistic but superficial appraisal of the position. The links between the trek Boers and the Cape Dutch had weakened over the years, not least because of the different experiences they had undergone. Smuts's understanding of Kruger's personality was also at fault. Although in the absence of enough Boers with the skill or interest to conduct the affairs of the Republic the President had imported Dutch civil servants, the country's policy was his own. He was fully aware of the difference in outlook between the immigrants (the *uitlanders*) and the Boers, but he feared neither mine-owners nor mineworkers. The former might complain of his outmoded fiscal methods, but Kruger knew that they fully appreciated the advantageous position they enjoyed with regard to taxation on profits and labour legislation. The mineworkers, too, might grumble, but they were well paid and their cost of living was low. There was no danger from that quarter. In Kruger's view the threat to the stability of South Africa came, not from his own attitude or from the internal condition of the Republic, but from outside. He knew of Rhodes's ambitions and he did not trust the man. It was Rhodes, not Kruger, who had nearly drawn Britain into conflict with the Republic over the railway dispute. Five years earlier, too, Rhodes had been instrumental in invoking British military intervention after Kruger had unwisely given his approval to the creation of two small republics outside the boundaries laid down for the South African Republic by the London Convention. To have been twice manœuvred into breaking a settlement by which he set great store had angered the President.

The London Convention had been drafted by the Earl of Derby, Britain's colonial secretary, in 1884 after the earlier Pretoria Convention had proved unsatisfactory. The British claim to undefined suzerainty over the Republic embodied in the earlier Convention was abandoned by Derby as, too, was Britain's right of intervention to protect the interests of the black population. What was left was, in the colonial secretary's opinion, the real substance of the arrangement. Britain retained control of the Republic's external relations to ensure that no hostile foreign power could obtain a foothold in the region. At the same time the boundaries of the Republic were clearly defined to east and west with a view to avoiding any further clash between Boer and African which might lead to a wider struggle between Black and White throughout South Africa. Kruger, too, had accepted the convention as an important safeguard against further intervention by Britain in the internal affairs of his country. He was not deeply concerned with external relations and he certainly did not wish to extend the Republic's boundaries or exert external dominion in a manner which might bring him into conflict with Britain. In any case, the Convention left him with room to expand northward if his people felt the need for more land. Or it had originally done so, until once again he had been foiled by Rhodes, who acquired a concession for his chartered company from the African ruler of the land beyond the Limpopo and thus pre-empted a Boer movement northward. Little wonder that Kruger felt encircled, and through the actions of the man he trusted least. Rhodes's plans were anathema to him. Conceived by such a man, they could not fail to threaten the spiritual foundations of his country's government and its very independence.

To Smuts, born in Cape Colony and educated in England, Kruger's attitude was incomprehensible. Though himself of Dutch descent, he, like the other Cape Dutch, did not see himself as a member of a people chosen by God to govern the land in accordance with Kruger's narrow interpretation of divine ordinance. Nor indeed did many of the Boers of the South African Republic, though in times of crisis they were ready enough to rally to their leader's exclusivism in defence of their independence. But the heart of Kruger's separatism lay in his fundamentalist Calvinist faith. It did not necessarily require physical segregation, but it insisted that the manner of government should be determined by God's people. Neither on the basis of his family upbringing nor on the basis of his education could Smuts accept that view. If, as he now believed to be true, the whole of creation was one, such separatism was unnatural. So Smuts sided with Rhodes in the dispute with Kruger, and, when the Bond leader, Hofmeyr, invited him to speak on Rhodes's behalf against those who accused the prime minister of using his wealth to promote selfish aims, he did so gladly.

He made the speech in Kimberley, the centre of the diamond industry from which Rhodes had derived most of his wealth. In it he pursued the themes for which he believed both he and Rhodes stood. The first of those themes was a call to foster a South African nationality in which all white men who believed the interests of their country were paramount might share. Rhodes, Smuts said, had done more to promote that national spirit than any other man had done. Together with Hofmeyr he had ensured that the potential division between farmers of Dutch descent and businessmen whose fathers had come from Britain had been avoided in Cape Colony. It still threatened in the South African Republic, but it was only by means of a union of the white races that the threat from the barbaric black population could be contained and the leadership

13

provided to bring those black hordes to a state of civilisation through systematic work and practical education. Left alone, as some self-styled well-wishers demanded that they should be, Africans were incapable of pursuing their own salvation. They needed help, but the education they required at their current stage of development was not of an intellectual character. All the evidence suggested that education of that sort destroyed the physical and moral stamina of the African urban population.[1]

This reference to the struggle of the Whites against the Africans recalled the article Smuts had written in Cambridge. But, although Smuts himself was unaware of it, neither the struggle itself nor the means he proposed to resolve it were in line with Rhodes's own view of relations between White and Black. Rhodes's handling of native affairs, like his handling of many other issues, was governed by expediency rather than consistency. Only to the principle of a South African federation did he remain constantly loyal. He had recently been responsible for the Glen Grey Act which, years later, Smuts was to describe as the foundation of sound native policy. In reality, however, it was no more than an experiment aimed at resolving the problems of one heavily populated area of the Eastern Cape. The intention was to give the Africans in the Glen Grey district an opportunity to learn the rudiments of British local government. Since there was not enough land to meet the needs of all who lived there, those who could not find employment in the district would be urged to seek paid labour on European-owned farms or in the mining industry. In this way, there would be an opportunity for some Africans to make progress in acquiring responsibility for conducting their own affairs, while others, together with their European employers, would benefit from taking part in a modern economy. Thus everyone would be satisfied – or so it was hoped – and, if the experiment proved successful, it might be extended to other areas. If not, Rhodes would no doubt produce an alternative scheme.

When speaking in support of the Glen Grey Bill in parliament, Rhodes did indeed claim that the native question was the foremost issue of the day. But for Rhodes other days always produced other issues, and one of them was soon to push the native question into the background for many years. In the early hours of 29 December 1895, Dr Leander Starr Jameson, Rhodes's close friend who commanded the force of men poised in Bechuanaland to co-operate at the appropriate moment with the *uitlander* rebels in Johannesburg, launched his attack on the South African Republic without waiting for the rising to take place. To make matters worse, the would-be rebels had never seriously contemplated a rebellion. Without their support the raid was bound to fail and, in so doing, it dealt a disastrous blow to Rhodes's hopes and to his reputation.

Chamberlain, who feared his own involvement in the plot might become known, was desperate to forestall criticism by achieving some measure of success. He therefore urged the British High Commissioner at the Cape, Sir Hercules Robinson, to intervene as Rhodes had originally hoped that he would. Robinson, however, quickly concluded that the best he could do would be to help the captured invaders. All hope of overthrowing Kruger's government had to be abandoned. Rhodes was in disgrace, if only briefly, and Chamberlain's own position was in danger. Kruger, meanwhile, had come to the conclusion that the London Convention, upon which he had rested his hopes of immunity from external intervention, could no longer offer protection. Not only his old antagonist, Rhodes, but even the British secretary of state for the colonies had seen fit to flout it. His longing to isolate his country from its neighbours was powerfully reinforced and that feeling was shared by most of his fellow-countrymen. The Boers of the Orange Free State and the Cape Dutch were also deeply sympathetic towards the Republic, with the unfortunate result that British feeling in Cape Colony quickly rallied in support of Rhodes. Thus British and Dutch in the colony were divided as they had never been for more than half a century.

Smuts's reaction to these tumultuous events took shape only slowly. The apparent collusion between Chamberlain and Rhodes certainly convinced him that Britain's claim to interfere by right in South African affairs must be firmly rejected. Yet, for a time at least, he continued to contemplate a future for himself in Cape Colony and he applied, unsuccessfully, for a lectureship in law in the South African College in Cape Town in March 1896.[2] He also wrote two articles which appeared on 12 and 19 March in *Ons Land*, a newspaper which, since its foundation in 1892, had been the mouthpiece of the Afrikaner Bond. In the first of these he again called for the consolidation of the white races in South Africa, but now his aim was to resist future imperial intervention. In the second article he expressed the hope that the revulsion of feeling in Britain against the raid might lead to the annulment of the London Convention and the total independence of the South African Republic.[3] Neither article suggested that there had been any revolutionary change in Smuts's thinking. The only significant innovation appeared in another article in the *South African Telegraph* for 25 March, in which Smuts referred for the first time to the malign activities of the capitalist-imperialists.[4] He used the term loosely, as he was to do frequently in the years which immediately followed. Indeed, its meaning appeared to vary to suit differing circumstances. Because of that lack of accuracy, Smuts was constantly to blur the distinction between the imperialism which some capitalists supported and imperialism as the natural and ultimate

15

development of capitalism. Consequently, until he himself came to hold a responsible position in government, he never attempted to understand the role of capital in South Africa.

A more important influence upon Smuts's future than the raid was a visit he paid to Johannesburg later in March which led to his decision to move to the Republic. Writing in 1902 he said, 'In the course of 1896, it became so clear to me that the British connection was harmful to South Africa's best interest that I feared my future position as a Cape politician would be a false one. I therefore left the old colony for good and settled in the Transvaal.'[5] Much had happened by 1902 to cloud Smuts's recollection. It was not the opportunity to breathe the pure air of political independence which alone brought about his decision to move. He gave up little in Cape Colony, for in 1896 his prospects as a politician there were far from bright. Nor did there appear to be any immediate political future for him in the South African Republic. There were few people there who were likely to support his plan for the union of the white races of South Africa, while, as a *uitlander*, he was unable even to obtain the franchise for fourteen years under the law of the Republic. It was, therefore, the livelier prospect of a successful legal career which might ultimately lead to politics that tempted him to take up residence beyond the Vaal River.

With those better prospects of earning a living came the opportunity to marry the young woman he had loved since he was at Victoria College, Isie Krige. The wedding took place in April 1897 during a fleeting visit by Smuts to the Cape and he returned at once with his bride to the Republic. The marriage was to be one of the most stable factors in Smuts's life. Isie remained an adoring and loyal wife, but she never lost her own identity. Her sound common sense had a lovingly deflating influence upon Smuts's more extreme conceits. She never travelled abroad with her husband when in later life he became an international figure, and she rarely visited Cape Town when his parliamentary duties took him there. In the earlier years of their marriage this was partly because she had to look after an ever-increasing family, but it also suited her to stay at home. The home she kept for Smuts to return to when opportunity allowed was a place of warmth and welcome. Like Isie herself, it lacked any sign of ostentation, even when visited by royalty. But it met Smuts's needs completely because he was never one to concern himself with outward appearances. When he was at home he could be a farmer and a family man and forget his other preoccupations. He found in marriage a profound sense of security. In his earlier years he liked to boast a little in order to impress Isie by his achievements. But he knew well enough that, though she loved and admired him for what he did achieve, she would never be unduly impressed by grand society or by the famous people with whom he came to mix. It was enough that he was her husband and that he was an honourable man doing his duty to the utmost of his ability. Although Isie was herself an intelligent woman, Smuts was later to find great pleasure in the admiration of other women, brilliant, beautiful and cosmopolitan, and he found friendship, spiced with romance, with a number of them. But, just as Isie had to be content to spend much of her time in the background of Smuts's public life, so too those other women were quickly forgotten when issues of national or international significance occupied Smuts's attention. In his relations with women, as in other aspects of his life, he could switch on the whole of his attention and as easily turn it elsewhere.

Soon after his move to the Republic the dynamic qualities of Smuts's mind began to make themselves felt. He occupied himself with trying out new approaches to problems he had as yet scarcely begun to understand. Enthusiasm, earnestness and naïvety led him to make mistakes. But he persisted, frequently unaware of his errors, determined to make his mark, to prove to himself that he had not betrayed the trust of those who had looked to him for moral leadership.

His first foray into public life came in a speech at the prize-giving ceremony of the *Afrikaansche Taalbond* – the Afrikaans Language Association – in Paarl in September 1896. For the first time he used the word Afrikaner, meaning people of Dutch descent, as distinct from the more commonly used expression, Afrikander, which included all white South Africans.[6] The nature of the occasion accounted to some extent for what some ill-disposed critic described as his overstatement of the case for Afrikaner resistance to imperial pressures.[7] But there is clear evidence that Smuts's attitude towards South Africans of British descent had undergone a change. Living in the atmosphere of the South African Republic he had already imbibed something of the spirit of Boer republicanism. Although for the first two years of his residence there he confined himself mainly to his legal practice, he had to augment his salary by coaching in law and writing for the press, and the latter activity directed his attention inevitably to political questions. He still thought of what he described as 'the moderate colonial population' as potential allies. But by the middle of 1897 he had concluded that the leadership of the movement to establish a white-ruled, united South Africa had devolved upon the people of Dutch descent and particularly upon those who lived in the South African Republic.[8] The fact that Kruger's government – and above all the President himself – had no interest in a united South Africa Smuts conveniently overlooked, and his view was strengthened by the proceedings of the parliamentary inquiry into the Jameson Raid which began in London in 1897. The guilt of Rhodes could not be concealed, but Joseph Chamberlain, who surprisingly was a member of the commission, strove with might and main to demonstrate that it had been the government of the Republic which was responsible for stirring up the rebellion by its repressive policies towards those who were not citizens.

Smuts's indignation when he learned of this led him to set out his views on what he believed should be the future relations between Britain and South Africa in an article which was not published at the time.[9] Although he set out to appeal to the sense of justice of the British people, he in fact presented a comprehensive argument in support of a united republic of South Africa. Chamberlain's claim that Britain, as paramount power, had the right to intervene in the internal affairs of the Republic he denounced as contrary to every tenet of international law. It had, he said, alienated the sympathy not only of the Dutch in South Africa but also of responsible British colonials. The protests of the jingoistic supporters of Rhodes were of no significance. The recent renewal and extension of the defence agreement between the South African Republic and the Orange Free State in March 1897 were a clear indication that President Kruger felt strong enough in the sympathy and support of the entire Dutch population of South Africa, and of a large group of English colonials, to start upon a bold policy of internal economic reform and external South African *rapprochement*.

The article contained a great deal of wishful thinking. Kruger certainly did not wish to add to his existing problems by becoming involved in an association with neighbouring states. The presence of so many British colonials in Cape Colony, together with the Cape's native policy, were more than enough to crush any desire to establish closer links than those which were already in force. Even his alliance with the Orange Free State was purely a defensive measure, whatever others might think. Smuts was equally wrong in his assessment of the attitude of the Cape Dutch, although he was one of their number. They were, indeed, deeply shocked by Rhodes's behaviour and they were equally unimpressed by Chamberlain's handling of events after the Raid. But Smuts was wide of the target when he spoke of their being concerned about the lack of political benefits arising from their colonial status. It was the stability and economic prosperity they enjoyed under British overlordship which attracted his fellow-countrymen to the imperial connection, rather than to the republicanism which he advocated.

The writing of the article coincided with the appointment of a new British high commissioner who was to confirm all Smuts's fears about

British policy towards South Africa. Sir Alfred Milner came with excellent credentials which in other circumstances might have resulted in an immediate rapport with Smuts. Indeed, in later life Smuts's own behaviour was to resemble closely that of Milner, but in 1897 these two men, both of whom relied so heavily upon intellectual insights, stood at opposite political poles in South Africa. Milner had learnt the business of finance and administration under Lord Cromer in Egypt and he had subsequently gained a sound grasp of fiscal issues as chairman of the board of inland revenue in Britain. He was widely respected by the leaders of both British political parties and, though this was unknown in South Africa, he had been instructed by a now wary Chamberlain to act with caution. But, as Smuts was soon to learn, he was personally committed to upholding and expanding the British Empire with a devotion which, in a man less coldly logical in his bearing, must have been described as passionate.

Initially Milner obeyed his instructions – looking, listening and learning rather than acting, but in the South African Republic he looked only for faults. He listened to its traducers rather than to its defenders. He sought evidence to support what he expected to learn, namely that the whole of South Africa could be administered more efficiently as an integral part of the British Empire. Administrative efficiency was the criterion by which Milner judged societies. By that standard the South African Republic appeared to him to be in urgent need of reform, and, because reform seemed unlikely, Milner informed Chamberlain in 1898 that, in his view, Britain's interests in South Africa would be best served by declaring war on the Republic.[10] Chamberlain hastily reminded Milner that his original instructions still held good. He had survived the parliamentary inquiry into the Raid only by dexterous manipulation of the commission's proceedings and he could run no more risks. Above all he was fully aware that there would be no enthusiasm in Britain for war with the Republic.

It was in this potentially dangerous situation that Smuts began to work his way into the forefront of the Republic's political life. The evidence suggests that he had been angling for preferment. The relatively simple demands of a legal practice in Johannesburg offered insufficient stimulus to a young man of his intellectual qualities who was also possessed by a powerful desire to play a significant role in public affairs. Smuts's son and biographer suggests that it was the intervention of friends which brought his father to the notice of President Kruger and resulted in his appointment as state-attorney in June 1898.[11] Though Smuts was only twenty-eight at the time, his appointment was not as surprising as in later life he himself was inclined to suggest. The Republic was not rich in talent and Kruger had frequently looked outside its borders for his officials. He had, too, a liking for intelligent young men whose ability complemented his own, and in the past had made a number of similar appointments. Though Smuts lacked the residential qualifications for first-class citizenship, which at the time stood at fourteen years, there was no problem about his being created a second-class burgher, and the post to which he had been appointed was not a political one and did not carry with it membership of the executive council.

Smuts's activities as state-attorney quickly won approval. He campaigned assiduously for the implementation of the laws against the indiscriminate sale of liquor to Africans and rejected complaints against a magistrate whose critics, he believed, had been bribed and incited by liquor salesmen.[12] He also tried with some success to put a stop to illicit gold-buying, though his task was made difficult because members of the detective service whose job it was to stamp out the trade were themselves involved in it. It was a triumph for Smuts when he was able to bring the service under his own control. From that time his reputation grew quickly, and with it his confidence. In October he was involved in a dispute over mining rights claimed by the firm of H. Eckstein and Company, the richest mining company on the Rand and a subsidiary of the powerful, London-based finance company, Wernher Beit. Relations between the mining companies and the government of the Republic were frequently strained and Smuts sensed that the situation provided him with the opportunity he sought to play a more significant role in his country's affairs. The negotiator on behalf of the company was James Percy Fitzpatrick, a partner in the company who was fast becoming an obsessive politician. He had been involved in a none too distinguished capacity in the abortive rebellion which should have accompanied the Jameson Raid, and had taken the opportunity to pose as something of a hero. Though legally barred, as a result, from further political activity until June 1899, he had had two lengthy conversations with Sir Alfred Milner in February 1898 during which he had stressed that, while Eckstein's was solely a business firm, he personally hoped that Britain would intervene actively in the Republic.[13] His ambivalence, his vacillation between the roles of businessman and political intriguer, made Fitzpatrick an unreliable consultant for his company and for Milner alike. Smuts, however, decided to use him as the agent through whose co-operation he himself would bring about a *rapprochement* between his government and the mine-owners. Accordingly, he invited Fitzpatrick to bring any further contentious matters directly to him.[14] It was a well-intentioned move though a naïve one. Fitzpatrick himself did not believe that Smuts could change the government's policy over any fundamental issue. But, characteristically, he saw that political capital might be made out of his own apparent readiness to negotiate.

Smuts, too, was not unaware of the magnitude of his task.[15] He was beginning to win Kruger's confidence, but that did not mean the President automatically adopted his recommendations.[16] His doubts on that score were quickly justified. Since early in 1897 Kruger had been convinced that, if his country's expenditure on railways and other public works was to be maintained at existing levels, more capital must be raised. Milner, learning of this, secretly intervened, via Chamberlain and some of the large finance houses in Europe, to ensure that a loan could not readily be raised by the Republic, and for a time the issue had to remain in abeyance. In 1898 Kruger looked at the problem again and decided to explore the possibility of raising the money he needed by a tax on mining profits, because for the first time the deep levels were beginning to produce gold in large quantities. Anxious to avoid disturbing the friendly relations he was trying to establish with the mining companies, Smuts tried to block Kruger's proposal and was largely instrumental in getting the proposed tax reduced from 10 to 5 per cent. When, in addition, the *volksraad*, the parliament of the Republic, reluctantly authorised the raising of a loan of £2.5 million, Smuts also suggested to Fitzpatrick that the mine-owners might secure a stronger basis upon which to argue future cases with the government by themselves advancing the loan. But when he made the same proposal to Kruger, the President rejected it firmly and immediately let it be known that he did not need to be taught his business by a youth.[17]

Smuts's dealings with another intermediary further underlined his political *naïveté*. In an attempt to put additional pressure on Kruger's government, Milner had recently brought charges of ill treatment of coloured British subjects in the South African Republic. It was an issue which aroused little interest, but on 22 December Smuts invited E. Fraser, the British Agent in the Republic, to call on him to hear the outcome of the executive council's deliberations on the subject. Towards the end of their conversation Fraser vouchsafed the remark that, after waiting two years for some improvement in the conduct of affairs in the Republic, Britain now intended to show who was master. The reason for that decision was that, in the parliamentary elections recently held in Cape Colony, the pro-imperialists had been heavily defeated. This, Fraser maintained, confirmed the view that Afrikaners throughout South Africa were in the mood to create a great Afrikaner republic in which the leading role would be played by the South African Republic. This constituted a threat to Britain's status as paramount power which could not go unchecked.

Though Fraser's interpretation of Afrikaner attitudes was largely erroneous, it coincided so closely with Smuts's own aspirations that he was disposed to take the comment seriously even had it not come from an apparently official source. The explanation for the Agent's seeming indiscretion is difficult to understand. It was certainly the case that Milner himself regarded Britain's attitude towards South Africa as deplorably supine. Summoned by Chamberlain, he had returned to England in November fully intending to stir up British opinion through the medium of the press to support firmer action. Chamberlain, however, though he might have been willing to appear bellicose in order to achieve his objectives, was in search of a diplomatic victory in South Africa rather than a military one. He was profoundly aware that any more decisive action would require the support of the cabinet and the public, and that was clearly lacking. For both those bodies, the exciting events in Egypt were of far greater significance than the grumblings at the remote southern tip of the African continent. In their eyes the defeat of the Mahdist forces at Omdurman and the set-back to French imperial ambitions at Fashoda were infinitely more stimulating than squabbles with a handful of presumptuous farmers.

Smuts, for his part, knew nothing of Milner's, or indeed of Chamberlain's, innermost thoughts, but he believed that Fraser's statement could not go unheeded. The delicacy of the situation became even more apparent when the British Agent raised another issue. Four days earlier an *uitlander* named Edgar, guilty of a violent assault upon another *uitlander*, was shot dead by an Afrikaner policeman whom he had struck fiercely over the head while resisting arrest. The policeman was himself arrested on a charge of murder but was released on bail by the public prosecutor who reduced the charge to one of manslaughter. At once the members of the Johannesburg branch of the South African League, a body first organised in Cape Colony in 1896 to promote British paramountcy in South Africa after the Jameson Raid had aroused anti-imperial feelings among the Cape Dutch, attempted to make a political issue out of the case. To defuse the situation, Fraser urged Smuts to have the policeman rearrested and Smuts, recognising the wisdom of the proposal, did as he was asked. Their joint efforts at peacemaking failed. The protesters held a public meeting and prepared a petition to be sent to the Queen but the Acting High Commissioner, General Sir William Butler, who was standing in for Milner, refused to receive the petition. He regarded the members of the League as puppets of Rhodes and interested only in stirring up trouble. A further protest meeting was then broken up by incensed republican burghers.

The mine-owners had refused to become involved in the turmoil and had pointedly refrained from signing the petition. Milner, meantime, vigorously condemned Butler's behaviour. Smuts was unaware of the High Commissioner's violent reaction. He was encouraged by the mine-owners' restraint, and by the willingness of Fitzpatrick, ostensibly speaking on their behalf, to continue discussions with him. The most contentious issue between the mine-owners and the government was the dynamite monopoly granted by Kruger to a nominally official company. His object had been to guarantee his government a reliable income from the manufacture of dynamite while retaining control of that strategic industry in government hands. In practice the monopoly had operated for the profit of private individuals, and the mine-owners believed that, as a result, they were paying a grossly inflated price for a commodity vital to their work. In December 1898 it was learnt that the *volksraad* was to discuss the renewal of the concession early in the following year. Milner, with Chamberlain's consent, urged the mine-owners to protest against any extension of the concession, but the mine-owners preferred to negotiate for the free manufacture of dynamite by offering an incentive of £600,000 to the government of the Republic.

Smuts seized upon the mine-owners' proposal with enthusiasm.[18] To demonstrate his good intentions, he suggested that a further dispute – over the right to mine underneath the land on which spoil from the mines was heaped – might be amicably settled along lines already proposed by the mine-owners. Fitzpatrick did not doubt Smuts's sincerity but believed he seriously underestimated the strength of the forces arrayed against him in the government.[19] Throughout his life Smuts', like Milner, tended to assume that, once he had seen what he believed to be a rational solution to a problem, others must see the issue in the same light. Their failure to do so could only be attributed to stupidity or outright hostility. He did not hesitate, therefore, to capitalise on what he saw as an excellent opportunity to improve relations between his government and the more influential elements among the *uitlander* population, an opportunity which appeared to have been enhanced by intervention from an unlikely quarter. Eduard Lippert, one of the leading beneficiaries of the dynamite concession, had approached Smuts and another politician, Leyds, with a plan apparently tailored to serve Smuts's purpose. Leyds, who might otherwise have been sceptical about Lippert's credentials for acting as agent in such a case, had had his critical faculties blunted by his recent experiences in Europe. There, as the agent of the Republic, he had been universally met with enquiries as to why his government refused to settle its differences with the mining community. Like Smuts, therefore, he listened to Lippert's proposal with a ready ear.

Lippert's plan was not wholly of his own devising. He had recently spent a holiday in Cape Colony with the experienced politician, John X. Merriman, who was anxious to improve relations between the colony and the Republic in order to discourage imperial intervention in South African affairs. Merriman had suggested that a South African conference should be held and that President Kruger might make it the occasion for offering some redress of the *uitlanders'* grievances. On his return to Pretoria, Lippert put the suggestion to Kruger. The President was wary of making gestures which he might be unable to implement but said that he was already pursuing some of the reforms Merriman had advocated.[20] It was at this point that Lippert approached Smuts and Leyds with a plan which he had modified in his own interests. His proposal was that the undermining issue should be settled according to the mine-owners' wishes, that the *uitlanders* should be given the franchise in some suitable form and that, as Merriman had suggested, the government should appoint a financial adviser who would be acceptable to all parties. In return, the mine-owners should be asked to agree to the extension of the dynamite concession. Doubtless Lippert mentioned that he had already had conversations with the President, though of course he had not obtained Kruger's approval for his plan.

Even evidence of prior consultation with the President could scarcely justify the energy with which Smuts now attempted to promote the scheme. When pressed by Fitzpatrick, he admitted that the executive had not been informed about the plan, but suggested that he might get agreement for it by springing it on the *volksraad* with the President's support. Challenged further about the franchise proposals, he swiftly produced a plan which would have involved the majority of the *uitlanders* in waiting seven years for the vote and then, equally precipitately, agreed to Fitzpatrick's suggestion that the vote should be given to all white adult males who had lived in the Republic since before 1890. In the light of this ill-considered improvisation, Fitzpatrick's doubts about the feasibility of Smuts's scheme were not surprising.[21] Yet some of the mine-owners were more hopeful. Lord Harris, chairman of Consolidated Gold-fields, told Chamberlain on 14 March that his company was prepared to accept Smuts's proposal unless the secretary of state objected. Chamberlain made it frostily clear that he did object, though claiming that he did so because public reaction to any such deal would undoubtedly be hostile.[22] In spite of this warning, a number of London capitalists with investments in South Africa offered to try to negotiate a comprehensive settlement with Leyds. Kruger, too, tried cautiously to prepare the way for a settlement in an address to the burghers of Heidelberg on 17 March, and a number of mine-owners put their own proposals to the state secretary, F. W. Reitz, two days later.

Up to this point Smuts's plans appeared to be going surprisingly well. The fact that tentative discussions were taking place had been concealed from the *volksraad* and the general public. In the suspicious mood of the burghers it would have been easy for ill-wishers to stir up trouble. But one ill-wisher there was, even among those party to the prospective negotiations. Fitzpatrick had all along been sceptical about the outcome of the proceedings. Now he intervened to wreck them by making them public. His motives are unclear. He may have distrusted the Boer leaders. More probably he believed he was promoting the grand aim of imperial intervention. He was fundamentally a foolish man who aspired to be both a leader of industry and a subtle statesman. By this action he did no service to his employers or to any other of the mining companies. He did, however, give a decided fillip to Milner's efforts to stir up trouble with the Republic.

As Smuts had feared, news of the negotiations immediately produced assertions and denials from all parties involved and destroyed all hope of a successful outcome. Chamberlain and Milner alone were pleased with events. They were both anxious that any negotiations with Kruger on behalf of the *uitlanders* should be conducted by the British government as an indication of Britain's paramount role in South Africa. Although the London Convention had expressly omitted any reference to British suzerainty over the Republic in favour of a more concrete definition of the nature of the relations between the two countries, Chamberlain was still atttempting to exploit the ill-defined powers implicit in suzerain status. Milner, meantime, was moving irrevocably, if as yet unilaterally, towards war. Whether the High Commissioner was responsible for encouraging the South African League to prepare a second petition to the Queen is not clear. It is certain that he let it be known that the petition would be forwarded to Her Majesty. With the aid of paid canvassers, more than 21,000 signatures were collected to a much more comprehensive indictment of the Republic's government than had been contained in the document rejected by Butler. Milner received the petition on 24 March 1899 and it was in Chamberlain's hands before the end of the month. A counter-petition, organised by the SAR government and signed by some 23,000 *uitlanders*, was dismissed by Conyngham Greene, the British Agent in Pretoria, as having no significance. Milner also blocked an attempt by Merriman to defuse the situation by summoning a conference of South African leaders to discuss mutual difficulties. It was only by enlisting the aid of President Steyn of the Orange Free State that Merriman had overcome the initial reluctance of Kruger to take part. William Schreiner, too, the Cape prime minister, had only

25

with difficulty been persuaded to support the proposal. It was, therefore, a great disappointment to Merriman that Milner's insistence upon being present at the conference ensured the rejection of the plan by the two republics.

Smuts, as yet inexperienced in the devious ways of politicians, was baffled and depressed by these events. He suspected that Chamberlain was behind all the machinations and was trying to force the SAR government to commit some unpardonable error which would justify British intervention. But, equally unversed in the ways of diplomats, Smuts believed that, even if Britain could trump up some *casus belli*, she would have to put 150,000 troops in the field, and that would give France and Russia, and possibly Germany, an opportunity to tackle her in another quarter.[23] Britain, he thought, could scarcely be unaware of that danger. He would have been less optimistic about Britain's probable behaviour had he known that, in what became known as the 'helot dispatch', Milner had written to Chamberlain on 4 May complaining vigorously about the treatment of British subjects in the South African Republic and had requested that Britain should give some striking proof of her intention 'not to be ousted from South Africa'.[24]

There were others in South Africa who had a keener insight into the country's affairs, notably Jan Hofmeyr, the leader of the Afrikaner Bond. Aided by Merriman and sometimes by Schreiner, and with the erratic assistance of a bewildered and increasingly belligerent Smuts, Hofmeyr set out to avert the conflict which appeared to be building up. With better sources of information than Smuts, he had learnt from Sir James Sivewright, a Cape politician who was then in England, that Chamberlain was trying to win support for a strong line in South Africa. Sivewright suggested a meeting between Kruger and Milner at which the former might offer concessions to remove *uitlander* grievances.[25] This suggestion Hofmeyr conveyed to Smuts. The latter replied that a seven-year residential qualification for the franchise, open at once to anyone who had lived in the Republic for ten years, might be acceptable to his government. Anyone seeking the franchise must, however, renounce his previous nationality. Yet surely, Smuts believed, Chamberlain must be bluffing. Prime Minister Salisbury was too cautious to be dragged unthinkingly into war. But if war were to come, the Republic would fight to the last, he added.[26]

Hofmeyr was deeply disturbed by Smuts's failure to recognise the extent of the danger and telegraphed urging him to adopt a conciliatory attitude.[27] Smuts replied in bellicose vein:

If England should venture into the ring without a formally good excuse, her cause in South Africa would be finished. And then the sooner the better; as we for our part are quite prepared to meet her. Our people throughout South Africa must be baptized with the baptism of blood and fire before they can be admitted among the other great peoples of the world. Of the outcome I have no doubt. Either we shall be exterminated or we shall fight our way out; and when I think of the great fighting qualities that our people possess, I cannot see why we should be exterminated. So, even if the worst happens, I am quite calm and await the future with confidence.[28]

Hofmeyr, unimpressed by such bravado, wired back to warn Smuts against pinning hopes on military support from the Cape Dutch.[29] Nevertheless, amidst all its rhetoric, Smuts's letter had contained a ray of hope. Kruger, it seemed, at the invitation of President Steyn, had agreed to meet Milner at Bloemfontein. Shortly afterwards, after consulting Chamberlain, Milner also agreed to the meeting.

To Smuts the discussions which took place between the President and the High Commissioner from 29 May to 5 June seemed wholly humiliating for the Republic. For the first time he saw Milner, rather than Chamberlain, as the chief threat to his country. 'There is something in his very intelligent eyes', he wrote to his wife, 'that tells me he is a very dangerous man.'[30] Kruger had not come to the conference empty-handed. He was prepared, as Smuts had indicated to Hofmeyr, to reduce the residential qualification for Whites from fourteen to seven years. Any adult male who had entered the Republic before 1890 might acquire the franchise in two years' time provided he became naturalised at once. Anyone else who had been in the country for two years might become naturalised immediately and obtain the franchise in five years. Under these terms no *uitlander* could be enfranchised immediately, but the proposals unquestionably provided the basis for negotiation. Milner, however, did not wish to negotiate. Instead he offered his own proposal – a five-year retrospective residential qualification or nothing. It is unlikely that many *uitlanders* would have availed themselves of the opportunity Milner's scheme would offer if it meant giving up their original nationality, but Kruger could not take the risk. He rejected the proposal and Milner broke off the conference. Under pressure from President Steyn, but with little hope of a successful outcome, Kruger asked for a further meeting with the High Commissioner, but, in spite of Chamberlain's request that he should keep the discussions going, Milner refused to see the President again.

Because of a delay in its transmission, Smuts had not yet received Hofmeyr's telegram warning him that he could expect no military aid from the Cape Dutch. He therefore appealed to Hofmeyr again. 'We

27

are setting our course,' he telegraphed. 'All eyes are now fixed on Afrikaner Bond. Will the ties of brotherhood become closer or looser? Afrikanerdom has never been at a more critical point than now.'[31] Hofmeyr
was worried. He had already wired Smuts urging him to try to induce
his government to abolish the dynamite concession and to introduce
other reforms in the hope of cutting the ground from under the feet
of Chamberlain and Milner[32] and he repeated his warning about the
lack of military support from the Cape. Puzzled and distressed by Hofmeyr's apparently lukewarm response to his own enthusiastic overtures,
Smuts asked that the Bond might at least pass a resolution supporting
Kruger's franchise proposal, even if they also suggested modifications.[33]
Hofmeyr was too shrewd and experienced to be deflected by the
demands of youthful pride. 'I can assure you', he wrote to Smuts, 'that
we strongly sympathise with you. ... But we are fully determined not
to let ourselves be moved by resentment, indignation, passion, or anything else, to the disadvantage of the cause of peace and therefore also
your own interests.'[34] It is not without significance, however, that Hofmeyr persisted in dealing with Smuts as the person most likely to persuade the Republic to accept a satisfactory settlement. Merriman, too,
though gently chiding Smuts – 'Do not make our task difficult by an
impossible attitude'[35] – still looked to him to persuade Kruger to make
reasonable concessions. Schreiner and another Cape politician, F. S.
Malan, added the weight of their advice along similar lines.[36]

Under these undoubtedly friendly pressures, Smuts responded well.
Hofmeyr was not unconscious of the fact that Milner's 'helot dispatch'
had been made public after the breakdown of the Bloemfontein conference. Although it had failed to convince either the cabinet or the British
public of the need for military action against the Republic, Chamberlain's
efforts to stir up feeling in England could not be ignored. Hofmeyr,
therefore, made a number of suggestions to Smuts about the way in
which Kruger's franchise proposals might be modified.[37] He was anxious
to get the approval of the Republic's government for his suggestions
before making them known to Milner lest the failure of the *volksraad*
to accept them at a later stage should be used by the High Commissioner
as further proof of Kruger's dissimulation.

While Hofmeyr now briefly held the centre of the stage, Smuts played
a loyal supporting role. It was Hofmeyr's view that Chamberlain would
accept a negotiated settlement if only he could demonstrate to the British
public that he had won the enfranchisement of some of the *uitlanders*
without a further period of waiting.[38] Among the suggestions he made
for the amendment of Kruger's franchise plan were, therefore, some
that might help Chamberlain to accept a compromise. Hofmeyr also

suggested that he himself might go to Pretoria to discuss his ideas with the *volksraad*. On his way there he talked with President Steyn and another prominent Free State leader, Abraham Fischer, and he also met Smuts. It was probably only the insistence of those men that induced Kruger and the executive *raad* to meet Hofmeyr. The President himself had unhappy memories of Hofmeyr's involvement in the Republic's affairs over the question of the administration of Swaziland. Kruger was not personally averse from amending his own franchise proposals, but he knew he would meet opposition from the *volksraad* which proudly defended the Republic's independence on all occasions. He therefore invited Hofmeyr to address a joint meeting of the *volksraad* and the executive *raad* on the evening of 5 July. Before an initially hostile audience, Hofmeyr insisted that any proposals for a revision of the qualifications for the franchise must be retrospective and must involve no delay between the time when a man, qualified by residence, took the oath of allegiance and was granted the franchise. He emphasised the horrors of war and reminded his hearers' that they could place no reliance upon military aid from the Cape Dutch. Supported by speeches from his fellow-Cape politician, A. J. Herholdt, from Fischer and from Kruger himself, Hofmeyr carried the day.

The visit to Pretoria had been a qualified triumph, but Hofmeyr was soon disturbed by the reaction of Smuts. Because the *volksraad* had agreed to make concessions, Smuts now expected the rest of Afrikanerdom to demonstrate its loyalty to the Republic's cause. Milner must be made to see that he could not increase his demands at will. 'Shall we now help Milner out of the confusion into which he has been brought by his own intrigues,' Smuts wrote. 'I leave him to the spirit of the Afrikanerdom which he has insulted in season and out of season.'[39] This was an attitude with which Hofmeyr had no sympathy. Having induced the *volksraad* to agree to concessions, he did not want the Republic to treat them as a final solution. In Hofmeyr's view they should be treated as a basis for negotiations with Britain. An inflexible statement would only lead to opposition from Milner. His idea was for Smuts to ask Schreiner to hand a copy of the *volksraad*'s revised position to Milner simply as an indication of the Republic's willingness to reopen discussions. In the meantime the *volksraad* itself might wish to look more closely at what was now proposed to ensure that no unforeseen difficulties would arise. Patience and flexibility were essential.[40]

Smuts was in no mood to propitiate the High Commissioner in the manner suggested by Hofmeyr, even if the *volksraad* had been willing to support the proposal.[41] But Hofmeyr persisted, suggesting that the text of their plan should at least be shown to Conyngham Greene, the British Agent in Pretoria, drawing his attention to the close comparison it bore to the demands made by Milner in Bloemfontein.[42] To this less ignominious suggestion, Smuts agreed. But, contrary to Hofmeyr's instinct, which was still to keep the proposals on a flexible basis, went ahead with preparing a draft bill which, in Hofmeyr's view, was open to misinterpretation: It was not Smuts alone, however, who did not wish to pander to Milner further. The *volksraad*, too, considered that it had conceded enough. The Bill was enacted without amendment. To satisfy Hofmeyr, Smuts included instructions to those concerned with the implementation of the Act in the government gazette which published the new legislation.[43] It was not enough. Milner immediately pounced upon the obscurities in the law and pointed out that the accompanying instructions had no legal force. He had already demonstrated that any proposal for a seven-year residential qualification would exclude, for a time at least, the large number of immigrants he had hoped to enfranchise by virtue of his five-year scheme.[44] The Republic's new plan in no way diminished his conviction that Kruger was trying to establish a Boer-dominated South Africa and that the Cape government, with its Afrikaner supporters, was sympathetic to his aims. The British government must not accept the franchise proposals without further inquiry.[45] Chamberlain, therefore, suggested there should be a joint inquiry into the implications of the scheme and induced the cabinet to send a token force of 2,000 troops to Natal as an earnest of their intention to negotiate from a position of strength. Meanwhile Milner took steps to brief Conyngham Greene about the points which, in his view, needed clarification.

Kruger, for his part, was not in favour of any further inquiry into what had already been decided by the *volksraad*, particularly in a matter which concerned the internal affairs of his country. The Orange Free State leaders, looking on, feared that war was inevitable.[46] At that critical moment Smuts took a series of bold initiatives, remarkable in one so young who had only recently come to office and who held no seat in the executive *raad*. With the approval of the *raad*, he called on Greene on 12 August to ascertain what Britain hoped to achieve from the joint inquiry. The following day Greene informed him, through an intermediary, that Milner's Bloemfontein proposals were again on offer. Smuts at once reopened discussions with the British Agent, but stressed that he was acting on his own initiative. He suggested that his government might indeed accept a five-year retrospective residential qualification and an increase in the *uitlander* membership of the *volksraad*, but only if Britain tacitly agreed to drop her claim to suzerainty and would not regard the arrangements as a precedent for interference in the internal affairs of the Republic at a later date. He would also try to persuade his government to agree to arbitration in the event of any dispute between Britain and the Republic once the franchise law had been enacted, provided no foreign elements were involved.

Smuts was certainly relying heavily upon his powers of persuasion in inducing the government and *volksraad* to accept his new proposals. But he believed that Kruger at least would be strongly influenced by the assurance that Britain would drop the suzerainty issue and give his country sovereign status at last. Milner, however, was not so easily convinced. Though he forwarded the news to Chamberlain, he commented dismissively that 'Nothing but confusion can result from this irregular method of negotiations.'[47] Chamberlain was not so bellicose as Milner and could not so easily ignore the likely response of the British public to the latest developments. 'They evidently constitute an immense concession,'[48] he commented, and not without a sense of relief went on to instruct the High Commissioner to inform the Republic that, if the proposals were submitted formally, they would be considered on their merits.

Kruger was pleased with the response and would have been even more so had he known that the British prime minister, Lord Salisbury, had written to Queen Victoria to say that war with the Republic was now improbable.[49] Though Milner still believed that Kruger's move had been no more than another attempt to avoid making any significant change, Chamberlain still clearly recognised that neither the cabinet nor the public wanted war. With the Republic apparently willing to co-operate, it would be impossible to persuade them that war was necessary.

Kruger's formal offer of a five-year retrospective franchise was submitted on 19 August. Two days later Reitz, in his official capacity as state secretary, made the mistake of requesting Britain to make the concessions which Smuts had suggested should be made unobtrusively. This amounted to a demand that Britain should openly renounce her role in the Republic. Chamberlain at once replied that such a request would impose heavy demands upon Britain and countered with the new demand that *uitlander* members of the *volksraad* should be permitted to use their own language, that the government of the Republic must be prepared to discuss with the British government any future proposals to change the method of election of the President or Commander-in-Chief and that the new scheme should be discussed fully with Greene.[50] Smuts knew that his government would never accept such terms and guessed that the two parties had reached the point when each suspected the other of merely proposing impossible conditions in order to avoid reaching a conclusion. Hofmeyr's view was that the Republic had gone further than was either wise or necessary in offering a five-year franchise, for, if Milner's forecast were correct, the Boers would soon lose control of their country. At the same time he considered that Reitz was asking far more than Britain could ever overtly concede. The conditions asked for by the Republic do seem to have been the turning-point for Chamberlain. Hitherto he would almost certainly have accepted a negotiated solution along the lines of Milner's Bloemfontein proposals. Britain's paramount role in South Africa would have been acknowledged – which was what he mainly desired – and he would have appeared to have achieved a remarkable victory for British prestige at a minimal cost. Now, however, he appears to have accepted that only the threat of military intervention would achieve the results he sought. Whether he thought the threat alone would suffice it is difficult to say, though that is the argument he put to the cabinet.

Faced with Chamberlain's apparent intransigence, the Republic withdrew its offer of a five-year franchise on 2 September but accepted that there might after all be grounds for a joint inquiry into the seven-year franchise scheme. But time was running short. On the same day Chamberlain asked Salisbury to summon a cabinet meeting at which he hoped agreement would be reached on sending an ultimatum. The cabinet met on 8 September, but was content to offer Kruger the terms he had himself submitted on 19 August, while adding that under no circumstances would the Republic be recognised as a sovereign international state. It was also agreed that 10,000 troops should be sent to South Africa – the first contingent to arrive in five weeks' time, the rest a week later.[51]

Although this was not the formal ultimatum that Chamberlain had sought, its impact on the Republic was likely to be little less striking. On hearing the news, Hofmeyr and Steyn urged the Republic to tread cautiously so as not to appear in the role of aggressor. Kruger's response was to declare the British demands both far-reaching and insolent.[52] His government, now fully expecting war, was already taking soundings regarding the likely reaction of several European powers. The response was not encouraging. Dr Leyds, in Brussels, reported that Germany would do nothing, that France was unreliable, but that there was just a possibility Russia might seize the opportunity to take action in Asia.[53] In spite of this gloomy forecast, Reitz replied to Chamberlain on 22 September, denying Britain's right to interfere in the Republic over the franchise issue and claiming for the Republic equality with Britain in South Africa.[54]

The British government, too, now expected war and played for time while preparations were made to send a full-scale expedition to South Africa. Chamberlain's problem was that he could not draft an ultimatum which would carry conviction with the parliamentary opposition[55] or with the British public as long as the Republic appeared willing to negotiate. His difficulty was resolved by Kruger himself. The President had finally concluded that war was inevitable. On 9 October he delivered his own ultimatum, hoping to be able to strike quickly against Natal before reinforcements arrived in the colony and so achieve a measure of success adequate to induce the British government to decide that peace was preferable to a prolonged struggle.

Smuts, who had been unable to exercise much influence over the later stages of the negotiations with Britain, was nevertheless in full accord with the President's decision. He was exhilarated by the prospect of war which, with the enthusiasm of a religious convert, he regarded as a heaven-sent test of Boer faith and discipline. Nor had he been idle during those days of tension. With a facility which was to mark the whole of his later career, he had already drafted a comprehensive plan of campaign which he presented to the government on 4 September.[56] He had, as Kruger now proposed, suggested a rapid strike to seize the port of Durban, which would make possible the defeat of the numerically weak British forces in Natal and the capture of their considerable supplies of arms and ammunition. This success might then encourage a rising of the Cape Afrikaners and the foundation of a third Boer republic in the colony. The corresponding blow to British prestige would shake the foundations of the Empire and deter Britain from moving her forces from Egypt and India for fear of unrest there. To this optimistic forecast Smuts added a warning that the republics must prepare a long-term economic programme in order to maintain themselves in the event of a lengthy and exhausting struggle. The treasury must not be allowed to become empty, the republics must be able themselves to produce adequate supplies of arms and ammunition, expert military advice must be sought from Germany, and an attempt should be made, with the help of Russia, to start a large-scale rising in India.

These excellent suggestions were accompanied by a wordy political polemic with the title, translated into English, *A Century of Wrong*. Though published under the name of Reitz, the book was the work of Smuts. It contained a highly tendentious account of the history of British relations with the republics and ended with the cry:

Even if we are exterminated the truth will triumph through us over our conquerors. . . . We now submit our cause with perfect confidence to the whole world. Whether the result be Victory or Death, Liberty will surely rise in South Africa like the sun out of the mists of the morning. . . . Then from the Zambezi to Simon's Bay it will be AFRICA FOR THE AFRIKANDER.

Wiser heads must have been shaken sadly at the publication of such adolescent rhetoric, which contrasted so sharply with the good sense contained in Smuts's military plan.

Yet there is no doubt he had made his mark in the years since his return from Cambridge. He had played a number of roles with varying success – in the legal profession, in journalism, as a diplomat and as a military strategist. In most of those roles he had, it is true, displayed considerable *naïveté* and some uncertainty. But he had zest and his determination never failed him. Perhaps he had taken himself too seriously, but the events in which he had become involved were of great moment for South Africa and seriousness of purpose was essential. He had had to abandon his attachment to Rhodes, but he had not lost the respect of Hofmeyr. Kruger listened to what he had to say, even if he did not always follow his advice. Smuts had made his mark and he had every intention of making it even more indelible in the dangerous years ahead.

3

The young soldier

In the opening days of the war it appeared that Smuts's military plan might succeed. The Orange Free State courageously threw in its lot with the South African Republic in accordance with the terms of their defence agreement and the forces of the two republics won early victories in northern Natal. This promising start was followed by a period of inactivity. The ageing SAR Commandant-General, Piet Joubert, was reluctant to press home the advantage his commandos had won. The drive to Durban never took place, and the British reinforcements landed unopposed. As a result of inept handling by their generals, the British troops suffered three disastrous defeats within a week in December, but, because the Boers did not hold on to their original initiative, the British reacted to their set-backs with an increasing determination to fight on until victory had been achieved.

During this period Smuts was not directly involved in military activities, but he maintained a lively, though not always informed, interest in events on the battlefield. In April 1900 he wrote enthusiastically to congratulate Louis Botha on succeeding Joubert as Commandant-General. He did not know how near the Boers had been to a rout in their recent retreat from the Tugela, and he was unaware that the tide was already beginning to turn against them when he wrote confidently, 'Do not forget that the enemy is at present in the same position as we, namely, with all his troops of any worth in the field, and if we are now to succeed in beating him back at the various points, our eventual victory is certain.'[1] Within two months Bloemfontein and Pretoria had fallen to the advancing British. The two republics were officially annexed and their names were changed to the Transvaal and the Orange River Colony.

Lord Roberts, who had succeeded the less aggressive General Buller as commander-in-chief, misjudged the nature of his achievement. Forgetting the military principle that the aim of war is to destroy the enemy's power to resist, he assumed that, with the capture of the two capitals, the Boers would surrender. The Boers could indeed no longer prosecute the war in the sense of fighting pitched battles. But anyone with Roberts' experience of the Indian north-west frontier should have been aware that campaigning did not consist only of set piece encounters.

The Boers' decision to continue the struggle as a guerrilla campaign met with Smuts's wholehearted approval. With Pretoria gone and the government operating from a temporary base in the eastern part of the republic, he had his first opportunity to sample military action. He had already been reluctantly forced to recognise that not all the burghers were filled with his own steely resolve and heady enthusiasm. Some had never even joined the commandos in the first place, while others had slipped quietly back to their farms after the initial success had been followed by heavy reverses. Smuts, therefore, took it upon himself to circulate a letter to all *landdrosts* (magistrates) urging them to encourage or if necessary to compel the burghers of their districts to rally to the defence of their country.[2] In July he was called upon to do some of the enforcement himself. The Boer leaders had decided to try to re-establish their authority in the Western Transvaal. General J. H. de la Rey was put in charge of military operations in the region and he asked for the assistance of Smuts. Together they put new life into the burghers of the western districts and conducted a number of small skirmishes against the British. Smuts still clung vainly to the hope that help would come from the Cape Afrikaners in spite of the limited response they had made when Free State forces briefly invaded the colony earlier in the year. But he was worried by the lack of news from his own government, cut off in the east, and by the rumour that Kruger had left for Europe. Unpalatable though this latter suggestion was, by October it was true.[3] Schalk Burger was elected Acting-President.

It was a gloomy period for Smuts, for about this time he learned of the death of his eighteen-month-old son in Pretoria in August. Yet he was enjoying his duties as political commissar to de la Rey. 'Disloyal officials are being dismissed and others appointed and everything is being done to let the burghers see that we are the lawful government,' he wrote to Reitz. He then added in a mood of exultation: 'The Lord God has destined great things for this little people.'[4] The first experience of war had, temporarily at least, revived something of Smuts's buried Calvinism.

Further south, in the Potchefstroom and Wolmaransstad districts, things were not going well. Acting in the name of de lay Rey, Smuts sought his superior officer's approval for assuming the rank of Acting Assistant Commandant-General in order to demonstrate that his authority overruled that of the combat general in the area and took control of the military situation. With the Lord's blessing, he wrote to de la Rey, he hoped to succeed in the task.[5] Like some divinely commissioned, though self-appointed, angel of judgement – a role for which he considered himself ideally suited – Smuts set about clearing up the problems of the district.[6] He dismissed a number of officers and set up a military court which dealt severely with, among other charges, cases of treason against the republic. By these methods he soon established order. Even though British troops were active in the area, he was able to mount guards at strategic points and to create a mobile force of 800 men from the hitherto disorganised rabble.[7]

Elated by his success and encouraged by the news of the enthusiastic reception given to Kruger in France, he raised again the suggestion approved at a meeting of commanders in October that the Boer forces should be concentrated to drive the British from the Witwatersrand. If that plan were not to be adopted, he proposed an invasion of the Cape,[8] with the aim of helping 'the Afrikaners in the execution of a general revolution and declaration of independence'.[9] For himself he envisaged a dual role – as combat leader and as political strategist. Had he not already, with de la Rey, won a convincing victory over the British in the Magaliesburg Mountains, west of Pretoria, in December? Had he not, too, on his own initiative, revitalised the forces in the south-west and led them in two successful battles to capture Modderfontein at the end of January and to defeat a numerically superior force commanded by General G. G. Cunningham on 2 February?[10] An invasion of the Cape would enable him to demonstrate the full scope of his military potential.

It was a severe blow to his self-esteem when Botha suggested that the expedition should be led by the more experienced General Beyers. Quickly he invoked his status as state-attorney to protect himself from the ignominy of serving under another commander. With complete self-confidence he wrote to his friend, N. J. de Wet, 'All the combat generals in the western Republic have asked to go to the Cape Colony under me as chief general.'[11]

By invading the Cape, Smuts hoped that a united South Africa might be created – under the Lord's guidance.[12] It was not, of course, a new theme for Smuts, but his hopes had been fuelled by the content of letters and newspapers he had captured from the British. In them he noted that England was deeply concerned about the situation in South Africa and that there was growing disquiet about the quality of the volunteer troops being sent to fight there. Britain's relations with France and also with Russia were becoming strained, while her war against the Ashanti on the Gold Coast had not yet been brought to a victorious conclusion. In the Cape itself, Afrikaners were said to be rising everywhere in response to the arrival of Boer commandos from the Free State.[13]

Smuts's political strategy was not put to the test. The accounts of conditions in the Cape and in Europe which he had read in the captured papers contained some truth, but they reflected more clearly the exaggerations which spring from the uncertainties of war. The British people were undoubtedly worried by the prolongation of a war which they had been led to believe would be over in a few weeks. Politicians were disturbed by the cost of the continuing struggle. There was lively criticism of the demand for unconditional surrender upon which Milner insisted. Did it not appear to encourage the Boers to go on fighting even while their country was being systematically destroyed by the farm-burning policy adopted by the British troops to prevent the commandos from obtaining food and shelter? But none of this meant that British public opinion was in favour of ending the war before the Boers had admitted defeat. In Cape Colony, too, the prime minister, Schreiner, had done his utmost to discourage Afrikaners from rising in response to the Boer invasion, and he had been largely successful. As Hofmeyr had warned, strong though the family ties might be between Cape Dutch and republican Boers, the former were not anxious to be incorporated into the great Afrikaner republic of which Smuts dreamed. Nor could Schreiner agree with Merriman that, with the exception of the leaders, those who did rebel should escape the total disfranchisement demanded by the British government, though he did urge that the punishment should be limited to five years rather than being a sentence for life.

The split over the role to be played by the Cape in the war widened, and in June 1900 Schreiner resigned. Sir Gordon Sprigg, ever on hand to take office when no one else was willing to respond, became premier. He was not popular among the Cape Dutch, who were already incensed by news of the farm-burnings in the republics. The imposition of martial law throughout the country at the time of the second ineffectual incursion by Boer forces at the end of the year aroused still more vigorous criticism of Sprigg's government. All this reinforced Milner's belief that the Cape Dutch could not be trusted, although their actions, if not their words, had been consistently restrained. Because of that error of judgement, his dispatches to England conveyed the impression that a more dangerous situation existed in Cape Colony than was truly the case. It was on the basis of Milner's reports that his Liberal critics challenged the British government's policy,[14] and this in turn helped to mislead Smuts when he tried to assess public opinion in England and South Africa.

So successful had the British forces been in fact that, late in February 1901, Kitchener confidently suggested to Botha that they should discuss peace terms. The Commandant-General, with the approval of his government – though to the dismay of the Free State leaders – met Kitchener at Middelburg. The discussions broke down, however, because Botha demanded independence for the former republics and an amnesty for those citizens of Cape Colony who had rebelled in response to the Boer incursions. Kitchener would accept neither demand, but so bad was the military position of the Boers that in May Botha convened a meeting of the Transvaal leaders, including Smuts, near Ermelo in the Eastern Transvaal. At the meeting it was decided to seek Kitchener's approval for sending a messenger to Europe to consult Kruger about future action. It was agreed, however, that President Steyn must be informed because the action of the Transvaal would affect the Free Staters equally. Reitz was the official correspondent, but Smuts appears to have written privately to Steyn suggesting that he himself should be the emissary to England and that, if Kitchener refused permission, he should go secretly.[15] He who had so recently affirmed his faith 'in that righteousness which has always triumphed in the struggles of humanity and which will not in our case be beaten by John Bull',[16] now appeared ready to put the case for surrender to Kruger. It was a betrayal which the Free Staters did not forget. Steyn treated Smuts's proposal with sorrowing contempt. To go to England secretly, he wrote, would seem like desertion. And, if the Transvaalers were to negotiate separately, 'What trust can we then ever again have in one another?'[17]

Smuts shrugged aside the rebuke. He had been prepared to wage the war to its bitter end as long as he could see himself emerging as one of the heroes of Afrikaner unification. Now that expert military opinion in the Transvaal had accepted that the struggle could no longer be carried on effectively, he changed his course. His role would be that of leading negotiator. For Kitchener did indeed refuse permission for a messenger to go to England, but allowed the Boers to communicate with Kruger by telegram. To Smuts fell the task of drafting the telegram which was sent in code via the Dutch Consul in nearby Standerton. Though admitting that the Free Staters were prepared to carry on the struggle, the telegram was otherwise couched in gloomy terms which virtually begged permission to bring the war to an end.[18] Kruger's reply brought little comfort or guidance. There was, he said, little prospect of intervention on the Boers' behalf by any European power, though opinion in England appeared to be becoming more hostile to the war. The attitude of the Cape Afrikaners – and here Kruger seemed to have swallowed Milner's propaganda – appeared favourable to the Boer cause. His advice, therefore, was to carry on the war, though he recognised that the final decision must rest with the commanders in the field, because they alone fully understood their capabilities.[19] On receiving Kruger's reply, a conference of the governments of the two former republics met at Waterval in the Eastern Transvaal. It was attended by Chief-

Commandant C. R. de Wet of the Free State and by Commandant-General Botha and Assistant Commandant-General de la Rey for the Transvaal. The result was a decision not to make peace unless the independence of the republics was recognised and the interests of the Cape rebels protected.[20]

While he was in Ermelo, Smuts learned that Isie had been moved to Pietermaritzburg and from Standerton he was able to send a letter to her on 2 June. It was carried by a British officer and was the first to reach Isie since they had been separated, though Smuts had tried several times to communicate with her. How much he had thought of Isie during their long absence from each other cannot be discerned from his correspondence. That he thought of her tenderly can be seen from the manner in which he now wrote about the death of their son and more recently of his own mother. Yet the role of devoted husband was quickly shed in favour of the more dramatic persona of the doomed warrior. 'Our future is dark,' he wrote, 'God alone knows how dark. Perhaps it is the fate of our little race to be sacrificed on the altar of the world's Ideals; perhaps we are destined to be the martyr race which must redeem our sordid money age from the charge of absolute worldliness and selfishness.'[21] Now, in Standerton, with Kitchener's help, Smuts was able to have a brief meeting with his wife.

Characteristically, Smuts doffed his negotiator's guise as readily as he had put it on. Once more he became the military commander and on 1 August launched upon the project which he had so long advocated, an incursion – it scarcely merits the description of invasion – into Cape Colony. It was a hazardous undertaking, skilfully executed. For a month he led his commando of 340 men along a zigzag route through the Orange River Colony, harassed at every step by British columns. Eventually he made a dangerous crossing of the Orange River and headed south-eastward. As an example of personal courage and endurance and of the tactical handling of a small mobile force in difficult terrain against vastly superior numbers, Smuts's campaign in September 1901 was a triumph. Again and again he eluded his pursuers. From time to time he struck unexpectedly, killing and wounding many of his opponents and capturing arms, ammunition and other supplies. Almost most important of all, he was able to replace his tired horses with fresh mounts. In many places he had a friendly reception from Cape Afrikaners, but at no time did there appear any likelihood of a mass rising in his support.

Having advanced to within 40 miles of Port Elizabeth by the end of September, Smuts turned westward. By mid-November he had crossed and recrossed the Olifants River to reach the North-Western Cape with a clear stretch of country ahead to German South West Africa. A rising by the Cape Afrikaners was now, for the time being, inopportune, Smuts decided. It would have drastic military consequences and could have an adverse effect upon eventual peace negotiations. Nevertheless, he insisted that thousands of Afrikaners wanted to join the commandos and were only prevented from doing so because the district had been cleared of horses by the British. Even now he was confident he could continue to harass the enemy by using small companies of 50 to 100 men provided he could get reinforcements from the Transvaal.[22]

Early in January 1902 Smuts sent Commander F. S. Alleman to Europe with letters for Kruger and a long letter to the Liberal journalist, W. T. Stead, accompanied by a detailed account of the background to the existing state of events in South Africa. He hoped his report might be published in order to awaken British opinion to the Boer view of the situation. The Boers, he said, were fighting with the calm resignation which sprang from the assurance that to do so was God's will. Adversity had converted their political creed into a religious faith. In particular he stressed the abhorrence felt by the Boers for the way in which the British had armed Africans to fight for them. The Boers knew well, he said,

that all the most serious complications which have arisen in South African history and politics are but aspects of the great Native question, the trail of whose shadow is black over the future as over the past of this dark continent. ... Far better than the English people can imagine, they understand the danger that looms before South Africa, when the Frankenstein Monster which a fatuous policy has created in this war will, as it necessarily must, get out of control.[23]

It was a reiteration of the old, instinctive fear of the African enemy, based not upon observable evidence but upon prejudice fed by memories of former battles, by more recent Darwinian theory and by an inner sensation which was irrepressible.

Having established contact with Europe through German South West Africa, Smuts turned his attention to harassing and sometimes capturing isolated British garrisons in the wasteland of the Northern Cape as far north as the Orange River. He did not venture south of the Olifants River again. Not only during this period but throughout the time since he had left Pretoria to take up arms in July 1900, he had managed to read extensively, often in books captured from the British. Apart from the Bible he had read works by Thomas à Kempis, by Augustine, Kant and Goethe, an astonishing achievement for one who had been so directly and continuously involved in the organisation and conduct of military operations.

Not all the Boers were still determined to fight on. Some had surrendered throughout the struggle and were called 'hands-uppers'. Kitchener believed that it was worthwhile trying again to test the views of the Boer leaders. He got in touch with Acting-President Schalk Burger who met President Steyn in Klerksdorp between 9 and 11 April. Steyn was adamant that he would only consider giving up a fight which he had undertaken on the Transvaal's behalf and which had led to the devastation of his own country if the independence of the republics was guaranteed. This proposal was put to Kitchener in Pretoria with a request for a general amnesty, equality for the English and Dutch languages and the offer of a perpetual treaty of friendship and peace supported by arbitration in all future disputes between Britain and the republics. Kitchener consulted the British government, which rejected the idea of independence for the republics. The Boer leaders then asked permission to call together representatives of their people to discuss peace terms on the basis of the surrender of their independence, coupled with other proposals similar to those suggested by Britain a year earlier at Middelburg.

Smuts, far away in the north-west of Cape Colony, first learned of these developments when, towards the end of April, he was summoned to attend a conference of Boer representatives in Vereeniging in his capacity as state-attorney. He travelled under safe conduct by a British ship to Simonstown and then completed the journey by rail. He met Kitchener at Kroonstad and learned from him the extent of the negotiations that had taken place. From the moment of his arrival at Vereeniging he became totally absorbed in the discussions between the Boer leaders, but found time to write to Isie a long letter which, in addition to gossip about family and friends, contained a nobly worded assertion of his intention to go on striving to do what was right.[24]

Just as, at Ermelo, he had transformed himself from aggressive military commander to wholehearted negotiator and back again to field commander, now he pushed thoughts of war to the back of his mind and became totally involved in the peace negotiations. The military leaders were asked to report on the strength of the forces still in the field. The overall number was not unimpressive but the condition of the men was weak. Steyn stoutly insisted that he would never compromise over independence, but the weight of opinion was against him. On 16 May Smuts and the Free State Attorney, J. B. M. Hertzog, were asked to draft proposals stating that the republics would be prepared to surrender control of their foreign affairs to Britain and accept the status of British protectorates. They would also surrender a portion of the South African Republic (the Witwatersrand and Swaziland) and would conclude a defensive alliance with Britain in respect of South Africa.[25] Having completed their assignment, the two lawyers, together with de la Rey, Botha and de Wet, presented the proposals to Milner and Kitchener in Pretoria. Milner countered with a demand that the Boers should surrender and acknowledge their allegiance to Britain after which the terms offered in Middelburg, suitably amended, would be presented to them. On this latter basis, Milner, Sir Richard Solomon, the Cape Attorney-General, Smuts and Hertzog began to draft an agreement.

In one important respect Smuts's personal contribution to these proceedings was to be of lasting importance. In Middelburg it had been suggested by Botha that the question of enfranchising the African population should be settled only after the introduction of representative government in the former republics. Chamberlain had accepted the proposal, adding that, if the vote were then given to Africans, it should be so limited as to ensure the just predominance of the white race. He did not include coloured people in this restriction. To them would be granted the legal position they had for long enjoyed in Cape Colony.[26] Now Smuts redrafted that section of the agreement to leave the whole question of the native franchise to be discussed only after self-government had been restored to the republics, which meant that the decision on the native vote would be taken by the republics rather than by Britain. Moreover, his use of the term 'native' – as opposed to 'kaffir' which was used in the earlier negotiations – opened the way to the exclusion of all non-Whites, coloured people as well as Africans, from the franchise. It is surprising, therefore, that the new draft was accepted without comment when it was subjected to careful scrutiny by the British negotiators. The rest of the terms of the agreement, apart from the demand for surrender and the recognition of King Edward VII as lawful sovereign, were designed to tempt the Boers, though the offer to teach the Dutch language in schools where parents requested it was not to prove quite as generous as was at first thought. The future of the Cape rebels, however, lay outside the terms of the agreement and would be decided by the Cape government. Milner informed the Boer leaders that the Cape government had decided upon the disfranchisement of all rebels, but he did not make it clear that they would be brought to trial. He did say that the leaders, together with those found guilty of crimes which did not arise directly from the war, would be liable to other punishments. Smuts was to take up that issue later.

The new terms were put to the assembled Boers to be accepted or rejected by midnight on 31 May. The discussions were intense and moving. It was the advocacy of Botha which finally converted de Wet. Smuts spoke with all the solemnity and conviction in favour of accepting the terms with which he had not long before argued for a continuation of the fight. 'Comrades, we decided to stand to the bitter end,' he said. 'Let us now, like men, admit that the end has come for us. . . . But we bow to God's will. The future is dark, but we shall not relinquish courage and our hope and our faith in God.'[27] He may not have been a minister of God, but he had fought, as he was ready to assert, as a soldier of God, and now spoke as God's statesman. He had certainly convinced himself of his own sincerity – it was essential to his faith in himself that he should do so – but his very firmness was remembered against him by those who, like Hertzog and de Wet, signed the agreement with hatred of the British still in their hearts. Steyn alone, who resigned the presidency which his followers continued steadfastly to recognise, refused to sign.

What had been gained by prolonging the struggle? Not a military victory. The fighting had brought profound suffering to South Africa, but it had not resulted in the creation of an Afrikaner republic stretching from Table Bay to the Zambesi as Smuts had confidently forecast in September 1899.[28] More than twenty thousand Boer women and children had died in refugee camps set up by the British. The greater part of the Transvaal and the Orange River Colony had been rendered desolate. The Boer people had been split into two hostile camps, the bitter-enders in one and those who had given up the fight in the other. Smuts and those like him had almost wilfully misjudged the probable reaction of the European powers and of the Cape Afrikaners. For the time being the prospect looked bleak. On the other hand, public opinion in Britain had come to admire the Boers' courage. Liberal leaders detested the 'methods of barbarism' which the British troops had used to bring the enemy to heel. Some of them were determined that, when they came to office, they would make amends. Indeed, concern for the Boers so fully occupied the hearts of their sympathisers in Britain that it excluded completely any thought for the non-Whites of South Africa whose lives had suffered equal disruption, who had died in equal numbers in the refugee camps and who yet, for the greater part, had loyally supported the British authorities. In them Britain showed little interest. Neither did Smuts.

The task of reconstruction in South Africa did not fall to Smuts. The responsibility was Milner's. Created a baron on 25 May 1901 and a viscount on 28 June 1902, Milner had given considerable thought to what the task might entail. As early as Christmas 1900 he had laid down the principles which were to guide his actions when victory had been achieved. His main aim was to create a South African federation under the British flag in which the dominant role would be played by men of British descent. To achieve that aim there must be large-scale immigration so that in time the Boers would constitute no more than 40 per cent of the white population. Most of the immigrants would settle in the towns, but, if the barriers which separated the races were to be broken, three out of every eight farmers in the former republics must be British. They must be men of some substance with plenty of farming experience and must not settle in an all-British enclave. He hoped that the immigrants would arrive quickly because he was anxious to postpone the granting of self-government until there was a clear British majority and he had established the sort of federation he wanted. He therefore urged Kitchener to make every effort to promote the federal idea at a practical level by keeping as many aspects of development as possible on an inter-colonial basis. Education, too, would make its contribution, with English as the medium of teaching except at the most elementary levels. Thus did he interpret the language clause in the Vereeniging agreement and in so doing stirred up acute hostility among the more nationalistic Boers.

The first step, Milner believed, must be the restoration of the mining industry to its full working potential. From that source alone could come the wealth upon which all other developments would depend.[29] Fortunately, with one exception, the Boers had failed to wreck the mines, though no gold had been produced since the outbreak of war. By October 1900 Milner was planning to start the mines working again, though guerrilla forces roamed the surrounding countryside. In December, in order to meet the shortage of African labour for the mines due to the demands made by military transport work, Milner made arrangements to enable the Transvaal Native Labour Association to recruit in Portuguese East Africa.[30] By the end of May 1901 the first three mines had recruited sufficient labour to start work.[31] When peace was restored, Milner directed all his vast energies into putting his plans into effect. He had become Governor of the Transvaal and the Orange River Colony in 1901, and in June 1902 civilian government was restored. Thanks to Milner's efforts, the majority of the Boers were able to return to their farms by the end of 1902, though severe and prolonged drought delayed the rehabilitation of the countryside.

Having set his plans for economic recovery in motion, Milner turned his attention to ways and means of achieving federation. He put in hand the construction of a uniform education system; he united the railways of the Orange River Colony and Transvaal under the supervision of an inter-colonial council which also controlled the schools and the South African constabulary; he created an experimental customs union and he appointed a native affairs commission under the chairmanship of Sir Godfrey Lagden, an experienced colonial administrator who had

45

served in West as well as in South Africa. This commission was ordered
to make recommendations which would enable the various colonial governments to adopt a common native policy. Milner's pursuit of efficiency,
his distrust of the Boers and his failure to appreciate the importance
of keeping in close touch with the people under his administration led
him to enlist the assistance of a group of able young graduates of Oxford
University to promote his plans. They were described disparagingly by
Merriman as Milner's Kindergarten, a title adopted with pride by the
young men themselves.

During this time Smuts's work lay in another field. Immediately after
the signing of the peace agreement he returned to the Cape and advised
the Cape Afrikaners who had joined him to surrender, informing them
that disfranchisement would be the most they would suffer if they had
acted according to the rules of war. He protested angrily when he learned
that they were also to be tried, but was assured that the cases had,
for the greater part, already been dealt with and the prisoners released.[32]
Only slightly mollified, he insisted that, while he himself had fought
for a united South Africa, everything now was being done to destroy
the Afrikaner identity. 'Let us try', he wrote, 'so to arrange our politics,
our administration and our legislation that a compact South African
nationality may be built up with the best elements of both parts of the
Colonial population.'[33] To his fellow-Afrikaner, Abraham Fischer, former
member of the executive council of the Orange Free State, he wrote
in a rather different vein, stressing the need to strive for the principle
of independence for which Afrikanerdom had always stood. It was essential, he said, to avoid the anglicisation of their children, if necessary
by making private provision for their education. But the moderate
English who were prepared to work with the Afrikaners must not be
estranged by extreme ideas.[34] Smuts's intentions seemed reasonable and
his sentiments were finely expressed, but he lacked a plan for achieving
the marriage of differing standpoints.

Towards the end of 1902 Joseph Chamberlain announced that he
intended to visit South Africa. Many of the Boer leaders believed this
was due to his dissatisfaction with Milner's handling of the situation
and they determined to make their views known to him. Characteristically Smuts drafted a circular inviting a number of prominent burghers
to a meeting in Pretoria at which the terms of a memorial to the secretary
of state could be agreed, and suggesting lines along which they might
make their representations. Most of Smuts's proposals were adopted
by the meeting and Smuts himself was chosen to present the address.
The meeting with Chamberlain took place on 8 January 1903 and Smuts
took the opportunity to deliver an explanatory speech in Dutch in which

he stressed the need to respect the feelings and traditions of the Afrik-aners.[35] His choice of language demonstrated both to the secretary of state and the assembled burghers where his immediate loyalties lay. He added that fair treatment would ensure the perpetual loyalty of all his people, a claim which he might have found difficult to justify in view of the attitude of the leaders of the Orange River Colony in particu-lar. The address itself called for an amnesty for all offences committed during the war and requested that government schools should be put under local management to ensure that parents' wishes could be made effective, particularly regarding the teaching of Dutch. The main concern regarding the native question was to make it clear that relations between Europeans and the rest of the population remained unchanged.[36]

Smuts's conclusion was that the meeting had been a dismal failure. Chamberlain had appeared unresponsive to every point that had been raised. Smuts himself was equally unco-operative when Milner approached him, together with Botha and de la Rey, inviting them to become members of the Transvaal legislative council. The polite reason given for rejecting the offer was that the country needed a time of quiet consolidation. Public discussion of potentially controversial issues could only have a divisive effect upon a society which all were seeking to unite. It would be obvious to all that power and responsibility still rested with the government.[37] It was this latter point which weighed most hea-vily with Smuts and his colleagues, who believed that their membership of a council of thirty could have little effect upon policy and might easily be misconstrued by their supporters. They therefore wrote a circular letter to explain their decision.[38] Smuts also wrote in more pretentious tones to former-President Kruger: 'Verily God's hand is heavy on our people. ... But however poor we may become, we shall with God's help summon up our utmost strength to preserve our nationality.'[39] He did not try to explain how this objective could be achieved within a united South Africa.

The question of preserving the Afrikaner nationality was taken up again a few months later when, on 2 July, a public meeting in Heidelberg passed a number of resolutions which were transmitted by Botha to Milner with Smuts acting as his amanuensis. One of the resolutions condemned the proposal to introduce Chinese labourers into South Africa on the ground that such action would be detrimental to the interests of Whites and non-Whites alike. The idea had first been mooted in May 1902 in response to the shortage of labourers in the gold-mines. Milner had seized upon it, not, as Smuts was later to claim, because he was being manipulated by the mine-owners, but because the urgent recovery of the mines was the foundation upon which all his plans for South

Africa's prosperity rested. Botha's objections were elaborated in a memorandum, again drafted by Smuts, which was submitted to a commission appointed by Sir Arthur Lawley, the Lieutenant-Governor of the Transvaal, to investigate the labour needs of the colony. The memorandum drew attention to the malign effects of the importation of Indian coolies into Natal where Indians now were a permanent feature of the population and were almost as numerous as Europeans. To compound the problem they were encroaching upon land formerly belonging to Europeans. The labour crisis in the Transvaal, the memorandum continued, was a temporary phenomenon, boosted by inaccurate figures. African labourers there were in plenty, but, because of the wealth they had accumulated during the war while working for the British, they were unwilling, for the time being, to quit their homes in order to work for wages. Even those who were squatting on European-owned farms were refusing to work for the owners because they regarded the Boers as a conquered people who could not enforce labour regulations. The temporary shortage should be met by employing Europeans who would strengthen the balance between Whites and Blacks. The long-term solution was to use the existing laws to force natives to work and to reinforce those tactics by gradually breaking up the native locations.[40]

If Smuts might, over his own signature, have used more discreet language, there is nothing to suggest that he disagreed with the view that Africans should provide the labour necessary to support European civilisation in South Africa. Merriman, who was engaged in an election campaign in the Cape in which non-white voters could seriously affect the outcome, was acutely embarrassed by the memorandum. He vigorously rejected the view that the lot of the Africans should be arbitrarily worsened to meet the needs of Europeans. His hostility to the importation of Chinese labourers was as strong as that of either Smuts or Botha. His fear was that their presence would enable the mine-owners to cut the wages of Africans still further and he also wanted to see larger numbers of Europeans working in the mines. He was not slow to point out that he had campaigned against Chinese labourers before Smuts had appeared conscious of the threat they presented. Even Smuts's old English friend, Emily Hobhouse, who had spoken out so vigorously in defence of the interests of Boer women and children in the refugee camps during the war, chided him gently for failing to go to England to make his opposition to Chinese labourers known in person. With some petulance Smuts replied that he could do nothing when the government only seemed concerned with serving the mining industry at any cost. In any event, he wrote, 80 per cent of the industry was a sham, perpetuated to swindle European investors and postulating a labour shortage where none existed.[41]

It was an indiscreet remark and it was untrue. Some mining companies existed primarily to promote share deals, but they accounted for nearer 20 per cent than the 80 per cent Smuts had claimed.[42] Unfortunately, in an earnest attempt to put the Africaner case before the British public, Emily Hobhouse sent his letter to *The Times*, where it was published. Smuts was taken aback by the news and admitted that his statement was an exaggeration. With a touch of bravado he added that he might soon have to fight for his dear life in defence of his stand. But he placed high hopes on the early return to office of a Liberal government in England. What he then wanted was immediate self-government for the Transvaal which would put a curb on Milnerism and the wrongdoings of the capitalists.[43] He had written in similar vein to Merriman, boasting that, if the financiers wanted war, he would make the fight worth while. Merriman was an equally vociferous critic of Hoggenheimer and Co., a designation he gave without distinction to anyone he saw fit to regard as a capitalist, and he concurred wholeheartedly.[44]

Most of Smuts's correspondence during 1903 had been couched in querulous tones. To those prepared to listen, he played the role of the defeated warrior suffering the pains of conquest. In his letters to Miss Hobhouse he played it fortissimo, sounding the depths of despair while not forgetting to mention his own courage and the fortitude of his fellow-Afrikaners. To Merriman, too, his letters were shrill in their denunciation of the enemy, but he took care in this case to present himself as the young statesman seeking to guide his people to their true if as yet not very clearly defined destiny. In 1904 there were signs of a change in Smuts's outlook. Plentiful rains had dispelled the drought and the fear of famine had subsided. Though Smuts was still heavily engaged in helping to resettle the last of the prisoners of war who had returned to the Transvaal in a state of destitution, he found time to involve himself in positive political action. Together with some of his colleagues, he assembled a congress in May which passed a resolution in favour of founding an organisation to appeal to fairminded Englishmen and encourage them to stand alongside the Boers.

Reporting these developments to Merriman, Smuts, for the first time in their correspondence, raised the question of creating a South African federation to stimulate a larger ideal of patriotism. It marked the beginning of a movement which was to be of the greatest importance for South Africa. Smuts's ideas differed from Milner's plan for a federation which would spring from the common economic needs of the South African colonies and would be the result of an imperial initiative. The united South Africa Smuts envisaged would develop in response to a deeply felt aspiration among the Boers, though it is unlikely that many Boers at that time had given serious consideration to what was essentially Smuts's own proposal. It was an idea with which Merriman sympathised, but for the time being he could do little to help in Cape Colony. As a result of the five-year disfranchisement imposed upon the Cape rebels, the Progressive Party, founded in 1897 to strengthen links with Britain, had narrowly defeated Merriman's South African Party in the elections held in February. Merriman, like Smuts, was not anxious to move in the direction of federation while Milner was on hand to channel any development into his own mould. As a plan for the future, however, he saw it as an important step towards freeing South Africa from the bureaucratic interference of Whitehall. Meanwhile he insisted that the main obstacle to any agreement between the colonies was the difference in their attitude towards non-Whites.

Merriman's enthusiastic response caught Smuts off his guard. He had as yet given little thought to the implications of his suggestion. He did, however, flatly reject the idea of representative rather than responsible government for the Transvaal as embodied in the Lyttelton Constitution of 1904, named after Alfred Lyttelton who had succeeded Chamberlain at the colonial office. The resignation of Chamberlain seems to have gone virtually unnoticed by Smuts, so convinced was he that Milner was now the main enemy of all for which he hoped. With Milner still in South Africa, representative government, which left ultimate authority in the hands of the executive even when the majority in the legislature were elected, offered no prospect of change.

In January 1905, in fulfilment of the decision taken by the congress held in the previous year, a Boer political party was founded and named *Het Volk* – The People. This was not the inter-racial body envisaged by Smuts, but that hope had been undermined by the formation in the previous year of the Responsible Government Association. This body consisted of English-speaking residents in the Transvaal who disliked Milner's efforts to deprive the population of a voice in the formulation of policy. Milner himself left South Africa in May and was succeeded by his long-standing friend, Lord Selborne. Selborne has often been compared to his disadvantage with his wife, the brilliant daughter of the Marquess of Salisbury. He was, in fact, an intelligent, thoughtful man to whose opinions too little credit has been given. His impact upon South Africa was diminished by the advent of a Liberal government in England when he had been in office barely half a year.

Not least in significance was the wise advice he was to give to Botha on native policy in the light of the report of the South African Native Affairs Commission which was published in 1905, and which, because of Milner's departure and the flurry of constitutional activity generated by the Liberal government, was largely ignored. Among the significant proposals of the Commission was the recommendation that natives, defined as aboriginal inhabitants of Africa south of the equator and including half-castes and their descendants – coloured people – should only be permitted to own land in reserves or in urban locations specially set aside for them. In addition they should be permitted to vote for a fixed number of European representatives in parliament.[45] Selborne's proposals were of a more generous character in respect of both Africans and coloured people.[46] Smuts, however, was far too concerned with the future of his own fellow-Afrikaners to take a serious interest in recommendations concerning the treatment of Africans. But he noted them, as did others, and drew upon them in later years.

On hearing the news of the fall of the Unionist government, Smuts at once determined to go to England to urge the Liberals to grant responsible government to the Transvaal and the Orange River Colony. In a letter to Steyn he concealed the reason for his trip, stating that he was travelling to England for reasons of health.[47] Again, as in 1901, Steyn deplored his dissimulation.[48] That Smuts was travelling on his own initiative there can be no doubt, and his visit to England was to have important repercussions upon his life outside as well as within the political sphere. He was a bad sailor and for a time suffered from seasickness. When he recovered he made the acquaintance of a fellow-traveller, Margaret Clark, a young Quaker woman, whose home was in Somerset and who was a granddaughter of the great Liberal, John Bright. Miss Clark had arrived in South Africa to assist Emily Hobhouse in a scheme for training Boer women in cottage industries. Now, returning home where she was soon to marry Arthur Gillett, a banker, she was attracted to Smuts as strongly as he to her. A deep friendship sprang up between them which was to last throughout Smuts's life. Together, they were able to stimulate each other's thinking and to exchange confidences without inhibition. Apart, they carried on a correspondence in which each wrote freely about their innermost thoughts. Of all Smuts's correspondents, apart from Isie, Margaret Clark probably understood him best, and in some respects Smuts was more at home when writing to her than to his wife. Isie shared more deeply the Afrikaner side of his nature. Margaret was to be the one who linked him most firmly with the wider world beyond South Africa. His nature craved the friendship of intelligent and beautiful women. He was never at ease to the same extent in the company of men, among whom he always felt the need to excel. To this generalisation his relationship with Botha was an exception, though, had Botha lived longer, Smuts mights have felt it increasingly difficult to accept the position of *secundus inter pares*.

Smuts's aim in going to England was to lobby members of the government. With that end in view, he prepared a memorandum in which he argued that, since the war in South Africa had ended, the balance of power had shifted in a wholly unsatisfactory direction. Everything had been done to promote the interests of the mining companies at the expense of the true residents of the Transvaal. To accept the franchise proposals contained in the Lyttelton Constitution would be to perpetuate the unhappy conditions which prevailed in the country. The idea of 'one vote one value' proposed by the Lyttelton Constitution ignored the women and children of whom there were far more among the Boers than on the Rand. It also ignored the hundreds of thousands of Africans, but that was a point Smuts did not mention, though Merriman, to whom Smuts had sent a copy of his memorandum, had warned that to ignore it would do their cause harm in the estimation of the British public.[49] Nor was Merriman Smuts's only critic on that score, but Smuts remained unconvinced.

His determination to destroy the power of the capitalists dominated Smuts's exchanges with the prime minister, Campbell-Bannerman, and the other Liberal leaders. Even his condemnation of Chinese labour seemed less of a moral or racial issue than a means of overthrowing the mining magnates.[50] When he reflected in later years upon the effect of his conversations upon the Liberal leaders, Smuts was inclined to claim more credit than he deserved. Campbell-Bannerman had been committed to the restoration of responsible government to the former republics ever since they had been annexed. But Smuts's memorandum and his personal representations convinced the prime minister and many of his cabinet colleagues of the need to look again at the franchise proposals contained in the Lyttelton Constitution which affected the distribution of seats in the legislative council between the European parties. As a result, the West Ridgway Commission which was sent to South Africa to make recommendations about the franchise gave the leaders of *Het Volk* an opportunity to seize power for which they had not dared to hope.

This did not at first seem to be the likely outcome of the inquiry. The visit of the West Ridgway Commission coincided with a Zulu rising in Natal which was put down by the provincial authorities with excessive harshness. The reaction of Merriman and Smuts differed only in emphasis. The former found his humane instincts profoundly disturbed by the actions of the Natal government which, he believed, reinforced his view that the only way to discourage imperial intervention in South Africa was to admit qualified Africans to the franchise. Smuts, though condemning the military campaign conducted by the Natal government, was less concerned with the misdemeanours of the Europeans in Natal than with their effect upon the visiting commission. What he particularly feared was that the Commission might recommend the Crown to retain reserve powers until non-Whites were given political representation. That, he believed, would be unacceptable to the overwhelming majority of Whites in South Africa.

Smuts's first impression was that the Commission's visit had been a disaster for *Het Volk*. Convinced that the Commission's recommendations would undermine his plans for the future, he again raised with Merriman the possibility of working towards federation at once or, preferably, union. Once again the older man warned of the dangers of moving too quickly and thereby inviting imperial intervention and again he stressed the need for native representation in any federal or unitary parliament.[51] Merriman's advice was sound. Milner's Kindergarten, led by Lionel Curtis, were already hard at work attempting to achieve the goal of federation along the lines laid down by their former leader. Because they isolated themselves from the world in their cocoon of intellectual superiority, they were unaware that others were contemplating the same goal, though for different reasons. It was fortunate for those who sought union by means of a South African rather than an imperial initiative that the Kindergarten remained ignorant of their plans until it was too late for Curtis to do other than co-operate.

The West Ridgway Commission having reported more favourably than the *Het Volk* leaders had anticipated, and with the prospect of elections in the Transvaal in the offing, Smuts deemed it expedient to adopt a moderate tone in his political utterances. Even his criticisms of Chinese labour had to be toned down to avoid antagonising voters in the mining areas. An alliance with the English-speaking Responsible Government party also seemed desirable if the forces of the mine-owners were to be successfully challenged. In the event and much to Smuts's surprise, *Het Volk* won an overall victory. The West Ridgway franchise recommendations had not proved as effective a deterrent to an Afrikaner victory as their proponents had intended. Even the alliance with the Responsibles had been unnecessary. Smuts recognised, however, that some seats had been unexpectedly won because his party had advocated a non-racial policy as far as the two European groups were concerned and he believed that policy must henceforward be honestly observed.[52] Even the Chinese question, it now seemed, deserved careful scrutiny before a decision was taken to repatriate the labourers too hastily. So an inquiry was instituted which was free to recommend deferment of repatriation if it were necessary, as a temporary expedient, to ensure the efficient operation of the mining industry. The responsibilities of office appeared to be modifying the outlook of the Boer leaders.

In announcing these views to Merriman, Smuts mentioned that he might himself have become premier of the Transvaal but had decided that it would have been a mistake to take precedence over Botha.[53] It was an understandable remark and revealed something of Smuts's ambition and self-esteem. But a mistake it would have been, even were it a possibility. The popular Commandant-General, who reacted instinctively to Afrikaner sentiment yet had the strength of character to mould it when he thought fit, would have been a difficult man for the intellectual Smuts to supplant. It is interesting that he believed he might have done so. But only Botha could carry the Afrikaners with him on a policy of co-operation with the British while simultaneously convincing the British of the Boers' sincerity.

Merriman, to whom Smuts confided his plans, had lost none of his waspishness. The Chinese labourers were still a scourge, whatever Smuts might say, he replied. Why could they not be replaced by Europeans? Smuts, however, now that a *Het Volk* government under Botha's leadership had been sworn into office on 4 March 1907, had to face facts. Reluctantly he acknowledged that there was some truth in the Chamber of Mines' contention that white labourers were both expensive and unreliable, though he was prepared to sanction an experiment by the labour leader, Fred Creswell, to see if a mine could be operated profitably using only European workers.[54] Merriman was not the only friend to challenge his new-found attitude of co-operation with the British. Soon after taking office, Smuts had produced an Education Bill for the Transvaal in which English was to be the compulsory medium of instruction at higher levels while Dutch might be employed optionally. Characteristically during those years when he was feeling his way he had sought the advice of several people before submitting his draft to the legislature.[55] Steyn and Hertzog had different plans for the Orange River Colony. Reluctantly Smuts had resisted Steyn's earlier appeal for greater assistance in setting up church schools, because he believed that to do so would alienate their English allies and might not please the majority of the Boers.[56] Hertzog, however, when his *Oranjia Unie* party took office, steadfastly pursued an educational policy which would ensure that the Dutch language would retain equal status with English. He was determined to ensure the survival of Dutch culture in the face of what he believed to be a concentrated attack by the pro-imperialists. Even in the Transvaal the Boers did not accept Smuts's policy wholeheartedly and there were instances of English teachers being harassed by local school boards who demanded that reports should be submitted in Dutch.[57]

The publication in 1907 of a document which became known as the Selborne Memorandum caused a stir among all those who wanted South Africa to stand on her own feet. Though it carried the imprimatur of the High Commissioner, the document was the work of Lionel Curtis, supported by other members of the Kindergarten. Their argument was predominantly an economic one and, although Merriman testily dismissed it as a 'windy effusion', Smuts recognised the validity of some of its claims. He could not make such an admission openly, however, for fear of surrendering the initiative to the imperialists, so he held his peace.

Over another issue he could not contain himself in silence. The presence of Indians in the Transvaal was a situation of which he profoundly disapproved. While he accepted that Africans had a place, if an inferior one, he believed there was no role for Asians in a country which was to be developed on the basis of European civilisation. The proliferation of Indians in Natal had caused him grave disquiet. In 1885 the government of the South African Republic had enacted a law debarring Asians from becoming burghers and from owning fixed property except in 'such streets, wards and locations as the government for purposes of sanitation shall assign them to live in'. They had also to pay a registration fee of £25 on entering the country. Though many had fled during the war, they had subsequently returned, and during the period of post-war upheaval many more had entered the country illegally. By 1904, 11,321 Indians were believed to be in the Transvaal. In that year a 'national convention' was held in Pretoria at which the Europeans who attended discussed the 'Asiatic invasion' and gave vent to their feelings of hostility. In 1906 the Transvaal legislative council passed an ordinance providing for the compulsory registration of all Asians living in the colony and their identification by means of fingerprints, but the Crown disallowed the ordinance.

Immediately after the introduction of responsible government, when the Crown was no longer in a position to intervene, Act No. 2 of 1907 was passed in almost identical terms. Later in the year another act restricted Asian immigration. The two Acts aroused vigorous protests from the Indian community, of which at least some were professional people who resented being required to provide fingerprint proof of identification. Others, to the number of five thousand, fearing a purge of illegal immigrants, fled the country. The more responsible Indians, having protested against what they regarded as a slur on their reputation as educated and respectable members of the community, refused almost unanimously to register. Their leader was a young Indian lawyer, Mohandas Karamchand Gandhi. Although Smuts as minister of justice had initiated those measures, he was, as so often in later life, not so much the originator as the codifier of public opinion on the issue of the relations between Europeans and other races. Lord Selborne wrote to him acknowledging the Transvaal's right to control immigration but pleaded that the rights of Indians already in the country should not be infringed.[58] Richard Solomon, the Transvaal's agent in London, also wrote to advocate a 'patient policy with regard to those [Indians] lawfully in the country' so as to disarm criticism in England.[59] Merriman, too, was, as always, concerned both with the injustices suffered by Indians resident in the Transvaal and with the effect of the Transvaal government's policy on public opinion in England.[60] A compromise of a sort was only reached after Gandhi had been imprisoned for leading the boycott on registration. Henceforward registration would be voluntary rather than compulsory. Gandhi and others then called for the repeal of the new Immigration Act so that educated Indians could enter and reside in the Transvaal on the same basis as Europeans. In spite of the warnings of Merriman and Solomon and the wise advice of Selborne, this was a step Smuts could not and would not contemplate.[61] His people did not want it, nor did he.

While the Indian question was still provoking argument, Selborne sent to both Smuts and Botha a detailed statement of his views on the treatment of coloured people and Africans. For its time it was a liberal document. The coloured population, Selborne believed, should be given the benefit of their European ancestry except where they clearly preferred to live in accordance with tribal standards. Africans should be divided into three categories. Those living in locations should be permitted to live in accordance with tribal traditions but should be offered educational opportunities, predominantly in the field of agriculture. Those working on European-owned farms should have the opportunity to enjoy secondary education and should be allowed to move freely from one farm to another provided they fulfilled their labour contracts. Africans living in towns should be given security of tenure for their homes, which they should be encouraged to improve, and they should be provided with good government schools. The responsibility for administering native affairs should not be left with a European parliament whose members, apart from the temporary nature of their appointment, would in any case pursue their own interests at the expense of the Africans. Instead there should be a permanent minister for native affairs assisted by an adequate staff. It should be his duty to meet representative gatherings of Africans regularly to hear their views. There would then be no need for an artificial franchise. At the same time, a panel of judges could be empowered to give the vote to any Africans who genuinely lived according to European standards.[62]

About the same time the commission appointed to inquire into the rising in Natal also published its report which, like Selborne's letter, made recommendations about African representation and administration. The commission differed from Selborne, however, in recommending that the tribal system should be gradually run down. One means of achieving that end would be to appoint a council for native affairs to advise the government on all legislation affecting Africans. To represent African interests, four white members, chosen for their special knowledge of Africans, should be appointed to the legislative council. Educated Africans should be allowed either to vote for those representatives or else to elect one unofficial member to the native affairs council. There should, in addition, be a system of local councils. These suggestions were intended to meet the needs of Natal, but were equally applicable to the Transvaal if the Transvaal government had been in the mood to adopt them. Botha and Smuts, however, were too deeply concerned with promoting South African union to give thought to native affairs, and Smuts still clung to the view that a union government would be better equipped to deal with such questions than were the four colonial administrations.

A spur to union had been given by the victory of Merriman's South African Party in the elections for the Cape assembly held in 1908. His supporters won sixty-four seats while Jameson's Progressives, renamed the Unionist Party in order to present themselves rather than Merriman's supporters as the party of South African unity, gained only twenty-nine. Merriman, however, still harboured suspicions that there would be powerful opposition to union from Milner and his supporters in England,[63] while Smuts, having tasted the burdens of office, reflected gloomily upon how little any government could achieve.[64] Such opposition as South African federation under the leadership of the likes of Botha, Merriman, Smuts and Steyn was likely to encounter in England was to come not from Milner but from those who, as Merriman had long feared, were concerned about the fate of the African population. But in response to a gentle enquiry from J. A. Hobson, Smuts obstinately insisted that no decisions should be taken on that issue until after union. In view of the opposition among Europeans to any improvement in the native franchise, elections to the first union parliament must be on the basis of the existing franchise in each of the colonies. Britain should trust the South African Whites, Smuts wrote, and if she did so they would recognise the gravity of their responsibilities.[65]

Merriman was deeply sceptical about the wisdom of Smuts's attitude, though he could think of no alternative scheme of representation for

Africans. Schreiner, the former Cape premier, urged Smuts in even stronger terms to take account of the rights of Africans, having himself been converted by a tour of Cape Colony in 1898 to a far more sympathetic view of the needs of the African population than he had previously held.[66] Their fears were unjustified.[67] Though some of the Liberal radicals in parliament, whose chief spokesman was Sir Charles Dilke, and the Labour members led by Ramsay Macdonald, were critical of South Africa's native policy, the leaders of both the main parties were anxious to promote South African union. Beset by bogies of their own creation, Smuts and Merriman, who together were fast becoming the chief architects of union, were unaware that the tide in England was flowing so freely in their favour. They did understand, however, that a liberal franchise for Africans would wreck any hopes of white South African support for union. 'On the question of the Native franchise,' Smuts wrote, 'my mind is full of Cimmerian darkness and I incline very strongly to leaving the matter over for the Union Parliament.'[68]

It was Merriman who suggested that there should be a national convention to promote the idea of union and typically it was Smuts who tried his hand at drafting a consitution for discussion by the delegates. He proposed that, in addition to the central legislature, there should be legislatures in each province, as the colonies were to be called. Representation in both central and provincial legislatures would be on a white population basis, with a redistribution every ten years following a census. Until the union parliament decided otherwise, the existing colonial franchises would remain in force, and legislation affecting non-Whites would fall within the province of the Governor-General, who might summon an assembly of chiefs and others who had special knowledge of native affairs to seek their opinions.[69] Merriman was critical of the proposal to elect provincial legislatures because they would involve unnecessary expense. He also disliked the idea of distributing seats on the basis of the European population and ignoring the rest because it would give undue influence to the urban centres which, in his view, were less representative of the true interests of the country. Unabashed, Smuts set to work with the assistance of R. H. Brand, another former member of the Kindergarten, to draft two possible constitutions for discussion, one of which retained the existing colonies as provinces while the other divided the Cape into three provinces and the Transvaal into two. He also set out to ensure that the Transvaal delegates, both Boer and British, were ready to present a unanimous front when the convention assembled.

When the convention did meet in Durban on 11 October 1908 the preparations made by Smuts were soon seen to have been vital to its success. In spite of a number of sharp exchanges, not least over Hertzog's insistence on the equality of the Dutch and English languages,[70] the delegates were able to reach agreement on most issues. Even the site of the capital, which aroused deep territorial jealousies, was settled on the basis of a compromise, if an unsatisfactory one, with Cape Town as the seat of the legislature and Pretoria as the administrative centre. A motion by Colonel Stanford, advocating franchise rights for 'all subjects of His Majesty resident in South Africa irrespective of colour, on the basis of such qualifications as the convention might deem appropriate',[71] was roundly defeated. The existing franchise in each colony was retained, but only Europeans would be permitted to stand for election to the union parliament, even in Cape Colony. The defence of African interests was to be left to senators nominated for that purpose. While Botha's soothing personality exerted a powerful influence upon the proceedings and Steyn's magisterial presence aroused deep emotions of loyalty, Smuts also made a significant contribution to the outcome of the convention by his indefatigable efforts in bringing members together for discussions and in drafting motions and amendments. He served on a number of committees, including that dealing with the administration of justice and, inevitably, on the committee given responsibility for drafting the constitution itself.[72]

Agreement at the convention was only the first step in the campaign. When the draft constitution was presented to the various colonial legislatures, new problems arose. Because of the care with which Smuts had prepared the ground before the convention met, he and Botha had a comparatively easy task in the Transvaal, although Smuts expressed his regret that it had been impossible to agree upon a uniform solution to the question of the native franchise. Initially the existing franchises would be retained and any alteration would only be possible with the approval of a two-thirds majority in a joint meeting of both the legislative assembly and the senate.[73] Smuts had foreseen the need for such a compromise a year earlier, but it is doubtful if it had enthusiastic support among Transvaal Whites generally. In Cape Colony Merriman encountered formidable opposition from Hofmeyr and Schreiner over the native franchise, while the Cape parliament demanded amendments which would give greater representation to the rural constituencies. Nevertheless, when the convention reassembled in Bloemfontein early in May, agreement was reached after only modest amendments had been made to the original draft.

It was not only a handful of liberal Europeans who opposed the decisions on the native franchise. News of the proceedings was one of the most important factors in mustering African opinion in defence of African rights. The Orange River Colony Native Congress, which had developed from a number of other African rights groups a few years earlier, took the lead by proposing a national convention of Africans to be drawn from the congresses which had sprung up in the other colonies during and after the war of 1899–1902. The members of the congresses, for the most part men of some education, had had high hopes of British rule and had offered loyal co-operation, but they had become increasingly disillusioned. African-language newspapers also criticised the recommendations made by the national convention of Europeans. The African convention met in Bloemfontein from 24 to 26 March 1909 and produced a number of resolutions criticising the proposed constitution for the South African Union. It also empowered the executive to organise a deputation to go to England to lay the African case before those responsible for making a decision. If necessary they might seek the assistance of Schreiner. These efforts produced no reaction from the various colonial governments so the deputation was assembled to pursue the case in Britain.[74]

There remained the final stage of converting a South African draft into a British Act of Parliament. Smuts was apprehensive that the Liberal government in Britain might not survive long enough to ensure the passing of the Union Bill. A Unionist government, however favourable to the idea of South African union, might prefer to see that union moulded in Britain. His fears proved unfounded. The South African delegation, of which Smuts was a member, met with a friendly reception in England, and, when the Union Bill came before parliament, Liberals and Unionists spoke contrapuntally in support. The deputation of African and coloured peoples' representatives, accompanied by Schreiner, made little impression. In the House of Lords only one peer, Lord Courtney, criticised the provision for native representation. In the Commons, Dilke and several Labour speakers made their voices heard, but to no avail. The Liberals were intent upon making amends to the Boers for what had happened in the war, and Liberals and Unionists alike looked forward to the day when South African Whites would cease to make demands upon the imperial treasury and upon the British army to defend them against the black menace. In such an atmosphere the rights of Africans had little chance of being seriously considered. There were clearly a number of members of parliament who were uneasy about the future of Africans, but they were not prepared to jeopardise the main aim of ridding Britain of responsibility for South Africa by voicing their doubts. Instead, pious hopes were expressed that there would be improvements in native policy once Europeans felt secure in their union. Such hopes replaced positive measures to protect African rights. Only one action was taken to salve the consciences of the legislators. They agreed that, for the time being, Britain should retain responsibility for the protectorates of Swaziland, Bechuanaland and Basutoland. The rest of South Africa's Africans must look to the Europeans – or to themselves – for succour. The loss of the protectorates was a blow to the pride of South Africa's white leaders, but they consoled themselves that they had got their union.

Smuts's role in that achievement had been of the greatest importance. Merriman may have provided the guiding hand which steered the venture in the right direction – particularly in advocating union rather than federation – and in ensuring that Smuts's unduly rigid views on the African franchise did not prevail. Botha and Steyn may have contributed the reassuring weight of their steadfast characters to give the whole enterprise its air of honourable compromise. But it was Smuts's tireless energy and fluent pen which provided the organisation, the adjustments and the modulations necessary to convert aspirations into legislation. The unity of the Europeans of South Africa had been his constant goal. As to the method of achieving it, he had had no doctrinaire opinion. He was never reluctant to hazard a solution and was equally ready to amend it when a more effective proposal was forthcoming. In those years during which Smuts was learning his trade as a political leader, there was nothing more striking than the dexterity with which he synthesised the ideas of others and came up with an answer which reflected popular opinion. Having done so, he had no difficulty in adopting the course he had proposed. As unofficial secretary-general of the union movement, he had been an outstanding success.

4
Minister and general

Smuts had been so completely absorbed in his campaign for union that he had given little thought to what should happen when it had been won. At times it had seemed as if union were an end in itself, a panacea for all South Africa's ills. But by September Smuts was back in Pretoria and anxious to implement the constitution which he had so pre-eminently formulated. He also moved his home from Pretoria to the outskirts of the small township of Irene. There he re-erected a bungalow, Doornkloof, which had acted as a British officers's mess in Middelburg during the war and which he had transported to its new location by cart, in sections. It was not an imposing residence, though beautifully situated. Smuts intended at some time to add enlargements and make improvements. The idea was only a fleeting one. His tastes, and those of Isie, were simple. He had little aesthetic sense. Even flowers and plants, which deeply excited him, did so for botanical reasons rather than because of their beauty. Though he developed a well-stocked library, the remainder of the furnishings of his home remained spartan. By this time they had four surviving children, Santa (Susanna Johanner), Cato (Catharina Petronell), Japie (Jacob Daniel) and Sylma (Sybella Margaretha). Twin daughters, born in 1898, had died almost at once. A second son, Jannie (Jan Christian), was born in 1912, and another daughter, Louis Anne de la Rey, named, in spite of her sex, after the great Boer commander, in 1914. Later Smuts adopted Kathleen de Villiers, the orphaned daughter of a friend. His closely-knit family background was a source of great strength to him. Though he was to be away from home frequently and sometimes for lengthy periods, to return gave him both a feeling of peace and the stimulus to go out again to do battle with his political opponents or his country's enemies.

Merriman, who had also contributed so much to the achievement of union and who was the most experienced parliamentarian in South Africa, wanted very much to be the Union's first prime minister. But the newly appointed Governor-General, Lord Gladstone, invited Botha to form a cabinet. It was a wise decision. In spite of Merriman's many qualities, he had many critics. His harsh financial policies in Cape Colony, though necessary, had not been popular even among his own supporters, and he would have commanded little following in the Transvaal or the Free State. By contrast, Botha had considerable influence in the Transvaal, he was respected in the Free State and greatly admired by the Cape Dutch. The decision was nevertheless a bitter one for Merriman, who refused office under his rival, believing that Botha lacked both the experience and the ability to undertake such an important task.

Without Smuts at his side, Botha might, indeed, have failed. The two men, close friends, were complementary. Botha's personality attracted loyalty and he had the talent to see what was needed and to make decisions. Smuts was an ideal staff officer who could draft the operational instructions needed to make Botha's ideas effective. His intellect enabled him to grasp the complexities of a problem and to suggest a variety of answers, but it was Botha who sensed which was the right one. At this stage of his life Smuts needed the more straightforward vision of Botha to show him what was practicable and what was not. Their roles resembled those of a minister and his trusted permanent secretary.

Merriman was not the only one to be disillusioned by the outcome of union. Jameson in the Cape, and the Transvaal Progressives too, claimed that Botha had led them to believe that, if he became prime minister, he would form a coalition or 'best man' government. Botha had certainly toyed with the idea when it was put to him by Jameson with a view to prolonging the amicable spirit engendered by the national convention.[1] On reflection he recognised that it would not be acceptable to his supporters in the Transvaal. But he did try to appease the Unionists as much as possible, though in so doing he was to split his Afrikaner followers. Merriman's judgement that Botha was 'a weak man ready to make promises, – rather like Laurier [the Canadian prime minister] without his brains', nevertheless did him much less than justice. It was a more accurate measure of the degree of Merriman's disappointment than of Botha's character.

What Botha hoped for was an amalgamation of his own *Het Volk* with the *Oranjia Unie* party and the Cape's South African Party to fight the elections planned for September 1910.[2] Some even of the more moderate English-speaking voters feared this might indicate a return to the political struggle between Dutch and English. The Unionists, for their part, loudly demanded a renewal of the 'convention spirit'. In trying to defuse this situation, Smuts admitted to Merriman that he sometimes had to explain the government's aims in a manner which lacked something of clarity – he might more appropriately have said 'frankness'.[3] Merriman had certainly been disturbed by the ambivalence of some of Smut's utterances regarding the prospect of a coalition government, not least because he, like Botha and Smuts, was strongly opposed to any such idea.[4] In an appeal to all moderates in South Africa and anticipating that, although Afrikaners would form a majority, their policies would not be of a character to antagonise English-speaking South Africans, Smuts had drafted a manifesto for a new South African National Party.[5] For one important section of the population the manifesto did not hold out great prospects. His proposal regarding Africans was that the government, 'while avoiding mere repression and uplifting Natives by all means suitable to their ideas and conditions will as far as possible prevent their political, social and industrial mixture with whites'. Later commentators might regard it as an illiberal statement. At the time, and perhaps today, it echoed the sentiments of most of the Europeans in South Africa. The voices which spoke up in defence of Africans represented only a small proportion of the European population. The pious hopes of British parliamentarians seemed to have little prospect of fulfilment.

In the event, Botha failed to achieve the amalgamation for which he hoped but instead led his own party into the elections in a loose combination with his hoped-for allies. Smuts professed to be far from confident about the outcome, but the three predominantly Afrikaner parties together won 67 seats while the Unionists gained only 39, the Labour Party 4 and independents 11. It was a great disappointment to the victors that Botha was defeated by Fitzpatrick. Although a safe seat was quickly found for him, Botha was convinced that he had lost many English votes because of the aggressive, Afrikaner education policy pursued by Hertzog in the Free State.[6] Hertzog's Education Act of 1908 had required both English and Dutch to be used equally as languages of instruction in the schools of the then Orange River Colony. Under the Union constitution all but higher education remained under the control of individual provinces, so that the provisions of Hertzog's Act remained in force. Botha was deeply aware of the resentment this aroused, but Hertzog was the hero of the Free State burghers and, when the time came to form a cabinet, he could not easily be omitted. An attempt was made to avoid his appointment by offering him a seat on the court of appeal, but when he rejected the offer Botha felt constrained to make him minister of justice.[7] Hertzog was in no way reconciled to the policies of the government which he now joined. In his opinion, Botha and Smuts had sold out to Britain in 1902. By their recent enthusiastic acceptance of a role for South Africa within the British Empire, he sincerely believed they had compounded their treason and had threatened the survival of Afrikaner culture. He was, therefore, an uneasy colleague from the outset. He accepted office only because he hoped to promote the Afrikaner cause more effectively from within the cabinet than he could outside it.

Smuts, upon whom devolved the three portfolios of defence, the interior and mines, was brought into contact with every aspect of the political conflict. So heavy was the burden of work which he undertook that there was no possibility of his accompanying Botha to England in 1911 to attend the imperial conference. But he revelled in the tasks which faced him. Though he wrote to Arthur Gillett, Margaret Clark's husband, that he longed for the time when he would be old enough to escape the demands of duty and spend his days in peace and leisure – a comment which he was frequently to make in times of stress – nothing could have induced him to accept retirement. While drafting a new Defence Bill and an Immigration Act aimed at preventing the entry of Indians into the Union, he still found time to acquire a number of farms in which he took more than a nominal interest. He also wrote a book, *An Inquiry into the Whole*, in which he developed the ideas which had first occupied his attention in Cambridge. To those varied activities was added, at Botha's request, the task of preparing the ground for the formation of a Union-wide South African National Party. On this and other issues the relationship between Botha and Smuts emerged clearly from their correspondence while the prime minister was in 'London. It was Botha who took the decisions, and Smuts was left to implement them. Botha determined the level of representation of each of the provincial parties at the meeting to be arranged by Smuts to launch the new party. It was Botha who ruled that Smuts should ensure that Africans paid a uniform poll tax and should slim down the civil service. It was he, again, who urged Smuts to see if Merriman could be prevailed upon to represent South Africa on a royal commission on trade,[8] an offer which Merriman turned down.

Smut's Defence Act won him both praise and criticism. As so often in his earlier career he prepared a draft and then circulated it to a number of friends for comment.[9] It was Merriman who offered some of the most constructive suggestions for amending the bill, insisting that the first concern must be to decide what money was available for defence and then to draft the plan in accordance with the available resources. He also pointed out that the next question must be to ask what the defence force was meant to do. The native population, in Merriman's opinion, constituted no serious threat, so the enemy to be countered must be an external one. Against such forces large numbers of half-trained troops, as envisaged by Smuts, would be less effective than a small body of highly professional fighters. These would bear the brunt of the fighting, but they would be powerfully reinforced by the traditional commandos of countrymen on horseback who would make up an unequalled guerrilla force. To call up townsmen would be a waste of time.[10]

Smuts did not accept all these proposals, but the innovations he introduced to replace some of the traditional methods employed by the Afrikaners caused some criticism in parliament because he did not explain in sufficiently simple terms the reasons behind the changes. This was a fault which was to bedevil Smuts throughout his life. When he wrote in irascible terms to Emily Hobhouse about the reaction of parliament, she gently chided him. 'Having thought out a matter and decided it was best, you just want to rush it through without criticism,' she wrote.[11] It was a perceptive comment. Smuts had frequently levelled a similar charge with less generosity against Milner only a few years earlier. Both men possessed powerful intellects on which they relied to solve their problems. They took little account of human nature, and, having decided upon a line of action, they tended to regard all contrary views as ill-judged or even malicious.

If Smuts was lacking in charity towards his critics, he could be more than generous to his friends, and Emily Hobhouse was one of those who benefited in a very practical manner from his kindness. She had been compelled through ill health to live in Italy in very straightened circumstances. A gift of £100 from Smuts enabled her to have medical treatment which she could not otherwise have afforded.[12] Though she tried to repay the sum, Smuts firmly refused her cheque.

Another old friend tried to offer sage advice. H.J.Wolstenholme, in Cambridge, to whom Smuts had sent the manuscript of his book for comment, was less than impressed by it. 'You seem', he wrote, 'to build from the apex downward, to proceed on the old pre-scientific plan ... of throwing out some brilliant speculation or flash of insight, and then trying ingeniously to make it plausible.'[13] To Smuts, who set such store by science, they were harsh words, but they contained more than a vestige of truth. With the simplicities of war far behind him the resurgence of the simple faith which had sustained him in battle had faded. It had become necessary once again to justify in philosophical terms the way of life he had adopted. Wolstenholme realised what Smuts himself could not appreciate, that no one, and especially a person as busy as Smuts, could hope to evolve an all-embracing philosophy which took into account the latest developments in scientific as well as philosophical thinking. Wolstenholme's advice was that Smuts should give up philosophy and instead should write the history of the Anglo-Boer war in which he had been personally involved.[14]

Brigadier-General Sir Charles Crewe, a Cape member of the House of Assembly, was one of those whose advice Smuts had sought over his Defence Bill. In August 1911 Crewe wrote to him again on another pressing matter. He had recently toured the reserves in the Eastern Cape and had been greatly impressed by the progress Africans had made since the war. He concluded that within twenty-five years they would be demanding the franchise and preparations must be made for that event. His suggestion was that, as a first step, the system of councils introduced in a limited area under the terms of Rhodes's Glen Grey Act should be extended so as to give Africans as much control of their own affairs as possible in areas specially designated for them. There should then be white areas in which no African might acquire land. As a next stage, delegates of the African councils might be permitted to elect a limited number of Europeans to parliament to represent their interests, while the European franchise remained a separate matter.[15] Crewe's proposals overlooked, or were intended to override, the existing constitutional position in the Cape where Africans might acquire land as freely as Whites, and could, if qualified, exercise the right to vote. At this stage Smuts had no direct responsibility for native affairs, but his retentive memory recorded Crewe's opinion which then became one more element in his thinking when native questions in due course fell within his sphere of activity.

With Botha back in South Africa, the government seemed suddenly to be assailed on every hand. The thread which held together the South African National Party which was formed in November 1911 was a tenuous one. There was no true focus of loyalty for the members of *Het Volk*, the *Oranjia Unie*, the Bond and the South African Party, who, together with the Natal independents and the Transvaal Nationalists, had joined together to form the new party. Within a month the Natal members of parliament were beginning to grow wary of what they felt to be an excessively Afrikaner influence in the formulation of government policies. Cracks appeared within the government itself in May 1912 when the Transvaaler, H.C. Hull, minister of finance, resigned in protest after criticising J.W. Sauer, minister for railways, for failing to consult either the cabinet or the treasury in the execution of his duties. Smuts was deeply distressed by these overt signs of disagreement. He had some sympathy for Hull's criticisms but believed that cabinet solidarity was all-important for the defence of South African unity. In supporting Sauer, however, he was aware that it might seem to his Transvaal followers that he was making an unnecessary concession to Cape opinion since Sauer was a leading Cape liberal. Botha, however, intervened decisively, insisting that Sauer should change his portfolio. In this way provincial sensitivities were appeased. For Smuts the outcome was that he added the ministry of finance to that of defence while shedding responsibility for mines and the interior.

If all the government's problems could have been handled so easily, life would have been relatively quiet for Botha and Smuts. Hertzog, however, presented a more difficult problem. In an attempt to win his confidence, Botha had offered him the ministry of native affairs. It was an act which indicated how little Botha himself cared for the rights of Africans, although he had already made his position clear on that issue in his comments to the Transvaal labour commission. Hertzog was not mollified. He continued to follow his own path, and in a speech at Nylstroom on 5 October 1912 referred to some English-speaking South Africans as foreign adventurers and claimed that he wanted to make Afrikaners masters in the Union. He attacked in particular Sir Thomas Smartt, leader of the Unionist Party, and in so doing enraged many of the government's supporters in Natal. Smuts, too, came under attack because his Transvaal Education Act had given precedence to the English language. Hertzog's fear was that the British, in their arrogance, would sweep aside all vestiges of Afrikaner civilisation. But, though he genuinely believed in that possibility, it was an embarrassment for his colleagues when he publicised his views. Two months later he launched an even more virulent attack on the government in a speech at de Wildt. His main object, he said, was to keep British and Dutch separated. He rejected all suggestions of conciliation and claimed that he accepted imperialism only in so far as it benefited South Africa. Sir George Leuchars, minister of commerce and industry from Natal, resigned in disgust, but Hertzog himself refused to resign or to apologise.

The immediate crisis was overcome when Botha himself resigned, and, when the Governor-General once more invited him to form a cabinet, he did not include Hertzog. But the breach among the Afrikaners remained, and, though de Wet and Steyn did not at once quit the South African National Party, their sympathies were clearly with Hertzog. Botha's attempts to unite Boer and Briton were not to go unchallenged. Nor did the appointment of Sauer to succeed Hertzog as minister for native affairs result in the adoption of a more enlightened policy. The Native Land Bill which was introduced in 1913 bore all the marks of Hertzog's planning. Sauer himself probably believed that a policy of dividing the Union into African and white areas and of forbidding the purchase of land by either Whites or Africans in areas allocated to the other race would protect Africans from unfair competition. He insisted, too, that, although an attempt had been made to ensure that enough land had been reserved for Africans, more would be made available in due course. But since the war many Africans had enjoyed squatting rights on land which by law they must now be called upon to surrender. Many more had farmed land owned by Europeans on the basis of half-share agreements, and this too must come to an end. The impact of the legislation proved to be uneven. In the Cape some of its provisions were ruled as being *ultra vires* by the courts. In the Transvaal and Natal many European farmers were reluctant to lose the services of squatters and their families. But in the Free State the Act had serious repercussions for many Africans who had occupied land or squatted on European farms and were now rendered destitute by being expelled from their homes.

There is no record of Smuts's response to the new legislation. He did not at any time wish to inflict hardship on Africans, but he unswervingly supported the policy of racial segregation. Trouble of another sort, more directly affecting his own ministry, occupied his attention. In July there was a strike of European miners demanding more pay. With trade union support it developed into a general stoppage along the whole Rand. Initially the government resisted requests from the mine-owners to intervene, but, as the strike spread, Smuts had the mortifying experience of having to request the Governor-General for imperial troops to guard the mines. His own defence force, which only came into being in the same month, was not prepared for the confrontation. It did not help him to know that his action was greeted with disapproval by his own Afrikaner supporters. Nor did the ensuing events enhance his reputation. A mass meeting of strikers to be held in Johannesburg was officially banned, but the miners ignored the ban. Violence was followed by arson and looting and a number of people were killed. The military claimed they could not contain the outbreak, so Botha and Smuts drove to Johannesburg to join Sauer who, as acting minister of justice, was already on the spot. There they signed a document drafted by the strike leaders which reinstated the strikers, recognised the trade unions and set up a judicial commission to investigate the miners' grievances. Smuts was deeply enraged by this submission to a disorderly rabble, most of whom were British. A letter of commiseration from Emily Hobhouse, voicing the hope that South Africans would bury the hatchet in time for the unveiling in December of a monument to commemorate the women who had died in the refugee camps during the Anglo-Boer War, arrived at a singularly unpropitious moment.

Miss Hobhouse had been invited by ex-President Steyn to unveil the monument in recognition of the way in which she had spoken out for the women in the camps and assisted them by organising supplies of food and clothing. Botha and Smuts had never been happy about the plan to erect a memorial. It seemed to them a divisive project, intended to play upon Afrikaner sentiments. The decision to hold the unveiling ceremony on 16 December, the Day of the Covenant, also seemed calculated to enhance rather than to reduce tensions between British and Dutch. That day was sacred to all Afrikaners because it commemorated their great victory over the Zulus in the Battle of Blood River. Miss

Hobhouse was unaware of the extent to which feelings between the two peoples had sharpened and was concerned only that the occasion should be a national rather than a provincial one. Ill as she was, she did not want to make the trying journey to South Africa unless by so doing she could promote the interests of the whole country. In fact the division between the die-hard Afrikaners and the supporters of Smuts was becoming steadily more acute. In November 1913 the supporters of Hertzog, led by former Chief-Commandant Christian de Wet, walked out of the annual congress of the South African National Party in Cape Town and servered their links with the organisation.

The unveiling ceremony went ahead nevertheless, and Smuts made a valiant attempt to calm the situation. Miss Hobhouse had made the journey to South Africa, but when she reached Beaufort West she was forced to cancel her further progress because of ill health. Speaking on her behalf, Smuts tried to set the occasion in the wider context of South African history rather than concentrating upon the events of the recent war. He stressed the reputation for courage and endurance which Afrikaner women had built for themselves since Afrikaners had first begun to settle in South Africa. He urged that the occasion should not be one of bitterness or hatred but of pride in the sacrifices made by the South African people. These were qualities upon which a strong South African nation would one day be securely founded. The Day of the Covenant he tried to turn to advantage by pointing out the opportunity which it gave for giving thanks to God for his unfailing aid in South Africa's days of darkness and difficulty. To the younger generation he gave warning that, whatever virtue they might as individuals enjoy, it would be useless if they themselves became hostile to the Church and to the faith. 'History teaches it again and again,' he said; 'nations that set God aside go under.'[16]

It was a magnificent speech, but, though it may have moved his hearers briefly, it made little impression upon the wider problems facing the Union, and these came from many quarters. The most persistent among them arose from the objections of the Europeans in Natal to the activities of Indians in that province. Indians had been brought to Natal in considerable numbers in the latter half of the nineteenth century to work as indentured labourers on the sugar plantations near the coast – a task to which Africans were in no way attracted – or to work in the coal-mines and on the railways. On the termination of their contracts more than half had stayed in South Africa. Some drifted to the Transvaal to open small shops or to take employment as semi-skilled workers, but most of them remained in Natal. As their numbers grew Europeans began to object to their presence in the towns. In an attempt to discourage

70

them from settling in urban areas, an act was passed by the Natal legislature in 1895 requiring them to re-indenture at the end of their five-year term of service or else to pay a tax of £3 per annum. The measure failed to achieve its object and in 1897 there were demonstrations in Durban against the landing of more Indian immigrants. This was followed by the passing of another act enabling local authorities to refuse to issue trading licences to Indians and to segregate Indian traders from European traders. Even that measure failed to satisfy the Europeans and in 1908 the Natal legislature passed still more drastic measures forbidding the issue or transfer of trading licences to Indians, and stating that all existing licences would expire in 1918. The Crown did not give its assent to the measure and it lapsed.

The year 1908 saw the low point of a depression which had seriously affected Natal. In April 1907, 2,000 Indians sailed to Angola to seek work on the Benguela railway. Nearly one-third of them died or left the work because of the brutal conditions of service. Meanwhile, in Natal starvation was common among the Indian population which by now was nearing 150,000. More and more Indians were forced to seek re-indenture, in spite of the overwork, malnutrition and squalid living conditions which they encountered on the sugar plantations. Those who could offer some skills to potential employers were better off because of the shortage of semi-skilled workers. Those employed on the railways or in skilled domestic work were relatively prosperous, though their working conditions left much to be desired. Protest against their working conditions was restricted by law. Indentured labourers could not move more than two miles from their place of employment without their employer's consent. Consequently, in spite of the difficulties they had to face, Indian workers were able to voice their grievances in only sporadic fashion.

This state of affairs began to change in 1911 as a result of the coming together of two strands within the Indian protest movement. Although Gandhi had been partly mollified by the amendment to the Transvaal Immigration Act, he had continued to campaign against its particular application to Indians. He had come to regard his cause as a moral issue and on that ground had won some support both in England and in India. Smuts was conscious of the bad impression the situation might create in England and in 1909 said that, if the imperial government would prevent more Indians from entering Natal, he would drop his registration campaign. Nothing came of that proposal and by 1911 Gandhi had begun to campaign more particularly for the repeal of the £3 tax on non-indentured Indians in Natal. He was not alone in taking up that issue. There were in Natal a few hundred Indians who had had an English-style education and who, for the most part, had entered the professions.

Hitherto they had not sought to establish a separate identity for themselves, but the depression and the efforts to exclude them from membership of the civil service alerted them to the need to fight for their position. They, too, took up the campaign against against the £3 tax. So did the Natal Indian Congress, composed mainly of traders, many of whom had begun life in South Africa as indentured labourers. Gradually, under the pressures of economic recession and social exclusion, these groups, the members of the professions and the Congress, began to come together – not to coalesce, but in common distress.

A new Immigration Bill drafted by Smuts in 1911 gave Gandhi the incentive he had needed to revive his hitherto flagging campaign. Lord Gladstone was sceptical about the wisdom of further legislation which he feared might strengthen Gandhi's hand.[17] Protests from the Viceroy of India bore out his argument, and the Union government agreed to a visit from S.K. Gokhale, the president of the Indian National Congress, who was also a member of the Viceroy's legislative council. The outcome of the discussions which took place while Gokhale was in South Africa, and in which Gandhi took part, was the decision to transfer control of Indian affairs from provincial councils to the Union government. The terms of the Bill were also to be amended so that the government would control all immigration on the basis of economic and educational considerations rather than on racial grounds. These changes were embodied in the Immigration Regulating Act of 1913, but Gandhi claimed that Smuts had also promised to abolish the £3 tax. Smuts denied this, saying that he had promised only to look at the tax, but the final decision must rest with Natal, a point which he claimed to have made clear in earlier discussions.

Gandhi determined to press his case to the limits of non-violent action. He believed that the tax issue would prove a unifying force for all Indians in Natal and that there would be widespread support for any action he might take. His decision was to lead a protest march from Natal to the Transvaal, thereby breaking the law against the movement of Indians from one province to another. At first Smuts gave orders to the police to avoid being provoked, thinking to kill the protest by ignoring it. But pent-up emotions burst out. In October, 20,000 Indian workers in Natal went on strike. This was not so much a response to Gandhi's call as a despairing cry of frustration. When the strike spread to the sugar plantations, Smuts ordered the strikers to be arrested and imprisoned. Gandhi himself was arrested and sentenced to three months' imprisonment, but was released almost at once when the Viceroy protested at the treatment of Indians who were passively protesting. Under this pressure, Botha agreed to appoint a commission under the chairmanship of Sir William Solomon to inquire into the Indians' grievances. Sir Benjamin Robertson, an experienced member of the Indian civil service, was invited to join the commission to represent Indian interests, but Gandhi objected to the absence of Indian members. He generously agreed to drop his protest when the government was forced to deal with another outbreak of strikes by white workers, but Smuts was determined to reach some conclusion which would prevent similar difficulties in the future. Working in close co-operation with Gandhi, he produced the Indian Relief Act No. 22 of 1914 which abolished the £3 tax and offered a free passage to India for any Indians wishing to return to their country. At this point Gandhi himself left for India – for ever, Smuts hoped. Throughout his campaign he had laid no claim to political rights for Indians. His aim was to achieve civic equality with the Europeans.[18] But even this Smuts could not accept. There must be no question of European culture being in any way threatened by the culture of India. In that spirit the Relief Act could in no sense be regarded as a final solution to the problem of the role of Indians in South Africa, though it was to be some years before the issue again captured Smut's attention.

More immediately there remained the problem of the striking workers to be dealt with. In January 1914 a strike had begun among the European miners working in the coalfields of Natal. It quickly spread to the railways where relations with the work-force had been seriously mishandled by the management.[19] The next area to be affected was the Rand with its goldfields. Smuts did not need the spur of a letter from Merriman[20] to induce him to take action. He had had time to ponder over his defeat in 1913 which rankled sorely. The government must never again be challenged successfully if national unity were to be preserved. Whatever the grievances of the miners, the strike must be crushed. Botha was far from well, so it fell to Smuts to deal with the problem on his own. He acted quickly. The strike leaders were arrested and their papers confiscated. Far from halting the strike, his action encouraged the union to organise a ballot with a view to calling a general strike. Smuts then declared martial law on 14 January. This time his defence force was ready for action. Under the leadership of General de la Rey a purposeful display of cannon quickly convinced the strikers that the government was resolute and the strike collapsed. Acting swiftly and without authorisation from the cabinet, Smuts deported nine of the strike leaders who, he claimed, were not South African citizens.

This latter action did not go unchallenged though there was considerable approval for the way he had put an end to the strike. Lady Courtney wrote from Britain after being disturbed by criticisms in the Liberal press.[21] Smuts's boast that not a drop of blood had been shed as a result of the intervention by the defence force brought some consolation to his old friend, Margaret Gillett, who was seeking to justify Smuts's behaviour, but she, too, was worried by the deportations.[22] Merriman was more outspoken in his condemnation.[23] When parliament debated a bill of indemnity for the government's actions during the strike and it was proposed to give the government power to deal with similar incidents in the future by means of an Undesirables Special Deportation Act, Merriman demurred. He gave generous praise for the manner in which Smuts had shouldered responsibility for handling a difficult situation virtually unaided, but the deportations, he said, had been a serious error of judgement and had flouted the constitution. Ironically, he was supported by Hertzog in almost identical terms. In reply Smuts demanded to know what else he could have done. If the ringleaders had remained in the country, they would have infected it with a malign disease. To check such a threat the government was entitled to set aside the law.[24] It was an authoritarian doctrine and not one to be voiced by a man secure in his authority unless he be a tyrant, and that Smuts was not. His behaviour was the over-reaction of a man who was not essentially a man of action. Nor was he a man of the people. Like the *predikant* his parents had wanted him to be, who would stand betwixt man and God, interpreting each to the other, Smuts now tried to demonstrate to man not the divine purpose perhaps but the product of his own pure reason. Like the *predikant*, he did not convince everyone.

One of the reasons for Smut's concern about the strike was his fear that it might spread to the African workers. There was no obvious ground for that fear. In 1911, as minister of mines, he had himself been responsible for legislation which prohibited strikes by contracted African labourers and reserved certain types of skilled work for Europeans. To the suggestion of a Unionist politician and former member of the Kindergarten that the only way forward was gradually to educate Africans along European lines and then to assimilate them, he made an unequivocal reply: 'The active civilising of the natives will not only accentuate all existing troubles, but will seriously threaten the white position in time,' he wrote. 'I believe in going slow as I don't have much faith in the native's capacity for permanent civilisation; and in the meantime I hope the doors of the country will be opened wide for suitable whites.' It was a view from which he never seriously diverged.[25] Throughout his life Smuts chose to ignore the fact that there were already Africans educated along European lines by the excellent missionary schools, especially in Cape Province.

Though they were few in number, some of them had made known their opposition to the provisions in the Union constitution for African representation in parliament. Smuts could not have been unaware of the deputation led by two editors of African newspapers, the Reverend Walter Rubusana and John Tengo Jabavu, which had tried unsuccessfully to present their case to the British parliament, but he closed his mind to its existence. He might be forgiven for his ignorance of a new develop-ment which took place in 1912, because it was not reported in any English- or Dutch-language newspaper. Yet there had been no attempt by the organisers to keep it secret, and the movement of large numbers of Africans must have been noted by the police. In January of that year a considerable concourse of Africans met in Bloemfontein and from their meeting there emerged the South African Native National Congress, dedicated to the defence of African rights and privileges. The moving force behind the summoning of the conference had been Pixley Seme, a Zulu who had been educated in America and in England, where he qualified in law. He, together with three other African lawyers who had trained in England, agreed that the time had come to put an end to tribal divisions and that this could only be done by a national union to parallel the union created by the Europeans.

The meeting in Bloemfontein was organised by those four men, and their hopes were rewarded by the presence of chiefs, lawyers, teachers, clergymen, clerks, industrial workers and others from all four provinces and from the protectorates of Bechuanaland, Basutoland and Swaziland. The proceedings were orderly and dignified, and the officers elected to lead the Congress were men who took their responsibilities seriously. The president-general was the Reverend John Dube, a Zulu who had been educated in America and who, on his return to South Africa, had established Ohlange Institute, an industrial college for Africans in Natal, which was financed by money he had collected by lecturing in America. Pixley Seme became treasurer-general, and another English-trained law-yer, Richard Msimang, chairman of the committee to draft the constitu-tion. The secretary-general was Solomon Plaatje, a self-educated journalist and newspaper editor, who spoke Dutch, English and German as well as his own native Tswana, while the speaker of the Congress was Thomas Mapikela, a carpenter and builder who had been a member of the delegation which went to London in 1909.[26] The aim of the Con-gress was totally opposed to Smuts's views on native policy. It was to seek by constitutional means to rid the Union of the colour bar in education, industry, in parliament and in the administration.

It was an enormous programme, which was checked almost as soon as it was launched, neither by government action, nor yet by any lack of will among the participants, but by external events. It is a measure of the restraint of the Congress leaders that, when war broke out in

75

1914, they decided to suspend their activities so as to avoid causing the government additional strain. It was, equally, a measure of the government's obduracy that, when the Reverend Walter Rubusana offered to raise a fighting force of 5,000 Xhosa to assist the government, his offer was coldly rejected. Already, however, before the outbreak of war, the Congress had organised protests against the Natives Land Act of 1913 which would make 90 per cent of the land available for Europeans while restricting Africans to 7.3 per cent. The government rejected all petitions urging the amendment of the Act, and the Governor-General said he was not empowered to withhold his consent. Funds were raised to send a deputation to England, but the Liberal colonial secretary, Harcourt, was indifferent to the Africans' pleading and referred them back to the Union parliament. Public opinion in England was more sympathetic, but the deputation returned to South Africa empty-handed. In the meantime more direct action had been taken. A number of African women in the Free State refused to carry the passes without which they were not permitted to move about the country. Their protest brought little benefit, for, although Botha himself promised action, nothing was done.[27] Smuts could have had little sympathy for the efforts of either the Congress or the women protesters, but he was engaged in dealing with other problems and seems to have closed his mind to all knowledge of African protestations. They were out of tune with his own ideas and so did not merit attention.

Smuts may have crushed the European workers' strike, but the repercussions of it lingered on. One early reaction was the success of the Labour party, led by Fred Creswell, in both the Johannesburg and Pretoria constituencies during the provincial elections. F.E.T. Krause, a member of the Union Assembly, went so far as to predict a Labour victory in the next general election.[28] It was an unlikely contingency and any prospect of its fulfilment was banished by the war. Creswell, a devout Christian, had been elected to the Union assembly in 1910. He had a profound admiration for Botha and an idealistic view of the character of the workers whom he led. This was based on his respect for the selfless courage shown by the miners and railwaymen in England during recent strikes when workers who were reasonably well off risked their jobs to support their lowest paid workmates. Railway workers in South Africa were, he thought, fairly well off because the railways were run by the state and questions could be asked in parliament. The miners, by contrast, were at the mercy of the owners, many of whom were consciously running precarious businesses and were in no position to guarantee adequate pay and working conditions, even if they had been concerned to do so.[29] Creswell's sympathies did not, however, extend to African workers. Like Smuts, his concern was to preserve the predominance of the Whites. Already the two had attempted to co-operate to achieve that end in 1906.[30] The following year Smuts had offered Creswell an appointment in the mines department and had suggested that a start be made at working at least one government mine so as to reduce unemployment and avoid undue dependence upon the mine-owners.[31] In spite of their differences over the strike, therefore, Smuts and Creswell had much in common and the latter could not bring himself to campaign against the government during a war such as that which began in 1914. Instead he accepted Smuts's offer of a commission in the defence force and performed with great bravery in action.

The outbreak of war brought another burden of work upon Smuts. Not everyone in South Africa thought that the conflict was any concern of the Union. Many hardline Afrikaners thought Britain had brought just retribution upon herself for her misdeeds as an imperial power. Emily Hobhouse wrote from England appealing to Smuts, 'For pity's sake don't let South Africa be dragged in.'[32] Not for the first time Smuts could not agree with his passionately idealistic friend. Even before Britain declared war, Botha had written to the British government accepting South Africa's responsibility for her own defence and releasing the imperial troops stationed in the Union for employment on other fronts. As minister of defence Smuts announced on 11 August, seven days after Britain's declaration of war, that the defence force was to be called out. It was also hoped to raise four volunteer regiments to take over the internal duties of the defence force which would thus be freed to respond to Britain's call for an invasion of German South West Africa and to seize control of the ports of Swakopmund and Luderitzbrecht. Botha explained that there was considerable opposition to South Africa's participating in the war, but the British government insisted upon the importance of occupying Windhoek, from which wireless communication was being maintained with German warships preying upon shipping in South African waters. Still filled with a deep appreciation of what he regarded as Britain's magnanimity in restoring responsible government to South Africa so soon after the Anglo-Boer war and in approving the Union, Botha could not reject such a plea. Nor could Smuts, who saw in South Africa's participation in imperial obligations a means to consolidate her statehood.

Parliament was not sitting and it fell to the government to order part of the defence force to launch the attack on South West Africa. It was a decision which did not command unanimous approval. Hertzog's party totally condemned the idea of South Africa's playing a part in the war. Even the commanders of the defence force were uncertain. The old

General de la Rey wondered aloud if it were not, after all, God's will that the Boers should oppose Britain rather than wage war on her behalf. Botha, Smuts and Schalk Burger tried to persuade him that the Boers could not honourably seek their independence by such means, but the old man was overcome by religious mysticism and felt only the desire to restore freedom to his people.

Worse was to follow, for de la Rey persuaded an initially reluctant General Beyers to join him in planning a rebellion.[33] On 15 September Beyers submitted his resignation as Commander-in-Chief of the defence force in protest against parliament's decision to launch what he described as an unprovoked attack on South West Africa. Britain, he said, had declared war in her own interests. He was prepared to fight in defence of South Africa, but to suggest that the war was being waged because of German barbarism was to ignore the barbarities perpetrated by Britain against the Boers. In a reply which he made public, Smuts denounced Beyer's criticisms, reminding him of the freedom now accorded to South Africa and pointing to the criminal invasion of Belgium by Germany. He condemned Beyer's attempt to divide the country and ended with a curt acceptance of his resignation. 'Botha and I are not men to desert England in this dark hour,' he wrote to Arthur Gillett.[34] At a meeting of parliament in September, Smuts spoke in support of the motion proclaiming the government's wholehearted determination to take all measures necessary for defending the Union and co-operating with His Majesty's Government to maintain the security and integrity of the Empire. His remarks were decisive in swinging the House of Assembly firmly behind the government and winning the vote by 92 to 12.

In spite of their parliamentary victory, the government's task was not an easy one. Hertzog's supporters were giving wide circulation to Beyer's letter of resignation[35] and were stirring up the Boers of the Free State by claiming that they were to be commandeered for service in South West Africa.[36] In reply, Smuts insisted that only volunteers would serve outside the Union. But feeling was further heightened when, on the evening of 15 September, General de la Ray was accidentally shot and killed when the car in which he was travelling with General Beyers failed to stop at a series of road blocks set up outside Johannesburg to trap three men who had killed a detective. The anti-government forces immediately accused the government of murdering one of the country's heroes. In spite of the denials of Botha and Smuts, Boers in the Free State particularly, but elsewhere too, began to take up arms. General Christian de Wet led the rebels in his own province, while S. G. Maritz, a colonel in the defence force, led a detachment of his troops, with the blessing of Beyers, to the assistance of the Germans in South West Africa.

Botha put himself at the head of troops loyal to the government and took the field against the rebels. Both he and Smuts appealed to Steyn to use his influence with de Wet to bring the rebellion to an end, but with little effect. Smuts felt he could not offer terms to the rebels, though he was deeply disturbed by the idea of taking up arms against his old comrades. He did, however, let it be known early in November that he would give careful consideration to any proposal from the rebels themselves to lay down arms in return for a promise that they would not be punished.[37] His attempts to negotiate a settlement were sharply criticised by Merriman who demanded, 'Are the crimes of robbery, sedition, and public violence merely venial eccentricities when committed by a certain section of the community? If anyone else had done these things, what a howl there would have been!'[38] But even after the defeat of de Wet in a battle on 12 November, Smuts was still prepared to offer an amnesty to anyone, except a leader, who was prepared to surrender within ten days. Merriman was disgusted. 'What, think you, must be the feeling of those who have done their best to maintain law and order when they see the very ruffians who have plundered them and shot their brothers quietly coming back to their homes like the prodigal son, – very possibly going back next week to the old game!'[39] Both Botha and Smuts, however, understood, if they did not agree with, the sincerity of the feelings which had led their former comrades to such acts of treason. Their grief at the death of Beyers by drowning was none the less genuine though the accident had occurred while he was trying to cross the flooded Vaal River to join the Germans.

Botha appealed to the British in South Africa not to press for the summary punishment of the rebels lest their demand should be attributed to race hatred. Only a man of his popularity could have made such a request. Smuts, nevertheless, felt it necessary to demonstrate the government's stern opposition to the rebellion, and, when Yosef Fourie, a captain in the Union defence force, was captured while opposing government forces, he was tried by court martial, found guilty of treason and shot. In spite of Fourie's guilt, his death aroused deep resentment among some of the Boers. Smuts was in a quandary. There were a number of others whose guilt was as great as that of Fourie. Were they also to be executed? And if they were, what would be the effect upon the loyalty of the Boers? Merriman, who was almost as deeply concerned about the vagaries of public opinion, urged Smuts to demonstrate the enormity of the rebels' offence by setting up a judicial inquiry and by stressing the links between German plots and the defection of members of the defence force.[40] Smuts's respect for his old comrades struggled with his anger at their disloyalty and he was further confused by the knowledge that Isie had an even deeper sympathy for the feelings of the rebels than he himself had. Christian de Wet had betrayed his country, but had not he, Smuts, urged surrender in 1902 when de Wet wanted to fight on? Circumstances had changed in the intervening years, but Smuts knew that de Wet's views had not changed. His burning affection for Afrikanerdom remained. For him the present struggle against the British Empire was the renewal of a war which he had earlier been compelled to abandon against his better judgement. So Smuts discreetly set his face against any further death sentences. Instead the rebel leaders were committed to prison, a decision which won the qualified approval of Emily Hobhouse. Nevertheless, she castigated Smuts and Botha for having missed a glorious opportunity to refuse to involve their country in yet another inhuman conflict. 'Those women, the women of the Free State, who forbade their men to go at your behest to fight a neighbour – *they alone were great,*' she wrote.[41]

Even with a rebellion to be crushed the business of running the country continued. As minister of finance, Smuts had to prepare the government's estimates for the forthcoming year, a task made more difficult by the unpredictable demands of the armed forces. Smuts was fully aware that he lacked the expertise to do the job and wisely sought the advice of Merriman. The High Commissioner, Lord Buxton, sympathising with Smuts, suggested to Botha that the cabinet should be enlarged, so as to share out the load which Smuts carried. Botha was not unaware of all that Smuts had to do, but he saw only too clearly that the country lacked men of experience or with suitable qualifications to replace him. After some hesitation he agreed to give the finance portfolio to the loyal and conscientious David de V. Graaf on 24 February 1915, whereupon Smuts, far from seeking respite, suggested that he himself might now become involved in the war in South West Africa.[42]

Botha who, after suppressing the rebellion, had taken command of the expedition against South West Africa, longed to have his friend with him. He did not, however, think highly of Smuts's strategic thinking, and, when the latter was rash enough to make suggestions as to how the campaign should be conducted, Botha did not hesitate to point out his errors.[43] On the other hand, he recognised Smuts's special skill in knitting together British and Boer troops who made uneasy comrades in arms. Smuts was therefore given command of the southern wing of a dual thrust against the German forces in April. After little more than a month, German resistance in the southern sector crumbled. The call for him to return to run the country in Botha's absence was too powerful for Smuts to ignore. Sending his men to reinforce the main army under Botha, he returned to Cape Town.

There was no shortage of work. In addition to keeping an eye on Hertzog and his followers, who were trying to turn public opinion against the government, Smuts faced a new problem from the British section of the population. The news of the sinking of the *Lusitania* had brought rioting mobs on to the streets of Cape Town and other urban centres and German property had been destroyed. In Johannesburg, on 15 May, a mass meeting demanded the internment or deportation of all Germans and the sequestration of their property.[44] Smuts moved carefully but deliberately. He saw he must respond to the clamour against the Germans in a way which would consolidate the support of the English-speaking community, but he must not overlook the pro-German sentiments of many Afrikaners. He decided, therefore, with praiseworthy discretion, that Germans in rural districts should be left alone as long as they behaved themselves, and magistrates and police were instructed to give the same relief to destitute German families as they did to other South Africans in a similar plight. Only in the towns, where feelings ran high, would some Germans be interned.[45]

This political tightrope walking was all the more necessary in view of the approaching elections to parliament. Botha and Smuts feared an ill-assorted alliance between Hertzog's followers and the Labour Party, though the only common ground between the two groups was their dislike of the government. The latter's actions since the outbreak of war had attracted the support of the Unionists, but its having done so had caused unease to many Afrikaners in the South African Party. De V. Graaf suggested that there might be collaboration with the Unionists to avoid a clash of candidates in the constituencies. Smuts disapproved of any blanket arrangement lest it should give the impression that there was to be a coalition. He did, however, wonder whether it was wise in any case to hold elections in the unsettled state of the country. Merriman, whose advice he again sought, had no doubt that elections should be held. To withhold them would give the opposition a genuine grievance, and he claimed, not over-confidently, to believe that Hertzog's challenge could be met.[46]

The surrender of the Germans in South West Africa on 9 July gave grounds for satisfaction and for hope, not always justified, that there would be less turbulence in the Union. Characteristically, Botha had been in favour of generous terms for the defeated enemy, but had met with opposition from the Governor-General, who had urged that such generosity might be misconstrued. In any case, it would give offence to Britain and her allies who were fighting Germany on other fronts.[47] For the support given by Smuts to his chief throughout the campaign Lord Buxton gave unstinting praise. 'The strain on you all these months has been tremendous,' he wrote, 'and I've often wondered how you've stood it.'[48] Smuts's capacity for work was indeed astonishing, but he felt an overwhelming sense of relief that Botha would soon be back to give a lead in political matters. Though growing in authority, he was still content to feel that final decisions would be taken by his friend. With the elections still to come, there were difficult issues to be dealt with. The strength of Afrikaner feeling was reflected in a petition supported by many thousands of signatures which was presented to the Governor-General by a deputation of Boer women from all four provinces requesting a remission of the sentences on de Wet and others.[49] The Nationalists were also actively circulating propaganda which included a poem honouring the work of Yosef Fourie. The newspaper, *Die Burger*, carried on the propaganda war, and a stream of pamphlets printed in Stellenbosch extolled the virtues of the rebels.[50] Nor was Smuts subject only to verbal attack. On the evening of 23 September he was fired upon from close range in the Johannesburg suburb of Newlands, but was saved by the intervention of plain clothes constables.[51]

Amid all this turmoil Smuts received the news that he had been elected to a fellowship at his old Cambridge college, Christ's. It was an honour he cherished profoundly. About the same time he was invited by the British government to take command of the forces operating against German East Africa. This recognition by the outside world of talents so varied marked the beginning of a transformation in Smuts, though its final consummation took several years. South Africa had so far made no contribution to the East African campaign, but at Britain's request was already recruiting a volunteer brigade to serve in Europe. In view of the troubled situation in South Africa, Smuts did not believe it would be right for him to go to East Africa. Nevertheless, it was decided that 20,000 troops should be sent to serve in that campaign in 1916.

Meanwhile, the elections took place in October and provided a disturbing result for the government which failed to achieve an overall majority. The South African Party won 54 seats out of a total of 130. The Unionists gained 39, the Nationalists 27 and the Labour Party 4. Significantly, the South African Party polled only 95,000 votes against 77,000 for the Nationalists, in spite of the greater number of seats they obtained, but that result suggested that Botha and Smuts might still have the support of the majority of Afrikaners. Henceforward, however, they would have to rely heavily upon the Unionists for support, and Hertzog and his supporters had made a point during the elections of stressing that there was no significant difference between the South African Party and the Unionists. By contrast, Hertzog had claimed that his party stood for the interests of South Africa. He was not, he said, pursuing a racial policy. What he disliked was the Jingo spirit which made the Unionists more loyal to Britain than to South Africa. Since union it had seemed that Botha was pursuing an identical policy of subordinating South African interests to imperial designs. He, Hertzog, wanted the Union to remain neutral in the war, if only to demonstrate that South Africa was not simply a British dependency. He was not opposed to English-speaking South Africans, but he did mistrust those who constantly looked to Britain for direction. He did not even insist upon a South African republic, but, if a country were truly free, the people could decide for themselves the form of government they wanted.

It was a compelling argument, and Smuts, who had been pleased by his own success in a constituency which, he claimed, consisted almost entirely of English and Dutch labourers who had been hostile to him ever since the strikes of 1913 and 1914,[52] was anxious about the strength of feeling which persisted among some of the Afrikaners. For that reason the government took the risky step of simultaneously releasing 118 rebels from prison. The subsequent triumphant behaviour of the Nationalists brought angry protests from Denys Reitz on behalf of the Afrikaners of the Free State who had remained loyal to the government and who resented their lack of representation in parliament arising from the success of Nationalist candidates in the Free State constituencies.[53]

When, in February 1916, the British government renewed their invitation to Smuts to take command in East Africa and in addition offered him the rank of Lieutenant-General, he felt he could no longer refuse in spite of the difficulties his government faced. He was attracted to the idea of a decisive intervention by Union forces in East Africa, hoping that a victory there might result in some exchange of territory with Portuguese East Africa to consolidate South Africa's territory south of the Zambezi and give the Union control of its northern access to the Indian Ocean.[54] He was convinced that right was on the side of the allied forces as he claimed in a rather sententious letter to Margaret Gillett to whom he wrote, 'I do sincerely believe that we are struggling for the preservation against terrible odds of what is most precious in our civilisation. I have passed through terrible times already but feel that there should be no hanging back when so much is at stake.' He went on, 'I shall do my best to succeed where several predecessors have already failed.'[55] His letter betrayed the humourless *gravitas* with which men impress their contemporaries while others, coming after, wonder how they got away with it. Mrs Gillett was certainly impressed, even while doubting whether civilisation could be saved by fighting in East Africa, or anywhere else. With the love that overlooks minor vanities, she looked forward to the day when Smuts would go to Europe to reconcile the factions there.[56]

To invite Smuts to take command in East Africa was a strange decision on the part of the British government. Nothing in his Boer War experience or in his brief action in South West Africa had prepared him for such a large command. Although he carried the title of general, he had never commanded large numbers of troops, and Botha had been sceptical about his ideas on strategy. Nevertheless, he had demonstrated his qualities as an administrator in civilian life and he had been a determined, courageous leader of a small, mobile force in the earlier war. These attributes were likely to stand him in good stead when dealing with troops from such varied backgrounds as Britain, India, East Africa, West Africa and South Africa, but his lack of experience of strategic planning was a grave disadvantage in the long term.

Smuts's orders were to conduct a successful campaign before the rainy season began in East Africa and it was important for him to win an early victory to establish his reputation among the troops he was to command. Soon after his arrival, therefore, he launched an attack on the German defences on the slopes of Mount Kilimanjaro near the Kenya border. It was not a complete success. Though the frontal attack was carried out with courage and determination, the flanking movement which was intended to cut off the Germans' retreat and destroy the enemy failed. Nevertheless, Botha was delighted by what his friend had achieved. Now their roles were reversed, not necessarily to the advantage of either of them. For while Smuts struggled with military problems, Botha faced the vigorous opposition of Hertzog's party and at the same time was anxious lest the Unionists should exploit the divisions among the Afrikaners to seek a majority at the next election.[57]

As Botha had done in South West Africa, Smuts met with jealousy among the officers under his command. Strongly supported by the British government as well as by Botha himself, he acted firmly to suppress the trouble. But, as the British forces advanced southward, he found himself increasingly cast in the role which Roberts had played in the Anglo-Boer War. To move and supply large bodies of troops across vast regions of inhospitable country called for immense organisation. To use those troops decisively against an elusive enemy, even one which lacked the mobility of the Boer commandos with which Roberts had had to deal, required even greater ingenuity and cunning. Like Roberts before him, Smuts found it easier to occupy enemy territory and to win numerous skirmishes than to destroy the opposition. In addition, casualties in the fighting round Kilimanjaro had been heavy, and with the onset of the rainy season in March large numbers of troops became incapacitated by sickness.[58]

After being held up by the weather while his South African troops were constantly harassed by the enemy, Smuts resumed his advance in May. He had in the meantime explained the military situation to Botha and had proposed a plan of campaign about which he sought advice.[59] Botha replied that it was difficult to express a useful opinion with the little knowledge at his disposal and then went on to offer a thoroughly professional plan of what Smuts should do. In keeping with the principles of war he emphasised the importance of striking a decisive blow against the main body of the enemy's army and of following it up vigorously with mounted troops to complete the destruction.[60] It was advice which Smuts found difficult to put into practice. Pressing southward by forced marches through thick bush country which tested the endurance of the soldiers to the limit and overstrained their tenuous supply lines, his leading troops occupied Morogoro by the end of August. But they failed to inveigle the enemy into a decisive battle. Smuts had hoped the Germans would make a stand at Morogoro, located on the central railway and backed by the formidable Uluguru Mountains. What he had not yet appreciated was that the German commander had accepted from the beginning that it would be impossible to defend the colony against overwhelming odds. His aim was to keep his force intact so as to be able to strike at his opponents whenever opportunity presented itself. In this way he could engage large numbers of imperial forces who might otherwise have been deployed in more significant areas of combat.[61]

Faced with the frustrations of war, Smuts lost some of the accommodating spirit which had appreciated British magnanimity. Instead he longed for an overwhelming victory 'which would for some generations to come cure mankind of this insane folly of war.'[62] Learning of the successful advance of Belgian troops into German East Africa from the Belgian Congo, he prematurely concluded that the campaign was about to enter its closing stages. All that was needed, he thought, was a decisive action and the hostilities would be brought to an end. The wish was clearly father to the thought. His decision to advance still further southward as far as the Rufiji River was in line with the instructions he had received from London,[63] but was open to serious question from a strategic point of view. His troops were exhausted, and any hope of using the central railway to supply them during the advance was ruled out for the time being because of the shortage of rolling stock and because of the damage done by the Germans to every bridge and culvert. By the end of September the advance had lost its momentum, and with the onset of the second rainy season of the year many of the British and South African troops had to be withdrawn to recuperate.

The arrival of reinforcements from Nigeria encouraged Smuts to try again to reach the Rufiji at the end of 1916. Another force, from Rhodesia, had invaded German territory from the south-west, so that, if one accepted the assumption that the occupation of German territory would lead to the collapse of German resistance, it could be argued that the advance Smuts projected would indeed be decisive. To gain his end he launched a frontal attack accompanied by a flanking movement and once again, after fierce fighting, the Germans withdrew before they were encircled. The Rufiji objective had been attained but the final action had yet to be fought. Further torrential rain in the spring of 1917 made the maintenance of a large force along the river an impossible task, and in the meantime the German commander was already exploring the possibility of retreating into Portuguese East Africa in order to carry on the campaign from there.

Smuts's claim that the campaign was now virtually ended was no more true than Roberts's statement when he said that the Anglo-Boer War was over after the capture of Pretoria. Nor can Smuts really have believed what he claimed. Years later he felt it necessary to defend himself against criticism by asking a historian of the campaign to stress the difficulties he had encountered in fighting in bush country where the enemy knew every inch of the ground.[64] Yet in 1917 he had no hesitation in claiming a victory, though the situation he handed over to his chief of staff, General Hoskins, was not dissimilar from that which Roberts handed over to his chief of staff, Kitchener, in 1900. The enemy was still in the field, still active and still determined to prolong the war. Smuts said nothing of this because he was now called upon to relinquish his command in order to represent South Africa at an imperial war conference to be held in London. Botha could not go because his presence was urgently needed in South Africa. Nationalist sentiment appeared to be weakening in the Transvaal and the Orange Free State, but the Cape gave cause for anxiety. Fortunately for the government, Christian de Wet had rejected a request that he should lead an ill-conceived attempt to launch a second rebellion and acted as a principal Crown witness against the organisers.[65]

But the East African campaign, consistently denounced by Hertzog's supporters, had provided ammunition for the critics of the government when the discomforts suffered by the troops were made public by the *Rand Daily Mail* and *The Sunday Times*.[66] The perennial question of the level of pay for troops serving overseas also caused embarrassment for the government. Botha had sought advice from the Canadian prime minister, Wilfred Laurier, who was suffering similar attacks from some of the French population of Canada. For some years his problems had paralleled those of Botha in that he had been criticized by his French fellow-countrymen for being too British and by the extreme British element for not being British enough. Since the outbreak of war he had been violently criticised by French-speakers for his loyalty to Britain but, as he wrote in reply to Botha's enquiries, 'To me, my course has been clear from the beginning; the triumph of Germany would be a menace to freedom in every land. England has nobly taken her part in standing at once by Belgium and France, and I have constantly and cheerfully exercised what influence I have in this country in support of her cause.'[67] They were reassuring words, wholly in accord with Botha's own sentiments, and they must have strengthened him in his purpose. During the East African campaign, however, Smuts had had little time to consider these issues, and he only occasionally found time to write to Isie about the management of his farms. Nevertheless, he had written to Wolstenholme to say that he had been giving serious thought to the question of holism during the campaign and believed that it had solved many problems that had been puzzling him.[68]

After a brief return to South Africa, Smuts was on his way to England in February with a military reputation enhanced more by his own accounts of the East African campaign than by his achievements as a commander. His hoped-for 'honeymoon week' with his wife and family at Doornkloof was spoiled for him by an attack of malaria[69] and he went on board ship with serious misgivings about the role he was to play at the imperial conference[70] and about the probability of seasickness during the voyage.[71] Isie had thoughtfully arranged for some of his friends to write letters which would be handed to him at intervals during the trip. She had probably not intended that they should remind him of the problems he was leaving behind, but he could not escape them completely. One correspondent stressed the urgency of countering Nationalist propaganda which, he said, was persuading the youth of the country that, if they were to be truly patriotic and true Afrikaners, they must join the Nationalist party. Even more mature men were becoming convinced that the government was trying to destroy the Dutch language and Afrikaner traditions. It was also said that the government had had prior knowledge of the rebellion of 1914 and could have nipped it in the bud, but preferred to let it take its course so that it could rid the country of some of its more troublesome opponents. 'I cannot support a government that deliberately allows Afrikaners to shoot Afrikaners,' one man had remarked.[72]

These were not cheerful thoughts to occupy Smuts's mind, and he had a similarly gloomy letter from Merriman who contemplated the possibility of a civil war stirred up by the Nationalists. Botha, he wrote, was building up trouble for the government by his proposal to make a free gift of £1,000,000 to the British government and by introducing a new Natives Land Bill which sought to make the provisions of the 1913 Act more stringent. The Bill was debated in the Assembly along British versus Boer lines and its defeat owed a great deal to the efforts of the Cape members whose presence in the House depended in part on African votes. In 1917 the Supreme Court ruled that Africans in the Cape must be free to buy land anywhere in the province because it was one of the qualifications they required to become voters under the South Africa Act. For the time being this gave the *coup de grâce* to Botha's efforts. As a final thrust Merriman cheerfully warned Smuts to reflect upon the failings of the Congress of Vienna while he danced attendance upon Northcliffe, the newspaper tycoon, and his old enemy, Milner, in the company of Milner's Kindergarten.[73]

5

International statesman

During Smuts's stay in England, which was extended from a few weeks to two and a half years, his career was to reach its climax and then go beyond it. His remarkable capacity for work and his skill at synthesising ideas and information enabled him to win international respect which he retained for the rest of his life. By 1918 his international influence reached a peak to which he could not later aspire. The war and its problems gave him the opportunity for service for which he had been craving and he responded wholeheartedly. The shadow of South Africa reached out to England briefly. During the course of the imperial conference Srinivasa Sastri proposed a resolution demanding all rights of citizenship for Indians in the dominions and Smuts found himself in a minority of one in opposing the resolution. In general, however, Smuts's welcome was of the warmest. Not only his friends – Arthur and Margaret Gillett; H. J. Wolstenholme, Olive Schreiner and Emily Hobhouse among them – but public figures and institutions alike greeted him with enthusiasm. Emily Hobhouse could not resist the sardonic comment that he would no doubt be joining Milner in an attempt to 'Russianise' Britain after the former High Commissioner's recent visit to the Czar's dominions.[1] But she was anxious to enlist her old friend's aid on behalf of her numerous causes and she took a house in London so as to be able to put her views to him in person.

Smuts's arrival in England was timely. The British people were profoundly depressed by the war. The campaign in France appeared to be making little headway and the shocking casualties suffered in the Battle of the Somme the previous year had left the country sick at heart. The Dardanelles campaign had reached a stalemate without any achievement to set against the losses suffered there. The army in Egypt seemed to lack any aggressive spirit, and the German submarine campaign was taking a heavy toll of shipping, which meant that food supplies were low. The appearance on this dismal scene of a handsome, exotic figure, who, not many years before, had led the British army in South Africa a lively dance but who more recently had led British and colonial troops in what at a distance seemed to have been a successful action, brought a gleam of hope which stirred men's hearts. It mattered little that the

89

East African campaign still lumbered tediously on or that, compared with the Western Front, only a handful of men had been involved. The British public longed for hope, and this former enemy commando leader seemed to offer it. In more than one of his letters to his wife Smuts admitted that he was getting more acclaim than he deserved. But he would have been less than human if he had not taken genuine pleasure in the warmth of his reception, and in spite of public demands he did not neglect the pleasure of visiting his friends.

Those demands were numerous and varied, and Smuts responded with his customary vigour. Edinburgh, Manchester and London all granted him the freedom of the city. His old university, Cambridge, awarded him an honorary doctorate. Mrs Alice Green, widow of the historian J. R. Green, sought to enlist his aid in the solution of Britain's differences with Ireland. The political writer J. A. Hobson invited him to address the League of Nations Society. L. S. Amery, on the staff of the war cabinet, also sought to interest him in the Irish question, as well as impressing upon him the need for a long-term strategy for the conduct of the war and a more forceful plan for the Palestine campaign. To all these requests and to many others Smuts gave his attention with astonishing speed, revelling in the opportunity to air his views on a new range of subjects.

First and foremost was the decisive contribution he made to the discussions in the imperial conference about the future constitution of the Empire. This was a subject upon which he did not wish to see a decision reached until after the war. Milner's Kindergarten, now reorganised as the Round Table, were of a contrary view. Federation was still their slogan as it had been in South Africa ten years earlier. For them it seemed a matter of urgency to establish an imperial federation if the Empire was not to disintegrate entirely. Smuts, on the other hand, believed that for such disparate nations to be run by a central parliament and a central executive would be to court disaster. To counter the Round Table he introduced a resolution which said that any adjustment of the imperial constitution should be based upon a full recognition of the dominions as autonomous nations in an imperial commonwealth and should provide effective arrangements for continuous consultation on all important matters of common concern. They should then take such necessary concerted action, founded upon that consultation, as the various governments might determine. The terms of his resolution sprang both from a spirit of high idealism and from bitter experience. Smuts longed for the willing co-operation of the nations of the Commonwealth, as he preferred to call the Empire, as a proof that wisdom resides in free spirits. But he knew all too well that any attempt to establish the sort of federation conceived by the Round Table would be vigorously opposed by Hertzog and his supporters, and possibly by other Afrikaners who hitherto had supported Botha and himself in their policy of co-operation with Britain. For Hertzog such a federation would have seemed like the enslavement of his people. Smuts carried the day. His resolution was adopted and discussion of the arrangements necessary to make it effective was postponed until the first imperial conference after the war.

Speaking in Edinburgh on 11 April after receiving an honorary degree from the university, Smuts next emphasised the virtues of magnanimity as demonstrated by the Boers' response to Britain's grant of self-government so soon after the Anglo-Boer War. As so often on subsequent occasions, he gave the impression that the policy he and Botha were so ardently pursuing reflected the general feeling of all Afrikaners. In stressing Boer participation in the present war on the side of Britain, he omitted to mention the far greater contribution of English-speaking South Africans and avoided all reference to the dissidents among the Boers who, even if they had taken no part in the rebellion, were reluctant to throw in their lot with the British.[2] These oversights were not due to a deliberate intention to deceive his audience. It was more like an act of self-deception. Increasingly Smuts was inclined to assume that any cause which he had adopted must reflect the views of his countrymen. He was the 'general will' of his people, in Rousseauesque terms. In other words, he was the will they would have if only they knew what was good for them. He was later to adopt a similar attitude towards wider issues as he came increasingly to regard himself as the world's wiser conscience. But that was in the future. At the moment he was engrossed in providing solutions to immediate problems.

An invitation from the prime minister, David Lloyd George, to go to France and submit recommendations for the conduct of the war on all fronts resulted in the sort of instant report for which, on a lesser scale, he had already demonstrated a remarkable aptitude in South Africa. His memorandum, like his earlier ones, was not entirely original in the ideas it presented. One feature which was his own, however, was the emphasis he placed upon the need to conquer world opinion by conduct which would win the admiration and respect of those not directly involved in the war. On a purely military note, he suggested that the main thrust of the campaign against Turkey should be switched from Salonika to Palestine. This would make it possible to supply the British forces from East and South Africa and from Australia without resorting to the dangerous Mediterranean route or to draining still further the declining resources of Britain. At the same time it would mean that the forces in Mesopotamia would be conveniently poised to assist at

91

the appropriate time. The main problem remained on the Western Front. The absence of any reserve there constituted a serious threat. It was, he wrote, a situation which had arisen from Britain's increasing commitment to the defence of France while French troops had become heavily committed in the Balkans. Smuts's solution was to leave a greater share of the burden of the defence of France to the French army so that British forces could be withdrawn to form a reserve which would be available to counter any unexpected German thrust or to reinforce any large-scale attack by the Allies.[3]

The strength of the memorandum lay in the skill with which Smuts had absorbed contemporary strategic thinking and had then synthesised it, adding a little embellishment which was entirely his own. In that way he was able to present the people with what they wanted to hear. His plan seemed to offer two strands of hope. First, he had suggested a means of breaking the deadlock in the west by seizing the initiative from the flagging hands of the French. Then, he had aimed to arouse the aggressive spirit of the forces arraigned against the Turks. The fact that the French were unlikely to approve the plan mattered little for the moment. Smuts had given a lead. The visitor from a distant land had breathed on the embers and the fire of British enthusiasm was rekindled.

The suggestion that he himself should take command of the Palestine campaign came at first as an unexpected pleasure to Smuts. His immediate reaction was to consult Botha to discover whether he could be spared from South Africa for an indefinite period. His friend responded warmly in spite of the problems he was facing at home, and urged Smuts to accept the offer as a tribute both to South Africa and to himself. But Smuts was already being diverted to more attractive fields of endeavour. He had seized with alacrity upon the opportunity offered by the growing interest in the idea of a League of Nations to draft a memorandum on the subject which had been discussed by the war cabinet on 26 April and accepted with only minor emendations.[4] Soon he was under pressure to join the war cabinet himself. In his letters to Isie he still wrote as the playful, loving, self-deprecatory – but not too self-deprecatory – young man who had wooed and married her. He would much prefer, he said, to return to his own little country lest his people should entirely forget him and come to regard him as English.[5] But to Botha he adopted a more arrogant tone, claiming that he had asked the British government to review the entire military position and to simplify its programme. Only after this had been done would he decide whether it was worth his while to go to Palestine. In any case, he would only accept command if it were treated as a first-class campaign and adequately supplied with men and guns. This might be good sense from a military point of view, but Smuts's military qualifications scarcely matched his self-esteem. Nor did his further suggestion – that Botha should impress upon the new commander in East Africa, General van der Venter, the desirability of finishing the campaign quickly – show him in a particularly charitable light. Van der Venter had been one of the most aggressive officers under Smuts's command and much of the success achieved in East Africa had been due to his dash and initiative. For Smuts now to imply that what remained was no more than a simple mopping-up operation was wholly unjust.[6]

Had all the adulation he had received gone to Smuts's head? Certainly he seems to have been regarded on all sides as something of a magician. On 15 May 1917, at a banquet given in his honour by both houses of parliament, he did much to justify that reputation. His audience listened with admiration when he addressed them on the need for fuller consultation with the leaders of the dominions in place of the four-yearly meetings of the imperial conference. Foreign policy, he said, should be discussed annually in meetings of the most important leaders of the Empire. A policy based on such a community of interests would not only benefit Britain and the dominions but would give a lead to the whole post-war world. Renewing the theme he had proclaimed with such success during the imperial conference, he said that the very term, 'Empire', was misleading. The dominions did not constitute one state. They were a community of states and nations which, together, were far greater than any empire that had ever existed.[7] These sentiments struck a sympathetic chord in the heart of L. S. Amery who, only a decade later, as secretary of state for the colonies, was to try to create the commonwealth of nations which Smuts now so earnestly advocated. The Liberal peer Lord Harcourt, too, was deeply moved by Smuts's speech, which he saw as a great liberal advance upon the theme of an imperial federation with an imperial parliament advanced by Milner's Kindergarten.[8]

A week later Smuts made another significant speech at a dinner in the Savoy Hotel. His theme on that occasion was South Africa, and he emphasised the unity which existed between British and Dutch and for which he and Botha had been earnestly striving. He accepted without equivocation the existence of a greater disunity – that between Africans and Europeans. Segregation was now South Africa's policy, he said. It was dishonourable to mix black and white blood, though in all the government's dealings with Africans it strove to observe the standards embodied in the Christian moral code. The old haphazard way of mixing Africans and Europeans had failed to uplift the former and had only degraded the latter. Now they were to be kept apart as much as possible. It was useless, he concluded, to try to subject Africans and Europeans to the same institutions of government or to the same legislation.[9]

The apparent logic of separate development was readily accepted by Smuts's audience, whose knowledge of South Africa was, in most instances, limited. The Chairman, Lord Selborne, may well have had doubts about the wisdom of Smuts's proposals, though he, like the other people present, would have accepted the desirability of ensuring that South Africa should be dominated by European standards of civilisation. Increasingly, however, when Smuts spoke, people in Britain listened.

At a more personal level, Alice Clark, sister of Margaret Gillett, wrote to ask him to make contact with the leaders of the Labour movement. Her hope was that he might be able to mediate between them and the government to find a solution to the strike of engineers in South Lancashire which was affecting the production of munitions.[10] In this instance Smuts, whose experience of dealing with strikes in South Africa had been less than triumphant, replied guardedly that he would try to get in touch with the Labour leaders but must take care that they did not think he was trying to take advantage of them. On the national level once more he was asked by the prime minister, Lloyd George, to preside over a conference to draft a constitution for Ireland. Here again Smuts felt the need to tread warily. He was all too conscious of the problems which could arise when two peoples with differing cultures inhabited the same country, though he was prepared to brush his doubts aside if circumstances demanded. Over the future conduct of the Palestine campaign he spoke with greater confidence since, having decided not to accept command there, he would not be involved in putting his plans into effect. In the international field, too, Smuts was increasingly to play the role of consultant, and his fertile mind was never slow to produce an answer – witness his proposal to use as a strategic reserve the American troops which would become available in due course as a result of the decision to enter the war taken by the United States in April.

In June Smuts entered the war cabinet believing that by so doing he could serve the Commonwealth best. To Isie he wrote, 'I do not see how I can be spared here in the immediate future.'[11] At the same time he was receiving frequent invitations to go to America to stir up interest in the more active prosecution of the war, and he had also been invited to go to Russia. A proposed weekend with the Gilletts had to be abandoned when he was summoned to Windsor Castle where he had a long talk with the King who advised him not to go to America but to remain to help in England until the end of the war.[12] Inevitably he was becoming more remote from the South African scene, though he confided in Isie that he hoped one day to win over the Nationalists, or their children, to the view that he was their best champion. He also noted, though from a great distance, that there was some talk of a coalition between the South African Party and the Unionists, though Botha was not in favour and his close supporters did not look favourably upon the idea.

Then, unexpectedly, came a telegram from the High Commissioner, Lord Buxton, summoning Smuts back to Africa. Botha, who had been diagnosed as suffering from a weak heart and a tendency to dropsy, had been under severe strain because of the opposition of the National-ists, while the sudden death of his brother had added to his worries. Lord Buxton had watched with growing anxiety the deterioration in the prime minister's health and on 17 September concluded that it was essen-tial for Smuts to be recalled to lighten the load on his friend and to give him the companionship he so badly needed. By the end of the month, however, Botha had recovered sufficiently to insist that Smuts should not be required to return in view of the importance of his work in England. Buxton, therefore, cancelled his request early in October.[13]

Smuts accepted the change in plan with some relief. It would have been a great blow to him to return to the small but immediate demands of South African government, and to leave the great opportunities offered by Britain at war. To Isie he wrote with that mixture of solicitude and masculine insistence upon the superior demands of duty which had characterised their limited correspondence during the Anglo-Boer War: 'This is hard on me: it is much harder on you, my dearest heart, but we are both on active service for humanity and we must strengthen our hearts to see all this separation through to the end.' Then, having justified his position to his own satisfaction, he turned immediately to practical things.

Yesterday [he went on] I made a speech about the military situation, and particularly about the air war, which is attracting much attention and has been cabled verbatim throughout the world. Roderick Jones, (Head of Reuters news agency) says he does not remember any other speech which has gained such a distinction. You are probably busy reading it now in South Africa. A sculpture of me is now being made by Tweed. ... He says he wants to make something good of me, and it looks very good. The portrait by Nicholson is also good and goes to Johannesburg Art Gallery; a copy of it goes to Cambridge University. Now you must not become too proud of your little Boer and remember that pride goes before a fall.[14]

But Smuts was more than a little proud of himself, and he certainly did not contemplate a fall in the immediate future. Was he not demon-strating beyond all question that his choice of vocation had been utterly right? His statement on air policy was certainly of the greatest significance and resulted in his being appointed chairman of a committee to set up an Air Ministry. Before long, too, he found himself in charge of the defence of London against air attack.

In spite of his prolonged separation from Isie, Smuts did not lack female companionship. Margaret Gillett kept a loving, sisterly eye on him and he also developed a strong attachment for her unmarried sister, Alice Clark. He described Alice, in the words of Goethe, as *ein Schöne Seele* – a beautiful soul – and he greatly enjoyed her company during weekends she spent with him in London. Between those meetings his life was as busy as ever. On the advice of Buxton and Botha he turned down the offer of a seat in the House of Commons lest it should seem to his fellow-countrymen that he had become wholly English. But he was at hand to advise Lloyd George to send four or five British divisions to Italy with all speed to show the Italians that Britain would stand by them after their defeat by the Austrians at Caporetto and Tolmino.[15] He also paid a visit to South Wales to investigate a miners' strike and, perhaps to his surprise, was received with wild enthusiasm. As a result of what he saw, he suggested to the government, sensibly enough, that the miners might respond more favourably if they were kept more fully informed about what was happening in the war.[16] Sometimes Smuts found it easier to advise than to follow his own precepts.

Scarcely had he returned from Wales before he was sent to Italy to attend a meeting of leading members of the British, French and Italian governments in Rapallo. His absence, and the continuing separation after his return to England because of his involvement in the proceedings of a committee on agriculture, distressed Alice Clark whose attachment to him had all the intensity of love. Smuts wrote to her frequently, letters full of affection, but also containing long disquisitions on his theory of the Whole. To such discursive ramblings only the blindest admiration could have produced the enthusiastic response contained in Alice's replies.[17] Margaret, too, happily married for ten years and with four children to occupy her attention, seemed nevertheless to have retained some of the romantic feelings for Smuts which had developed during their voyage to England in 1906. But in the intervening years those feelings had matured into something more akin to comradeship. To both those devoted women Smuts owed the comfort, peace and stimulus which sent him back renewed to his work time and time again.

One of Smuts's public utterances provoked a comment which was to have far-reaching effects. In a paper on Peace Conversations he had suggested that Germany's captured colonies should not be returned to her because they were essential to British communications. Philip Kerr,

Lloyd George's secretary and a former member of Milner's Kindergarten, at once remarked that such a proposal would be unacceptable to the USA because, by implication, it meant that every coaling station throughout the world should belong to Britain for the same reason. While he agreed that Germany should not be allowed to recover her colonies, Kerr thought it would be wiser if they were to come under the control of a neighbouring power or country with colonial experience or even be internationalised.[18] It was advice which Smuts took to heart and from it sprang the germ of Smuts's later scheme for mandates which was to win widespread acceptance, though for Smuts himself it meant partial defeat because he would dearly have liked to annex South West Africa to the Union.

It was not long before Smuts was again on his travels, this time to Geneva to attend a meeting with the Austrian emissary, Count Mensdorff, to discuss, on behalf of the war cabinet, the possibility of a separate peace with Austria–Hungary.[19] The discussions reached no conclusion. Mensdorff, acting on explicit instructions, introduced the question of peace terms for Germany but the subject was firmly vetoed. So, too, was any idea of a greater Germany embracing Austria. Smuts made it clear, however, that there was no wish in England to destroy Austria–Hungary. His own view was that the Habsburg Empire should be transformed, using the British Commonwealth as a model, so enabling the Allies to fulfil their promises to the Serbs and Romanians. Mensdorff, who believed that Germany could not be defeated, asked for time to consider the proposals, and there Smuts's personal involvement in the negotiations ended.[20]

To the delight of his friends, Smuts was back in England in time to spend a joyful Christmas at the Clarks' family home at Millfield, in Somerset, where he went for long walks with Alice on the morning and afternoon of Christmas Day. On his return to London he swiftly drafted a statement of war aims in response to the possibility that a general peace conference might be imminent because negotiations were taking place between the Russians and their German and Austro-Hungarian enemies at Brest Litovsk. It was a statement which, he believed, would cause a sensation. It certainly won the approval of the French premier, Georges Clemenceau, and formed the basis of a speech by Lloyd George. Its object was to ensure that justice should be done to those who had suffered as a result of the war without insisting upon the total destruction of the enemy. It was a view which Lloyd George shared until later in the year when the desire to appear responsive to public opinion induced him to take a much harder line against Germany.[21]

In February 1918 Smuts was in Cairo at the head of a mission to plan the further campaign in Palestine and Mesopotamia. Although he was working against the background of a separate peace between Russia and Germany, he felt exhilarated. Having crossed France and northern Italy by rail, he had boarded HMS *Liverpool* at Taranto to face the twin hazards of a submarine attack and the even greater certainty of seasickness. The party had arrived safely in Alexandria, however, and, after a visit to the pyramids and a meeting with the High Commissioner in Cairo, the party set out for Palestine and General Allenby's headquarters. They were able to get as far as Jerusalem but could not reach the front line because of bad roads. Smuts was thrilled to be in the Holy Land and found time to soak in the atmosphere of a country about which he had read so much in his Bible and had come to love. Its far horizons reminded him so vividly of his own homeland. But the main business was his consultation with Allenby and it was carried out carefully but expeditiously. On his return to Egypt Smuts was also able to visit Luxor and the Valley of the Kings before arriving in Cairo. There he had further talks with General W. Gillman, who had just arrived from Mesopotamia with the information Smuts needed to formulate his plan. By 26 February he was back in London and was immediately summoned to important discussions in the war cabinet. Soon afterwards his report was discussed by the cabinet and accepted without reservation. As usual Smuts's personal contribution to the draft had been largely one of synthesis. His ideas closely followed those presented to him by the commanders in the field, but by presenting the argument in cogent style and by giving his name to the plan he supplied the elements needed to induce the cabinet to support opinions already held by those in command in Palestine and Mesopotamia.

All other considerations were hastily pushed into the background by news of a great German thrust towards the channel ports which began on 21 March. Smuts readily appreciated how finely balanced the outcome must be, and how vital success would be to either side. A German triumph could not be dismissed as out of the question. But if the attack failed, German hopes of ultimate victory must be at an end. It was no time to accept an invitation from another old Cambridge acquaintance, now President of the Massachusetts Institute of Technology, to go to America to try to stir President Woodrow Wilson into a more vigorous prosecution of America's contribution to the war,[22] desperately though that help was needed. Although America had officially been at war with Germany for a year, she had made no contribution to the fighting. Wilson himself had spent most of the time trying, without any obvious success, to induce the combatants to accept 'peace without victory'. In January he had announced to congress the principles upon which he believed the war should be brought to an end, his 'Fourteen Points'. They included an agreement on open diplomacy; freedom of navigation of the seas unless closed by international action; the removal of economic barriers; a drastic reduction in armaments; a free adjustment colonial claims; the evacuation of Belgium and of French and Russian territory occupied by the Germans; an adjustment to Italy's boundaries; the creation of an independent Polish state; freedom for non-Turkish nationalities at present in the Ottoman Empire; and the creation of an association of nations under specified covenants to afford mutual guarantees of political independence and territorial integrity to great and small states alike. Compared with the terms offered by Germany to Russia, the Fourteen Points were very generous. But Germany, unlike Russia, was prepared to fight on for an even better result, and the advance in March was an earnest of her intention to do so.

Smuts sketched out his own ideas about a settlement in a speech delivered in Glasgow on 17 May when he received the freedom of that city. There was, he believed, no place for a negotiated peace. There were some things, such as the restoration of Belgium, over which there could be no negotiation. On the other hand, he believed that to destroy Germany would be impossible without many more years of warfare, and to do so would not in any case be in keeping with the purely defensive purposes for which Britain and her Allies were fighting the war. He hoped, however, that the failure of the great German offensive, with the hideous loss of life that that entailed, would convince the German people of the bankruptcy of the military ideal for which their leaders stood. Germany might then accept the terms without which the Allies could not contemplate an end to the war.[23] There was, he was convinced, an imperative need to inflict a heavy reverse upon the German army. Without that, the Germans might seek to negotiate peace while they were at the height of their success over Russia. This would leave their military prestige at its peak and would provide no foundation for future stability in Europe. But the Allies were too exhausted to launch any vigorous attack unless the American army were to be brought into action. Smuts did not regard General Pershing as the man to lead such an undertaking and so privately suggested his own appointment as field commander of the American forces to Lloyd George.[24] The acclaim Smuts had received in all his recent advisory roles had scarcely prepared him for such a post. Nor had his military experience demonstrated his obvious suitability. Lloyd George does not appear to have pursued the initiative further, which on military grounds was probably wise and from a political point of view was certainly tactful. Instead he suggested Smuts might usefully be sent to Russia. This, too, came to nothing.

The war, meanwhile, was moving more rapidly to an end than was generally appreciated. On receiving the news that an armistice was to be agreed, Smuts at once urged the prime minister to show generosity by sending food to the famished millions of Europe. 'May God in His great love remove from us all smallness of heart and vitalize our souls with sympathy and fellow-feeling for those in affliction – the beaten, weak and little ones who have no food,' he wrote.[25] Unfortunately, his call for a magnanimous gesture was rendered ineffectual because Lloyd George had already committed himself to a policy of demanding retribution from Germany.

For Smuts the armistice held out the possibility of release from so many burdens and the prospect of a return to South Africa, leaving General Botha to look after the Union's interests at the peace conference. But again he encountered problems. He had, for some months, been chairman of a demobilisation committee set up by the war cabinet, and that work now took on a greater urgency. In addition, in such high esteem was he held as a thinker and a draftsman that the cabinet invited him to prepare the British case for the peace conference. The aims which he had already touched upon in his speech in Glasgow and in correspondence and conversations with the prime minister he now elaborated in an address given to a number of representatives of the American press on 14 November. He began by stressing the ruined state of European civilisation lest his hearers, who had stood upon the fringes of the war, should be unaware of the extent to which the European powers had suffered. A terrible tragedy had befallen Germany and history had pronounced its solemn judgement on Prussian militarism, he said. That was what the Allies had been fighting for, but in victory they felt no vindictiveness, only weariness. If a new world was to emerge from the ruins, Europe needed American help. The Allies' struggle might have saved the soul of civilisation; now it was urgently necessary to save its body. Not only the smaller states but Germany too must be helped at once to recover. An international organisation must be set up to combat hunger. Numerous tiny nations were emerging as a result of the breakup of Russia and Austria–Hungary. They would need to be protected against the stronger powers in the long term and against each other's ambitions immediately. Again, an international body was needed which might delegate to one of the greater powers responsibility for dealing with particular problems in its own neighbourhood. A League of Nations, widely accepted as a worthy ideal, had become a necessity. Turning again to the theme of conciliation, he once more evoked the somewhat questionable example of the aftermath of the Anglo-Boer War.[26]

His involvement in preparing for the peace conference changed

Smuts's views about an early return to South Africa, even though Botha had arrived in England on 16 December. He had become deeply concerned about the shape which the treaty should take and he now accepted beyond all doubt that only a League of Nations could ensure lasting tranquillity among the powers. Although he sought leave to quit the war cabinet in mid-December, he busied himself in the preparation of a pamphlet entitled 'The League of Nations: A Practical Suggestion', which embodied his ideas on the structure of a League. He was in no way a pioneer in that field. In September 1916 the *New Statesman* had published an article advocating an international organisation which might, among other duties, hold the German colonies in trust, thereby guaranteeing free and equal economic access to all nations. By the end of the year, J. A. Hobson, in his *Towards International Government*, had described many of the essential features of trusteeship. The British Labour movement also became involved in the debate and in 1917 the *Manchester Guardian* published articles on methods of preventing future wars. The Round Table also took up the question of trusteeship and Lord Robert Cecil outlined his own scheme for a League of Nations to the war cabinet in May 1918. Two months later the Phillimore Committee made its report to the cabinet on the same subject. In America, too, a variety of ideas had been under discussion, so that by the time Smuts produced his pamphlet the ground had been well prepared. Once again, however, he demonstrated his remarkable powers of synthesis to ensure that ideas which were already widely accepted were presented in a compelling form.

It was Smuts's own idea to suggest that the British Commonwealth provided the best pattern upon which to found the constitution of the League, and L. S. Amery, one of those to whom Smuts circulated his pamphlet, fully endorsed it. But Amery was more sceptical about Smuts's proposals for the limitation of armaments and further suggested that the smaller new nations which were to be created out of the old Russian and Austro-Hungarian Empires should be banded together into lesser leagues under the trusteeship of the League of Nations. This, he thought, might prevent the new states from dissolving into anarchy and would divide the world into a more manageable number of larger units.[27] Lloyd George was less critical. He described Smuts's pamphlet as one of the most able state papers he had ever read and it was agreed by the cabinet to present it to President Wilson as an indication of Britain's views.

His creation as a Companion of Honour in mid-December caused Smuts some embarrassment. Boer principles opposed the acceptance of distinctions of that sort, but for Smuts they were quickly submerged in his satisfaction that his many services to Britain had been formally

recognised. When he left for Paris in January 1919, however, he was·
far from well. Winter's maladies had undermined even his rugged phys-
ique. Both Alice Clark and Margaret Gillett wrote anxiously to urge him
to take care of himself, but the excitement aroused by the prospect of
the discussions in which he was to take part was, for Smuts, a more
effective stimulant than any medical prescription or the admonitions
of those who cared for him dearly. But what he did not realise was
that his years of wartime triumph were at an end. While he had been
working for the British government, he had been acclaimed on all sides.
In Paris he was to operate as an individual. His views were often to
conflict with those of the men with whom he had hitherto worked in
closest harmony. Soon he was to find himself on the outside, looking
in, when important decisions were taken. His vision and idealism, well
suited to winning the war, were an ill match for the bitterness, fear,
selfishness and sheer short-sightedness which seeped through the committee rooms of the Paris Conference.

At first Smuts moved tentatively. In spite of the victory over the enemy,
the atmosphere in Paris was just as subdued as it had been when he
had visited France in 1917. There was fear in the air, fear of the dark
forces lurking in the background and preparing to tear down the plans
of statesmen and soldiers alike.[28] But there was one hopeful sign. Wilson
had taken up his plan for a League of Nations and, according to Lloyd
George, was inclined to regard it as his own. It was not surprising that
he did so. Smuts had drawn upon the wisdom of many others in producing his draft. The American President, who had been absorbed in plans
for a League for many months, could scarcely have noted the distinguishing marks in Smuts's pamphlet save for the clarity of its exposition.
Another cause for satisfaction was the knowledge that South Africa,
along with Canada and Australia, was to be allowed to send two members
to the conference exactly like the smaller independent nations such as
Belgium and Serbia. Smuts was pleased to note that, while the Nationalists were noisily demanding independence for South Africa, his government had quietly achieved the substance of independence by co-
operation rather than by adopting a hectoring policy. The Union was
taking her place as of right among the nations of the world assembling
for the peace conference.[29]

The first regular meeting of the conference quickly dispelled any feelings
of euphoria Smuts might have originally enjoyed. The opening speech
of the French president, Raymond Poincaré, was not concerned with
magnanimity but with meting out punishment for the crimes committed
against the Allies. Smuts may have noted the fearful atmosphere abroad
in France, but he had underestimated its effect upon the French people

who had twice seen their country invaded by the Germans within half a century. Fired by his vision of a community of nations, he understood their feelings as little as he comprehended those of Hertzog and his supporters in South Africa. There was some consolation to be drawn from the knowledge that the League of Nations was to be the first item on the agenda, but Wilson's enthusiasm for the League did not, as was soon made evident, extend to the idea that Germany's colonies should be annexed by the Allies. It had been one of the main tenets of Smuts's programme that the Union should take control of German South West Africa. He had hoped, too, to improve the Union's northern boundary by some exchange with Portuguese East Africa in return for a portion of German East Africa. Now he began to oscillate between hope and deep concern. Concern, but not despair, for, without abandoning his belief in the importance of the Whole, he seemed increasingly to rest his faith on the ultimate power of God during that period of extreme trial.

Action, however, quickly pushed doubts into the background. Smuts was appointed to the committee which was to hammer out the form which the League of Nations should take. With an eye to the more specific interests of South Africa, he also argued for the Union's claim to retain South West Africa, stating with unconvincing disingenuity that the territory was after all little more than a desert and quite unworthy of the attention of so august a body as the League of Nations.[30] Wilson was adamant, but finally succumbed to the idea of extending the proposed system of mandates to the former German colonies. It was a qualified triumph for Smuts, for Wilson would never have accepted the idea if it had come from any other source. Later, too, Smuts was able to ensure that the C-type mandate under which the Union would administer South West Africa was defined in such a way as to approximate very closely to annexation. Philip Kerr's warning against making too overt a demand for Germany's colonies had prepared him to adopt more subtle means of pressing his case. So the committee, sitting day and night under Wilson's chairmanship, moved rapidly ahead.

Elsewhere Smuts sensed there was an evil spirit abroad which threatened to reduce the League of Nations to little more than an alliance built upon fear and mistrust which would ultimately become an instrument of reaction.[31] By 10 February, with the first draft of the League Covenant almost complete – Wilson preferred the title 'Covenant' to 'Constitution' – Smuts again felt optimistic, but not for long. A brief interlude in England with the Gilletts saw him once again a victim of influenza and of doubt. Refusing to give in, he returned to Paris full of concern over what might have happened in his absence. The situation was even worse than he had anticipated. After taking a few days to get up to date with developments, he wrote urgently to Lloyd George. If Germany were to be destroyed, he argued, Europe would be undermined. It could only be saved if Germany were allowed to co-operate with the other nations. Yet everything that was being suggested at the conference seemed to lead inevitably to Germany's destruction. An army limited to 100,000 men could not possibly control seventy million Germans. Many of them had been trained as soldiers and they were unlikely to remain silent when their country was threatened by extreme internal disorder and by a Bolshevik invasion from the east. The plans for the territorial dismemberment of Germany were equally unrealistic. How could an ancient German town like Danzig be incorporated into Poland, together with other areas containing millions of Germans? And why should the wholly German Saar Valley be transferred to France along with Alsace-Lorraine? Such proposals, if implemented, would be fatal to any hope of securing peace, in the present or in the future. They would only encourage the desire for revenge. Neither Poland nor Bohemia could survive without the goodwill and assistance of Germany. Recent events in Hungry had given a clear warning of what might happen in Germany too. In Hungary, an initially co-operative government had resigned rather than accept reduction of territory, and it had been replaced by a Bolshevik revolutionary council. In trying to break up Germany with a view to creating a number of small national states, the Allies were bound to fail. 'We shall get no peace now', Smuts wrote, 'and Europe will know no peace hereafter. And in the coming storms these new states will themselves be the first to founder.' Regarding both the proposal to punish individuals deemed to be guilty of war crimes and the plan to demand reparations from the defeated enemy, Smuts counselled moderation. Germany could only pay – and would only agree to pay – a large indemnity if the Allies promised to supply raw materials and to restart German industry. Germany must indeed be made to pay heavily and must accept responsibility for maintaining peace in the future. But if she were to do those things, she could not be dismembered and left to face servitude and pauperism. She must become a member of the League of Nations from the outset. Again he insisted that the present policy would bring failure for the conference and could spell ruin for Europe.[32]

Those fine sentiments, sound though they may seem in retrospect, found little favour with Lloyd George. Though Smuts wrote to Margaret Gillett that to do one's duty and leave the rest to God produced great serenity of mind, he was soon to have whatever serenity he had acquired through writing to the prime minister rudely shattered. For Lloyd

George, Smuts's opinions were ill-timed and embarrassing, and the prime minister suggested that his uncomfortable grey eminence should go to Russia or Serbia where urgent problems demanded attention.[33] Hastily Smuts pointed out that, having been appointed plenipotentiary on behalf of South Africa on 1 January 1919, problems arising from South African demobilisation prevented him from leaving Paris.[34]

Undeterred by the prime minister's coolness, Smuts next presented him with a scheme for dealing with reparations. To avoid disagreement at the outset, the plan proposed that no actual sums should be specified in the treaty itself. Instead a reparations committee should be set up, preferably by the executive council of the League of Nations, with power to determine all questions of loss and damage. The treaty itself should contain a scale setting out the rate at which reparations should be paid off, though it might be varied by the committee where circumstances made it necessary to do so.[35]

It was an ingenious scheme, but it was unlikely to be immediately acceptable to France, or even to a number of other countries, as the question of reparations began to dominate the whole of the conference proceedings. Having made his electioneering promises, Lloyd George was anxious to appease both parliament and the British public by ensuring that Britain got her share of any disbursements Germany might be forced to make. Britain had clearly not suffered as directly as Belgium and France, however, so that if she were to receive an adequate share of the reparations – or even any share at all – it could only be by insisting that Germany should be responsible for paying the pensions of war widows and persons incapacitated by the war. Smuts had first opposed such an extension of the interpretation to be put upon the meaning of reparations, but, when Lloyd George put Britain's case and asked him to draft a legal opinion on what was meant by the expression 'damage done to the civilian population of the Allies and their property by the aggression of Germany by land, by sea and from the air', he responded at once. Later he claimed that he had approached the task in a detached, legal manner and that his reply was not a personal but a legal opinion. He did admit, however, that, if he had not expressed himself in the terms he had presented to the prime minister, there was a danger that France, as the chief sufferer at the hands of Germany, might have been able to claim all the reparations available. This was simply a repetition of the argument put to him by Lloyd George, and it is clear that others assumed his opinion represented a case for treating Germany harshly to ensure that Britain came out of the negotiations reasonably well.

Developments in South Africa made a brief intrusion into the work of the peace conference, but Smuts seems to have been little involved.

With the end of the war the South African Native National Congress believed the time had come to make further claims on behalf of the African population. Arguing that they had remained loyal throughout the rebellion of 1914 and had made a not inconsiderable contribution to South Africa's war aims in a non-combatant capacity, they now asked for a hearing. Three of their number were sent to Europe to petition the King and to present a plea to the peace conference. One of their requests was for an increase in African representation in parliament and they also urged that the protectorates of Swaziland, Bechuanaland and Basutoland should not be incorporated into the Union against the wishes of their inhabitants. The people of South West Africa should also be consulted before the future of the former German dependency was decided, and, if the Union were at any time to seek to become a republic, the King should only give his approval when the majority of the African population of the Union and the protectorates had given their consent.[36]

The tone of the requests echoed the distrust which educated Africans felt about native policy in the Union, but their efforts ended in failure. Botha simply replied that the procedure followed by the Congress was unconstitutional and that any alteration in the constitution could only be made by the Union parliament. He added that any proposal for the future of the protectorates should be addressed to the High Commissioner and that in any event he could not see how the peace conference could be concerned with the internal affairs of South Africa. He remarked, too, that his impression was that the Congress leaders did not represent the inhabitants of the protectorates.[37]

Whether Smuts assisted in any way in formulating Botha's response it is impossible to say, though he would have agreed with its sentiments. L. S. Amery, under-secretary for the colonies, gave a similarly negative reply. The Congress leaders pleaded for the removal of the colour bar in South Africa, claiming that, since union, British ideas about the treatment of Africans had been replaced by those of the Dutch. They also stressed that they were strongly opposed to the Nationalists' demand for South African independence. Amery's response was to inform them that the South Africa Act could not be changed at the request of one section of the population. He suggested that, as educated Africans, they should work within the constitution to gain influence. It was an answer which did not satisfy the deputation, not least because it was the constitution which prevented them from exerting any influence. Defeated, they expressed their disappointment that the King could do nothing for them.[38]

During these negotiations Smuts was in Eastern Europe. Lloyd George had, after all, prevailed upon him to undertake a mission to Hungary to investigate the situation there. For Smuts, Bolshevism was a disease which had arisen from the horrors and sufferings of war,[39] but he found Bela Kun, chief commissar for war and foreign affairs in Budapest, responsive to the Allies' proposals. Kun's co-operativeness did not spring from an undiluted love for the Allies. For him Smuts's visit was, in its local context, a diplomatic triumph because it gave him the appearance of having been accepted internationally as the leader of his people. Hungarian newspapers stressed that Smuts had come, not as a soldier to threaten, but as a diplomat to negotiate with the recognised government which had the support of the whole might of the proletariat. Smuts would see for himself that peace and order were the fruits of Soviet rule and he would doubtless report that fact when he returned to Paris.[40] Smuts was unaware of these undercover struggles for power and of the extent to which he himself was being used by the contending parties. He was convinced he had won Kun over to the Allies and kept him away from Russia, but he did report that Kun had difficulties which the Allies might not previously have appreciated. He added optimistically that, within these limits, Kun was prepared to observe the Wilsonian principles of nationality and self-determination.[41]

What affected Smuts far more than the conversations in Budapest were the tragedies he encountered as he passed through Vienna and visited Prague. To Margaret Gillett he wrote: 'Nothing so burns up every particle of self as the sights I have passed through during the past week.'[42] Unfortunately the Allies were not as impressed by Bela Kun's claims as Smuts had been, nor did they accept Smuts's recommendations that there should be an immediate economic conference of all the states of Central Europe to produce a plan for the economic reconstruction of the region. It was a bitter blow to him, for it seemed to be one more indication that the powers were more concerned with vengeance than with planning for future peace. Selfishness dominated the discussions. Italy protested, as she felt justified in doing, when Wilson insisted that Dalmatia should form part of the new state of Yugoslavia. For Dalmatia had been promised to Italy by Britain and France on 26 April 1915 as a reward for her entry into the war. As the reports poured in from the various committees, Smuts was depressed by the pettiness of many of their recommendations.

The speed with which Smuts had executed his mission to Hungary meant that the telegram from Lloyd George requesting him to extend his operation to take in Serbia and Russia failed to reach him before he was on his way back to Paris. Nevertheless, the prospect of attending a meeting of the Supreme Economic Council to discuss the situation in Austria–Hungary filled him with despair. 'Will the Lord never rid us of these debating societies?' he wrote to Alice Clark. 'Oh, for an ounce of action.'[43] The problem was that he now represented only a minor nation. He could exert influence only by persuading the leaders of the great powers, and they were deeply divided in their attitudes towards the objectives of the conference as well as having to keep a watchful eye on their own electorates. Moreover, skilled though he was in the scientific preparation of a written statement, he was less adept in the arts of persuasion. By passionate oratory he could stir up a sympathetic audience to the heights of enthusiasm. For more sceptical listeners, he had little patience.

Driven by his desire to serve mankind Smuts was always ready to propose ways of dealing with Europe's problems, but those who made the decisions seemed less and less inclined to listen to him. The revised Covenant of the League of Nations and the section of the peace treaty dealing with the international regulation of labour were approved on 28 April, but the rest of the treaty left Smuts in despair. His efforts to provide financial aid for Europe appeared to be permanently bedevilled by disagreements among financiers. It seemed inconceivable to Smuts that the British government could genuinely believe that the destruction of Germany, for long one of Britain's most important markets, could assist British industry.[44] The hope of a brief respite from the negotiations and the prospect of spending a few days with the Gilletts in London in May had to be postponed, as such meetings had been on a number of occasions, because of the pressure of work.

The refusal of the Americans to accept a plan to give financial aid to Central Europe on the ground that it was pointless to do so while the Allies were deliberately setting out to ruin Germany and Austria by their demand for reparations spurred Smuts to prepare a memorandum for Lloyd George in which he suggested a number of amendments to the draft treaty. These would, he believed, make the treaty acceptable to the Germans without undermining the principles upon which the Allies were determined to stand. There was little in the memorandum for which he had not already pressed on a number of occasions, but now the urgency attached to his proposals was desperate. He wanted a saner approach to the boundary proposals, larger military forces for Germany and more time for the payment of reparations. Surely, too, the surrender of the Saar was an adequate restitution to France for the destruction of her mines without demanding that Germany should hand over still more coal.[45] He followed his memorandum with a passionate letter addressed to both Lloyd George and Woodrow Wilson in which he pointed out that both the western and eastern territories of Germany were to be controlled by the country's hereditary enemies. How could peace be achieved by an arrangement of that sort, he asked. The devastation suffered by France called for some recompense, but there simply had to be a more reasonable plan if peace were to be secured.[46]

On more than one occasion Smuts had told his friends that the prime minister relied heavily upon his advice, and that had been true when Smuts was carrying out Lloyd George's wishes. But now the views he so strongly advocated were at odds with Lloyd George's promises to the electorate and Smuts sensed that the prime minister was no longer susceptible to his persuasions. Wilson, too, had seemed unwilling to accept the logic of Smuts's arguments. 'I fear the Prime Minister is definitely against me now,' Smuts wrote to Alice Clark, 'and I get no support from Wilson. I do not even know whether he really agrees with me.'[47] To Isie he confided his doubts about putting his name to what he believed was not a peace treaty but a war treaty. He had done his utmost to amend it, he said, but he had failed. Yet he was worried about the repercussions which might be felt in South Africa and indeed in the rest of the world if he were to refuse to sign. He must, therefore, go on striving to get the treaty amended. 'I am bitterly disappointed,' he added, 'in both Wilson and Lloyd George, who are smaller man than I should ever have thought.'

He was profoundly worried that, if Germany refused to sign the treaty, the naval blockade which had been used so effectively during the later stages of the war would be renewed, with the result that millions would starve. France had insisted that the blockade should continue after the armistice in the hope of forcing Germany to accept the peace terms and the German leaders had contributed to the suffering by refusing to make their merchant ships available to collect supplies of food. Only the passionate intervention of Lloyd George had brought the blockade to an end in March. If he were to keep a clear conscience, Smuts knew he must oppose such action at whatever cost. It would not be easy for him to stand alone, but in the event of Germany's refusal to sign he said he would start a press campaign to get the treaty amended. Germany might deserve a hard peace, as Woodrow Wilson himself had said, but Smuts was anxious to avoid one which would bring the world to ruin. If necessary he must resign his ministerial post in order to conduct his campaign, and to make up for the loss in salary he could sell one of his farms.[48]

When he wrote in similar terms to Margaret Gillett she was delighted. 'Your letter was as the sound of trumpets and the colour and movement of flying banners,' she replied enthusiastically.[49] But, though the rhetoric may have been stimulating to his friends, and even to Smuts himself, the reality of his struggle imposed a heavy strain upon him. He had only contempt for Arthur Balfour's single-minded pursuit of what he conceived as Britain's interests. Unable to recognise that the British foreign secretary might have a different objective from his own high-minded goal, Smuts wrongly attributed his attitude to a total ignorance of the situation. Lloyd George, too, seemed to Smuts to have developed an exasperating obtuseness, asking him to prepare yet another memorandum to explain what was worrying him.[50] In fact the prime minister was tiring of Smuts's importunity. Restraining his feelings of frustration, Smuts laboriously spelled out once more the reasons for his disquiet. The proposal to occupy the west bank of the Rhine and the Saar Basin for at least fifteen years posed a clear threat to peace and stability, he wrote. Both those areas were patently inhabited by Germans, who would become increasingly resentful of foreign occupation, while the absence of any limit upon the size of the French army of occupation could mean that the cost of maintaining the whole of the French army might have to be borne by Germany. On the eastern frontier there were similar potential dangers. The new Poland would incorporate large numbers of Germans and Russians and, in time to come, sandwiched between a resurgent Germany and Russia, she would be heavily dependent for her survival on their goodwill. Then the reparations clauses, and particularly the demand for coal, were far too harsh. While it was reasonable to punish people for war crimes, he could not believe that the pride of the German people would permit them to accept what was now proposed. Again, a German army restricted to the degree suggested would be incapable of maintaining law and order. The controls on the rivers of Germany were equally unrealistic and unnecessary. The Germans must be given an opportunity to put their point of view, preferably to a small committee which would in turn explain the Allies' case and then report to the Supreme Council. In that way, any suggestion of negotiation would be avoided, and the Allies would retain the initiative while gaining a clearer idea of the Germans' position. The outcome of such a procedure would, he hoped, be that the moral authority of the treaty in its final form would be more compelling.[51]

For a fleeting moment Smuts believed he might be able to wield some influence by putting his case to a number of American representatives at the conference who believed Lloyd George was too prone to give in to the excessive demands of the French.[52] It was a forlorn hope. With a total disregard for Smuts's criticisms, the prime minister invited him to sit on the commission dealing with Austrian reparations. Smuts could only reject the offer, believing as he did that it was ludicrous to try to impose financial penalties upon countries as broken and bankrupt as Austria or Czechoslovakia. He even wondered whether the prime minister was deliberately trying to compromise him by making such a suggestion.[53] Lloyd George's written reply to Smuts's memorandum did, indeed, demonstrate how far apart their attitudes had become. The war had to be paid for, the prime minister argued. Was it right that the payment should be made entirely by Britain and the Empire?[54] Smuts did not disagree with that statement, but considered it irrelevant to his main point, which was that the defeated powers had themselves suffered appalling losses and had the same leeway to make up as had Britain and France. Though they were the aggressors, it was widly unrealistic to expect them to make good all the Allies' losses.

Amidst these disturbing battles of conscience, Smuts had remained unaware of the arrival in Paris of a Nationalist delegation led by Hertzog until his attention was drawn to what was happening by a letter from Isie.[55] Inspired by a statement in favour of national self-determination made by President Wilson early in 1916 and apparently endorsed by the British government, the delegation had come to Europe to demand the restitution of republican status to South Africa. Lloyd George received their petition early in June and on that occasion sought the advice of Smuts in earnest. Smuts drafted a reply which the British prime minister embodied in his own response to the delegation. In it he laid stress upon the advantages of the dominion status which South Africa enjoyed and which gave the Union full control of her own destiny while allowing her representatives to take part, on a basis of complete equality, in the deliberations which determined imperial policy. How far those views had been accepted by Lloyd George himself it is difficult to say. They certainly accorded closely with Smuts's own interpretation of dominion status, which he was anxious to establish on a firm constitutional basis as soon as possible to counter republican propaganda. So the Nationalist delegation returned to the Union empty-handed.

From that brief foray into South African affairs Smuts was swiftly recalled by Margaret Gillett who sensed that, for all his fine words, Smuts might be persuaded to sign the treaty. She understood all too well that his lively intellect, which saw so many sides to every problem, might discover compelling reasons why he should go along with the other signatories. 'Please don't sign the thing unless you are sure,' she wrote. And again, 'Yes, I know I do not know what not signing that Treaty means, but I feel I know enough of what signing means to make me believe you cannot do it and ever have peace in your own being over your own life.' He had given enough warning to the Allied leaders, she added, so that it would come as no surprise to them if he were now to refuse to sign.[56] Certainly for Smuts the struggle was not yet over. The Germans had argued that any peace formula must fall within the spirit of Wilson's Fourteen Points. In the light of that claim Smuts had written to the American President to demonstrate that, in some measure at least, the peace proposals fell short of those principles. The war, the Allies claimed, had begun because they believed that promises were something more than mere 'scraps of paper.' How could they then let it end by themselves treating the Fourteen Points as another scrap of paper?[57]

Suddenly light seemed to break in. On 31 May Lloyd George summoned all available cabinet members to meet him in Paris. In a lively meeting he was given a free hand to change the peace terms as he thought fit. The following day all the members of the Empire delegation met in the prime minister's flat and Smuts led a strong plea for revision. Everything seemed to have prepared the ground for a new approach to the treaty.[58] Smuts was extremely angry, therefore, when the report of the meeting made reference only to the minor points upon which agreement had been reached and failed to mention the major criticisms which he had voiced. In the strongest terms he wrote to Lloyd George, who countered by questioning Smuts's interpretation of what had taken place. Again the prime minister blandly asked for a memorandum setting out Smuts's reasons for criticising what had happened, and with rather more acerbity demanded to know if Smuts were prepared to surrender South Africa's claims to South West Africa and to German East Africa in order to satisfy the needs of the Germans.[59] If Lloyd George thought by those tactics to weaken Smuts's resolve, he had underestimated the latter's tenacity. Though exasperated almost to the limit, Smuts once again detailed his proposals, brushing contemptuously aside Lloyd George's reference to the former German colonies in Africa as of total insignificance compared with the terrible threat to world peace presented by the tone of the peace proposals.[60]

Lloyd George's behaviour seems to have been utterly perverse and is explicable only on the assumption that he believed he had a surer grasp of British parliamentary and public opinion than had the other members of his cabinet. And what parliament and public wanted, he thought, were reparations. While he had no strong feelings about other issues, he believed Clemenceau would not countenance any change in the proposals regarding Germany's frontiers or the size of her army, so there was no point in pressing for revision there. It is surprising, however, that Woodrow Wilson was not moved by Smuts's appeal to the Fourteen Points, more particularly because the President generally respected Smuts's opinions. The suggestion of A. Lentin seems to offer a likely explanation. Wilson, he said, came to Paris to see justice done. He listened to all the arguments and had slowly absorbed the atmosphere of the conference to such a degree that he was convinced that justice had been done.[61] His own sincerity blinded him to the self-interest and spirit of revenge which had moulded the peace treaty.

Smuts, however, was still not prepared to surrender. When he learned that the British economic adviser, Maynard (later Lord) Keynes, had quitted the delegation because of his inability to convince the leaders of the folly of their economic proposals, he urged him to write an account of his experiences and to comment upon them in language which could be understood by the ordinary reader. The result was *The Economic Consequences of the Peace* which was published in December 1919. Smuts himself did not consider resignation, though he told Alice Clark he was tempted to slip away to South Africa and abandon any idea of making further speeches against the treaty.[62] Alice sympathised with his weariness and did not recognise that his desire to be involved would always outweigh any desire to escape. She therefore insisted that he owed it to those who had trusted in him to make some statement before leaving Europe. Margaret Gillett, more perceptive than her sister, or less blinded by her feelings for him, sensed that Smuts was preparing the way to sign the treaty, however vehemently he continued to protest that he would not do so. Unlike Alice she knew that he would never resign and leave others in charge. Like Alice, therefore, but for different reasons, she emphasised his moral obligation to tell those who believed in him that he was not satisfied with the treaty.[63]

For two or three more days Smuts's resolution appeared on the surface to be as firm as ever. He telegraphed Botha on 21 June to say that, as he would be unable to sign the treaty, consideration must be given to whether he should first resign his position as a South African delegate so as to avoid embarrassing his government.[64] Two days later he was still assuring Margaret Gillett that he would on no account sign the treaty even though the effect would be that he could never succeed Botha as prime minister when his friend resigned, as he intended to do in the near future.[65] Margaret, however, had now concluded that Smuts was protesting too much. Gently she scolded him. 'I am not sure that I quite approve of the way you throw all responsibility on the Almighty, after your colleagues and you have landed in such an awful mess! . . . It is still strong in my mind that you must not break off without a word of explanation of how the world has got to this point and where we must now be looking.'[66]

Margaret's prognostication proved correct. On the very day after he had sworn on no account to sign the treaty, Smuts decided to put his signature to it. He hastened to say that it would be impossible for him to take a different line from Botha, and that he intended to make a statement to the press explaining his decision.[67] It was a precipitous descent from the heights of idealism though the explanation he gave was undoubtedly sincere. More fundamental, however, was his fear of being excluded from playing any role in the future conduct of world events. That was made clear by the theme he was henceforward to promote, that the treaty was only the end of the war; peace was something to build in the future. In that building Smuts was determined to play his part. He must demonstrate that he could exert influence for good as a diplomat in peacetime as he had as a member of the war cabinet when the conflict was at its height. Was that not fulfilling God's role for him in the most effective way? But he must not parade his self-righteousness, so he wrote to Alice Clark: 'I feel I am no better than the others, and that I must stand in the dock beside them. And God be merciful to us poor sinners.'[68] To C. P. Scott, editor of the *Manchester Guardian*, who had sympathised with his efforts to amend the treaty, he also wrote describing the treaty as 'thoroughly bad, impolitic, impracticable in the case of Germany and absolutely ludicrous in the case of German Austria'.[69] The Austrian Empire had been shorn of four-fifths of its population, some of them Germans, and reduced to a land-locked state of six and a half million Germans whose request to be united with Germany was rejected.

Margaret Gillett had no time for such posturing. Even before she learned that Smuts had decided to sign the treaty, she warned him of how to behave when he did so. He must avoid the doubtful phrasings he had used during the war in his effort to keep as broad a base of sympathy as possible. Those phrasings were part of the deceptiveness of the passion of war and there must be no mistake about the deep, compelling sincerity of the path he now took.[70] Smuts did in fact send Margaret a draft of the statement he intended to issue to the press. But, though he asked for her comments, he did not wait for her reply before releasing the statement immediately after signing the treaty on 28 June.

Margaret was not wholly enthusiastic about what he had written. She believed he should have made a much stronger indictment of the treaty. There was little point in appealing to a new spirit in the world without giving a clear explanation of how that spirit should work, she wrote.[71] The statement contained the highminded principles and stirring phrases which the world had come to expect of Smuts, but Margaret Gillett's criticisms were not without justification.[72] Its warm reception from people in all walks of life owed more than a little to the fact that the call Smuts made was spiritually uplifting but contained no specific demand for action from his hearers. There is no doubt that fighting a losing campaign had left him emotionally exhausted and his weariness was reflected in a letter to Keynes in which he wrote: 'After giving the matter my closest consideration, I have seen no great profit in a regular attack on the Treaty. It is past and nothing can undo it except time and the great Mercy which works away all our poor human follies. Better to be constructive.'[73]

Before leaving for South Africa Smuts was able to spend some time with his English friends. He also visited Manchester to receive an honorary degree and while there he met C. P. Scott. Smuts, Scott recorded, said that he was returning to South Africa a defeated man. He had fought persistently for a better settlement but had failed. The British election was the root of the trouble. He had advised Lloyd George that his popularity was such that he had no need to offer the people too much. But the prime minister, exhorted by his election agents, had played upon the war weariness and anger of the electorate and then had had to redeem his promises when he returned to Paris. Wilson, in Smuts's view, had proved to be a second-rate man. In fact, he shared Smuts's qualities of idealism, intellect and a preacher's fervour, but in this instance he happened to be preaching what Smuts considered to be a heretical doctrine. Balfour, Smuts continued, had been a tragedy, a mere dilettante – but that was because he had not shared Smuts's idealism. Clemenceau, by contrast, had known exactly what he wanted and he had got it. Though his actions were opposed to Smuts's aims, he nevertheless gained some approval from Smuts simply because nothing more had been expected of him. Even the League of Nations, which Smuts regarded as the best hope for the future, might become entirely futile, he thought, if it did not start off on the right footing. Unfortunately the diplomats were all against it, regarding it as a toy to amuse and mislead the public while they continued to play their old games. To be effective the League must meet constantly and be represented by first-rate men from all the countries party to it.[74]

On 18 July Smuts set out on his long-delayed journey home. Before leaving England he issued a further valedictory statement to the press in which he bore in mind the advice given him by Margaret Gillett and Alice Clark. He warned England that she could not ignore the suffering and anarchy in Europe without endangering herself. The democratic government of Friedrich Ebert in Germany must, he said, be given support if the example of Russia and Hungary were to be avoided. Russia should be left alone to solve her own problems without military intervention from the West. The dominions, as a result of the part they had played in the war and in the peace negotiations, had been successfully launched among the nations of the world, but a solution remained to be found for India and Egypt, to whom the dominion solution could not apply. Possibly native self-government could be reconciled with a system of expert advice and assistance. Nearer home, the problem of Ireland should not be too much for statesmen who had just been dealing with similar racial problems in Europe. Finally he urged the people of England to reject the materialism which had seemed to achieve so much in the Victorian Age but which had just ended in the deaths of millions of young men. The Commonwealth must win a moral victory so that the ideals which had shaped its destiny might become the common heritage of the League of Nations and of Europe.[75]

The statement still contained more exhortation and less practical guidance than Margaret Gillett might have wished, but it was the most that Smuts felt capable of saying. His perception told him that he had failed to achieve the sort of peace for which he had hoped. His conscience told him that he had failed to make the gesture which would have demonstrated his distaste for the spirit of the peace treaty. Neither of those facts brought solace to one who set himself such demanding targets. With a half-hearted attempt at self-justification, he wrote to Margaret Gillett from on board the *Edinburgh Castle*:

> It is no use disguising the facts. I *have* suffered defeat. Not the lost endeavour, not the lowered banner – thank God. It is partly because I tried to keep the faith, to keep aloft the banner of the spirit that I have failed in my purpose. But then, victory along the lines I wanted would have been so tremendous. It was not really possible. . . . And so I go in peace.[76]

It was not a very convincing epitaph to what had been a great endeavour. He had not even stayed in Europe for the signing of the treaty with Austria, still less with Turkey. But it is difficult to see how he could have done better. As long as he had a seat in the war cabinet, he had a power base from which to operate. When he surrendered that base after hostilities ceased, he became no more than the representative of a minor state. Though his reputation and his ability permitted him to communicate with Lloyd George and Woodrow Wilson with a freedom which no one else enjoyed, it was they who in the last analysis made the decisions, along with the French leaders. They were compelled, or so they thought, to take careful account of the views of the British and American public and, inevitably, of the fears of the French people. High ideals were admirable in their way, but practical issues must take precedence, while powerful prejudices could not be ignored. Perhaps they were too conscious of those pressures. On the other hand, they might reasonably have argued that Smuts was not sufficiently aware of them. He had, it was true, helped to carry the majority of his countrymen with him in bringing South Africa into the war for the sake of an ideal

Jan Smuts, State Attorney of the South African Republic, 1898.

Smuts (centre) on commando in Cape Colony during the Anglo-Boer War, 1902.

Jan Smuts with his wife, 'Isie' and daughter, 'Santa', 1904.

J. X. Merriman, Prime Minister of Cape Colony, 1908–10.

General Louis Botha, Prime Minister of the Union of South Africa, 1910–19. This photograph was taken at the beginning of the First World War when Botha led a Union army against the Germans in South West Africa.

General Smuts with his cabinet, 1921.

General J. B. M. Hertzog, Prime Minister of the Union, 1924–39.

Sir Patrick Duncan, formerly a member of the Unionist Party, then a member of Smuts's cabinet, 1921–24, and later deputy leader of Smuts's South African Party. The photograph was taken about the time of Duncan's appointment as Governor-General of the Union in 1937.

African National Congress Conference, 1930. Pixley Seme, founder of the Congress and later President-General, is on the extreme right of the front row of those seated on chairs.

General Smuts and Isie Smuts (extreme left of picture, dressed in voortrekker costume) at the laying of the foundation stone of the Voortrekker Monument, Pretoria, 1938.

Houses of Parliament, Cape Town, scene of many wordy battles between Smuts and Hertzog.

Dr D. F. Malan, who had just become Prime Minister of the Union after his National Party had defeated Smuts's United Party in the elections of 1948.

Field Marshal Smuts with Winston Churchill, Mrs Churchill and his son, Captain 'Japie' Smuts, 1943.

ield Marshal Smuts, Chancellor of Cambridge University, 1949.

The unveiling of a memorial to Field
Marshal Smuts in Parliament Square,
London, 7 November 1956.

Statue of Jan Smuts, Botanical Gardens,
Cape Town.

of loyalty to the Empire. But a vocal minority had rebelled against him and were still actively opposed to all he had done. He had spoken frequently of the virtues of magnanimity, but they had clearly made little impression upon Hertzog and his associates. Smuts may have stood for the right, but they had stood for the practicable. Above all, they could not overlook the deep-seated apprehensions of the French and they had, after all, pursued Wilson's principle of national self-determination, even though in retrospect it might be said they did so to exaggerated lengths.

So Smuts returned to the peace of Doornkloof, profoundly weary and secretly ashamed, not of his failure to amend the treaty, for he had done all, and more, than any man could hope to do in that respect, but of his failure to denounce it. His lay *predikant*'s conscience would not let him forget that. Because he had chosen his own way of life and established his own philosophy instead of accepting the traditional Christian standards of his youth, it was vital that he should not fall short of his own ideals. Failure could not be accepted humbly as a chastening experience. It was too important for that. So humility ceased to be a virtue. Smuts felt he must forever put himself to the test and he came to resent those who challenged him.

But that was still ahead. Now was a time to relax at home. His house had changed in no whit from the unassuming structure he had had carted in sections from Middelburg in 1909. The furnishings, too, were still as spartan as ever. But Isie, the self-styled farmer's wife, who had worked humbly and generously for the people of her own country while her husband played his central role in the tragedy of the world, welcomed him with warmth and without ostentatious display, as was her manner.

6

The prime minister

The time allowed for recuperation was short. Little more than three weeks after the arrival of Botha and Smuts in Cape Town, Botha died. Within days Smuts became prime minister. The task that faced him was formidable, though it seemed like having to drive a Model-T Ford after helping to design a chauffeur-driven Rolls Royce. He had returned to a hero's welcome from his supporters, but there were many Afrikaners who believed his efforts in Europe had brought little benefit to South Africa. Was he not, for example, the main author of the mandates system which prevented the Union from annexing South West Africa? How could his critics know the struggle he had had with Wilson to achieve even mandatory status for South Africa? Still worse, was not Smuts insisting that the Union had no right to secede from the British Empire? That was a view which could never be acceptable to the Nationalists. In their eyes, the co-operation between the South African Party and the Unionists during the war only underlined Smuts's willingness to remain subservient to British interests. On that issue Hertzog made his position clear by riding into Johannesburg on 20 November 1919 at the head of a thousand men and making a speech extolling 'the ideal of ultimate and absolute independence'.

How Botha would have handled such critics it is impossible to determine. Smuts knew he was no Botha. He lacked both his personality and his temperament and he had never exercised the sway over Afrikaner loyalty that Botha enjoyed. But his experience in England had given him a confidence in his own ability which was gradually to envelop him in a protective cloak of intellectual rectitude, not unlike that worn by Milner during his stay in South Africa. While Smuts never ceased to cull ideas from many sources, henceforward, when he had absorbed them into a pattern of his own devising, his pronouncements were uttered in terms which appeared to suggest infallibility. For a time, however, he progressed carefully.

The Africans who had remained quietly loyal through the war, now began to make demands which a government controlled by Whites could not accept. The main grievance of the Africans was levelled against the laws which required any of them moving outside the reserves to carry a pass which must be presented on demand. This, in practice, meant that only Africans employed by Whites could travel outside the reserves and even pass-holders were constantly harassed by the police. Immediately after hostilities ended in Europe, sporadic passive resistance to the pass laws broke out in scattered areas in the Transvaal and the Free State. The police and white civilians reacted firmly and sometimes violently to these demonstrations which were quickly suppressed. The body which might have co-ordinated them, the South African Native National Congress, though reactivated after the war, was still primarily concerned with the question of the franchise, and gave no lead to the African workers. Nevertheless Smuts, minister for native affairs and for justice as well as being prime minister, could not ignore the manifestations of discontent.

There were ominous rumblings from the Labour Party, too. The price of gold had risen sharply at the end of the war and the National Labour Congress, held in Pretoria in late November and early December 1919, hoped to take advantage of the situation by pressing for an increase in the wages and an improvement in the working conditions of European employees. A disturbing political note was sounded in the discussions when a resolution was adopted which maintained that the private ownership of South African industries was against the best interests of the people. It urged that the industries should be taken over by the state and subsequently be managed and controlled by local district and national boards composed of equal numbers of representatives of the unions and the state.[1] Meanwhile, a report had recommended increases in the pay and allowances of civil servants and railwaymen which would cost the Union £2.5 million a year. It all added up to a daunting prospect. Nevertheless, when Smuts contemplated the appalling situation facing political leaders in Europe, he was able to write, gratefully if somewhat ruefully, to Merriman that he could 'accept even my Hertzog and Creswell'.[2]

Briefly, in November, he escaped to a setting in which his efforts were appreciated without reservation. A reception was given for him in Johannesburg by the South African Zionist Federation and the South African Jewish Board of Deputies. Before an enthusiastic audience he was able to indulge in the fine rhetoric and high idealism which had roused support in England, though it had been accorded a more sceptical reception by his fellow-Afrikaners. In spite of the tribulations suffered by the Jewish people, he said, they had survived and the day would come when the words of the prophets would come true and Israel would return to her own land. This was not vain encouragement. Among the many other tasks he had performed in England in 1917, he had been instrumental, along with Lloyd George and Arthur Balfour, in securing from the British government the pledge which became known as the Balfour Declaration. The idea behind the declaration had originated with the Jewish leader, Dr Chaim Weizmann, whose hope was that Palestine should once again become the home of the Jewish people. A friendship had developed between Smuts and Weizmann, and the former had been attracted to the proposal both because of his biblical studies and because he responded readily to the call to support an oppressed minority. The idea had also commended itself to Lloyd George and Arthur Balfour and a letter had been sent to Lord Rothschild on 2 November 1917 stating that the government would do its best to make Palestine a Jewish national home on the understanding that the rights of non-Jewish inhabitants would be safeguarded. The pledge had subsequently been taken up by America and France, and the grant of the Palestine mandate to Britain, which Smuts confidently believed would soon take place, would mean that the plan could be put into effect. He warned that it would be a slow process because of the need to avoid misunderstandings between newly arriving Jews and the existing Arab population. He and his hearers might not live to see the day when the whole of the Jewish people had returned to Palestine, he said. But, increasingly, the country would become a Jewish national home. He spoke, too, of his own visit to Palestine, of how the fine, clear air and the wild scenery had reminded him of South Africa, and he had been able to understand why the Jews in South Africa felt at home. South Africa had given a great deal to the Jews, and Jewish citizens had much to offer to South Africa – not only in a material sense, but also by giving the sort of spiritual lead which had provided the driving force of the Jewish people in biblical times. The Afrikaners, he said, were a people of the Old Testament and added – without, it must be said, any evidence to support his statement – that there was a close bond between the two peoples.[3]

The speech was a *tour de force* which gave Smuts the same temporary feeling of exhilaration as it gave his hearers. But he was quickly confronted by Afrikaners who did not feel strong bonds even with himself. He knew he must soon call a general election and he had little hope of improving the government's position by doing so. For several years the South African Party government had been forced to rely upon the support of the Unionists in resisting the more extreme demands of the Nationalists. The Unionists were willing, even anxious, to convert that informal liaison into a coalition, but Smuts knew that such an arrangement would be unacceptable to many in his own party. He also retained a lingering hope of some *rapprochement* with the Nationalists, both because of his own Dutch ancestry and because he thought it would be more likely to promote the unity of the British and Dutch races than would a closer association with the Unionists. That would only encourage the Nationalists to become more bitter in their opposition.

The results of the election quickly destroyed his illusions. The SAP gained only 41 seats, the Nationalists 44, the Unionists 25, the Labour Party 21 and 3 seats went to independents. Some of Smuts's colleagues wanted the government to resign, but Smuts insisted that the fight against republicanism must go on.[4] His position was made more difficult when the British foreign secretary stated in the House of Commons on 30 March 1920 that, if the dominions wished to secede from the Empire, Britain would not try to stop them. 'Dominion Home Rule means the right to decide their own destinies,' he said.[5] This view was at variance with everything Smuts had stood for, and seemed to concede the Nationalists' case completely. Smuts managed, nevertheless, to hold out until the end of the parliamentary session of 1920 and was successful in enacting a considerable amount of legislation, including the Native Affairs Act, No. 23 of 1920.

The Act was the first step in Smuts's campaign to implement the native policy he had sketched in outline in his speech at the Savoy Hotel in 1917. It was characteristic of his approach to native problems that the measure was formulated without consulting Africans and without any consideration of the issues which were agitating them at the time. The proposals contained in it were drawn from a variety of sources, including the South African Native Affairs Commission's report of 1905 and the advice given by Lord Selborne to Smuts and Botha in 1908. Those gleanings were combined to produce a statement which conformed with Smuts's idea of how the relations of Africans and Europeans could be managed, an idea which bore little relation to the realities of the situation. The main provision of the Act was that it created a Native Affairs Commission, empowered to advise the government on any aspect of native administration. This was intended as a means of alerting those responsible to problems which required attention. The Act also contained enabling clauses which made possible the extension of Rhodes's Glen Grey scheme of administration, introduced in 1894 to a limited area in the Transkei, to the rest of the Union. Under that scheme Africans were entitled to elect councils which in turn could send representatives to superior councils. At each level the council would be responsible for local government and for recommending legislation to the central government. They would operate only in areas set apart for occupation by Africans, so that the new measure in that respect was not in conflict with Sauer's attempt to achieve segregation in 1913. In those areas only there would be opportunities for private ownership of land. This would, it was thought, provide a stronger incentive for the improvement of farming methods than was possible under the traditional system of communal ownership. The local government system would, in Smuts's estimation, give Africans their own institutions which would enable them to develop a sense of responsibility for the conduct of their own affairs. His aim was to foster an indigenous African culture or system of cultures and to avoid forcing Africans into a European mould.[6]

What Smuts failed to understand was that the Glen Grey plan, upon which his own proposals were based, was itself a novelty to the African population. It was essentially an attempt to transfer the British system of local government to Africa, for it deprived traditional authorities of their power and replaced them by elected councils. It was little wonder that Africans were slow to respond, and the terms of the Act were a clear indication of Smuts's unwillingness to apply himself to the understanding of African society, even when his goal was to ensure that segregation worked for the benefit of both Europeans and Africans.

If the majority of the African people found Smuts's proposals totally alien, the educated minority found them equally unsatisfactory. In spite of Smuts's assurance that he was trying to give a constitutional outlet for their grievances, educated Africans could see no prospect of their further enfranchisement or of finding any effective opening for participation in the country's political life. Patrick Duncan, a leading Unionist, thought the Act had possibilities, but he ruefully added that it could not be as liberal as Smuts tried to make it out to be or his party would never have accepted it.[7]

The question of a *rapprochement* between the South African Party and the Nationalists was still being discussed in September 1920, although an exchange of letters between Smuts and Hertzog in April had convinced the two leaders that there was little hope of advance along those lines. The main stumbling block was their disagreement over the Union's relations with Britain. For Smuts, membership of the Empire gave South Africa both independent status and a significant voice in world affairs. For Hertzog, independence and the British connection were irreconcilable opposites. By the time the rank and file of the Nationalist party decided at a conference in September that reunion was impossible, Smuts was already looking in a different direction. He had now come to the conclusion that the only way forward lay through co-operation with the Unionists. He was opposed to the idea of a coalition, because that required a constant review of every decision. Instead, he invited the Unionists to join his party. The Unionist leader, Sir Thomas Smartt, was afraid such a proposal would alienate the 'advanced democratic wing of his party'. But the majority of Unionists were in favour of Smuts's proposition, because they believed the country was in grave danger of splitting into too many factions. So willing were they to co-operate that they did not question Smuts's offer of two seats in the cabinet, to be increased to three later.[8] Some members of the South African Party hesitated over the merger, as Smuts expected that they would, but it took place in November. Smuts claimed a great, historic victory for South Africanism. The party of Rhodes and Jameson, which had exacerbated the feelings between Boer and Briton, had been dissolved and a new level of unity achieved, he said.[9] It was an exaggerated claim, and, although Smuts put out feelers in the hope that some of the Nationalists who were not in favour of secession from the Empire might respond, there was little prospect of any wholesale movement to join the new party from that quarter.[10]

Smuts was aware that his victory was as yet only a parliamentary coup. If it were to have real significance, the people as a whole must demonstrate their support for his efforts to unite British and Dutch and to maintain the imperial link. For that a general election must be held. Before it could take place, Smuts's thoughts were once again diverted to wider issues. President Wilson was due to retire from office on 4 March 1921 and Smuts was asked to write an appreciation of his career. In spite of the criticisms he had levelled against the President during the peace conference in 1919 and of Wilson's failure to obtain the support of the American electorate for either the peace treaty or the League of Nations, he undertook the task willingly. Wilson had, after all, had ideals, even if they had been lost from sight in the bitter discussions in Paris. To some extent, too, Smuts looked upon himself as the President's mentor, at least in respect of some of his noteworthy achievements. In his heart of hearts, Smuts confided to Margaret Gillett, he regarded the League of Nations as his own child, though, if it were to prosper, there was nothing to be gained by questioning Wilson's paternity.[11] Smuts had certainly made a great contribution to the formal creation of the League, but only the authority of the American president could have imposed the idea on a hostile France and an indifferent Britain.

A less pleasant reminder of Smuts's membership of the wider world appeared about the same time in H. V. Temperley's *A History of the Peace Conference of Paris*. Smuts it was, the author claimed, who had recommended the provision in the treaty which made Germany responsible for reimbursing pensions and allowances paid to civilians as a result of the war. Smuts was not greatly troubled by the accusation. With the conscious rectitude of one whose conscience is clear, he reminded Margaret Gillett that he had been asked for his legal opinion and had given it. In any case, he added, he had always opposed heavy reparations.[12] Conveniently he dismissed the possibility that others might have used his 'legal' opinion to ensure that France would not be able to claim all the reparations from Germany. The ability to ignore the responses of others, while believing he could justify his own motives in the minutest detail, would create problems for Smuts throughout his political life, and contributed to the distrust and uncertainty he aroused among his critics.

These echoes from the outside world aroused in Smuts the desire to recapture something of the excitement he had enjoyed during his two years in England. 'If there were a good man in South Africa,' he wrote to Margaret Gillett, 'I would like to come to London myself [as High Commissioner] and devote my time mainly to the League.'[13] To escape from South Africa and to play a central role on the international stage was a desire which frequently overtook him. That he did not succumb to it was due in part to his conviction that he alone could lead the Union along the path it should follow, a path which he had devised for it, and that he had a duty to be his country's leader. It was also due to the conclusion, drawn from his earlier experience, that personality and ability alone could not influence world events unless backed by power. The Union did not itself supply an adequate power base, while the Empire, which alone might wield sufficient influence to counter the opposition of France and America, seemed lukewarm about the League of Nations and the high ideals of world peace which Smuts himself cherished.

Relegating such dreams to the inner recesses of his consciousness, Smuts turned to face the problems arising from a convincing victory by the new South African Party in the 1921 elections. Although the party had won 79 seats, the Nationalists had captured no less than 45, which suggested that there would be a lively opposition in parliament. Support for the Labour Party had apparently declined and one of the casualties was Fred Creswell, the Labour leader, who had taken time off from electioneering to get married, with unfortunate results for his immediate political career. Smuts did not approve of Creswell's political views, sincerely held though they may have been. But he respected his loyalty during the war and admired his distinguished military service. He therefore wrote to his opponent, regretting his defeat and expressing the hope that some other Labour member might stand down in his favour.[14] Proud and prickly, even disdainful, in the face of opposition, Smuts never took pleasure in the downfall of an opponent.

The South African Party's victory coincided with the retirement from the colonial office in London of two men in whom Smuts reposed considerable trust and to whom he had looked confidently for support in all his efforts on behalf of the Empire and the League of Nations. His former enemy, Lord Milner, converted by time and a change in Smuts's own outlook into an ally, had married Lady Edward Cecil who had become his friend during the Anglo-Boer War. The under-secretary, L. S. Amery, had been a war correspondent during the same war and had then become a close associate of Smuts during the First World War. Now he moved to the Admiralty. The departure of both from the colonial office was a blow to Smuts,[15] but at least the situation in Europe seemed a little brighter, because on 11 May Germany accepted in full the reparations scheme. Smuts himself was due to visit England in June for a meeting of dominions prime ministers and he looked forward to that as another opportunity to press for a clearer definition of dominion status.

Though he might thrill to the prospect of dealing with issues of such importance, he responded less than skilfully to a minor problem at home. An African religious sect, styling themselves Israelites, had been recently formed in the Eastern Cape. Some members of the sect established a settlement at Bulhoek, near Queenstown, and religious festivals were held there which attracted large numbers of people. As long as the members obeyed the law, no action was taken against them, but it was stipulated by the administration that when the celebrations were over all non-residents should return to their homes. After the ceremonies in 1920 the participants did not disperse. Instead, large numbers of squatters built houses and settled down there. The local farmers complained of stock thefts, but when the Israelites were ordered to leave they refused to go, claiming that they were on the Lord's ground at his behest. They asked for an interview with the prime minister, but Smuts said he was too busy to see them immediately. Instead he sent members of the recently constituted Native Affairs Commission to negotiate. After the Israelites had ignored an offer of free travel to their homes, the commissioners telegraphed a request for a strong force to be sent to put the law into effect. Smuts responded by dispatching a large body of armed police, hoping that their presence would induce the Israelites to give up their resistance. His hope was not fulfilled. The police subsequently claimed that while they were still 200 yards away from the crowd the Israelites charged them, armed with sticks. The police opened fire and 163 people were killed and more than 100 wounded.[16]

Smuts, who was minister for native affairs as well as prime minister, was answerable to parliament for the massacre, but by the time the subject was debated he was already in England. This allowed his critics ample opportunity to advance their charges, prominent among them

125

being the claim that he was more concerned with the affairs of Europe than with those of South Africa. The prime minister, his opponents argued, should have gone to parley with the Israelites instead of going overseas to talk about the League of Nations. It is easy with hindsight to criticise Smuts's behaviour, and it should be said that his critics in parliament were less concerned with the fate of the Israelites than with seizing an opportunity to attack the government. The police had certainly used considerable violence as the casualties indicated, and it could well have been that the appearance of Smuts himself, as minister of native affairs if not as prime minister, would have given the Israelites the satisfaction of airing what they believed to be their grievances and that might have defused the situation. Smuts did not shrink from the encounter through cowardice and he could not have anticipated that the police would over-react as they did. Nevertheless, his decision not to confront the Israelites in person is a pointer both to his attitude to African affairs and to his personality. He did not think an issue of that sort important enough to require his personal involvement. It was a matter for administrators to deal with. Decisions about native affairs were taken by government, but their implementation, he believed, was best left to officials. In any case, he did not enjoy negotiating. He preferred to draft memoranda or letters. In a cold rage he could intervene severely, sometimes too severely. But he was not at ease with other men except in the role of director. The physical separation of a platform, or the notional separation provided by an officer's uniform, alone gave him the confidence to present his case in an inspiring form.

Smuts's visit to Europe demonstrated again those varied aspects of his character. His immediate reaction to the news of the prime ministers' conference was to prepare a lengthy memorandum for another conference, to be held in 1922, at which it was hoped the constitutional relations of the Empire would be determined as projected in 1917. For Smuts it was vital that the status of the dominions should be made clear without delay and in a manner which would satisfy the aspirations of the young nations. Otherwise, the republican movement in South Africa would gain momentum.[17] His fluent pen failed to convince the other prime ministers, however, and in the discussions which followed he was unable to carry the day. The plans for a conference in 1922 were rejected. It was a great disappointment for him. He had hoped that the position achieved by his country's participation in the war and by being represented in its own right at the peace conference could now be formally acknowledged. He could then demonstrate to his fellow-Afrikaners that membership of the Empire brought freedom and strength rather than subservience. By contrast, the other dominions' prime ministers believed that they had everything to gain by an informal relationship which allowed them to assert their independence when need be and to claim British assistance in an emergency. They did not have a strong republican opposition to deal with.

The reputation Smuts had built up during the war still counted for something in Britain, however. Even before he reached England, he had found a bundle of correspondence awaiting him in Madeira. The writer was an old friend, Tom Casement, who had sent the letters to inform Smuts about the desperate situation in Ireland and to entreat him to help. The Government of Ireland Act of 1920 had provided for two parliaments, one for the six counties of the north and one for the twenty-six southern counties. Elections were arranged for both assemblies but proved unnecessary in the south where every constituency save Trinity College, Dublin, which returned four members, returned a member of the Sinn Fein party unopposed. The Sinn Feiners' hostility towards partition meant that the southern parliament could not function. Military rule by Britain continued, therefore, in the southern counties, with violence from each side leading to reciprocal violence from the other.

Casement was not the only one to look to Smuts for help. The leader of the more moderate Irish, Horace Plunkett, sent him a copy of a memorial which had been submitted to Lloyd George without eliciting a response. It called for a constituent assembly and for a firm offer of dominion status for Ireland which, Plunkett claimed, would have been acceptable to all sections of opinion throughout Ireland before the elections had taken place. He recognised that the situation was now more difficult, but still believed that a solution could be found by using the memorial as a basis for discussion.[18] King George, too, through his private secretary, tried to interest Smuts in the Irish question. True to form, Smuts responded swiftly by penning a declaration to be embodied in the speech from the throne at the opening of the Northern Ireland parliament. The object of the declaration was to demonstrate beyond doubt the King's desire that the ideals of freedom and co-operation upon which the Empire rested should be extended to the whole of Ireland. Smuts then sent the draft to Lloyd George, emphasising that the promise of dominion status by the King would only have validity if it were clearly adopted by the government as its policy.

Lloyd George responded by inviting Eamonn de Valera, the Sinn Fein leader, and Sir James Craig, prime minister of Northern Ireland, to a conference in London. De Valera asked Craig for a preliminary meeting between the two of them, but Craig, who was prepared to go to London to negotiate with Lloyd George, would not agree to a private encounter with de Valera. The latter then invoked the aid of Smuts, requesting him to go to Dublin to discuss Ireland's problems. Smuts complied and, face to face with de Valera and some of his closest associates, urged them to attend the London conference proposed by Lloyd George. Not to do so, he said, would turn world opinion against the Irish. To de Valera's protest that he could not accept the partition of Ireland, Smuts responded that Southern Ireland's future could be better determined without Ulster. He also challenged de Valera's claim that the only satisfactory solution would be for Ireland to become a republic, even if that meant she must be bound to Britain by a treaty because of their close economic links. South Africa's experience of such an arrangement had been disastrous, Smuts said. De Valera then showed some interest in dominion status for Ireland and Smuts returned to London feeling that he had made at least a slight impression on him.[19]

His optimism, mild though it was, was quickly shattered. After reflecting upon their conversation, de Valera wrote saying he still wanted a preliminary meeting with Craig, and he still aimed at a united Ireland. Smuts tried to meet the first of these requirements, but without success. Craig was adamant. Smuts then saw no further advantage in his involvement in the Irish question if de Valera were to remain intransigent. He wrote firmly to the Southern Irish leaders to say that there was no prospect of Ulster's joining Southern Ireland at present, and that Ulster could not be coerced. Nevertheless, if Southern Ireland prospered, Ulster might come to see that it was in her interests to change her attitude. The delay could be repugnant to Irish patriots, but a wise man bows to the inevitable without surrendering his ideals. A humble acceptance of the facts was often the only way of finally overcoming them. That had proved to be the case in South Africa, where the republican ideal, for which unheard of sacrifices had been made, had given way to another form of freedom. Lloyd George had offered that same freedom – dominion status – to Southern Ireland, and it was a status other nations had gladly accepted. South Africa herself had accepted a far less generous offer and had used it as a foothold from which to improve her position. Today South Africa was a happy, contented, united and completely free country.[20]

Hertzog would have strongly contested Smuts's description of conditions in the Union, and it was characteristic of Smuts that he should have attempted to brush aside the obvious disquiet of de Valera and his supporters in the same way that he dismissed the opinions of the South African Nationalists as misguided and therefore unworthy of serious consideration. His delight at the immediate results of his letter to the Irish leaders seems also to have been rather less inhibited than the circumstances would appear to justify. Some of the leaders, it is true, were prepared to attend a conference in London on 6 December 1921, and as a result articles of agreement for a treaty between Britain and Ireland were adopted. The terms were then accepted by the Southern Irish parliament on 7 January 1922, but, ominously, by a majority of only 64 to 57. It looked like a step in the right direction, but Smuts's triumph in announcing that the agreement was along the lines he had advocated[21] was to prove premature. He did not understand the Irish, however clearly he might see the solution to their problems.

Soon he was back in South Africa, and the 'happy, contented, united country' of which he had boasted was not living up to his description of it. His absence had aroused strong criticism, and a speech he delivered in Pretoria on 21 October 1921 gave further ammunition to his opponents. His aim while in England had been to stress the need for dominion status to be defined in the form in which he himself desired to see it. He now pointed out that the United States had invited Britain to the first great international conference since the peace conference, but no invitation had been sent to the dominions. Britain had offered places in her delegation to dominion representatives, but that was very different from the role played by the dominions in Paris. It was a valid argument, but delivered in the wrong quarter. Addressed to the British government it might have produced some response. In Pretoria it only served to convince the Nationalists that they had been right all along in insisting that membership of the Empire meant that South Africa was merely a subsidiary of Britain. Merriman, no friend of the republican movement, was aghast at the ineptitude of Smuts's timing. 'I think it is a pity that he will think that he is born to ride abroad redressing human wrongs,' he wrote to Fred Creswell. 'Now he thinks it necessary to make a speech on every topic from "status" (God help us!) downwards.'[22] Confident that his own assessment of South Africa's needs was correct, Smuts had once again failed to take into account the strength of his opponents' feelings.

There were some issues about which Smuts did not speak enough, or not sufficiently explicitly, or not to the right people. One of them was his economic policy, a field of operations in which he was never wholly at home. Throughout the world the threat of inflation had followed hard upon the heels of the post-war boom and was beginning to spread ruin in several European countries. In 1920, to counter the threat, Smuts acted on the advice of a financial conference he had summoned and took a number of severe measures. The gold basis was suspended for three years and a new central reserve bank was set up. Smuts himself regarded these steps as purely temporary expedients to deal

129

with a transient problem. He was anxious to return to the gold standard as soon as possible, but believed that to do so too hastily would have disastrous repercussions on the country's economy. He was aware, also, that the Union's banking system was inadequate for the purposes for which it was used, and he had held frequent discussions with a view to making changes which would meet South Africa's expanding requirements.[23] He did not, however, make these ideas known to his opponents, or even to some of his supporters. Hertzog was ready to admit that there was a need for deflation, but he believed that the reserve bank's restrictions on credit had been misdirected. They had damaged small, bona fide businesses, leaving farmers and other small businessmen at the mercy of the big financiers.

I have no feeling of antagonism against capital [he wrote to Creswell], . . . but I detest and dread the influence of capital on government. Our government having so consistently during the past years derived their support from the financial houses rather than from the people, I fear they are by this time far too much compromised through their various actions and measures, to ever again assume that free and independent attitude which alone can save us against capitalist influence.[24]

It was a criticism which Smuts himself might have levelled against Lord Milner less than twenty years earlier. The grounds were the same – lack of appreciation of the government's problems due to lack of consultation and explanation by the government.

Independently of Hertzog, Creswell had reached a similarly critical view of the government's policy. He, too, recognised South Africa's dependence upon the world's economy, and he believed that the government's behaviour had accentuated the Union's problems. He, too, considered that the banking system operated in the interests of a few large companies which used the banks to control credit. At a time of labour shortage they would be unlikely to adopt measures to encourage new enterprises which might make demands upon a limited labour supply. Like Smuts, though unknown to him as his views were to them, Creswell and Hertzog looked to an extension of banking facilities to improve the situation.[25] With less restraint, Merriman voiced similar criticisms. 'I can just imagine Farrar and all the mob of bureaucrats making things comfortable all round and landing us in the bottomless pit,' he wrote to Creswell, who was to attend an economic conference convened by Smuts towards the end of 1921. 'But for goodness sake my dear fellow do stick to hard money and preserve us from the printing press.'[26] Even making allowances for Merriman's delight in donnish petulance, it does seem clear that Smuts had not explained his position with sufficient care.

The edifices Smuts had tried to build in Europe also appeared to be crumbling. The Anglo–American guarantee which had been offered to France in 1919, and which had led Botha and Smuts to express serious reservations on behalf of the Union, had broken down. In 1921, however, Lloyd George agreed to an Anglo–French pact with the more amenable Briand, who briefly succeeded Poincaré in office. Smuts was horrified and wrote at once to Lloyd George to say that the Union could under no circumstances be a party to such a breach of the ideal of collective security for which he and others had worked so single-mindedly at the peace conference. His concern on that score was short-lived. Poincaré returned to power and rejected the terms upon which the pact had been based, so that it lapsed.[27] The Irish settlement, meanwhile, had proved even more fragile. Following the London conference in December 1921, Arthur Griffith had led a provisional government in Southern Ireland. De Valera, however, had never accepted the dominion idea and soon set up a new republican party in opposition to Griffith. The two leaders then agreed to hold elections at which the new constitution would be put to the voters. Smuts was depressed by the news. 'In Ireland Griffith again has compromised with de Valera,' he wrote to Margaret Gillett, 'and I imagine all the good work there is in gravest danger. There are occasions beyond all compromise, when men and nations have to be put to the test, whatever the issue.'[28]

Those sentiments were written from the heart, for at home Smuts was himself engaged in a new struggle in which he believed, once again, that he stood for rationalism and progress against the forces of conservatism and self-interest. On New Year's Day 1922, the white coal-miners of the Transvaal had gone on strike in response to a call to take a cut in pay from 30 shillings to 25 shillings a day in order to help in the struggle against the economic problems facing the Union. Civil servants, gold-miners and railwaymen had all accepted reductions, but the coal-miners refused to follow suit. Ten days later the European gold-miners also went on strike, after being asked to accept a reduction in the proportion of European employees to Africans in semi-skilled jobs in order to cut costs. The world price for gold had fallen steeply and the many low-grade mines brought into production to meet wartime demand were no longer an economic proposition. A meeting between the South African Industrial Federation, representing the employees, and the Chamber of Mines failed to reach an agreement, but shortly afterwards the Chamber made a new offer with regard to the proportion of African and European workers. This the miners' leaders rejected, but they asked for further discussions. The strikers had already begun to form unofficial commandos and to have drill parades in a number of Rand townships, ostensibly to keep the men fit and to keep them together so that they could not be enticed back to work individually. That the commandos might be used for more sinister purposes was obvious, but the government took no steps to check their activities. One commando, led by a Labour member of parliament, was particularly active in preventing men from going to work, and at a strikers' meeting in Johannesburg on 5 February it was proposed that a republic should be proclaimed in association with Labour and Nationalist members of the assembly. The motion was adopted but was rejected by a meeting of Labour and Nationalist MPs the following day.

Many Nationalists were, however, giving encouragement to the miners, partly to embarrass the government and partly in defence of the white workers' campaign against the employment of Africans in semi-skilled jobs. A secret report claimed that Hertzog himself had attended a meeting of the strike committee on 31 January and had said that his party would call up armed burghers to assist the strikers.[29] Hertzog was undoubtedly on the Rand at the time and, when Smuts later said in parliament that he did not believe the Nationalist leader would have involved himself in violence, Hertzog remarked ill-temperedly that he was a fool if he did not.[30] In fact the armed burghers he was said to have promised did not put in an appearance, but Hertzog was without doubt deeply disturbed by the government's policy. He was convinced that Smuts's failure to take action to settle the strike was an indication that he was working with the mine-owners to oust the Whites in order to employ cheap labour. In Hertzog's opinion, the government should announce categorically that its segregation policy included industrial segregation.[31] Smuts himself believed that both sides in the dispute were at fault. The mine-owners had adopted too dictatorial an attitude in their dealings with their employees, while the white miners should have realised that their unrelenting opposition to any change in the ratio of Whites to Africans must lead to the closure of many uneconomic mines. Even at that early stage of the dispute, the strike had caused serious damage because the failure to keep the pumps working had caused flooding in some of the mines.

When Smuts eventually decided to intervene, his actions were far from reassuring to the miners or to his parliamentary critics. His attempts at mediation having failed, he called on the miners on 12 February to return to work, offering them police protection. The dispute would then be sorted out by an impartial board and by parliament. A number of miners responded to his call, but it was argued by others that to return to work on the terms offered by the owners would compromise their case even before the impartial board had met. On 22 February Hertzog moved in the assembly that a select committee of parliament should be appointed to investigate the causes of the dispute and to make recommendations for a settlement. Smuts, however, was convinced that a growing number of miners were returning to work in answer to his appeal, although neither side had nominated members to sit on the board of inquiry. He was anxious to keep the question as an industrial dispute and to avoid the political implications of a select committee. The Nationalists, he believed, were simply trying to make political capital out of the strike.

On 4 March the Chamber of Mines added fuel to the flames by rejecting any further discussions and by setting out its own standpoint in uncompromising terms. The Augmented Executive, which had organised the strike among the miners, had been considering whether to call for a ballot to determine the amount of support among other workers for strike action. It met on 7 March to reach a decision, but its deliberations were upset by a mob led by a group calling themselves the Council of Action. This latter, some of whose members were Communists, was hoping to turn the strike into a political confrontation with the government. It succeeded to the extent that, under pressure from the mob, the Augmented Executive agreed to call a general strike and Smuts concluded that the strike had become a revolution. The mob, he afterwards claimed, was in no way representative of the workers, who had a genuine grievance, though the timing of their actions was inopportune. The mob, he said, consisted of unemployed, uneducated Afrikaners, who had gravitated to the city in a fruitless search for work, together with labourers from overseas who had little understanding of South African ideas of government.[32] It was the sort of explanation to which Smuts was prone, and it demonstrated his remoteness from the mass, even of Europeans.

Control of events on the strikers' side now fell into the hands of the Council of Action. Violence broke out, beginning with attacks on African workers. Within three days unofficial commandos were attacking police and citizen forces all along the Rand. On 10 March Smuts declared martial law. An aeroplane was sent to reconnoitre one of the worst scenes of violence, at Brakpan, where five mine officials, three policemen and an African worker had been killed. The plane was fired on and the observer was killed. Other planes which followed were also attacked and one was shot down. By the following day it seemed that the whole of the Rand was under the control of the revolutionaries. On 12 March Smuts took personal command of the government forces. Commandos were rapidly assembling in response to the declaration of martial law and were hurrying to the government's aid. Heavy fighting followed, and by 14 March the rebellion had collapsed. More than fifty members of the government forces had been killed and 237 wounded. Other casualties, which included not only rebels but also innocent people killed by the rebels, as well as some who suffered accidentally from the aerial attacks by government planes, amounted to 169 killed and 354 wounded.[33]

Opposition members of parliament vigorously attacked what they claimed to have been improper action by the government and by government troops. A leading Nationalist, N. C. Havenga, drew attention to the death of three brothers after being arrested by soldiers. Privately, N. J. de Wet, minister of justice, informed Smuts that the shooting had been done by members of the Transvaal Scottish, acting under instructions from their officer, who had ordered them to deal in that way with any snipers caught red-handed. To explain that to the satisfaction of a hostile opposition was impossible. It was easier to answer accusations that the trial of rebels had been improperly conducted because they had taken place in the cells instead of in the courtroom. There had, de Wet pointed out, been no ulterior motive behind the arrangement. It had been difficult to transport large numbers of prisoners under adequate escort through the streets to the courtroom because of the turmoil. Now it was possible to transfer the trial to the ordinary courts within a week,[34] and four men, found guilty of murder, were hanged.

More serious were the general criticisms of the government's handling of events. They ranged from accusations of undue hesitancy to the charge that excessive force had been used by government troops. Smuts replied that, until the declaration of a general strike, he had had high hopes that the strikers were about to return to work. Under those circumstances, it would have been wrong to take premature action. He had, throughout, been influenced by considerations of humanity and by kindly feelings for the workers,[35] and he had not found it easy to recommend to the Governor-General that the sentence of death passed on the four men found guilty of murder should be carried out.[36] With the outbreak of widespread violence, however, determined action had been essential, and the amount of arms captured from the rebels was a clear indication of the seriousness of the situation and fully justified the degree of force used by the government troops.

A judicial inquiry gave its support to the actions taken by the government, but one is left with the feeling that the situation might have been handled more skilfully than it was. The difficulty lay in the fact that Smuts believed that the mine-owners were talking sense when they demanded economies in the cost of producing coal and gold, and he was consequently reluctant to try to influence their conduct. While he could sympathise with the European workers who feared for their jobs

134

and their economic status, he had no answer to their difficulties. Because he sympathised with them, however, he failed to intervene quickly and firmly to squash the unofficial commandos before they could pose a threat to stability. So the government seemed to the strikers to be allied to the mine-owners yet too indecisive to prevent the more rebellious among the strike leaders from seizing the initiative. When Smuts decided upon intervention, he did so with extreme severity because the situation had got out of hand. 'There was madness in their blood,' he wrote to Alice Clark, 'and in the end bloodletting became necessary.'[37] It was not the remark of a strong man confident of his position, but rather of a weak man driven to fury.

Politically, the most important result of the strike and the government's handling of it was that it laid the foundations of an improbable alliance between the Nationalists and the Labour Party. The post-war economic problems had forced many poor Afrikaners to abandon hope of finding employment on the hard-hit farms and to seek work in the towns, more particularly on the Rand. There they had come to share some of the frustrations of the white workers already in the mines and in industry. But the *rapprochement* between the two political parties was based primarily upon the shared belief that Smuts's government was too closely identified with the capitalists and was not conducting the affairs of the country in the interests of the white population as a whole. Beyond that they had little in common, but the feeling was strong enough to have serious repercussions in the near future.

From this tumultuous scene Smuts switched with his customary facility to a new role – to the more constructive task, he hoped, of chairing a conference of representatives from Rhodesia and the Union government to ascertain the terms on which the Union would be prepared to incorporate Southern Rhodesia in the first instance and Northern Rhodesia at a later stage.[38] This was a scheme to which Smuts was deeply attached. It was, he believed, an extension of the civilising mission for which, long ago, he had admired Rhodes. He was convinced that it was in the economic and strategic interests of both parties to promote such a link, and he was not unaware of the benefit to his own policies in South Africa of incorporating the predominantly British white population of Rhodesia to strengthen the opposition to the Afrikaner republican movement in the Union. Consequently, the fortnight-long conference from 3 to 17 April 1922 was an enterprise to which he could direct his energies unreservedly. The result was a proposal that Southern Rhodesia should become a fifth province of the Union.[39] Not surprisingly Smuts failed to carry either the Nationalists or the Labour Party with him in the enterprise. Both Hertzog and Creswell believed that the negotiations

135

with the Chartered Company in Rhodesia were part of Smuts's general campaign to ally his government with all the big financial interests operating in Southern Africa, to the ultimate detriment of the white population as a whole. So another link was forged in the chain which was to bind the extreme poles of white political opinion in the Union together[40] in opposition to the South African Party.

In the event, the discussions with the Rhodesians came to nothing. Though the British secretary of state for the colonies, Winston Churchill, had given the conference his approval, he had almost certainly made its efforts abortive by having previously appointed a committee, under the chairmanship of Lord Buxton, to consider the future of Southern Rhodesia. The committee had recommended that the country be granted responsible government if it was shown, by means of a referendum, that the white population wanted it. Its recommendation had been adopted, and a majority of white Rhodesians were attracted by the prospect of managing their own affairs. Many, too, disliked the policies advocated by the Nationalists in the Union and the bilingualism practised in South Africa.[41]

The Rhodesians' decision was a great disappointment for Smuts and a serious set-back to his plan 'to round off the South African state with borders far-flung into the continent'.[42] Even after the referendum he did not give up the struggle, however, having convinced himself that Southern Rhodesia could not survive alone. Within a few years it would be seeking to join the Union – unless financial aid came from Britain! Obviously Britain must be warned against offering such assistance, so Smuts wrote urgently to the new prime minister, Bonar Law, and sent a copy of his letter to the under-secretary for the colonies W. G. A. Ormsby-Gore.[43] To no avail. Southern Rhodesia clung obstinately to responsible government and in 1924 Northern Rhodesia became a British protectorate, further beyond the reach of the Union than even Swaziland, Bechuanaland and Basutoland, which Smuts also coveted.

Before the decision of the Rhodesian voters was known, the Union government had suffered another disaster. For some time there had been unrest among some of the inhabitants of South West Africa who had previously clashed with their German overlords. This group, the Bondelswarts, claimed that the Union, as mandatory authority, had encroached upon land guaranteed them by the Germans. An investigation indicated that there was no substance in the grievance, but the report did not satisfy the Bondelswarts, who were also protesting against a long-standing tax on dogs which they used for hunting and to help control their herds. The tax had been halved by the mandatory administration in 1921 but the dissatisfaction was kept alive by Jacobus Christiaan, one of the leaders of the rebellion against the Germans, who had been banished but had returned without permission in 1919. In May 1922 an even more prominent figure in the earlier rebellion, Abraham Morris, also returned illegally from exile and the Bondelswarts refused to surrender him to the authorities. When the Administrator, G. R. Hofmeyr, tried to enforce his order, the Bondelswarts took up arms to resist. With only a limited police force at his disposal, Hofmeyr resorted to an aerial bombardment of the village where the Bondelswarts had gathered. Heavy casualties were inflicted and when the Bondelswarts fled Hofmeyr ordered his forces to pursue them and punish them further.

To Smuts the news came as a serious blow. He had had high hopes of being able to arrange a closer assimilation of South West Africa within the Union as an extension to the terms of the mandate, but he knew that to do so he must suitably impress world opinion with the manner in which South Africa carried out her mandatory obligations. Events such as these could only arouse doubts in the minds even of impartial observers. He telegraphed hastily to Hofmeyr urging him to parley with the Bondelswarts, but by the time the Administrator received the instructions Morris had been killed, Christiaan wounded and taken prisoner, and the remaining Bondelswarts had surrendered. In spite of Smuts's efforts Sir Edgar Walton, South Africa's High Commissioner in London and permanent representative at the League of Nations, found himself having to plead with the Assembly of the League not to leap to conclusions on the basis of newspaper reports which censured the conduct of the mandatory administration on insufficient evidence. He was also at pains to restrain the protests of the Aborigines Protection Society which had taken the lead in sponsoring the press campaign against the Union government, but his efforts at conciliation were not helped by the unsatisfactory nature of the report submitted by Hofmeyr which at the time was the only evidence available to the League.[44] The League Assembly agreed to do as Walton advised, but asked the South African government to do all they could to alleviate the sufferings of the victims and to assist in reconstructing the economic life of the Bondelswarts.[45]

The entire incident came to an end within a few days, but the repercussions were felt long afterwards. A three-man commission appointed to investigate what had happened added to the difficulties of the government by letting it be known, in advance of the completion of its report, that it intended to condemn Hofmeyr's administration root and branch. Later it admitted that, on closer scrutiny, the evidence did not justify such action, but as far as the government was concerned the damage had been done, and, in any case, two of the three commissioners remained critical of Hofmeyr's behaviour.[46]

When the report was eventually debated in the Union parliament, Labour Party members, still smarting from Smuts's vigorous suppression of the general strike, condemned the government for using excessive force,[47] referring to Smuts as 'the murderer of Bulhoek'. The Nationalists, who also wished to annex South West Africa, remained silent, and Smuts could confidently ride out the storm of Labour protest. It was the reaction of the League – *his* League – that worried him. He was deeply hurt, though not wholly surprised, when the Permanent Mandates Commission reported unfavourably on the Union's handling of events.[48] The Council of the League felt bound to accept the report of the Commission, but under pressure from Walton and Lord Robert Cecil, president of the League of Nations Union, agreed to accept South Africa's assurance that she would seek to fulfil the request made by the League the previous year regarding the future treatment of the Bondelswarts. It was a courteous statement, but the reproach was clear enough to Smuts.[49] Less than a year earlier he had written proudly to W. E. Rappard, director of the mandates section of the League: 'I wish you all success in your very responsible work. And from me you will always have full support. I believe in the League as a new instrument of human progress.'[50] It was with chagrin that Smuts saw his fine statement thrown back at him.

The statement had been made with the best of intentions. When South Africa had been granted the mandate, Smuts, with deliberate generosity and in contrast to what was done by other mandatories, had permitted the German colonists to remain in the country. Unfortunately the colonists had refused to co-operate with the administration, remaining aloof and clinging to the Fatherland as if South West Africa were still a German dependency. Instead of accepting that, under the terms of the mandate, the Union government had full powers of legislation and administration, they demanded their own legislative institutions. A committee of the League, invited to adjudicate over the issue, strangely concluded that the colonists were still German citizens. The illogicality of the ruling was pointed out by Smuts, who said that the implication of it was that the indigenous inhabitants of South West Africa must also be German citizens by right of conquest, which in terms of the mandate was absurd. To solve the problem he sensibly proposed to pass a nationality law which would include South West Africa in the same category as the rest of the Union and leave it to individuals who wished to do so to register their desire to retain German nationality. To this proposal the Council of the League was delighted to give its assent in April 1923 and by so doing to escape an embarrassing muddle.[51] It was an intelligent solution, but, as time was to show, it did not work.

Nor did it conclude Smuts's problems with the League. Coinciding with the discussion of the Bondelswarts affair, Indian political spokesmen were making representations in support of equal political status for Indians in South and East Africa. Concerned at the political capital made out of the situation in Africa by Indian critics of British administration in India, the Indian government felt obliged to protest to South Africa, and to the British government in respect of East Africa, regarding the treatment of Indians in those two countries. Though he was not optimistic about its probable outcome, Smuts was prepared to accept, as far as India itself was concerned, the relevance of Abraham Lincoln's statement about America that the country 'Cannot endure half free and half slave'. India, Smuts reluctantly admitted, was travelling the same road to self-government as Egypt and with just as little capacity for it.[52] But the position of Indians in the Union was a different matter. They could not, in Smuts's view, be given equality of status with Europeans under any circumstances. Apart from the practical consideration that to make such a concession might give Indians a preponderant voice in the affairs of Natal, there remained the fundamental issue of what type of civilisation was to prevail in South Africa. For Smuts, that question was already settled. It must be a civilisation based on Christian – and European – principles. Indians could have no role to play in any such scheme of things.[53] In 1924 he even went so far as to introduce a Class Areas Bill aimed at segregating Indians from Europeans in urban areas, but his government fell from power before it became law. Though he had no means of interfering directly in the affairs of East Africa, he telegraphed the British colonial secretary to emphasise that, if the demand for civic equality between Indians and Europeans were conceded in that region, together with unrestricted Indian immigration, it would be impossible for the Union to control the situation. 'From the point of view of the Union,' he concluded, 'I can only counsel extreme caution in dealing with Indian demands outside of India.'[54]

One direct result of the Bondelswarts rebellion was the attention it drew to native administration in South Africa generally, a topic with which Smuts never felt at ease. The commissioners who reported on the rebellion had been drawn from the Native Affairs Commission appointed under the legislation of 1920. Their dilatoriness in producing the report, and their verbal indiscretions while hearing evidence, convinced Smuts that a review of the personnel of the Commission was urgently needed.[55] His opinion was reinforced by a letter from Bishop Talbot of Pretoria calling for improvements in the administration of native affairs. He replied assuring the bishop that he intended to take action regarding the staff of the department. He also hoped that new legislation which he proposed to bring to parliament would improve the administration of native affairs in the towns and act as a prelude to improvements in rural areas.[56]

The Native Urban Areas Bill to which Smuts referred was mainly based upon the recommendations of the Transvaal Local Government Commission, better known as the Stallard committee, after its chairman, the lawyer Colonel C. F. Stallard. That committee had argued that the towns were essentially the creation of Europeans and that Africans should only be allowed to enter them to minister to the needs of the Europeans. The indiscriminate mingling of the races led to the degradation of both African and European. The existing law did not cover situations where the races lived together, so they must be kept apart. These were sentiments which coincided with Smuts's own and were almost certainly shared by a large proportion of Europeans in South Africa. It was in no way strange, therefore, that the Native Urban Areas Act, which became law in 1923, stated that only Africans employed as labourers should be admitted to towns, and that they should live in separately administered and financed locations outside the towns.

The Act, like the Native Affairs Act of 1920, proved ineffective in practice. Educated Africans in Cape Province opposed a law which threatened the rights they had enjoyed for generations, while the attractions of paid labour in the urban areas meant that other Africans simply continued to make their way to the towns from an increasingly impoverished countryside where they could not find enough land to sustain them. Employers, too, were reluctant to place any curb upon the free flow of labour which helped them to keep wages low.[57] But the legislation was the final proof, if any were needed by African leaders, that they had nothing to hope for from Smuts's government. In addition to the Acts of 1920 and 1923, qualifications for admission to apprenticeships had been tightened in 1922, making it virtually impossible for any but Europeans to achieve the required standard. Then, as a final gesture, in 1924, an Industrial Conciliation Act was passed which restricted the machinery of arbitration to Europeans.

The South African Native National Congress, which in 1923 became the African National Congress, passed a vote of no confidence in the government. Smuts dismissed the gesture on the ground that the Congress was unrepresentative of the African people. In this he may not have been wholly wrong, though he himself had never hesitated to pursue policies which he believed to be sound merely because many of his own people, in their blindness, could not see the wisdom of them. His reaction was significant on other grounds. Once again it demonstrated his inability to recognise the existence of Africans already educated to a level which placed them alongside many of the leading Europeans. Instead he dreamed of a system of segregation which would ensure that Africans only developed along traditional cultural lines. It was an attitude of mind which was shared by many British colonial administrators in other territories. There the theory of indirect administration obscured the degree of Europeanisation which was taking place both in methods of local government and in the schools run largely by missionaries who believed in the close links between Christianity and European culture. Like the officials in tropical Africa, Smuts was prepared to discount any developments which did not fit into the pattern of life which he believed to be suitable for Africans.

From this disturbing series of emergencies, Smuts was able to escape to a wider stage in September 1923 when he was again required to attend an imperial conference in England. It was something of a relief to him to be greeted by the almost excessive adulation of the British press after the unalleviated criticism he had had to endure in his own country. Even during the most turbulent moments in South Africa, he had maintained his interest in events in Europe. It was not wholly surprising that he had written to Brigadier-General C. P. Crewe in 1922 that he would like to take a holiday and give South Africa a respite, meaning, more probably, that he would like to take a respite from South Africa.[58] With his unique capacity for finding relaxation from his problems by contemplating others, he sought solace in reflecting upon the difficulties faced by his counterparts in Europe. Lloyd George, he believed, had been too prone to give in to Poincaré since the time that negotiations began after the armistice. Yet he could sympathise with the British prime minister's position. He had, in Smuts's view, no support from his Liberal colleagues, who were not only devoid of courage and audacity but lacked even conviction or first-class intelligence.[59] Nevertheless, by co-operating with Poincaré, Lloyd George was ignoring the fundamental need to restore Germany to a place of responsibility in the world. Germany *must* be admitted to the League of Nations.[60] The attitude of France, Smuts consistently believed, was the chief obstacle to a truly peaceful settlement, though the refusal of America to join the League of Nations had weakened almost irreparably the effectiveness of that body as an instrument for keeping the peace.

Lloyd George's tenure of office was brought to an abrupt end in October 1922 when his personal decision to support Greek claims against Turkey in Asia Minor almost involved England in war. Smuts had little confidence that his successor, Bonar Law, would take a stronger line in dealing with France, so he wrote to the new prime minister warning him against those who might argue that it was not French ambitions which must be watched but French fears which must be soothed. The French spirit, he argued, was alien to all true ideals of international peace and co-operation. South Africa would, of course, respect Article 10 of the Covenant of the League, which bound all members to protect the territory and independence of other members against external aggression. It would be no party to any exclusive alliance which conflicted against the ideal of collective security for which the League had been created. All foreign policy issues should be determined only after consultation with the dominions if the Empire was to have any meaning.[61] Bonar Law replied that he was in general agreement with Smuts, but Smuts still feared 'the madness of France'.[62] To Stanley Baldwin, who replaced Bonar Law in May 1923 when the latter resigned because of ill health, Smuts wrote in even more forceful terms. If France would not retract her claims to the Ruhr, he urged, Britain should formally renounce the *entente* and, in consultation with the dominions, open negotiations with Germany to determine exactly how much that country could afford to pay. The sum should then be apportioned among the Allies in the proportions already agreed, after which a separate peace treaty should be made with Turkey.[63] It was a bold suggestion for breaking the deadlock over reparations, and, although the foreign secretary, Lord Curzon, was unable to adopt it in the form presented by Smuts, he did, later in the year, attempt to hold discussions with Germany.

Smuts yearned for an opportunity for the Empire to intervene decisively in European affairs. 'If I could help in this respect,' he wrote to Margaret Gillett, 'I would not care a farthing about my position in South Africa.'[64] It was a comment which throws considerable light on Smuts's character. Though a loyal South African and convinced that he was needed there, he was never at ease in the routine of politics. His clever brain battled ineffectively with problems which called for human understanding rather than intellectual sublety. His idea of the Empire roused in him feelings of exaltation. He could make stirring speeches about it as long as he was not directly involved in administering it. On those occasions when he did try to realise his ideals in a practical fashion he came up against the idiosyncracies of his fellow prime ministers from other dominions and the selfish interests of the dominions themselves. Faced with such obstacles, the fine rhetoric evaporated and Smuts became as ineffective as was Lloyd George when dealing with Poincaré. And more so, because the keenness of his own intellect prevented him from understanding the doubts and obscurities which made it difficult for others to see through a problem with the clarity which he himself was able to command and left them uncertain about his motives as well as his aims. The question, then, is why did he not abandon the routine of South Africa to seek employment on the world stage. It was partly that he sincerely believed that, without him, European civilisation, as opposed to Afrikaner separation, would never survive in South Africa. It was partly, too, that he loved being in South Africa. Perhaps also he feared that, without a political power base, he would be ineffectual. Had not that been his experience at the peace conference? Personality and ability counted for a lot, but not for enough. They might enable him to be a consultant, but he would never be the one who made the final decision.

Nowhere was this weakness more obvious than in Smuts's efforts on behalf of the Jewish claims to Palestine. In his view, Britain's role in Palestine was vital, not only for the sake of world Jewry and for the ideals for which Britain had fought in the First World War, but more practically for her own position in Egypt. To Smuts the objective was clear, and, because it was so clear, the lurking shadows which lay along the path to its achievement must be ignored, even though that they concealed grave hazards. Smuts the efficient staff officer was now replaced by Smuts the visionary. He firmly believed that his own blueprint for the future of Palestine, etched into the Balfour Declaration, was the only just answer to the problem of finding a national home for the Jews. But the British government was seeking for ways of pulling out of its obligations as mandatory authority because, in the view of those who had to carry out those obligations, they were an expensive and dangerous entanglement. For them, Smuts's arguments may have sounded impressive, but they ran counter to practical politics.

Meanwhile, France had occupied the Ruhr in response to Germany's failure to meet the reparations demands. Britain reacted by sending a note on 11 August 1923 proposing that a group of experts should examine Germany's capacity to repay and indicating that France's action had been illegal. It was a mild reproach, but Poincaré rejected both suggestions. Smuts, however, was cheered by the British government's efforts. Now, he believed, in the light of the French initiative, Britain was free to take the lead in mobilising European opinion behind a new policy. Perhaps the imperial conference which he himself was due to attend could play a vital role in encouraging such an initiative.[65] When the conference opened on 1 October, therefore, he boldly called upon the Empire to use the weight of its influence and authority to achieve a settlement in Europe. The League of Nations, too, must be supported, he said. Turning his attention to the preparation of a memorandum, he then proposed in it a conference to fix the amount of reparations Germany should pay and to impose a moratorium on that payment which would give Germany time to recover and to face up to a more realistic task.

143

If France and Belgium refused to take part, the conference should go on without them, but the participation of the United States was essential to the success of the undertaking.[66]

Many were deeply impressed by Smuts's appeal. The volatile and loyal Emily Hobhouse implored him to forget about South Africa long enough to throw himself wholeheartedly into the settlement of Europe's problems.[67] Former President Wilson also appealed to him to find a solution. Though stirred by these requests, Smuts hesitated, excusing himself on the ground that it would be wrong to initiate action for which he could not himself take responsibility.[68] He claimed he was urgently needed in South Africa yet painted an optimistic picture of the Union's recovery from its economic problems and political turbulence in a speech to the South Africa Club at the Savoy Hotel on 23 October. Still more strangely, in view of those statements, he went on to say that his main doubt about South Africa's recovery centred upon Europe's capacity to absorb the Union's products.[69] Clearly he hankered after an international role but recognised that the lack of response from official quarters meant that he could expect little support there. So he confined himself to making speeches, and it should be said that they won widespread approval – even from Lord Curzon, the foreign secretary, and M. P. A. (later Lord) Hankey in the cabinet office – though how far it was possible to translate personal approval into official policy was open to question. The economist, Keynes, for example, was doubtful whether Germany could even pay the reduced sums which Smuts might envisage.[70] The American financier, Bernard Baruch, however, enjoyed reading Smuts's address, as too, did the German foreign minister, Stresemann, who invited him to Germany to discuss that country's position along with other contemporary problems. But again, enjoyment and discussion were not followed by action.

Smuts's brief visit to Europe impressed upon him even more deeply than before the desperate state into which Germany had lapsed. Before leaving for South Africa he wrote to *The Times* on 14 November once more urging England to take the initiative, in co-operation with the United States, in summoning a conference to discuss not only reparations but also the means whereby Germany's finances could be put on a workable footing. Even if the French were unhappy about the proposal, he considered that Britain and the United States had a moral obligation as well as a financial interest in assisting Germany to save herself.[71] With that parting advice, Smuts returned to South Africa to face problems which he was unable to observe from a fine judicial distance. The challenge to the South African Party government had been immeasurably strengthened by a pact between the Nationalists and the Labour Party.

The apparent incongruity of that arrangement concealed the fact that both Hertzog and Creswell believed that the government's policy was based upon a 'Big Finance' view of what was needed to solve the Union's economic problems which was both injuring the country's welfare and jeopardising its destiny as a civilised society. On the basis of the shared conviction, each party agreed in 1923 not to contest constituencies in the next elections where the other had strong support.

Both Hertzog and Creswell accepted the fact that their parties would differ over many issues. They were not contemplating a coalition. Creswell was particularly anxious, however, that the Nationalists should announce formally that, for the duration of one parliament at least, they would not pursue the question of secession from the Empire. Hertzog was prepared to accept that condition, though there were members of his party who did not agree.[72] Smuts's opponents seemed to be aiming at the same goal as Smuts himself – co-operation between the European races – but without Smuts. Smuts would have subscribed to Creswell's view that 'the real religious difficulty to people in our day is to realise the fact that the reality in us is spiritual and that the reality in which we live and move and have our being is spiritual and not material'.[73] But Creswell communicated his opinion to his wife and not to Smuts, and, as was so often the case, there was no dialogue between them. For Creswell, as for Hertzog, Smuts's intentions were shrouded in mystery. They could only guess what they were and they usually guessed incorrectly.

Co-operation between the Nationalists and the Labour Party was not easy. At the National Party Congress in September 1923, two prominent members, Tielman Roos and Piet Grobler, vigorously reaffirmed their belief that the goal to be aimed at must be the complete independence of South Africa. The editor of the *Natal Witness* argued that the Labour Party, though doubtless acting in all sincerity, had been grievously misled by the Nationalists.[74] Creswell denied this, maintaining that individuals were free to speak as they wished, but the parties would remain loyal to the compact. Both parties must strive to ensure that South Africa was governed in such a way as to enable men and women of the white races and civilisation to live there in increasing numbers. There must be no more dismissals of Whites from the great industries in order to make room for Africans from Mozambique. Natal, too, must be rescued for the Whites by offering generous inducements to Asiatics to return to their mother countries. All this could be achieved only if English and Dutch South Africans forgot their ancient prejudices and pursued their national duty.[75] To all this Smuts would again have said 'Amen' and Hertzog was grateful to Creswell for his generous attitude towards the vagaries of Roos and Grobler.[76] Smuts, meanwhile, was conscious of the increasing pressure on the government and for that reason refused an invitation to attend a South African Zionist conference in Johannesburg while parliament was in session. He informed the secretary of the Zionists, J. Alexander, that he had discussed their concern with Dr Weizmann during his recent visit to London. Subsequently he had raised the question of the Jewish national home with the other dominions' prime ministers and as a result the British government had reaffirmed its support for the project.[77]

To strengthen his own party's position, Smuts looked round for 'new blood, new ideas, courage and the forward look'. All this he hoped to discover in J. H. Hofmeyr, a young man whom he now adopted as his protégé.[78] He did not expect Hofmeyr, then aged thirty, to go into politics immediately. Instead he prepared the way for him to do so later by appointing him Administrator of the Transvaal. Then, with the parliamentary session almost at an end, he planned a political tour of the Transkei and the Eastern Cape, in the course of which he hoped to find the time to pursue his hobby of plant-collecting. The tour took on greater importance when Smuts decided early in April to dissolve parliament and appeal to the country for support. In a manner which was to become increasingly characteristic, he acted without consulting his colleagues after his party had suffered defeat in a by-election in the Wakkerstroom constituency. He knew he was taking a risk. His handling of what he described as the revolution of 1922 and his policy for dealing with the country's economic problems had aroused a storm of criticism. 'You do not reap a harvest of appreciation for these things in South Africa,' he wrote to a friend.[79] In a speech full of venom delivered in his home constituency of Smithfield, Hertzog bore out that claim by attacking all the things Smuts had listed and more. Moreover, though the pro-government *Cape Times* might deplore the epithets levelled at the prime minister by the leader of the opposition,[80] the words found an echo in many quarters.

Even in the middle of a violent election campaign, Smuts did not lose sight of the greater issues troubling Europe. A committee appointed in December 1923 under the chairmanship of an American general, Charles C. Dawes, had submitted proposals on 9 April 1924 for stabilising Germany's finances and reducing the reparations as Smuts had suggested while in England. The recommendations received widespread international support, but Poincaré, on behalf of France, persisted in making demands for sanctions against Germany. Smuts found his behaviour unacceptable and wrote to the British prime minister, Ramsay MacDonald, urging him not to let the French hold up a settlement any longer and to avoid at all costs involving Britain in a common policy with France which could only bring her discredit and ruin.[81] Hopes that this might be possible were enhanced when the French premier, Poincaré, was replaced by Edouard Herriot, who was of a more amenable disposition. But Poincaré's overthrow coincided with Smuts's defeat in the elections held in June, so that Smuts, too, was in a less effective position to make his voice heard in world affairs.

The South African Party won only 53 seats to 63 for the Nationalists and 18 for the other member of the Pact, the Labour Party. Smuts had not been sanguine of the outcome, but it was a humbling experience. Mrs Violet Carruthers, a woman who had gratuitously taken upon herself to keep Smuts informed about events in Britain, now wrote urging him to take a long rest. Her impression during a recent visit to South Africa was that the South African Party leaders were tired men. Smuts himself was, she said, a great world asset. He needed to recharge his batteries in order to bring the qualities of a statesman, rather than those of a harassed politician, to the consideration of the new forces which were shaping the world.[82] Arthur and Margaret Gillett had also hoped that a defeat might give Smuts an opportunity to indulge in more restful and more stimulating activities, and for a brief moment Smuts allowed himself the pleasure of contemplating a future away from South African politics. But it was a pleasure of a very fleeting character. He could never bear to surrender the stage to others whom he considered less able than himself. The long-running show might have experienced a series of disasters, but he still believed himself to be the actor–manager. His company and his public needed him. 'I felt at once that under these distressing circumstances I ought not to clear out, that the South African Party might go to pieces in the rout, and that irreparable mischief might be done to South Africa,' he wrote to Margaret Gillett.[83] As always he was, in his own opinion, indispensable to the Union. He might not be prime minister, but he was prepared to upstage anyone else who might try to play the role.

147

7

Leader of the opposition

While the Nationalists and Labour Party proceeded to form a government in which both parties preserved their identities, Smuts gave himself a short rest from public life. He still wrote ten to twenty letters a day, but he had time to go out walking and riding, to add to his store of botanical knowledge, to read extensively and to revise his book on holism. Nor did he neglect what was going on in Europe. He was pleased to learn of the overthrow of Ramsay MacDonald's government in October 1924. MacDonald's decision to drop all ideas of imperial preference seemed to Smuts to be in conflict with his own concept of imperial unity. Nor did he take kindly to the suggestion of the Labour colonial secretary, J. H. Thomas, during a visit to the Union in September 1924, that Hertzog's love for South Africa equalled Smuts's own. It was consequently a matter of some satisfaction that, with the fall of the Labour government, Thomas was replaced at the colonial office by Smuts's old friend, L. S. Amery, who shared his views on the Empire and the League of Nations. In a letter of congratulation on his appointment, Smuts urged upon Amery the importance of developing a white dominion in the highlands stretching from the northern border of the Union to the southern frontiers of Ethiopia. There was, he maintained, ample land for Africans on the flanks of the highlands. The existing policy, however, appeared to favour the emergence of an African state with an Indian trading aristocracy in charge. This was contrary to all his hopes for the future of the African continent.

Turning to other issues, Smuts expressed concern at the Conservatives' plan to build up a naval base in Singapore. He recognised that there was pressure for it from Australia but, prophetically as events were to show, he argued that at a time of crisis the British fleet would not be big enough to divide between the Pacific and European waters.[1] The Labour government had left another legacy which also worried him. On 2 October MacDonald and the French premier, Herriot, had put before the assembly of the League of Nations proposals which would make arbitration compulsory in all international disputes. Nations failing to comply would be subjected to an economic boycott at least. The assembly unanimously recommended the adoption of the proposals, which became known as the Geneva Protocol. Smuts was convinced that the idea would prove unacceptable in practice because national pride would reject it.[2] To his delight the new Conservative government was of the same opinion and turned down the proposal.

By the beginning of 1925, Smuts was back in action in the South African Assembly. The government had introduced a Mines and Works Amendment Bill to limit the grant of certificates of competence in a number of skilled occupations to Whites and members of the coloured population. Their aim was to legalise measures which Smuts himself had tried to introduce with his Mines and Works Act No. 12 of 1911, but which the courts had decided were *ultra vires*. Now, however, Smuts proceeded to attack the government's actions, not it would seem because of any disagreement with the aims of the legislation, but simply to embarrass his opponents by criticising the clumsiness with which they presented their case. As a result, discussion of what came to be called the Colour Bar Bill dragged on for many months. Many of the government's errors Smuts attributed to pressure from Labour Party members who were anxious to protect white workers from competition. Their attitude was further reflected in the Wages Act No. 27 of 1925, which provided machinery for fixing the wages of unskilled labourers and distinguished between those with 'civilised' and those with 'uncivilised' habits of life.[3] This was a question over which Smuts himself was ambivalent. He sympathised with the objective of protecting the interests of the Whites, but he saw the mining industry in particular as the main source of the country's wealth, and he did not wish to take any measures which would make the running of the industry less economic. At this stage, however, distinctions of that sort were unimportant to him. His main aim was to attack the government whenever the opportunity arose.

The activities of the British government were also causing him concern. The Locarno Pacts, signed on 16 October 1925, seemed to offer the prospect of more stable relations between France and Germany but at the same time threatened to precipitate a European war as a result of friction between Germany and Poland. Smuts accepted with cautious optimism the mutual guarantees of the Franco-German and Belgo-German frontiers, but he regarded the guarantees of mutual assistance between France and Poland and France and Czechoslovakia with the greatest suspicion. He had always looked upon the Polish Corridor and the free port of Danzig as unfair to Germany and therefore as hostages to fortune. 'In Poland,' he wrote to Sir Austen Chamberlain, the British foreign secretary, 'we have not only an unstable, but an inequitable, situation and trouble arising there will and indeed must involve military movements and war in the West, too.'[4] Fourteen years later his forecast was

149

confirmed. He was worried, too, that Britain had become a party to the guarantee of the Western frontiers, while allowing the dominions to claim exemption from any obligation to support her. This, Smuts believed, would encourage the dominions to take an ever-decreasing interest in British foreign policy and that would be bad in every way for the Empire. Furthermore, it would weaken his own position in South Africa, where he had consistently stressed the importance of strong imperial links in the face of a powerful separatist movement.

One of the preconditions of Germany's acceptance of the Locarno agreement was her admission to the League of Nations and to permanent membership of the League Council. There was a general acceptance of this proposal, but the move was jeopardised when Spain, Poland and Brazil demanded that they, too, should become permanent members of the Council. Germany protested and seemed on the point of withdrawing from the arrangement. Smuts was deeply distressed, fearing that, if the League acquiesced in the proposal to increase the Council's permanent membership so markedly, its position and effectiveness would be gravely weakened. Once again he bemoaned the non-participation of the United States. 'My fear is deep that the League has arrived at a critical point,' he wrote to his friend, Professor Gilbert Murray, 'and that a fatal turn may be taken not only in her fortunes but in those of Europe and civilization too.... The chance for another effort like the League will not come again until the world has been once more engulfed.'[5] Prophetic words! In the event a compromise was reached. Only Germany became a permanent member of the Council, but the elected membership was increased from six to nine, three of whom might be re-elected for further periods at the end of their three-year tenure of office.

In South Africa Smuts showed less foresight and statesmanship. He still resented being out of office and he spent his time in political infighting while professing to deplore political divisions. When Hertzog proposed early in November 1925 that the South African Party should join the Nationalists, Smuts's response was ambivalent. He claimed to be in favour of union but wanted the Nationalists to take the initiative. There was no racial division between the parties, he said, but such divisions as did exist were the result of political hatred for which the Nationalists were principally responsible. The country was tired of the situation, and in the rural areas even some of the National Party's own supporters had, he claimed, been shocked by their leader's cynical alliance with the Labour Party.[6] It was a confused and confusing statement of Smuts's position, but it achieved his aim, which was to suggest that his party was prepared to consider union while ensuring that the National Party rejected his overture and was seen to do so.[7]

In a similarly obstructive frame of mind, Smuts entered into an unprofit-able wrangle with Hertzog over native policy. On 13 November the prime minister outlined possible developments in a speech in Smithfield. He envisaged the provision of more land for Africans in line with the terms of the Act of 1913. Local councils, recommended by Smuts's Act of 1920, must be encouraged wherever possible and better educational provision should be made to enable Africans to administer themselves in their own areas. The annual Native Congress, meeting in Pretoria, which had also been provided for in the 1920 Act, should be converted into a mainly elected council which, though at first advisory, should in time be given legislative powers in purely native affairs. At the same time, the Cape Native vote should be abolished and instead Africans throug-hout the Union should elect seven Europeans to represent their interests in the house of assembly. The coloured population in the northern pro-vinces would then be given the same voting rights as those in the Cape.[8]

The proposals closely resembled the policies pursured by Smuts's gov-ernment, though the suggestions about the African franchise were new and there was some vagueness about how it would operate and about the powers of the Europeans elected to represent the Africans. Neverthe-less Smuts was unco-operative, as he continued to be for many years. He and his friends, he said, were of the opinion that drafts containing the whole of the government's proposals should be placed before parlia-ment before consultation could take place. In any event, he considered a national convention would be the best body to consider a matter of such importance.[9] The executive of the South African Party was afraid that Hertzog might try to place the blame for any breakdown in discus-sions upon his opponents if it did not announce its own position unequi-vocally. It was also aware that within its own party there would be considerable division of opinion on an issue which so closely affected all its members, if in different ways. So Smuts avoided committing either himself or his party and did so in an increasingly ungracious exchange of correspondence with his rival. Although he insisted that his idea of a national convention was intended to avoid party strife over a potentially contentious issue, he gave no indication as to why that particular proce-dure would be less prone to conflict than any other save, perhaps, that participants need not, by implication, be bound by party allegiance. Not surprisingly, Hertzog brought the correspondence to a close early in 1926.

Smuts's response to the government's proposals for the segregation and repatriation of Asians was equally disingenuous. His own government had introduced a Class Areas Bill with the object of empowering the Governor-General, on the advice of commissioners appointed by the minister of the interior, to designate urban areas as restricted to one race for residential or commercial purposes. The Bill was aimed at the Asian community because Europeans feared commercial competition and disliked the presence of Asians in residential areas which they themselves occupied. Hertzog's Areas Reservation and Immigration Bill was brought forward as part of the bargain with Creswell's Labour Party at the time of the Pact and it contained little that was new. Nevertheless, Smuts denounced its proposals as being as dangerous and unpleasant as any that had been before parliament. Over that issue Hertzog was under pressure from another quarter. The Indian government, also, claimed that his policy was objectionable and the Viceroy suggested that there should be a conference between representatives of the Union and the Indian governments. Hertzog procrastinated, claiming like Smuts that the South African government must be free to determine its own policies over internal matters. So far as Asians were concerned, its policy was to reduce the number of them in the Union by prohibiting further immigration and by encouraging the repatriation of those already in South Africa.[10] But the Viceroy persisted, and Hertzog ungraciously agreed to a conference provided the aims he had propounded were not overlooked. Pending the outcome of the discussions the Areas Reservation Bill was withdrawn.

The conference met in Cape Town in 1927 and formulated the Cape Town Agreement. The main feature of it was that there should be an intensification of the assisted emigration scheme introduced by Botha's government with a view to reducing the Indian population to a size which could be comfortably integrated into the Union. At the same time, the Areas Reservation Bill was dropped and the government gave an undertaking to improve the conditions of those Indians who remained legitimately in South Africa. Finally, the Indian government was to appoint an agent to look after the affairs of Indians in the Union. With none of this could Smuts have been in disagreement and for the first eighteen months after the signing of the Agreement the number of Indians emigrating from South Africa increased sharply. But the increase was not maintained, and the high Indian birth-rate, coupled with the legal immigration of minors and their mothers to join men already resident in South Africa, more than balanced the number of emigrants. Though the government of India fulfilled its side of the bargain, many Indians in South Africa resented the ruling under Act No. 37 of 1927 that anyone legally domiciled in South Africa who left the country for more than three years would be deemed to have surrendered his right of domicile. Minors, too, would not be permitted to join their fathers in the Union unless accompanied by their mothers.[11] When, therefore, the Agreement came up for review after five years, as laid down at the Cape Town conference, the Union government claimed that it had failed in its objectives and should not be renewed. It was particularly concerned that the presence of an agent of the Indian government gave the impression to Indians in South Africa that they could appeal at any time to the Indian government for support against the Union government and this encouraged non-co-operation with South Africa's efforts to deal with the problem.[12]

As far as Smuts was concerned, the government must fight its own battles over the Indians. It was native policy which occupied his attention more fully. The Colour Bar Bill eventually became law as Act No. 25 of 1926, but not before Smuts had opposed it with a vigour that was only equalled by his inconsistency. It was twice rejected by the senate and was only adopted by invoking a joint sitting of both houses. A number of prominent churchmen, headed by the Archbishop of Cape Town, had addressed a memorandum to the government claiming that the Bill violated both moral and religious principles,[13] and in the debate in the joint sitting Smuts added his voice to the opposition protests. He was greeted with cries of 'Traitor' and 'Judas' from the government benches, not entirely without justification. Hertzog, who also criticised the clergy's memorandum, described Smuts's intervention as contemptible.[14] The Natal Native Congress, however, gave Smuts its full approval. Its general secretary wrote: 'The Natives here greatly admire your effort and we hope that you will ever stand for what you consider is right for all sections and races in South Africa.'[15] It is doubtful whether Smuts fully merited the congratulations. He was not insincere in his opposition to government policy and he doubtless saw some difference in emphasis between the new legislation and his own which was not immediately obvious to less subtle minds. Yet his main concern was less with the rights of the Africans than with the hostility to the Whites which Hertzog's policy threatened to stir up among the Africans.[16]

The publication on 23 July 1926 of four more bills embodying further aspects of the government's native policy gave Smuts a further opportunity to maintain his attack. 'On the great question I fear the Nationalist influence is thoroughly reactionary and bad for the future of the country,' he wrote to Margaret Gillett.[17] He then drafted a memorandum criticising the bills, which he presented to his party for consideration.

The memorandum attacked the Natives Land Act (1913) Amendment Bill because, in recommending the provision of more land for Africans, it suggested that such land might be purchased by people of any race.

This would force Africans into competition with Whites and ran contrary to all Smuts's views on territorial segregation which had been the mainstay of his own land policy since the passing of the 1913 Act. His criticisms were clearly not of a liberal character.

Smuts's comments on the Representation of Natives in Parliament Bill seemed equally reactionary. He strongly challenged the legality of Hertzog's plan to deprive the already enfranchised Africans of Cape Province of their right to vote for members of parliament on equal terms with Whites. But he condemned the proposed method of electing representatives of the Africans by the votes of chiefs nominated by the government not only on the obvious ground that this was a travesty of true representation, but also for the less plausible reason that the system would encourage Africans to elect the wrong sort of people to parliament, people who would stir up trouble. Such representatives might be in a position to hold the balance between parties and so could determine policy. In any case, he added, the whole indirect system of electing representatives implied that Africans were not ready to play their part in parliamentary government. He was, moreover, even prepared to see the Cape franchise for Africans phased out provided those already entitled to the vote did not lose that right. Once again the impartial observer was left in grave doubt about the true nature of Smuts's aims.

His comments on the Coloured Persons' Rights Bill were mainly concerned with the clarification of a number of anomalies, but in general they showed little evidence of a liberal attitude towards that section of the population. He rightly pointed out that the definition of a coloured person was an absurdity. Only persons classed as coloured *before* the Bill became law would in future be recognised as coloured. People of similar racial mixture born *after* the enactment of the law would be classed as natives. Enfranchised coloured people in the Cape would retain their voting rights, while their counterparts in other provinces would be enfranchised for the first time but for seven years would elect their representatives on a communal roll. After that they might be given the vote on the same basis as Whites. This, Smuts thought, might possibly give them an undue influence at elections, though his scruples seem unwarranted if no additional coloured people were to be recognised in future. The Bill did contain one further anomaly, he added. While Asians in the Cape were to retain their right to vote, no provision was made to enfranchise those in Natal and the Transvaal where most of them lived.[18] This was true enough, but it is doubtful whether Smuts favoured any increase in the scope of Asian representation. The Union Native Council Bill, the fourth of the measures proposed by Hertzog, which aimed at extending the policies of the 1920 Act, aroused no response from Smuts.

In the event all four Bills, together with Smuts's comments on them, were relegated to the background for a time because Hertzog had to leave for England to attend an imperial conference at which, like Smuts in 1921, though for different reasons, he was at pains to secure a more formal definition of dominion status. While Smuts had wanted to demonstrate that membership of the Commonwealth strengthened South Africa's role in the world while not seriously impeding her freedom of action, Hertzog placed the emphasis on freedom rather than upon mutual responsibility. In the prime minister's absence, Smuts delivered a funeral oration when the ashes of his great friend, Emily Hobhouse, were buried at the foot of the Women's Memorial outside Bloemfontein. While extolling the virtues of one who had done so much for the women and children who had suffered during the Anglo-Boer War, he was at pains to show that Miss Hobhouse had criticised the actions of her own people because there were considerations which transcended national loyalties. It was a lesson, he said, which his own people, the Boers, should take to heart.[19]

It was an inspiring address, at odds with his carping attitude towards Hertzog's efforts in Britain. 'Botha and I', he wrote to Philip Kerr, 'always availed ourselves of these great occasions to put our best foot forward on behalf of our country. But Hertzog remains as *gauche* as ever.'[20] Smuts's friend, Amery, took a less jaundiced view. After discussions with Hertzog, he came to the conclusion that their differences were of emphasis rather than of substance.[21] This view seemed to be borne out when even Tielman Roos, one of the more republican members of the National Party, was overcome by enthusiasm for the Empire after reading the report of the Imperial Relations Committee which was published in November 1926. G.R.Hofmeyr, whose earlier attempt to encourage union between the Nationalists and the South African Party had been dismissed by Smuts as 'simply stupid',[22] felt sufficiently moved by Roos's euphoria to conclude that the time was ripe to renew his efforts. To that end he wrote to both Smuts and Hertzog,[23] adding hopefully to the former that, in the new atmosphere which seemed to prevail, the Nationalists might be prepared to retain the Union Jack as part of the national flag. Hertzog, in fact, suggested that a crown, rather than the Union Jack, should be included in the South African flag, because the Crown was the key element in the imperial association. Smuts, however, treated Hertzog's attempt at compromise with a mixture of amusement, scepticism and wariness. To F.S.Malan he wrote: 'It looks to me as if our English friends are completely losing their heads over Hertzog in their joy at his now having accepted the Empire faith. We have every reason to be careful. Hertzog has given us very little indication of what he really means. He may honestly mean a new orientation. But he may also in his self-satisfaction, only be using pretty phrases.'[24] In a similarly cautious vein he addressed Patrick Duncan:

It is difficult to see what is behind Roos's somewhat wild statements and we must await Hertzog's arrival and declarations before the air will be sufficiently clear to enable us to take stock of the situation. Recent developments ought to have finally killed the National Party and in any well-educated electorate that would certainly have happened. But here they can actually hold up their crushing defeat as an epoch-making victory and justification.[25]

Smuts insisted that the decisions of the imperial conference had made no significant change in the relations between Britain and the dominions, and, in spite of Hertzog's claim that he had ensured South Africa's virtual independence, it must clearly be demonstrated that this was not the case. To Amery, who was relieved that Hertzog had given up the idea of secession from the Empire and was consequently prepared to tolerate any political capital the South African prime minister might try to make out of the imperial conference,[26] Smuts wrote with pedagogic disapproval: 'It would be most mischievous to let the impression take root either in South Africa or Canada that a radical transformation of the Empire has been brought about, and that the Empire in fact has ceased to exist except as a mere collective name. This mischievous impression may easily become the cause of new separatist troubles in the future.'[27] From the last remark it is clear that Smuts's attitude was not due to pique alone, but also to his fear of Nationalist support for Afrikaner separatism. In the debate on the results of the imperial conference in the house of assembly in March 1927, he stressed once again that the inter-imperial committee had not spoken of independence. In spite of the violent attack made upon him by Hertzog for the views he had expressed, he acknowledged the good work the prime minister had done at the conference and invited the government to work with the South African Party for the good of the country now that the idea of secession, one of the great areas of disagreement, had been removed.

Though this seemed like a genuinely conciliatory gesture, it was more in the nature of a tactical move. Smuts was still wary of any close co-operation with the Nationalists. The reunion of his party with its rivals seemed likely to call for too great a sacrifice. 'We should have to go into the cabinet with three or four seats as dependants of the Nats and include all they have already done. Our party would not accept that,' he wrote.[28] To another correspondent who had pressed for the reunion of the two parties he admitted that he would prefer not to discuss the matter further. It was bedevilled by too many pitfalls.[29]

In April Hertzog brought his four Bills on Native Affairs to the house of assembly for their second reading and they were duly referred to a select committee of which Smuts was a member. The committee's task was a difficult one, but Smuts was less than just in attributing its problems solely to the ineptitude of the draftsmen who had prepared the Bills. In spite of his repeated claim to want a solution to the native question, he had little to contribute to that solution which differed markedly from the ideas of the majority of white South Africans at that time. His disagreements with Hertzog, though sometimes wrapped in rhetoric calling for fair treatment for Africans, were in the end only legal quibbles. His cry of 'What a bankruptcy after the great era through which we have passed,'[30] was at best an epitaph to aspirations unfulfilled rather than a lament for achievements now threatened. It was unjustified even in respect of the failure of the Dutch- and English-speaking sections of the population to reach agreement over the design of the national flag, though in the event an accommodation was reached over that question.[31] It was still less appropriate when applied to the differences between the native policies of the two political parties.

Smuts derived little pleasure from the resolution of the flag dispute. Out of office he felt nothing but frustration. He needed the stimulus of involvement in great affairs to arouse his enthusiasm completely and to justify himself in his own eyes. As a member of the opposition he could be only marginally effective even in the concerns of his own country, and he had little claim to a voice in world affairs. His triumphs at the end of the war were now in the past, and the League, to which he had given so much thought, was already struggling. At home he was innately incapable of accepting the greatest challenge which might have engaged his attention, that of dealing with vision with the native question. Instead he bemoaned the fact that the world was in turmoil and he himself was helpless to put it right. Poincaré was up to his old tricks, he claimed, poisoning the atmosphere of Europe with his narrow hatreds and fears, and the Conservative government in England was short-sightedly supporting France in her disastrous policy.[32] 'All political ambition – if I ever had any – is dead in me,' he wrote to Margaret Gillett. Again he talked of quitting politics – this time if the reunion of the Nationalist and South African Parties ever took place.[33] But it was only the voice of frustration that spoke. Smuts did not really want to leave the stage. What he hankered after was the leading role.

Smuts's behaviour during the early part of 1928 underlined his problem. During conversations with Hertzog in February and March he did indeed appear to make constructive suggestions about the native question, and Hertzog readily listened and tried to assess the merits

157

of the ideas put forward. Briefly it seemed that progress was about to
be made, but then Smuts withdrew a little. He insisted that his suggestions were no more than that. He was in no way committed to them.
Hertzog was undismayed, even though Smuts's behaviour effectively
undermined the political significance of the discussions. Over the question of the franchise, the prime minister admitted that he could not
go far as Smuts had suggested and still retain the support of his own
party. What Smuts had proposed was that a franchise based on wages,
salary or occupation tests should be introduced for voters of all races.
The qualifications should be sufficiently low to ensure that only the poorest Whites were excluded while ensuring that the vast majority of Africans were debarred. In addition, he thought it appropriate that all non-
Whites should be subjected to a civilisation test before being granted
the vote. This would guarantee that European standards were secure
for all time. In view of his insistence upon the territorial segregation
of Africans and the absence of any provision for their education along
European lines – save for that available in mission schools – his proposals
could not be regarded as unduly liberal. Yet, if he meant them sincerely,
he seemed to have moved from his former, entrenched position.

Hertzog, however, believed it would be impossible and inappropriate
to restrict white manhood suffrage by imposing even modest financial
qualifications. Nevertheless, he said that he himself was prepared to
give the vote to anyone who met such qualifications and, additionally
in the case of Africans, passed a civilisation test. Over the right of all
who already had the vote in Cape province to retain that right and to
vote on a common roll, the prime minister was willing to defer to Smuts's
view. New lists would be prepared for other Africans meeting the qualifications required of them and they would vote for their own representatives on a communal roll. In the Cape those representatives, all Whites,
to a maximum of five, would sit in the house of assembly. The African
voters in the other three provinces, voting together, would elect five
white members to the senate.

It was a muddled arrangement, and Smuts noted that the proposals
regarding African votes in the three northern provinces constituted a
backward step from Hertzog's earlier suggestion that they should be
represented in the house of assembly, but he did not press the point.[34]
Nor did he overlook the fact that the prime minister appeared to contemplate allowing coloured people in all four provinces who met the franchise qualifications to vote along with Europeans. He did point out,
however, that it would be illogical to exclude qualified Asians from voting
in view of the Cape Town Agreement and of the fact that all other races
could qualify to vote.[35] Hertzog was unable to accept this argument,

but it was an issue over which Smuts had no strong feelings. Like Hertzog he could see no lasting place for Asians in South Africa and that opinion was strengthened still further as Asians became more critical of the conditions under which they were required to live in the Union. A similarity of attitude between the two leaders was also to be seen in Hertzog's willingness, on Smuts's advice, to postpone indefinitely his plan to compensate Africans for the limitations on their representation in parliament by converting the informal, annual native conference into an official Native Council. Smuts's fear was that a council of that sort might consist of agitators who could have an unsettling effect on the African population. In an equally compliant mood, Hertzog agreed it would be wise to look again at the means he had suggested to provide more land for Africans because he wanted to avoid the possible complications to which Smuts had drawn his attention.[36]

The prime minister could be forgiven for thinking that the differences which still existed between Smuts and himself over the native question were of little significance. They were certainly not of such an order as to justify the claim that they fell short of the 'substantive justice' Smuts claimed to be seeking for the African people.[37] Indeed, Hertzog was convinced that he had made such changes to his original scheme on Smuts's recommendation that he should have no difficulty in winning sufficient support from the South African Party to secure the two-thirds majority of both houses of parliament needed to change the constitution. Smuts, however, thought otherwise. It is difficult, therefore, to understand why he ever took part in the discussions with Hertzog, particularly in view of the fact that he claimed he had made it clear to the prime minister that he was only discussing possible improvements to the latter's plan so as to ensure that whatever was decided would be acceptable to members of all races. It was an improbable argument, and when he went on to insist that any view that he had expressed was of a purely personal nature and that he would have to consult his colleagues before reaching any decision, the whole exchange of ideas appears to have been little more than a charade so far as Smuts was concerned. Clearly he had no intention of helping to perpetuate the Nationalist government even by assisting in the solution of such a fundamental problem as native policy. He was contemptuous of all the Nationalists stood for and he was anxious to wield power himself. For that reason the overthrow of Hertzog was essential. He may well have been surprised by Hertzog's own apparent willingness to co-operate. It was not what he would have expected of his rival. It was rather as if both men had been bidding against each other in some political poker game, only to discover that neither had the money to back his stake.

Over another issue the two men crossed swords even while their apparently amicable discussions on native policy were taking place, and on that further question there could be no offer of compromise from either side. On 8 March 1928, Hertzog introduced into the house of assembly a motion approving the report of the imperial conference on dominion status. In the course of the debate which followed, he laid particular emphasis upon the union's right to remain neutral in the event of Britain's becoming involved in war. Smuts regarded this as an extremely questionable aspect of the report and, as he wrote to Amery later in the year, deplored the fact that the prime minister always seemed more concerned with South Africa's right to secede from the Empire than with co-operation and comradeship between Britain and the dominions.[38] He was, too, dissatisfied with the arrangements made for flying the Union Jack under the terms of the Flag Act of 1927. The Act had said that the Union Jack should fly along with the national flag over the houses of parliament and over the main government buildings in the provincial capitals and in such places as the government might determine. Smuts regarded this decision as niggardly and his view was shared by others who favoured closer integration within the Empire.[39] He was also angered by a treaty signed between the South African government and Germany on 16 November 1928 which provided for mutual freedom of trade and a most favoured nation agreement. In spite of all he had said about the need to restore Germany's economy, he could not countenance such a threat to imperial preference. That, he believed, was one of the cornerstones of imperial unity.[40]

It was the native question, however, rather than differences of opinion over South Africa's place within the Empire, which was to dominate the elections which took place in 1929. Smuts believed that he had scored a political triumph in his discussions with Hertzog about native policy. He was convinced that the northern provinces would never accept Hertzog's idea of extending the franchise to Africans outside Cape Province. He would not, therefore, alienate support for the South African Party in that quarter if he continued to oppose Hertzog's Native Bills.[41] But, by skilfully criticising every clause of the legislation when it came up for debate, he was able to give the impression that it was he rather than Hertzog who stood for the principles of justice and fair treatment for the African population. As a result, the government failed completely to obtain the majority needed to change the constitution.[42] It was a hollow victory for Smuts, nevertheless. He had to admit to Margaret Gillett that he had no alternative plan to offer. 'It seems to me', he wrote, 'that it is demanding almost too much of human nature to ask Black and White to be just and fair and generous to each other.'[43] It was a despairing comment, but it threw light not only upon Smuts's attitude to race relations but also upon that of many other members of the Anglo-Saxon race when faced with the problem of living with large numbers of people whose pigmentation differs from their own. Even to some of the more liberal-minded people of his day Smuts's conclusion, that 'We must do our best and act up to our lights, and God will fulfil himself in ways now dark to us', probably sounded less sanctimonious than it does today.

Hertzog did not forgive Smuts for what he firmly believed to be a cynical betrayal of their agreement over native policy and, for wholly sincere reasons, he distrusted Smuts's desire for a close association with Britain. In a vicious electioneering speech in Smithfield, the prime minister accused the South African Party of being crypto-Unionist. Then, turning Smuts's claim to defend the rights of Africans to his own advantage, he maintained that Smuts and his supporters were trying to give Africans equal voting rights.[44] It was a clever move and, although Smuts counterattacked fiercely, he was, from that moment, on the defensive. He tried hard to refute the charges in a speech he made in Pretoria on 30 April 1929. He charged the prime minister with holding dangerously racist views. Had he not condemned Smuts for inviting English-speaking South Africans to join the South African Party in 1920, implying that such people were still foreigners to whom the interests of the Union meant nothing? Such a man could not unite the European races of South Africa which was the all-important goal. The prime minister's statements about Smuts's views on native policy were equally false. Never at any time, said Smuts, had he himself advocated equal voting rights for natives – a claim which was very nearly true, and, in any case, election speeches do not recognise the finer shades of dissimulation. What his party aimed to do, Smuts went on, was to improve and make better use of the reserves and native locations and to extend local self-government in native areas. But Africans did not claim, and the Whites would certainly never concede, equal franchise rights. He accurately represented the views of the Whites in saying this, but ignored the claims of the African National Congress. What was needed, he went on, was a national convention to deal with native policy outside party politics, though once again he vouchsafed no explanation of how a national convention could achieve that aim. As for the charge that his desire to create a great British dominion from the Cape to the Equator meant that he wished to see South Africa absorbed in a kaffir state, he could only answer that it bore no relation to his hope for a white dominion in which European standards of civilisation would prevail. He then went on to condemn the Nationalist government's handling of the economy and its squandering of the country's resources. He criticised the arrangement made with Mozambique for supplying labour for the mines, because it fell far short of what was needed. He upheld the view that there should be no further Asian immigration and that Asians already in South Africa should be repatriated as swiftly as possible. He defended Empire preference and condemned the treaty with Germany, and finally he called for the enfranchisement of European women.[45]

It was a powerful speech and, except for the remarks about the Empire, seemed calculated to appeal to all sections of the white population. But Hertzog had sown the seeds of doubt in many hearts. His warning of a 'black peril', and his claim that Smuts was a party to it, had stirred deeply held fears for the security of white domination. In the eyes of his critics, Smuts's position was further weakened when the Archbishop of Cape Town, together with Sir James Rose-Innes, Henry Burton and a number of others, issued a manifesto in May 1929 which led to the formation of the Non-Racial Franchise Association to defend the Cape franchise and to work for its extension to the rest of the Union.[46] Smuts protested in vain that the group did not represent the views of the South African Party. It was enough for many of the electorate that he had spoken for the retention of the vote by those Africans already enfranchised and had apparently recommended a general franchise qualification for all races.

The result of the elections was almost a foregone conclusion. The South African Party polled a majority of votes throughout the country, but the distribution of parliamentary seats defeated them. The rural constituencies, in which opposition to all forms of advancement for Africans was strongest, tilted the scales. The Nationalists won 78 seats, the South African Party 61, the Labour Party, divided and weak, only 8, and one seat went to an independent. 'We have lost the fight but have saved our soul,' Smuts claimed somewhat unjustly, 'aye, the soul of South Africa.' Possibly with more justice he wrote; 'Hertzog has stampeded the people into racialism with his black bogey, and has an awful responsibility before history.'[47] Looking to England, Smuts sought consolation in the victory of the Labour Party in the elections there 'after the stupidities of the Austen Chamberlain regime'.[48] Perhaps a visit to England would rescue him from the backwater in which he was stagnating after five years in opposition, he thought.

The motive for such a visit was to be found in an invitation he had had to deliver the Rhodes Memorial Lectures in Oxford in the Michaelmas Term of 1929. The topics he chose for the three lectures were all important to him – European settlement in Africa, world peace and native policy. He submitted the draft of his last lecture to Patrick Duncan enquiring whether it was likely to cause any problems within the South African Party. Duncan read the lecture carefully. He was aware that Smuts's views on the handling of native policy were apt to vary unpredictably when he was out of office. Earlier in the year he had had occasion to caution his leader about a speech Smuts had made on Union Day in which he seemed to commit his party to maintaining the Cape franchise although in his discussions with Hertzog he had not insisted on that point.[49] The draft of the lecture promised no such hazards, but in Duncan's opinion it did contain serious errors of fact, and it advocated developments which he thought inappropriate under South African conditions. Smuts was wrong, for example, in suggesting that the system of local government introduced by Rhodes into the Transkei and subsequently extended to other areas by Smuts's own Act of 1920 was aimed at encouraging the development of native institutions. In practice it fostered a British system of local government in a manner thought to be suited to African requirements. The local councils were in no sense extensions of chiefs' courts, as Smuts suggested they were. Their procedure was an adaptation of British methods, and under that system chiefs had to a large extent been deprived of their former authority. Nor would it even be desirable to try to use local government to encourage the development of a distinctive African nationality, as Smuts advocated. What was needed in the Union, in Duncan's view, was the gradual adoption of European standards of civilisation by the African population. This was already being achieved to a limited extent by the involvement of Africans in white-owned industries and by their working on white-owned farms. But undue pressure must not be put upon Africans to leave rural areas in order to hasten what, if it were to succeed, must be a gradual process. On that account Duncan was at one with Smuts in arguing that more land should be made available for Africans in rural areas.[50] He fully understood that the Whites of South Africa would not accept government by an African majority. That was why he regarded the extension of the Cape franchise, even with qualifications, as a dead end. Only a policy of assimilation based on the education of Africans on European lines, and introduced very slowly, held any prospect of being accepted as a very long-term solution.

Smuts had not agreed with Duncan's ideas in 1912 and he rejected them now. Nor did he take any account of his valid criticisms of the interpretation he, Smuts, had put on Rhodes's local government policy. Instead he delivered his lectures in their original form, advocating more European settlement in Africa in order to create a new British dominion and recommending the policy of territorial segregation for Africans. Some of the latter might, he said, be permitted for limited periods to work for Whites, but they must not be accompanied by their families lest they be tempted to abandon their traditional way of life. Ignoring Duncan's warning, he extolled the virtues of Cecil Rhodes's local government policy, incorrectly representing it as having preserved traditional African society while providing a blueprint which South Africa was now following in its local government policy.[51] Perhaps the fact that he was delivering a Rhodes Memorial Lecture provided some justification for Smuts's flights of fancy. It did not justify his blindness to what was really happening in South Africa. Educated Africans had for years been trying, against innumerable obstacles, to adopt European standards of behaviour. Africans, with their families, were living on white-owned farms. Only the large mining companies had been successful in limiting their labour force to men, without their families, who worked for only limited periods in the mines. Driven by a shortage of land in rural areas, however, other Africans had sought to supplement their incomes by seeking temporary employment in areas reserved for Whites. In its revelation of Smuts's hopes, rather than of the true situation, his lecture was in the same self-deluding vein as the claim he so often made in Britain that the Europeans of South Africa had been happily united by Britain's magnanimity and by the efforts of Botha and himself.

Though the lectures were acclaimed by his English audience, Duncan was not alone in South Africa in finding Smuts's views on native policy wide of the mark. The *Cape Times*, a newspaper which usually supported the South African Party, remarked that the native policy described by Smuts with such enthusiasm had made little headway. 'The picture, for instance, of the native question in South Africa which General Smuts presented to the guileless and unworldly eyes of Oxford, seemed to South Africans to have almost scandalously little resemblance to local realities,'[52] an editorial commented. In an article in the same paper the historian, Dr J. S. Marais, said that the absence of any clash of interests between European settlers and Africans claimed by Smuts might be achieved one day, but only if the colonists became wholly altruistic beings. So far the whole history of colonisation had been one of clashes. Nor was the additional land which Smuts said should be given to Africans in any way adequate for their needs if they were to pursue the traditional way of life which he wished to encourage.[53]

Smuts was deeply hurt by the criticisms, attributing them to some campaign which was being waged against him.[54] He was unable to comprehend that anything about which he felt so strongly could be wrong, or even that there might be a valid difference of opinion about it. Like Milner before him, he believed that men of intelligence and goodwill could not fail to share his views. It was the error of the intellectual who mistakes the concept for the reality and cannot be convinced of his error. In conversation with the elderly colonial administrator, Lord Lugard, he continued to argue for territorial segregation and separate administration for Africans and Europeans, even in Kenya. There, because the number of European settlers was small, the difficulty of justifying his policy was proportionately greater.[55]

If Smuts felt he was not adequately appreciated in his own country, he could not doubt that his qualities were amply recognised in other quarters. King George repeatedly invited him to stay at Sandringham, and he received numerous invitations to visit America. He spent a day with the British prime minister, Ramsay MacDonald, and he received a long letter from Chaim Weizmann setting out the errors of the British administration in Palestine and seeking his aid, as the main instigator of the Balfour Declaration, in urging the British government to fulfil its responsibility for establishing a Jewish homeland in Palestine.[56] In the end Smuts gave in to the importunities of his American admirers and spent a lively three weeks in the United States at the beginning of 1930. He enjoyed his visit immensely. He had a royal reception, he told Isie in one of his letters to her. To his friend, T.W. Lamont, an American banker whom he had first met at the Paris peace conference, he said he could not understand why he had not gone there ten years earlier.[57]

On his return to England, Smuts addressed a meeting of the Empire Parliamentary Association. He stressed the importance of countering talk of the independence of the dominions, which might lead to the Empire's disintegration, while making it clear that real unity existed within the Empire. He also spoke of how he had tried to explain to the Americans the real nature of the League of Nations. It was an idiosyncratic interpretation which, if correct, meant that events might easily get out of hand before decisive action could be taken. Explaining how he had put the case, Smuts said that the Americans were suffering from a severe reaction against their involvement in the First World War and were deeply suspicious of the continuing friction between the European powers. In that frame of mind they had come to regard the League as a coercive body which interfered in the affairs of nations and by so doing increased the likelihood of war. That was why he had been at pains to emphasise the League's conciliatory role. He had pointed out, he said, that only when every effort at *rapprochement* and arbitration had failed would there be any resort to economic sanctions or more strict coercion. He had had to admit that the covenant did not entirely measure up to the interpretation he was putting upon it, but he had countered by pointing out that, if the peace pact recently engineered by the American secretary of state, Frank B. Kellogg – which over sixty countries had adopted and of which the Americans were justly proud – were to be effective, there must be some means of enforcing it. Good intentions alone were not enough.[58] All too soon, events were to prove him right.

On his return to South Africa in February Smuts immediately became involved in the native question. Fortified by the new mandate he had received in the recent elections, Hertzog appointed a select committee to look at his Bills on native policy once more, and Smuts became a member of the committee. Reaction was in the air, partly because of the speeches Hertzog had made during the election campaign and partly because of clashes between Europeans and Africans in Durban in November 1929 when police, pursuing tax defaulters, had used tear gas to disperse spectators. Possibly in response to the criticisms to which he had recently been subjected, Smuts entered upon the new deliberations with the appearance of greater flexibility of outlook and a more sympathetic view of Africans' needs. But he was still pessimistic about the outcome. 'The way out is as dark as ever,' he wrote to Margaret Gillett, but continued more positively:

My own thought is beginning to come to acceptance of Hertzog's scheme for the Cape only, *plus* the removal of the colour bar of the South Africa Act (so that natives can sit in Parliament and represent their own people) and *plus* a provision which will enable Natives with a certain education qualification to remain voting with the whites instead of in separate native constituencies.[59]

This was probably the most liberal pronouncement Smuts ever made on the native question. In the same vein, while rejoicing over the enfranchisement of European women in 1930, for which he had himself campaigned, he regretted that the new law had introduced yet another colour bar. He claimed, too, to have been moved to the edge of despair by the Riotous Assemblies (Amendment) law which had been enacted by the government in the atmosphere of unease arising from the disturbances in Durban. The law gave the minister of justice power to expel from any district a person whose presence he believed might lead to hostility between the races. In a letter to Margaret Gillett, Smuts suggested that there remained little for him to do but to drift with the tide.[60] Mrs Gillett was not prepared to indulge defeatist sentiments of that sort. If he no longer found any purpose in South Africa, she replied, why did he not quit the country and work for the League of Nations or some other international project?[61] It was a reasonable question, but Smuts did not respond. As always, in spite of his concern for world affairs, and especially for the League, he shied away from the idea of becoming permanently involved in events outside South Africa. It was as if he feared such a degree of commitment, preferring the role of oracle to that of administrator.

Meanwhile his spirits had been briefly raised by a letter written to the press by D. D. T. Jabavu, virtually the only African leader whose existence Smuts recognised. Jabavu had argued that there should be no change in the Cape franchise until Africans were allowed to take their seats in parliament. This was an idea with which Smuts had himself been toying. Now, fortified by the opinion of Jabavu, he wondered whether the proposal, if implemented, might not offer the prospect of reducing hostility between the Africans and their white rulers. If it were adopted, might it not then be reasonable, even in African eyes, to insist upon a differential franchise for the two races since Africans so heavily outnumbered Europeans? But caution prevailed. Even in a moment of enthusiasm Smuts felt it impossible to follow his idea to its logical conclusion. It would be wrong, he thought, for African representatives to sit in the house of assembly. Their place should be in the senate.[62] Instinctive prejudice triumphed over reasoned argument, even in a private letter. Nevertheless Smuts did not openly oppose his own party when, under Duncan's direction, it advocated the retention of a European majority in the electorate while permitting Africans who held the required qualifications to vote along with European voters for European members of parliament.[63] It was a policy which was difficult to reconcile with Smuts's own views on territorial segregation and on African social development along traditional lines. But with Smuts, logic went overboard when the native question was under discussion. Humane considerations pushed him in one direction, instinct in another.

Fortunately, perhaps, further consideration of the matter was deferred until the next session of parliament after the select committee had failed to make any progress in its deliberations. Without leaving South Africa Smuts was able to escape, at least intellectually, to a wider field of endeavour. The South African Jewish community had, since the previous year, been protesting about the bias they claimed was shown by British administrators in Palestine against their co-religionists who wished to settle there or who were already resident in their national home. Duncan considered the arguments exaggerated, but Smuts felt obliged to act on the Jews' behalf. A White Paper, published in October 1930, which set out British policy in Palestine, provided the occasion for a telegram to Ramsay MacDonald. In it Smuts accused Britain of failing to meet her obligations and called for a reaffirmation of the Balfour Declaration.[64] Simultaneously he telegraphed Lloyd George asking him to make similar representations.[65] MacDonald replied that, if Smuts were to read the full text of the White Paper and the report of Sir John Hope Simpson upon which the paper was based, he would realise that Britain was already fulfilling both aspects of the mandate. Efforts were already being made to establish a Jewish national home and those efforts would continue. At the same time, Britain must protect the interests of the Arab population of Palestine, and that was not an easy task in the changing circumstances resulting from Jewish immigration.[66] With that reply Smuts expressed himself satisfied.[67]

Smuts also grudgingly admitted, but only to Margaret Gillett, that Hertzog had been 'less stupid and provocative than some of his colleagues'[68] during the 1930 session of the imperial conference, but that in no way prevented him from reopening the party struggle when the prime minister returned to South Africa. He did so by an act which was mischievous rather than malicious, though he must clearly have anticipated the outcome. The occasion was a statement by Hertzog that, having finally settled the status of South Africa, the next great task was to effect a reconciliation between Boers and Britons in the Union with the aim of achieving national unity. It was an indication of the prime minister's sincerity that he went so far as to attack the republicans in his own party for resisting such unity. Smuts, however, could not refrain from pointing out that his own party had, all along, taken the lead on both those two issues and it was the Nationalists who had dragged their feet. Hertzog, the most courteous of men in private conversation, lacked a sense of humour and could easily be provoked in parliament where he felt himself to be on public display. At once he rounded on Smuts in an angry, sarcastic tirade and, although his tormentor swore that he had given the prime minister total credit for his sincerity, all hope of a *rapprochement* initiated by the Nationalists was dashed.[69]

Soon after the reopening of the new parliamentary session in 1931, a select committee was again appointed to look into the Native Bills, but little progress was made. Smuts's view was that public feeling among the Whites was so strong that Africans were likely to be totally denied representation in the house of assembly if the committee reached a decision in any way favourable to them.[70] How far that opinion reflected Smuts's own feelings about the franchise it is impossible to say at a time when his ideas, it not his opinions, had oscillated widely. Generally his views coincided more closely with European attitudes towards native policy than they did over other issues because that was a matter where his instinct prevailed over his intellect. Nevertheless, in his confused state of mind he was glad when the parliamentary session was over. The frustrations of being in opposition drained him far more completely than did the responsibilities of office.

With parliament adjourned Smuts was able to make a more complete break with South African affairs than he had done even twenty months earlier. Recently he had been elected President of the British Society for the Advancement of Science for its centenary year. He had at once suggested that the occasion should be marked by inviting leading scientists from the dominions to attend the annual conference to be held in 1931. He himself then prepared the presidential address on the subject 'The Scientific World Picture of Today', which he delivered in London on 23 September. It contained a formidable survey of recent developments in mathematics, physics, biology, physiology and astronomy. This was followed by a leap to philosophy and theology, which was achieved by skilful sleight of hand rather than by academic argument and he ended by emphasising the scientist's role in bridging the gap which had opened between scientific advances and ethical development.[71] It was a *tour de force* for one who had been so heavily engaged for so many years in political affairs on both a national and international scale, and for a few days Smuts revelled in mixing with scientists and being accepted by them. Though he wrote with appropriate if rather forced modesty that he thought he had managed to conceal his errors and shortcomings with some success, he had obviously enjoyed playing a new and exhilarating role before an appreciative audience. What matter that the appreciation was more courteous than critical!

With customary ease he turned his back on his triumph and at once became absorbed in European politics. His first impression on arriving in England had been that the people were rattled. Repayment of the war debt was imposing a crushing burden on the country and the people were wilting under the weight of taxation. The only answer appeared to be to adopt a protectionist policy.[72] A crisis in the cabinet, with Ramsay MacDonald, the prime minister of the National government formed on 21 August 1931, threatening to resign, led to an urgent telephone call from the King requesting Smuts to present himself in London to give his advice. Smuts arrived the following morning to find the crisis had been resolved during the night.[73] The government had decided that it was essential to seek a mandate from the electorate if it was to deal adequately with the desperate financial situation in which the country found itself. Three weeks later elections were held and the government won a landslide victory.

Meanwhile, in mid-October, Smuts visited Germany, his expenses being generously paid by Arthur and Margaret Gillett. He had talks there with several leading politicians and financiers and the impression made upon him by what he heard and saw disturbed him deeply. There appeared to be every likelihood of an imminent political and financial crash. France had Germany at her mercy, while America seemed to have lost interest in Europe and Britain was wholly absorbed in her own affairs. In those circumstances Smuts felt he had an obligation to stay in England a little longer to try to impress upon the new government the gravity of the situation on the Continent.[74]

He had, too, another important task. In November 1930 the then Labour government had summoned a round-table conference to discuss the effectiveness of the 1919 Government of India Act in the light of a report recently submitted by Sir John Simon. The Congress Party had boycotted the conference, but some progress had been made early in 1931 when Ramsay MacDonald had induced the Indian princes to agree to the future federation of the states over which they ruled. About the same time, M.K.Gandhi, now the leading figure in the Indian National Congress, began talks with the Viceroy, Lord Irwin, which were continued in England during a second round-table conference starting in September. Early in November, Gandhi wrote to Smuts asking him to discuss India's problems with him. The two men met on a number of occasions and Smuts also had talks with MacDonald. He quickly came to the conclusion that Gandhi had reached a stage in his thinking which might make it possible for the conference to reach a successful conclusion.[75] He did not underestimate the difficulties still ahead. Though the political issues were not insoluble, the temper and temperament of the Indian people were unpredictable. Gandhi himself, in Smuts's view, was a great asset in the negotiations. He was an honest man in spite of his vagaries. He was, too, the only Indian leader with any real influence among his fellow-countrymen. It was worthwhile, therefore, to show patience in dealing with him even if it meant that there would have to be innumerable conferences and discussions in which Indians took such great pleasure. A settlement was possible, Smuts believed, though they were dealing with a very tiresome and suspicous people.[76]

He was wrong. Communal issues, which he thought he had persuaded Gandhi to shelve, proved a total stumbling-block. The conference broke down and Gandhi returned to India to resume his campaign of civil disobedience. Smuts himself attributed the breakdown to MacDonald's failure to follow his advice, though he admitted the Congress leaders were 'quite impossible'. He had, he claimed, presented the prime minister with an agreed constitutional solution and MacDonald must have let success slip through his fingers.[77] His own experiences in South Africa of the gap between negotiations and their successful implementation might have led him to take a more charitable view of the prime minister's efforts.

By the time the conference came to an end Smuts was back in the Union and deeply involved in his own political troubles. On the voyage home he had taken the opportunity to read Bertrand Russell's *The Scientific Outlook*, C.G.Darwin's *The New Conception of Matter* and, most important of all, L.S.B.Leakey's *The Stone Age Culture in Kenya Colony*. For a time his mind had been totally absorbed by scientific speculation. Politics were forgotten, and there emerged the idea for a lecture he was to give six months later to the South African Society for the Advancement of Science on 'Climate and Man in Africa'. Once on shore, however, he took up his campaign against the government at once, charging them with killing the exporting industries and bringing business to a standstill by their insistence upon restoring the gold standard.[78] Duncan agreed with his criticisms and, writing to his old friend, Lady Selborne, added that the farmers, too, had suffered from the government's policies. To appease them the government had unwisely adopted a policy of granting ever larger bounties and, as a distraction, it was proposing to introduce a decimal coinage to demonstrate South Africa's independence from Britain.[79]

Before Smuts could come to grips fully with the prime minister over the economy, another matter claimed Hertzog's attention. The Cape Town Agreement, dealing with the treatment of Indians in South Africa, had come up for review. The second round-table conference on the subject, which opened under Hertzog's chairmanship in January 1932, quickly revealed that Europeans were still looking for a reduction in the size of the Indian population, but the assisted emigration scheme was not achieving that aim. Indians, on the other hand, were claiming the right to attain to any position or civil status to which their capacities enabled them to rise in fulfilment of the terms of the Cape Town Agreement as they interpreted them, a claim which the government would not recognise. In view of those differences, the outcome of the conference was a minor triumph for Hertzog and for those responsible for drafting a statement obscure enough to be acceptable to all parties involved. Its main recommendation was that every effort should be made to find some other country where South African Indians might settle and acquire land with a reasonable prospect of economic prosperity and social advancement.[80] It was neither an ambitious nor an imaginative scheme, but it served the immediate purpose of avoiding open conflict.

The parliamentary session had opened in the fourth week of January and the opposition saw a glimmer of hope for the economy when Hertzog announced the appointment of a select committee to look at the question of the gold standard. The hope was short-lived, for the prime minister quickly made it clear that his intention was merely to demonstrate the need to resist any change in policy.[81] The skill with which he silenced critics among his own party not only depressed Duncan but also led

171

him to reflect upon the nature of Hertzog's hold over his supporters. His power 'certainly does not come from intellectual endowment,' he wrote to Lady Selborne.

When he tries to argue out some point a rising fog seems to envelop himself and his hearers alike. The ideas which attract him are almost always the most obvious and superficial. He is the apostle of the short view. But that is also the religion of most of his followers. And in sentiment he shares with them that latent sense of racial grievance which makes them cherish the memories of wrongs and look for slights from the other section. To all this he responds like a tuned string . . . . So perhaps I have already explained his ascendancy.[82]

From this perceptive comment the differences between Smuts and Hertzog emerge clearly. It also explains why they were for so long at loggerheads. Both were equally sincere in their views, but neither could believe in the sincerity of the other because neither could understand how the other reached his conclusions. While Hertzog responded to and reflected the views of his supporters, Smuts, with his powerful intellect and penetrating vision, produced his own ideas and expected men of intelligence to agree with him. Many years earlier someone had written a jingle which ran: 'He longs to be an autocrat does Smuts, To rise above all party tiffs and Rule without annoying "Ifs" or "Buts".'[83] There was little truth in those sentiments at the time they were originally uttered. Only in his later years could it fairly be said that Smuts looked for loyalty rather than ability in his supporters. Earlier in his career he had certainly grown impatient when others did not see issues as clearly as he did himself, and he had deplored, as he continued to do, the fact that so many Afrikaners defended their racial exclusivism. Though he saw himself as fulfilling his true vocation by leading South Africa into the paths of righteousness, as he defined them, he yearned for others to go along with him willingly, and he had always been ready, in his early days, to seek advice from those he knew had greater experience than he had himself. Later in life, as he became more aware of his intellectual superiority, he grew more remote from popular feeling. It was by chance rather than by design that his views on the Empire coincided with those of the British population of South Africa. It was equally by chance that his views on the native question sometimes sounded an echoing chord among his fellow-countrymen. Because these occasions were infrequent or because insufficient numbers responded to his call, Smuts became irascible. Lacking the qualities needed by a politician, he tended to react in an authoritarian fashion. Instead of explaining himself, he relied on assertions which, however sincere, often seemed inscrutable even to his admirers. In opposition this characteristic was still further tempered by frustration and it was increasingly difficult for people to know him. Hertzog, by contrast, could always appeal to Afrikaner nationalism to win support, and it was a much more powerful motivating force than those who attribute all political alignments to economic causes are prepared to admit. In Duncan's opinion even the gold standard was used by Hertzog's government as an instrument of national independence rather than as a significant economic determinant.

Hertzog himself, however, was beginning to lose support. As the farmers increasingly came under pressure from the economic crisis, numbers of unskilled Europeans, many of them Afrikaners, as well as many Africans, were again beginning to drift to the towns in search of employment. But there was no work to be found in the towns and unemployed Europeans began to listen to the voices of the Labour Party leaders who were denouncing the Chamber of Mines because of the apparent prosperity of the mining industry at a time when so many South Africans were hard pressed. In so doing they ignored the stern fact that it was the steady output of gold which alone was holding the country's economy together during a period of world-wide economic stress.

With the opening of the parliamentary session it was the native question which again occupied Smuts's attention, as a new select committee began its abortive investigations. Once again Duncan put his finger on the essentials of the problem.

The people of South Africa – the European people – will not give up the idea that the country is theirs, the only home they have for themselves and their children [he wrote to Lady Selborne]. They do not consider that they are here as invaders with no title as against the natives but that of conquest . . . . But of course it is not really a question in the end of title, legal or moral. In the end it is a question of survival in numbers and on that ground our prospects here do not look very bright. But the point here which makes our position different from most is that we are here as a minority having built up the country out of barbarism and established conditions under which the other race could flourish in peace, and we claim the right to rule not as trustees but as a dominant and civilised race ruling their own country and with it the subject race which partly for the comfort and partly for the embarrassment of the rulers will persist in inhabiting it.

Smuts would doubtless have agreed with most of this outline, though he might have wished to make some play with the idea of a civilising mission which Duncan more realistically avoided. He would, however, have taken issue with Duncan when he went on to write:

173

That works all right so long as the under race is content with its primitive state and does not feel the stirrings of national and political feelings. When they do – as they are beginning to do here now – the trouble begins and grows apace. What the end will be, whether we will slowly evolve into a Jamaica or be the ancestors of a new brown race no one can tell. But it certainly seems unlikely that the white man will be able permanently to maintain the outlook to which he clings now.[84]

To such defeatist sentiments Smuts would never have succumbed, and, while blindly ignoring the growth of African political consciousness, he continued to reject firmly the ideas both of miscegenation and of African rule. As always he was baffled by two conflicting emotions – the desire to give justice to all men and a deeply ingrained conviction that Africans and Europeans were fundamentally different, which made co-operation on equal terms impossible.

From the obscurities of the native question Smuts was diverted to another racial problem about which he felt he could act with confidence. Faced by financial difficulties for which it seemed impossible to find a solution, the provincial council of the Orange Free State had threatened to resign. Dr D. F. Malan, minister of the interior, responded by proposing an inquiry into the provincial system which, Smuts feared, might threaten the degree of independence which the provinces still enjoyed.[85] If Smuts was worried, Natal was thrown into a panic. The predominantly English-speaking European community had always been suspicious of an Afrikaner government. They went in constant dread of secession from the Empire and were anxious to preserve their freedom of manoeuvre in such an eventuality. They had been worried by the underlying implications of the decimal currency proposed by a Nationalist government which they saw as savouring of republicanism. Now, Malan's plan for a commission of inquiry into provincial government seemed even more menacing. Natal members of parliament – who were also members of the South African Party – met on 4 June and decided to form a separate Natal federal group, as a wing of the party, with a view to protecting the province's interests. Their leader, G. Heaton Nicholls, a front-bench member of the opposition in parliament, went further, writing to Smuts to say that the people of Natal would like to see a federal relationship introduced for all four provinces. They would not, he wrote, presume to insist on this, but they were anxious that Natal at least should be granted federal status.[86]

Smuts consulted Duncan, who thought the Natal proposals would create an impossible situation for the South African Party.[87] Smuts was in total agreement. He had fought for union and he was convinced that a federal relationship would weaken still further the ties between Britons and Boers. It was equally important to avoid any amendment to the South Africa Act lest such a breach should destroy the whole. In October Smuts visited Natal, and by the force of his arguments appeared to have brushed the rebellion aside. Unfortunately, no one was sure at the end of the discussions exactly what had been decided. Duncan commented sceptically that it would be as easy for the South African Party to carry out those decisions as it had been for the Allies to live up to Wilson's Fourteen Points.[88]

Nicholls was far from content to let Smuts dispose of the Natal protest without rejoinder. In a speech in Empangeni he denounced Smuts's efforts to build up a South African nationalism. Smuts countered this challenge vigorously, both in a speech delivered in Turffontein, near Johannesburg, and in a letter to Nicholls himself.[89] At the same time, he made it clear that the South African Party held no brief for the government's provincial policy, and he introduced a resolution at the party's congress in Bloemfontein in December which sought to uphold the existing rights of the provinces.[90]

It was less easy to defeat the challenge offered by Hertzog who, in an attempt to undermine Smuts's apparent success in Natal, started a rumour that, in the course of his negotiations, Smuts had bound himself to destroy South Africa's national status and to change the agreement which guaranteed the equality of the English and Dutch languages. The prime minister's aim was to tempt some Afrikaners from their allegiance to the South African Party and he was delighted when a number of English-speakers in Pretoria and elsewhere reinforced the rumour by forming British leagues to protect the English language.[91] It was a difficult time for Smuts, and the fact that he was forced to formulate a policy at his party's congress which, in Duncan's words, 'should mean two or three different things without altogether meaning any of them'[92] was a clear indication that traditional differences within the party were not dead. The South African national spirit did not always manifest itself in unsullied form, even in what Smuts would claim was its natural home.

In the meantime, the select committee on the Native Bills had failed to reach any conclusion after a third parliamentary session. So the Governor-General, the Earl of Clarendon, appointed the members of the committee to a commission which would carry on and, it was hoped, speed up the work by presenting a report. To clear the way Hertzog agreed not to proceed with his Coloured Persons' Rights Bill.[93] Smuts, however, came to the conclusion that no advance would be made along lines which he would find acceptable and advised those of his own party who were members of the commission to resign so that the South African Party

175

would not be associated with the proposals contained in the final report.[94] Duncan alone rejected the advice, believing that to boycott the proceedings was a negative gesture. Instead he took part in the discussions with vigour, arguing that the segregation policy advocated by Hertzog – as, indeed, by Smuts, though Duncan did not draw attention to that fact – really meant that Europeans wanted the labour of Africans but not the Africans themselves. He was prepared to accept segregation, he said, if the National Party members of the commission would begin by getting rid of the African labourers on their farms. His comments rapidly brought the deliberations to an inconclusive close,[95] which satisfied Smuts, though he could not have been in sympathy with the case which Duncan had presented.

If the South African Party had its problems, the Nationalists, too, now began to show signs of weakness. First, several members of the Labour Party who had co-operated with Hertzog's government were now in despair over his economic policies. Finding themselves ineffective as critics under the existing party alignment, they were persuaded by Smuts to join the South African Party.[96] Next, trouble arose as a result of the machinations of that flamboyant and unpredictable figure, Tielman Roos. Roos had retired from the government in 1929 because of ill health, and he had later been promoted to the bench to avoid the embarrassment of having him once again on the political scene. The judiciary did not satisfy his restless spirit and he soon let it be known that he would like to return to politics. Hertzog made it clear that he would not have him in the cabinet and Roos then started rumours that he would be prepared to form a coalition government in alliance with any group willing to accept his leadership. Smuts, whom he approached, was wary of committing his party to such an unreliable ally, though he was not averse from undermining Hertzog. He watched hopefully, therefore, while Roos made his impact upon some of the Afrikaners who had hitherto supported the prime minister. Roos had always been a popular if rather unprincipled politician and he knew how to cultivate the press. He was thus able to arouse immediate and vocal support from many who simply wanted a change from the apparently endless economic problems from which the country was suffering. They had little idea how such a change might be effected, but their strident voices stirred unease and speculation. At length the government was forced to abandon the gold standard which, as proof of South Africa's independence, it had defended so vigorously. In an attempt to conceal what he had done, Hertzog simultaneously imposed restrictions on exchange transactions, but the cover-up deceived no one and there were loud demands from the opposition for his resignation on the ground that he had abandoned the policy which his government had regarded as the foundation stone of all its actions.[97]

When parliament opened on 20 January 1933, Roos was still making extravagant gestures to win support. Smuts shrewdly estimated that the frenzy of his campaign was an indication of declining confidence. The government had weathered the immediate storm arising from the abandonment of the gold standard and Roos seemed to have shot his bolt. Smuts guessed, however, that Hertzog had been profoundly worried by what had taken place and might be more amenable to friendly overtures from the South African party. On 24 January, therefore, he proposed a motion in the house of assembly advocating the formation of a national government. He gave no indication as to how the government would be constituted or who would be prime minister, and Hertzog decided he could not accept such a vague proposal. The motion was defeated, but the prime minister, sensing the likelihood of defeat in the forthcoming elections, had decided that the Nationalists had much to gain from co-operation with the South African Party. He also feared that to reject all consideration of coalition would drive Smuts into a closer alliance with the more extreme imperialist element among the population and thus pose an even greater threat to the hopes of the Afrikaners. When, however, he raised the idea of discussing coalition in his cabinet, members were sharply divided. Nevertheless, after pondering further, he determined to approach Smuts in what, in spite of opposition, he firmly believed to be the interests of the National Party. Smuts accepted his overture, and on 16 February talks between the two leaders began, Hertzog being accompanied by his minister of finance, N.C. Havenga, and Smuts by Patrick Duncan. There was little disagreement between the two parties except over the question of native policy. Smuts was anxious that no legislation should be enacted on that subject during the period of co-operation lest the South African Party be associated with measures of which he did not wholly approve. For a time the discussions seemed in danger of foundering over that one issue, but Smuts finally compromised and the two leaders were able to announce to their supporters the terms on which a coalition might be contemplated.[98]

It remained to be seen whether the two men could carry their parties with them. Hertzog knew that Dr D.F. Malan was only prepared to agree to a coalition so long as it upheld Nationalist principles, and Malan had considerable support among Cape Afrikaners. The prime minister was very conscious of the fact that, in the course of his discussions with Smuts, he had conceded that South Africa should remain a loyal, co-operative member of the British Commonwealth of Nations – a title

177

which was beginning to supercede that of 'Empire'. Fortune favoured him, however, for Malan was convinced that, in spite of Roos's blandishments and the economic problems of the farmers, Hertzog still commanded the support of the vast majority of his party and that it would be impolitic to challenge him at the next elections. He must bide his time, while continuing to insist that nothing should be allowed to threaten the Union's right to remain neutral in the event of an imperial war and, if necessary, to secede from the Commonwealth.[99]

Smuts, too, had his difficulties, but, in spite of the doubts and uncertainties to which the plan for a coalition had given rise, he could still, it seemed, rely on the loyalty of most of his party, though some had their doubts and Natal had greeted the idea with horror.[100] The country members in the Transvaal had for some time been engaged in a bitter political struggle with their fellow-Afrikaners of the National Party. This had resulted in deep social and political divisions, so that Smuts's decision now puzzled them greatly. But the fact that he had committed himself to coalition was enough to convince them that it was right.[101] Had he not led them in the war against the British thirty years ago? And had they not, nevertheless, followed him into a coalition with the pro-British Unionist Party in 1920? Clearly they could not desert him at this time of crisis. There was some discontent, it must be admitted, among those members of the South African Party who had hoped for ministerial office in the event of an election victory, and among others who believed they would have won seats in parliament if they had been allowed to contest them.[102] But there was no doubt that the country's economic problems remained to be solved, and the more moderate elements in both parties recognised the fact. Gradually they came to accept the idea of coalition, leaving those on both sides for whom the political struggle had become almost a religion to continue in opposition.

For Smuts the coalition held promise. Though he had agreed that Hertzog should lead the government, he would himself be back in office, as minister of justice, after nine frustrating years in opposition. He had, it is true, enjoyed the opportunities he had had during that time to read widely and to pursue his interest in botany and philosophy, but even in office he always made time for those pursuits. Certainly his statement to Margaret Gillett that he wished his life could continue as it had done recently 'to the end'[103] was far from representing his real feelings. The opportunity for action was both a pleasure and an obligation. He would have been denying both his personal predilections and his deeply felt vocation to have stood on the side lines indefinitely while his country was governed by others. By bringing his party into a coalition with the Nationalists he was convinced that he had taken one more vital step towards the fulfilment of his enduring aim to unite the European races of South Africa.

8

The collaborator

Even amid the grave political struggles in which he was involved in South Africa in the early 1930s, Smuts's concern for events in other parts of the world, and particularly those affecting the League of Nations, remained as strong as ever. Japan's attack on Manchuria in 1931 and her subsequent withdrawal from the League in March 1933, after having been called upon by the assembly to return her conquests to China, had struck a heavy blow against the policy of peace through negotiation. Hitler's barbarous treatment of the Jews in Germany, where he had become Chancellor on 30 January 1933, sickened Smuts, who looked upon the Jews both as founders of modern religious faith and as a constant civilising factor in Western society for over a thousand years.[1] In June he had an opportunity to make his voice heard in an international forum as one of three South African representatives at the world monetary and economic conference which met in London, but it was to no avail. The conference adjourned without achieving any measure of agreement. As always, however, Smuts was in demand as a speaker on academic occasions and at meetings concerned with international affairs.[2] One other event also gave him pleasure. On 8 June he received an invitation to travel in the royal carriage procession with the King and Queen to the opening of South Africa House in Trafalgar Square, when it was his duty to present the South African High Commissioner to Their Majesties.[3]

During his absence from the Union the new government faced a heavy assault from some of its own supporters as well as from its opponents. The reason for the attack was the rise in the level of taxation on mining profits which had resulted from the abandonment of the gold standard.[4] The protest was short-lived, because the price of gold continued to rise and activity on the share market recommenced. By August the recovery in the mining industry was so great that some of the Nationalists began to accuse the government of not taxing the industry sufficiently severely.[5] The coalition was beginning to work, and was achieving widespread acceptance. When Smuts returned to South Africa he found a growing movement, particularly among Afrikaans-speakers, in favour of carrying things further by fusing the two parties. The supporters of the South

African Party who lived in the towns, and particularly the British, were inclined to hold aloof through fear of being swamped by the rural Afrikaners.[6]

Smuts himself was suspicious of the move, mainly because Hertzog seemed to be strongly in favour of it. Inevitably he assumed that the prime minister had espoused the idea for purely selfish reasons.[7] He had misjudged his man. There can be little doubt that Hertzog genuinely believed that a union between the two parties would produce a more effective government, and he had no ulterior motive. Challenged by Malan, who still feared that anything stronger than coalition would threaten the survival of Afrikaner principles, Hertzog made it clear that he was not contemplating any casual fusion between every element within the two parties. He wanted a union only of those members who were prepared to put South African interests first. He was confident that, if a union of that sort were achieved, there could be no threat to the ideals which Malan cherished so dearly. He could see no objection to members of a union government advocating republicanism if they wished to do so, though they must achieve a two-thirds majority of both houses of parliament if they wished to make their policy effective. As for Malan's concern to protect South Africa's right to remain neutral in time of war and to secede from the commonwealth if it wished to do so, were not those rights already implicit in the Kellogg Pact, which had renounced war as an instrument of policy, and in the Union's membership of the League of Nations in its own right?[8]

The nature of Hertzog's discussions with Malan were unknown to Smuts and his supporters, who feared lest the prime minister should be forced to agree to a compromise which would be unacceptable to the South African Party. Contrary to those expectations, Hertzog put his own opinions openly to the test at a meeting of the Cape congress of the National Party in Port Elizabeth on 4 October 1933. Malan, on his home territory, took up the challenge, and his resolution opposing the fusion of the two parties was adopted by 142 votes to 30. Deeply distressed, Hertzog left the congress and quitted Port Elizabeth by the next train.[9] Malan was emboldened by his success and openly challenged Hertzog to split the National Party.

For a moment, in February 1934, it seemed that the prime minister was wavering. In an exchange of letters with Malan the impression was gained by South African Party observers that he had conceded his rival's demands and that any united party would adopt as a principle South Africa's right to neutrality and to secede from the Commonwealth. Smuts wrote at once to ask Hertzog if the agreement on which the coalition had been established still held good. The points upon which he laid stress were the status of the Union as a fully co-operating member of the Commonwealth, the British nationality of citizens of the Union – which Malan had called into question – and the rejection of official party propaganda in support of a republic.[10] Hertzog was not dissimulating. In his view he had made a clear distinction in his letters to Malan between the right of individuals to express their opinions and the policy of a united government. He had no difficulty, therefore, in accepting the points raised by Smuts.[11] Hertzog no longer seriously contemplated the possibility that imperial interests would supersede those of the Union unless too aggressive a campaign for a republic were to cause a backlash of pro-British feeling. He was far from pleased, therefore, when Smuts published their correspondence as a counter-blast to Malan's propaganda.

Smuts made amends by speaking strongly in support of the second reading of a Status of the Union Bill which Hertzog introduced into parliament. His aim in doing so was to silence the doubting voices, some of them vociferous, among his own supporters, and to reassure Hertzog's followers that he was not at loggerheads with their leader. Once the Bill was enacted as Law No. 48 of 1934 the two men were able to set about producing a programme of principles on the basis of which their two parties could unite. It was published on 5 June 1934. Its main result was to convince Malan and his Cape Afrikaners, together with a small group from the Orange Free State led by Dr van der Merwe, that, if republican Afrikanerdom was to survive, they themselves must take the initiative and break with Hertzog, raising their flag as an independent movement.

It was an important step for both sides in the dispute. It could now be clearly seen that Malan's party did not represent all Afrikaners, but only those who, like Hertzog fifteen years earlier or Kruger in the 1890s, saw their future in a limited, Afrikaner republic rather than in a united South Africa. For the newly formed United Party, Malan's group provided the sort of opposition which had been lacking in the brief coalition period. It also permitted the government to define its standpoint more clearly.[12] Malan and his supporters were not, however, the only breakaway section among the Afrikaners. Others, mainly unskilled farm workers, who had failed to find employment in the towns, began, for the first time, to transfer their allegiance to the Labour Party.[13] Though their numbers were comparatively small, their action indicated the range of opinions now current among the Afrikaner population. About the same time the Germans of South West Africa were beginning to demonstrate a lively enthusiasm for Adolf Hitler. In spite of the relatively generous treatment given them by Smuts after the war, they had refused to take part in the administration of their country. Recently, they had organised themselves under a *'führer'* who claimed to take his orders from Germany. Within the Union itself there was a covert but widespread anti-Semitic agitation, which drew encouragement from the alarm the movement aroused among the Jewish community.[14]

In spite of these problems, the formation of the United South African National Party gave Smuts a sense of hope for the future. Simultaneously, industrial expansion became possible because of the high price paid for gold. This meant that mines hitherto deemed uneconomic because of the poor quality of the ore could again be worked.[15] The supply of African labourers from within the Union had grown steadily because of the shortage of land for Africans in the rural areas, and due, too, to the increasingly effective methods of recruitment used by the mining industry. As a result, within the general framework of labour legislation, control of labour relations was effectively taken out of the hands of the government and left to the mining companies. Meantime, the demand for labour from Mozambique having fallen, it was possible for the government to let the agreement with the Portuguese authorities lapse when it came up for renewal in 1934.[16] Six years earlier the National government had agreed that, in return for the supply of 80,000 labourers for the mines, the port of Lourenço Marques should be permitted to handle 50–55 per cent of all trade to and from the mining areas of the Transvaal. Now the ports of the Union were no longer required to face such competition.[17]

Dr Malan's break with Hertzog did not prove as immediately disastrous for the latter's authority as might have been expected. Not all the Cape Nationalists joined Malan, though he was strongly supported by *predikants* and school teachers. At the other end of the political spectrum, Colonel Stallard and a few ultra-British members of the South African Party, particularly in Durban and East London, campaigned vigorously against the union of the parties, but the majority of Smuts's supporters remained loyal.[18] In an effort to attract Afrikaner support, the Labour Party also campaigned vocally against the union, but as prosperity began to percolate downwards throughout the European community its propaganda became less and less effective.[19] In a significant by-election in Heilbron in the Free State, Hertzog's candidate polled 1,000 more votes than his closest rival, a supporter of Malan, while the Labour and Roos candidates captured only 500 votes between them.

Only the native question threatened to cause dissension. The difficulty did not arise from any action by Africans. Although they had suffered even more than the poorest Whites from the effects of the world economic recession of the early 1930s, they had not used the occasion to promote any demand for better living conditions. This was mainly due to dislocation among those agencies which normally gave a lead to African opinion. Anti-Communist sentiment among some of the leaders of the African National Congress had led to the resignation of the president-general, J. T. Gumede. His successor, Pixley Seme, the founder of the Congress, who had been elected primarily to reunite the party, became involved in clashes with other leaders when he condemned strikes, demonstrations and the burning of passes as a means of attracting attention to the plight of Africans. The Communist Party, which favoured direct action of that kind, made an attempt to encourage a pass-burning campaign, but, because it was launched prematurely and did not have the wholehearted approval of the Congress, it gained little support except in Durban. There the protesters were given sharp treatment by the police and the demonstration quickly fizzled out. Any further prospect of a successful, Communist-inspired initiative was destroyed by the heavy-handed intervention of Moscow, which, in an endeavour to insist upon conformity to party dogma, caused the expulsion from the party of most of the South African leaders who commanded respect and support. With the parties in disarray and the economy once more flourishing, organised African discontent was not a factor of any significance for the government in 1934.[20]

Danger threatened when the United Party held its first congress in December 1934. Northern Province members wanted membership of the party to be restricted to Whites. With the precedent of the South Africa Act as its guide, however, the congress wisely averted a split by leaving each province to determine the criteria for its own membership. Malan and his supporters at once claimed that the United Party was betraying the cause of the Whites, but their efforts made little impact on public opinion.[21]

Smuts was able to fly to Britain in October 1934 to be installed as Rector of the University of St Andrews with reasonable confidence that the situation in South Africa was stable. He was concerned, nevertheless, that the disturbed state of Europe might adversely affect South Africa's export trade. In a speech at a dinner of the Royal Institute of International Affairs held in the Savoy Hotel in London on 12 November he undertook a characteristic survey of the world's problems. Europe, he said, was suffering because the victors in the First World War still feared their former enemies, while the vanquished were suffering from an inferiority complex which tended to make them act aggressively to compensate. His solution was for them to follow the advice of Freud and bring their feelings into the open and, through discussion, to dispel them. In Smuts's view the League of Nations was the ideal agency through which to carry out that treatment. But, with American opinion very much in mind, he went on to stress that the League must not be thought of as a military machine. Even economic sanctions should only be employed on a limited basis. It was an appeal which had great attractions for an England where the pacifist movement was very strong, but it took little account of Hitler's emergence on the German scene and above all of Germany's angry withdrawal from the League the previous year.

Turning to the problems of the Far East and the Pacific Ocean, Smuts again proposed a policy of non-aggression. Japan's action in invading Manchuria, he said, had threatened the treaties made by Britain, the USA, Japan, France and Italy in Washington in 1922 to guarantee a naval equilibrium and the integrity of China, and an open door to the potentially enormous markets of that country. It would have been more accurate if he had said that the Japanese had actually broken the treaty. For him to suggest that a friendly appeal to Japan to refrain from any further action which might heighten the danger was a wholly ineffective way of upholding the authority of the League. Once more, however, he was hoping to win the support of the USA by his conciliatory remarks, because he regarded America's absence from the League as a damaging blow to its prospects of success.[22]

Coming from a man who had for so long pursued the goal of unity in his own country and who, it seemed, had achieved so much success by his methods of friendly co-operation, Smuts's remarks impressed many of his hearers as profoundly sensible. Several of them, including Violet Bonham Carter, said they wished he might become Britain's prime minister or at least foreign secretary.[23] Smuts hastily disclaimed all desire for office in England – or even in South Africa, he added. Would he, however, have been so adamant if he could have been sure of genuine political backing, as distinct from the blessing of the League of Nations Union idealists?

The immediate problem facing the new party on Smuts's return to South Africa was that of deciding upon its response to Hertzog's Native Bills. The decision of the party congress to allow provincial congresses to determine the qualifications for membership had been taken while Smuts was in England. Commenting on it, he had written to Margaret Gillett that he hated the colour distinctions insisted upon by the northern provinces and which could only be attributed to fear on the part of the Europeans.[24] This was not the complete reversal of opinion which it might appear to have been. It sprang from Smuts's annoyance that disagreement within the party might stir up discontent among Africans and the coloured population. Essentially he still stood for the franchise laid down by the South Africa Act, and, so far as Africans were concerned, he believed the main aim should be to improve their living conditions by making better provision for their health and education and by a fairer allocation of land[25] rather than worrying about the franchise. He must have felt the strength of his view when he received a letter from the African journalist, academic and political leader, D. D. T. Jabavu, who wrote to applaud him for his defence of the rights of Africans and to urge him to leave the franchise as it was while concentrating upon the question of land for Africans and upon making the Native Conference created by the Native Affairs Act of 1920 more effective.[26]

That was the line Smuts adopted during the discussions of the native Bills which took place in 1935. It was a good time to consider those measures because there was little pressure from Africans and the government was free to reach a balanced decision without appearing to be giving in to protest or criticism from those who would be most directly affected by the legislation. Smuts was still firmly attached to his policy of racial segregation, however violently he appeared to vacillate over other aspects of native policy. Now he seemed prepared even to abandon his opposition to the abolition of the Cape native franchise, and instead concentrated upon convincing the government of the importance of converting the Native Conference into an elected council, a move which at one time he had opposed. In a more co-operative frame of mind he claimed that the council would provide a platform for intelligent African speakers and a compelling means of making informed African opinion known to parliament.[27] There is little wonder that observers were sometimes hard pressed to know what Smuts really did want. But his insistence upon European control, over which he differed not at all from the overwhelming majority of Whites in South Africa,[28] demonstrated beyond all doubt that now, as always, he rejected any idea of the assimilation of Africans educated according to European standards. Only in 1928 had he appeared to diverge in any way from that approach, and that had been an aberration, arising from his attempt to confuse his rival, Hertzog.

Had Smuts tried to act in any other way, his efforts would have been abortive. As Duncan admitted, native policy was not a policy at all, but a hand-to-mouth expedient on the part of the Whites. They enjoyed the benefits which accrued from the subordination of African interests to their own whenever they came into conflict. They vaguely hoped that something could save them from domination by Africans[29] and, because they had made their home in South Africa and firmly believed the country's development was entirely due to their initiative and efforts, they would never tolerate the extension to Africans of political rights which might one day enable them to control the government.[30] Smuts's motives were probably less pragmatic and more instinctive, and they did embody a more humane acceptance of the material needs of Africans than was evident among his opponents and many of his supporters. But he unhesitatingly accepted that the races differed fundamentally, and he had an unswerving conviction of the superiority of European civilisation. In 1934 as in 1912 he did not consider that Africans should be assimilated into that civilisation.

As Smuts had anticipated, he was defeated over the issue of retaining the Cape native franchise for the Union parliament, though enfranchised Africans might still vote for representatives in the provincial council. Though he had for so long opposed any change, he does not appear to have been unduly worried by his defeat. He had not defended the Cape franchise because of any concern with the right of Africans to vote. He had certainly had legal scruples about depriving those who were already enfranchised, and he had been worried lest a breach of the South Africa Act might undermine both the unity of the white population which that Act sustained and South Africa's links with the Commonwealth. With these latter worries removed he was prepared to accept the recommendation of a select committee that Africans should have increased representation in the senate and that some of the additional senators should be elected by Africans. This, he said, would, in the long term, be of greater value to the African population than were the existing arrangements. Meanwhile, he devoted his energies to convincing the government that the Native Conference should be converted into a Native Council which would meet regularly and advise parliament on all matters affecting African interests. He also supported the recommendation that more land should be allocated to Africans and that land scheduled for their occupation should be vested in a Native Land Trust. The trust would be empowered to acquire by voluntary purchase, or if necessary by expropriation, additional land to a total of 7,250,000 morgen (*c.* 15 million acres).

Smuts was not wholly confident that the proposals contained in the two Bills would receive unanimous approval from Africans, and he was not alone in his doubts.[31] It was decided, therefore, that, before the measures were enacted, an attempt should be made to test African opinion. Accordingly, conferences were held in Pretoria, Pietermaritzburg, Mafeking, Umtata and King William's Town, at which the secretary for native affairs, D. L. Smit, sought the views of representatives of the African population. In Pretoria, the spokesman said they had not had time to grasp the implications of the Bills. In Pietermaritzburg, they asked for more senators but otherwise seemed satisfied. In Mafeking, little was said about the franchise, the main argument being directed towards the acquisition of more land. In Umtata, the representatives said the offer of additional land was inadequate. But it was in King William's Town, where African voters were fairly numerous, that the strongest criticisms were made. There the representatives voiced their unqualified opposition to the abolition of the Cape franchise. Behind the right to vote, they argued, lay the principle of freedom and full citizenship for Africans. Implicit within that was the acknowledgement of African loyalty to those in power. The existence of income and property qualifications for the franchise was, in any case, a guarantee that the vote would be restricted to people with a stake in the country's stability. African votes had always contributed to the election of men of high quality, such as William Schreiner, J. X. Merriman, Sir Charles Crewe, Sir James Rose-Innes and J.W. Sauer.[32]

In spite of the criticism, the government determined to go ahead with the legislation during the 1936 session. The moribund African National Congress decided, therefore, that it must take up the challenge. The president-general, Pixley Seme, felt disinclined on account of his age and his involvement in other problems to lead the campaign, so help was sought from D. D. T. Jabavu. It was he who was mainly responsible for summoning an All-African Convention in Bloemfontein on the Day of the Covenant, 16 December 1935. The Convention was attended by Indians and coloured people as well as by a few liberal-minded Whites, in addition to the numerous African representatives. The attempt of a small number of militants to call for strikes and demonstrations was defeated. Instead the majority voted in favour of a qualified franchise for Africans throughout the Union. A deputation led by Jabavu was sent to Cape Town to present the Convention's decision to the prime minister. Hertzog was worried that he might not get the two-thirds majority he needed in parliament to change the constitution because the members from the Eastern Cape, who depended on African votes, were unwilling to go against the clear wishes of their African consti-tuents. He greeted the deputation with great courtesy, nevertheless, and tried to urge them to accept his proposals. Meanwhile, the Eastern Cape members of parliament produced what they described as a com-promise. The Cape native vote should not be abolished, they said. Instead, in addition to the senators to be elected by African electoral colleges, Cape Africans should be put on a separate electoral roll to vote for three white members of the Assembly.

The so-called compromise was a denial of the qualified Cape Africans' right to vote alongside Whites for the same members of parliament. But Jabavu and his fellow-members of the deputation seem not to have appreciated the implications of the change immediately, or else were anxious to co-operate with the members of parliament who had for so long represented them and who were urging that these were the best terms they could hope to get. They were joined, however, by two less accommodating members of the Congress, Dr A. B. Xuma and James Moroka, who successfully turned the scales against acceptance of the compromise. There was some support for their stand from European churchmen and others with a sympathetic attitude towards the enfranchisement of Africans, but the prime minister adopted the compromise on behalf of the government and proceeded with the legislation.[33]

The government had lost a great opportunity of winning African support for its native policy, but had it taken it, it would almost certainly have been denounced by the bulk of its own supporters, whether former Nationalists or members of the South African Party. Smuts's own comment was revealing. 'I view these bills with a detached spirit,' he wrote to Margaret Gillett, 'as a matter decided for me in far-off days by my temperament and outlook which cannot be affected by what passes or happens today, but of course I see the rocks ahead quite clearly.'[34] Africans might not be content with their lot for ever, but Smuts could not change his intuitive beliefs on that account. The man who relied so confidently upon the powers of the human intellect when dealing with international problems which defeated others, used different criteria when considering the relations between Africans and Europeans in South Africa. As the debate on the Bills drew to its conclusion, he distanced himself still further from the issue. 'I cannot manage to feel any great interest,' he wrote to Margaret Gillett at the end of March 1936. 'I cannot say there is great excitement in parliament, and so I have stayed away tonight to read the mail papers which arrived this morning, and to write this letter.'[35] Then he turned to discuss the situation in Germany.

It was appropriate, nevertheless, that Smuts should be the man to open the first meeting of the Natives' Representative Council in December 1937 which Hertzog was unable to attend. It was he who had originally urged that a council of that sort would be the most satisfactory forum for debating issues affecting Africans and the most effective channel through which to present the views of Africans to parliament, and he had only briefly taken an opposite view. Now he was particularly happy with the composition of the Council. 'The body contains all the most prominent Native leaders,' he wrote to Margaret Gillett, '. . . big chiefs, educated plebeians, journalists and even capitalists – like Baloyi who owns a big bus and cab service in Johannesburg. So, like Galileo's earth, the world is still moving, and I hope this movement will mean sound and wholesome progress.'[36] He was pleased, too, by the senators chosen to represent African interests, and he concluded that, in spite of his earlier doubts, the two Bills of 1936 had produced excellent

189

results.[37] His opinion was not entirely the product of wishful thinking. Although the leaders of the African National Congress had been disappointed by the enactment of those measures, they had decided to co-operate with the Council, at least to see if it worked. Another law, passed in 1937 and affecting the rights of urban Africans, was to test their patience to the limit.

The growing prosperity of the white community and the increasing poverty of Africans in the reserves had attracted ever larger numbers of Africans to the towns. Their prospects in the gold-mines were not as good as they had hoped. Early in 1935 the Chamber of Mines had obtained government permission to recruit a small number of labourers from Bechuanaland and Southern Rhodesia and even from further north in Nyasaland. Ostensibly the aim was to meet a shortfall in the labour supply.[38] In practice it enabled the mine-owners to resist the government's proposal to establish a minimum wage of 50 shillings a week. Their argument was that such a measure would upset the balance between the wages of Europeans and Africans and that, feeling their position threatened, the Whites might turn against their employers. In bland contradiction to this claim was the further statement that the position of African workers would be put at risk by the introduction of such a high minimum wage because employers would be tempted to replace Africans by lowly-paid Europeans.[39]

In spite of these developments the flow of Africans to the towns continued and in January 1936 a departmental committee, consisting of two experienced members of the native administration, submitted a report on African residents in urban areas. The two men, J. Mould Young and A. L. Barrett, had taken their task seriously. When they were first appointed, they protested that their terms of reference assumed that only Africans who were needed to meet the labour requirements of Whites should be permitted to reside in urban areas. This was a principle which had been enunciated in 1921 by the earlier commission chaired by Colonel Stallard which had maintained that co-mingling between Africans and Europeans was detrimental to both races. It was upon that basis that the Act passed by Smuts's government had been moulded. The new committee denied Stallard's contention that the towns had been created solely by Whites. To continue employing Africans in towns while treating them as if they should not be there was, they said, both illogical and short-sighted. It was essential to admit that Africans had a place in towns. The employers of Africans should then have an obligation to house their employees adequately. Other Africans needed to sustain the labour force – ministers, teachers, doctors, traders and artisans – must also have their place. At the same time, new arrivals should only be admitted to urban areas where there was a labour shortage, lest they should throw long-term residents out of employment by offering to work for lower wages. Africans who had lived in towns for long periods had, for the most part, abandoned their traditional way of life. This should be recognised. In any case there was no room for them in the reserves, and settlements should be created for them outside the towns where they could own small plots of land on which their families could live while the men worked in the towns. Pre-eminently, if a further drift to the towns was to be prevented, the amenities of rural areas must be improved.[40]

The views of the committee commended themselves to Smuts and were, henceforward, to form the basis of his own attitude to the treatment of urban Africans. They reinforced his belief in segregation and the need to make better provision for rural Africans while advocating an improvement in the material condition of African workers. He was unhappy at the drift of Africans to the towns, but was gradually coming to acknowledge that it was inevitable. Nevertheless, urgent measures were needed to control the exodus from the reserves lest the increasing contract between Africans and Whites should have a revolutionary effect upon both races.[41] 'Justice', he commented to Margaret Gillett, 'comes, either in good time with good sense, or else ultimately as the avenger and the wrecker.'[42] The law which was enacted on the basis of the committee's recommendations seemed to Smuts unduly harsh in its requirements, but he consoled himself with the belief that those who would implement it would do so temperately and with a genuine understanding of African needs. In this he was not far wrong, for if the mine-owners effectively determined labour recruitment policy within the broad limits laid down by the government, the character of native administration was equally formed by officials of the native affairs department, who manipulated legislation to meet the local situations in which they found themselves. To that extent it could be said that legislation was not essentially the brain-child of governments. Their task was to put into generalised legal form the ideas of those Europeans concerned with any particular aspect of South African life.

Acting briefly as minister for native affairs late in 1937, Smuts was himself able to demonstrate the effective paternalism of the department. In September a number of acts of violence occurred in scattered areas in the Transvaal and Natal. The motives behind them varied – resistance to a police raid on illegal drinkers in Vereeniging or to tax collection in Natal – while some were merely the result of minor crimes in the Johannesburg area. In all cases police, some of them white, were the main sufferers. European outrage exploded and there were demands for vengeance, no less vociferous for being irrational.[43] The incident in Vereeniging was immediately attributed to Communist propaganda, and there was a fear that Communism would spread dangerously among the African community.[44] An investigation carried out by the Natal police on Smuts's orders demonstrated beyond doubt that the disturbances in that province at least were not the result of Communist influence but had simply arisen because Africans believed their wages were too low and that taxes were too high.[45] The news did not reassure those who wished to apportion blame to others rather than to themselves, and Smuts was heavily criticised when he released four hundred Africans who had been arrested because they did not have passes or tax receipts. Believing his own views to be correct, he took little account of the protests, and during his four-month tenure of office went on to introduce a number of minor improvements for Africans over matters of health and land and in the organisation of local councils.[46]

Though his incursion into the realm of native affairs gave Smuts some satisfaction, his return to office in Hertzog's government did not commit him wholeheartedly to South African problems. Without ultimate responsibility for the government of the Union, he could, even less than before, satisfy within South Africa his longing to be involved in great issues, to make a significant contribution to the direction of the human race. Yet his contact with the reality of the outside world was becoming more tenuous. Increasingly, and against all the evidence, he put his faith in transforming the League of Nations into a meeting-place of rational beings where unruly elements would be converted to righteousness by the power of good sense. In the hope of inducing the USA to join the League, he was even prepared to water down Article 16 of the Covenant which called upon members to impose economic sanctions in certain circumstances. Article 10, requiring members to respect and preserve the territorial integrity and political independence of all other members, he declared to be a dead letter.[47] France, he believed, was still the main stumbling-block on the road to peace and he commended Philip Kerr for his initiative in speaking with Hitler.[48] For the time being, it seemed, his concern for the Jews in Germany must be deemed to be secondary to the pursuit of peace in Europe. He was, too, beginning to look more kindly upon the Locarno Pacts though still only in so far as they related to Britain's commitment to peace between France and Germany. What had originally looked like an Anglo–French alliance against Germany, he said, now seemed to offer the prospect of British intervention to assist Germany against France. He was also satisfied that the Pacts had not, after all, weakened the dominions' influence on British policy,[49] though it is difficult to see how he could justify his statement.

192

Though his opinion that Britain should pursue a resolute policy of appeasement and reconciliation[50] coincided with that of the pacifist lobby in Britain, it was out of line with the views of the British government, which was becoming increasingly aware of the growing dangers in Europe. A white paper had stressed the need to increase expenditure on the defence forces in response to German rearmament. France, meanwhile, had doubled the period of conscript service and Germany, in contravention of the Versailles treaty, had introduced full conscription and had admitted to the existence of a German air force. But Smuts still insisted that Britain could have only one role – that of peacemaker.[51] 'We shall only save Europe from war', he wrote, 'if Great Britain declared [sic] herself out of it and exerts all her immense power and prestige as the peacemaker.' He was even prepared to reopen the question of Germany's right to colonies in Africa – though with a view to the possible surrender of Togoland and Kamerun, not of South West Africa or Tanganyika. He did, however, recognise that his proposals omitted any reference to satisfying the demands of Italy and Japan.[52]

By July 1935 some of Smuts's optimism seemed to have leaked away. 'It may be that we have been wrong about the way out,' he wrote to Philip Kerr. 'I have firmly believed in the League and on the human principles on which it is founded. But I see plainly as anyone its weaknesses and its inadequacy to the heavy tasks of the post-war world.' He was in a dilemma. He was convinced that Kerr's advocacy of a world super-state was doomed to failure in view of the momentous drive towards nationalism embodied in the Nazi and Fascist creeds. But all he could do was to urge Kerr not to 'decry the League in this crisis but back it to the full. It is the symbol of goodwill and co-operation among men.'[53] It was a statement of faith rather than a reasoned argument, for he admitted to seeing a new paganism in Germany and Russia which ran counter to the spriritual doctrines in which he believed. Christianity, he wrote to Arthur and Margaret Gillett, had gone underground and a new conviction of the spirit was sorely needed. 'We who believe in God', he went on, 'must also believe that inner forces are working themselves out beyond our vision or understanding.'[54]

What Smuts did not know was that as early as 1933 Mussolini had decided to extend Italy's possessions in Africa, even if that meant war with Abyssinia. Goodwill and co-operation were not ideals which commended themselves to the Italian dictator. By September 1935 his intentions became clear in spite of an attempt by the League of Nations to formulate a compromise solution. Following upon Japan's attack on Manchuria, the League's position would be gravely weakened if Italy were permitted to pursue a similar line of action. When he realised that, Smuts swiftly abandoned the idea that Britain should adopt a resolute policy of appeasement and urged that the best way to stop Italy would be to close the Suez Canal to Italian shipping – contrary, it should be said, to international agreement. If only Britain and France would co-operate to enforce sanctions, he added ruefully. It was a change of view dictated by circumstances.

Smuts had been too remote from the European situation for too long, but at last the realities of power politics were beginning to impress themselves upon him. Yet he still hoped there might be some way of saving civilisation from violence and shipwreck. He was cheered by the news that Sir Samuel Hoare, the British foreign secretary, had made a speech in Geneva on 11 September affirming Britain's intention to 'stand for the collective maintenance of the covenant in its entirety and for resistance to all acts of unprovoked aggression'.[55] But, after giving such a lead, it was vital that Britain should not weaken. This was the final test of the League's credibility. Failure would be fatal.[56] Amery, more conscious of the nuances of the diplomatic scene, chided Smuts for his rapid change of stance from pacifism to belligerence, and for his failure to appreciate the realities of the situation. Hoare's speech, he reminded his friend, was utterly at odds with the opinions Smuts had expressed as little as ten months earlier. The British government had, in fact, tried to conciliate the pacifist lobby by insisting that war must be prevented by the League and only by the League, as Smuts himself had previously demanded. But in practice the members of the League were unlikely to agree to anything but the mildest form of sanctions against Italy, and in the meantime Hoare's speech had inflamed relations between Britain and Italy to little avail, because the outcome was likely to be an Italian triumph in Abyssinia and a diplomatic humiliation for Britain.[57]

The problem was that the British government saw its relations with Italy as a far more complex issue than Smuts could accept, concerned as he was for the reputation of the League. In the first place, Italy might prove a useful ally to Britain in her efforts to restrain Germany. Secondly, though Britain was anxious to ensure that an Italian victory did not jeopardise Egypt's water supply from the Blue Nile, she was equally anxious lest an Italian defeat at the hands of Abyssinia should encourage opposition to all the colonial powers in Africa. For Smuts, whose idealised view of the duty of the League was reinforced by his desire to protect South Africa from an Italian threat, machinations of the sort in which Britain saw fit to indulge were a deviation from the true faith. His reply to Amery was, consequently, both equivocal and disingenuous, reflecting the confusion into which he had been driven by contact with the convolutions of international diplomacy. The light of pure reason seemed inadequate to penetrate the surrounding gloom. Modifying if not wholly contradicting his earlier statements, he now insisted that he had never opposed sanctions. He was, he said, a supporter of the Covenant to its full extent, including Article 16. What he *had* been opposed to was any attempt to endow the League with a defence force of its own, which would have made it into a super-state capable of enforcing its decisions without reference to its constituent members. It was a specious argument because nothing of that sort had ever been contemplated.

Nevertheless, Smuts would not withdraw his support for Hoare's speech. Italy, he said, must not be allowed to carry out her aggressive policies lest the League be reduced to a position of futility.[58] The ineffectiveness of the League was soon demonstrated, however, when German troops occupied the demilitarised zone of the Rhineland on 7 March 1936. Although the Council of the League declared Germany guilty of a breach of her international obligations, the signatories of the Locarno Pacts made no move to support that statement with any sort of pressure either military or economic. Smuts resignedly suggested that the best line of action would be to negotiate an air pact with Germany, together with a twenty-five-year peace agreement along the lines Hitler was now suggesting.[59] Smuts's hope that Hitler would regard British restraint as a severe warning of the risk Germany had taken in occupying the Rhineland seems excessively naïve, even by the standards of the 1930s. That he willed himself to believe in Hitler's sincerity, there is little doubt. His insistence that Hitler's peace proposals deserved investigation sprang from his desire to see Germany back in the League. He was still suspicious of France and continued to castigate the counter-proposals she put up.[60]

Towards Italy Smuts was, as always, less charitable than he was towards Germany. He was cheered when the League imposed limited sanctions and deplored Britain's suggestion that they should be dropped in order to encourage collaboration between Britain, France and Italy to keep Germany in check while at the same time negotiating with Germany in the hope of avoiding any serious clash. Equally, he brushed aside Britain's anxiety about reducing the pressure on the British fleet in the Mediterranean, which, it was feared, might be vulnerable to air attack by Italy. He could see the immediate practical value of the policy, but he was distressed that individual interests should be permitted to undermine Britain's attachment to the Covenant as the keystone of her foreign policy. To accept such a prospect was to pose a direct threat to world peace. If sanctions against Italy were lifted, Article 16 of the Covenant would cease to have any effect. 'Make no mistake,' he wrote to Philip Kerr, 'if Article 16 goes all that remains is a sort of Kellogg Pact of pious aspirations.' The effect upon the Commonwealth would be disastrous. Endowing his own objectives with an innate moral authority, he had always looked upon the cement which the League provided for the Commonwealth as one of the strongest justifications for the League's existence. It had bound the dominions together by enabling them to share in one great international treaty. If the Covenant were to go, the dominions would be tempted to take independent action and the Commonwealth would cease to be a valid institution.[61] For that reason if for no other, the League must be upheld.

L. S. Amery thought him naïve to expect members of the League to fulfil the obligations which their membership entailed. France, he argued, simply could not afford to quarrel with Italy beyond a certain point. Britain may have been foolish not to try to enforce Article 16, but in practice actions such as that of Italy in invading Abyssinia could only be restrained by the immediate action of those countries directly concerned. As for the League, its only role was to try to create an atmosphere of international understanding and to provide improved machinery for conciliation.[62] Though this was very much the line Smuts had pursued in America in 1930, he was reluctant to see his ideal of a community of nations being replaced, as the logic of the argument demanded, by the old system of alliances and rearmament. But he had no workable alternative to offer. His problem was that the god-like detachment with which he was able to suggest ideal solutions was due to the fact that he was six thousand miles away from the problems he was trying to solve. Those on the spot may not have been in a position to offer such detached wisdom, but they had a more acute awareness of what was feasible and what was not.

Two issues linked South African affairs more directly with those of Europe. First was the problem of South West Africa. In 1923, when he had generously insisted that Germans should be permitted to remain in their former colony, Smuts had also maintained that nothing short of a fully democratic regime would be appropriate for the European inhabitants of mandated territory. The system had not worked because the economy of South West Africa was too dependent upon that of the Union. A commission appointed to look into the affairs of South West Africa reported in 1936. It recommended that the Union government should exercise a more direct control over the allocation of funds within South West Africa, with the particular object of promoting the development of the African inhabitants. It also proposed that there should be no further automatic naturalisation of Germans in the territory.[63] Successive administrators, as well as the legislative assembly, had been less than liberal in making appropriations for services which would benefit Africans. But Smuts appears to have done little other than note that section of the report and Hertzog was unlikely to make an issue of it.

The problem of the German population seemed to call for more urgent attention. Either voluntarily or under duress, the overwhelming majority of Germans in South West Africa supported the principles of Nazism. Because of their allegiance to Germany they were unwilling to co-operate with the South Africans who had settled in the territory. Through the agency of the legislative assembly, the latter had urged in November 1934 that the territory should be administered as a fifth province of the Union or in some other way as an integral part of it.[64] This proposal did not contradict the terms of the C-type mandate under which the territory was administered and Smuts had always hoped for an arrangement of that sort, but Hertzog was disinclined to take action.

Smuts himself did not consider that there was any real danger that Germany might interfere in South West Africa, in spite of the feelings of the German settlers there. He was not wholly convinced that Hitler was interested in the recovery of Germany's former colonies. If, as Smuts believed, Hitler was sincere in wishing for friendship with Britain, he would not persist in stirring up trouble in Africa. He must, therefore, be using disaffection in the colonies as a bargaining point which he was prepared to surrender to win support for his policy in Central Europe. The most obvious aspect of this, as Smuts had anticipated as early as December 1917 in Geneva, was the reunification of Austria with Germany, the *anschluss*. This he regarded as inevitable and not wholly undesirable. It could, therefore, be accepted with good grace. He even hoped it might be a means of obtaining a guarantee of the permanent security of Czechoslovakia from German aggression.[65] He could write confidently: 'South West Africa will *not* go to Germany. The thing does not worry me. The consequences not only for South Africa but for the British Empire would be too grave. So let that rest. This bit of desert will not upset the apple-cart.'[66]

Smuts could not be so complacent about a further issue which linked South Africa with events in Europe, and particularly with Germany. In May 1936 he had been conscious of strong anti-Jewish feeling in the Union assembly during a debate in which he had been accused of banning South African Nazi (Greyshirt) meetings and conniving at Jewish attempts to suppress free speech in the Union.[67] He was aware that other leading figures in South Africa, including his close associate Patrick Duncan, were critical of the behaviour of many Jews in the Union. They considered that even those whose general conduct they respected were more deeply concerned about world Jewry than about the country in which they had chosen to live. Those same Jews also appeared unwilling to support any restriction upon the immigration of other Jews whose presence would not be welcomed by the rest of the white community in South Africa.[68] The secretary for external affairs, responding on behalf of the prime minister to an appeal for help from the South African Jewish Board of Deputies, produced similar criticisms, but assured the Jews of his protection.[69] Hertzog's own views had recently been greatly influenced by Hilaire Belloc's book, *The Jews*, which had been recommended to him by Creswell. He thought it the only publication on the subject worth reading, and it had brought home to him the danger of permitting the unrestricted immigration into South Africa of hundreds of people every week who were incapable of being assimilated into the South African nation.[70]

Against that background, Smuts considered it unwise to speak out too forcefully in the house of assembly, but he was far more sensitive to Jewish feelings than were the other cabinet members. The news that Britain contemplated a total suspension of Jewish immigration into Palestine pending an inquiry by a royal commission distressed him deeply. He therefore wrote to Amery in the strongest terms, urging him to oppose the plan lest it should weaken British influence in the Middle East.[71] On the same day he wrote to Lloyd George, addressing him as another surviving member of the war cabinet which had formulated 'that great policy' embodied in the Balfour Declaration. The government's intention would inflame Jewish people throughout the world, he argued, and would turn them into critics if not enemies of the British Commonwealth.[72]

It was the travail of the Jews in Germany which first aroused Smuts's doubts about the feasibility of negotiating with Hitler. He deplored the revival of 'Prussianism' and the birth of 'paganism' in Germany, writing to Margaret Gillett: 'Can anything good come out of a country whose deliberate policy is to persecute Jews and Protestants? Is there not a fundamental vitiation there which poisons everything? ... France is hopelessly unwise, but fundamentally stands for human freedom and conscience like Great Britain.' Britain must co-operate with France, but only on condition that Britain assumed the leadership. He believed that both Hitler and Mussolini were bluffing, but their bluff must be called. For the present, however, the League had no role to play.[73]

The situation obviously still confused him, in spite of his apparently confident utterances, and a few months later he was following a different tack. In the meantime his fears for the Commonwealth had been sharply aroused by the crisis surrounding the proposal of King Edward VIII to marry the American divorcee, Mrs Simpson. The Union government strongly supported the line of the British prime minister, Stanley Baldwin, to whom Smuts drafted a minute on behalf of his cabinet which said:

They [the cabinet] most earnestly implore His Majesty not to take a step which would deeply shock public opinion of all shades in the Union and produce more lamentable and mischievous consequences in the Union and, by lowering the high esteem in which the Throne is held, might produce incalculable effects for the whole of the British Commonwealth.[74]

The subsequent abdication of the King aroused mixed feelings in South Africa as it did in Britain, but nothing further could be done and Smuts again turned his attention to mainland Europe. There were a number of factors, he thought, which gave rise to hope. Though the USA must be left out of the picture, Britain was in a stronger position than might at first appear. Hitler seemed sincere in his desire for Anglo-German co-operation. In any case Germany could not hope to carry on a lengthy war because her four-year plan for economic development had been a disaster. There was, of course, the danger that such total failure might lead Germany to take desperate action, so that if Britain intended to intervene she must do so at once. After America she was the richest country in the world and she held many bargaining counters, among them her willingness to return some of Germany's former colonies, to accept German union with Austria and to admit that Danzig and Memel had been temporary makeshifts. If Britain were to enter into a comprehensive accord with Germany, France and Russia would be given the security they sought and the unnatural alliance between Germany and Italy would collapse. The Mediterranean would then become as safe as the North Sea.[75]

Not everyone accepted Smuts's instant remedy. Opposition in Britain came from three quarters, he calculated. There were the traditional anti-Germans; there was the Left, mad about anti-Fascism; and there was the foreign office, pledged as always to the French view of European politics.[76] None of these seemed to appreciate as he did that even an armed, truculent Germany must be given justice, and quickly. Japan would then recoil before a powerful Russia and a resurgent China. The Far East, in Smuts's opinion, had become an even more serious threat to peace than were the upheavals in Europe. It was an interesting comment, for, although Britain had been wary of Japan for some time because she feared there might be an attempt to block the Suez Canal, it was only in 1937 that Japan in fact came to look upon Britain as a probable enemy.

For Smuts, however, the bombing of Canton by the Japanese was a matter of the greatest moment. He felt only despair when Britain accepted the Japanese statement that strict instructions had been given against the bombing of civilians.[77] Britain, he thought, had let the world down badly for many years by refusing to show firmness when it was patently needed. Now rearmament was essential if Britain wished to exert any influence in international affairs. Italy's bluff must be called. Britain and France must demand the withdrawal of all volunteers fighting in the Spanish Civil War. Britain, jointly with the USA, must challenge Japan's behaviour in China and mobilise world opinion against Japanese aggression. At the same time Britain must discuss the world situation frankly and boldly with Germany which, with its rickety internal condition, might well be grateful for overtures leading to a new settlement and a fresh start.[78] He would have liked to discuss these ideas in person with Britain's leaders, he said, but his first duty was to South Africa.[79] It was a statement which conveys an air of self-doubt. It was unlikely that the situation in South Africa would crumble, as he professed to believe. But he recognised that he carried little influence with Stanley Baldwin or with his successor, Neville Chamberlain. He now saw that, in spite of his remarkable vision, he was too remote from the scene of action to be able to assimilate the intricate web of diplomacy which bound the European nations together and seemed to strangle some of them in the process.

Even in an area in which in the past he had played such an important role he felt helpless. In July the Royal Commission on Palestine recommended that the country should be divided between Jews and Arabs. The territory to be allocated to the Jews was not, in Smuts's opinion, large enough to survive as an independent unit, even though Weizmann had accepted the proposal. If the scheme were to work, Britain must retain a mandate over both parts in order to protect the Jews.[80] His protests were in vain. Palestine was not immediately partitioned, but only because the Jews rejected the idea. A commission appointed to work out the technical details also reported against the plan in October 1938. In May 1939, Smuts saw what appeared at the time to be the final blow delivered against the Balfour Declaration. In order to appease Arab sentiment, Britain decided that Palestine should not, after all, become a Jewish state; instead it would attain independence in about ten years' time, with a government in which both Arabs and Jews would share.

Meanwhile Japanese victories in China were increasingly threatening the stability of the Far East and there seemed to be no prospect of any Western alliance to check Japanese ambitions. In despair Smuts confided yet again in Margaret Gillett that he longed to retire from public life, an opinion which was reinforced by the news that Gandhi had announced his intention to quit politics and seek obscurity among the simple people of North-West India.[81] Like Gandhi, however, Smuts was not due to take his curtain-call in the immediate future. Jettisoning his earlier proposal for negotiations between Britain and Hitler, he now suggested that to keep Germany in check the Commonwealth must seek a closer association with the USA. Amery pointed out that America's tariff system might have serious implications for the dominions, but for Smuts the need to co-operate with America superseded economic considerations. Smuts had never really understood economic issues and, in any case, it was Australia and New Zealand which, in this instance, would have been hardest hit by America's tariff policy. But Smuts insisted that even they must be aware of their military weakness and their need for American protection.[82]

The shock of Hitler's forcible annexation of Austria in March 1938 underlined the strength of Smuts's case. He had always accepted that the unification of Germany and Austria was inevitable. What filled him with anger and frustration was the knowledge that, by blocking any peaceful move in that direction, Britain and France had paved the way for Hitler's act of violence. What the German leader had done was on a par with Italy's attack on Abyssinia and with what both Italy and Germany had done in Spain. And on each occasion the Western powers had responded half-heartedly.[83]

At last Smuts saw clearly that what was happening was the fulfilment of the plan set out by Hitler in his book, *Mein Kampf*.[84] Like Amery, he suspected that Czechoslovakia would be Germany's next objective. Britain herself was in no immediate danger, but Smuts was afraid she might become embroiled in a struggle over Central or Eastern Europe which would not have the support of the dominions. He urged, therefore, that for the time being Britain should remember she was not a continental power and that she had no role to play in checking Germany's eastward advance. Her main concern must be to defend the Commonwealth and the trade routes upon which the Commonwealth depended.[85]

For one so committed to the Commonwealth as Smuts, these were anxious times. Few others in South Africa apprehended the danger as acutely as he did. Most people were involved in local issues which Smuts could only consider trivial. For example, a disturbance blew up over the singing of *Die Stem van Suid-Afrika* along with God Save the King. Hertzog, as zealous for South African sovereignty as were some of his critics for the Commonwealth link, casually suggested that *Die Stem* might become the national anthem if people wanted it. Smuts sat in gloomy silence, regretting Hertzog's lack of sensitivity to the views of the English-speaking supporters of the United Party in the shadow of the forthcoming elections. He need not have been so apprehensive. The elections brought an overwhelming victory for the United Party, but friction continued when only the South African flag was flown at the military parade on Union Day, 31 May 1938. Smuts refused a request to summon a meeting of all English-speaking members of the party to discuss the matter further, but the government was attacked by Afrikaners when it was suggested that God Save the King might be sung at the celebrations on 16 December to mark the centenary of the Great Trek. It was therefore decided that, on that day, the Governor-General should not attend the laying of the foundation stone of a *voortrekker* monument to be built on the outskirts of Pretoria. It would not then be regarded as a state occasion and no national anthem need be sung.[86]

A more important and equally untimely dispute affecting South Africa's links with the Commonwealth was stirred up by Hertzog when he tried to secure the transfer of the protectorates of Basutoland, Bechuanaland and Swaziland to the Union, as had been envisaged by the South Africa Act of 1909. His request met with a sharp refusal. The British government was more concerned than its predecessors had been in 1909 about South Africa's native policy. Patrick Duncan, who had become Governor-General in 1936 on Hertzog's nomination, despaired of the prime minister's clumsiness. Smuts, too, though he sympathised with Hertzog's views on the protectorates, could only deplore the timing of the prime minister's demand. 'I have a nose for things,' he confided to Saul Solomon, 'and believe that before long our allegiance to England will be on trial – to meet that day I am going to stick in the Cabinet until I am kicked out – I know people are saying that I surrendered to Hertzog and condemn me for it. But I have my reasons.'[87] He could not, therefore, approve the decision of his friend and erstwhile protégé, J. H. Hofmeyr, to resign from the cabinet in protest against the appointment of an unsuitable person to represent African interests in the senate. In Smuts's view that savoured too much of running away when much was at stake.[88]

Hofmeyr's concern was fully justified. The government had shown a total lack of interest in both the Natives Representative Council and the views of those chosen to represent Africans in parliament. The African National Congress had, nevertheless, made every effort to give the system of representation introduced in 1936 an opportunity to prove its effectiveness. They were not unaware of its shortcomings, but they were prepared to give it a fair trial. It was essential, therefore, that Africans should believe that their representatives were the best available. The government, however, was not profoundly concerned about African issues, thinking them of minor importance in face of the calamity which threatened the world. Even while Hofmeyr was making his protest, Hitler had prepared the way for the invasion of Czechoslovakia. Already Smuts had felt impelled to state in parliament that, although it was for the house to decide, he firmly believed that South Africa must go to the defence of Britain in the event of war. But, he had added, even now, patience, forbearance and compromise were the weapons most likely to triumph.[89] This was another change in his approach to world problems and it marked the beginning of a revival of his interest in the League of Nations. The League must not be deemed to be dead, he once more insisted. There must be no drastic amendment of the Covenant. Even the use of sanctions should be regarded as in only temporary abeyance. The totalitarian states might reject the League completely, but that was no reason for its supporters to become weary in well-doing. Again, as long before, he blamed American defection for the weakness of the League, yet still he dreamed of tempting the USA into collaboration – though he admitted he did not know how it could be done.[90]

Such fluctuations in Smuts's opinions reflected his acute sense of helplessness and of remoteness from those regions where important decisions were taken. Yet his uncertainty can be forgiven when one recalls that Sir Maurice (later Lord) Hankey, secretary to the cabinet, could write, 'I am less troubled than most of my friends about the international situation. ... All my news from Germany and Italy is that the mass of the people don't want war. The very thought gives them the "jitters". I can hardly believe that the dictators are such fools as to go into a war without a much stronger popular opinion than they have for war.'[91] Hankey, it is true, drew solace as far as Britain herself was concerned from *Mein Kampf*. After all, Chamberlain and the French premier, Edouard Daladier, had been to Munich in September, and had agreed, without consulting Czechoslovakia, on the surrender of the Sudetenland to Germany. It seemed not unreasonable, therefore, to assume that Hitler would be satisfied that Britain would acquiesce in his plan to extend Germany's frontiers eastward.

Hankey seemed to have read the situation accurately, for, when Hitler invaded Czechoslovakia on 15 March, Chamberlain made only a nominal protest. Smuts's dismay was matched only by his bewilderment about whether anything could still be done to avoid war. He had accepted the Munich concession because he believed Germany had some sort of claim over the Sudetenland. But Hitler's forcible annexation of non-German Czechs, contrary to his promise at Munich, could not be accepted. Reluctantly Smuts was coming to the conclusion that, as a last resort, Britain must, after all, be prepared to go to war and that South Africa must reconsider her position even if she were not likely to be directly affected by hostilities.[92] In that frame of mind he was worried by the likely repercussions on the Commonwealth of Chamberlain's announcement on 23 March that, if Poland's independence were threatened, Britain would give all support in her power. Was that not going too far, far beyond Locarno? Could the Commonwealth feel any responsibility for events in Eastern Europe? How could he, Smuts, defend Britain's stance before a critical audience in South Africa?[93]

As the storms gathered he still found time to read philosophy and to study again the New Testament. He also commiserated with the Jews over British concessions to the Arabs in Palestine and wrote to Amery urging him to enlist all possible support in an effort to prevent the abandonment of the Balfour Declaration. He was, too, deeply conscious of concealed movements in South Africa which threatened to divide the country, and he was determined to be prepared for the moment when the Union's loyalty to the Commonwealth was put to the test.

The dismissal of the Russian commissar for foreign affairs, M. M. Litvinov, who had seemed well disposed towards the Western powers, suggested there had been a shift in Russian opinion in favour of Germany. While pondering that riddle, Smuts had the confusing news in May that the British and French ambassadors in Moscow had begun to discuss a mutual assistance pact with the USSR. He was suspicious of entanglements with Russia but he sensed that, if the talks were successful, they might lead to a balance of power in Europe which would make war less likely.[94]

Against that shifting background of alternating hope and despair for Europe another local dispute emerged to harass the government. Many Whites believed that Indians were infiltrating areas reserved for Whites and that the numbers involved were increasing. In response to their complaints, the Union government passed the Asiatics Transvaal Land and Trading Act which imposed severe restriction on the right of Indians to reside and trade in the Transvaal. A section of the Transvaal Indian Congress protested to Smuts as minister of justice,[95] while the Viceroy of India appealed to the Governor-General[96] and Gandhi sent a reproachful telegram to Smuts reminding him of their agreement of 1914.[97] To add to Smuts's embarrassment, J. H. Hofmeyr, who had already resigned from the cabinet over one racial issue, now resigned from the party caucus in protest against the new Act. Smuts did not consider Hofmeyr's reaction was in any way justified by the contents of the legislation, but felt some obligation to support his friend even though it meant opposing the prime minister. That was something Smuts was anxious to avoid because he did not want to encourage friction within the party. The unity of the white races was far more important, in his estimation, than minor issues of Indian rights.

Yet there *were* divisions. Malan and his supporters had shown their sympathy for Germany by announcing that they were prepared to see South West Africa handed back. Meanwhile, in Hertzog's own Orange Free State a group had set up the *Ossewa-Brandwag* (Ox-wagon Sentinel) in October 1938, ostensibly to promote Afrikaner traditions and culture, but it had quickly developed into a semi-military organisation. On both developments Smuts kept a watchful eye, remembering the disloyalty of some Afrikaners in 1914.

In Europe events were coming to a climax. Smuts's forebodings were realised on 23 August when Russia and Germany signed a non-aggression pact. He would have been even more disturbed had he known of their agreement to partition Poland. When Britain signed a defence agreement with Poland on 25 August, war seemed certain. The question was, how would South Africa respond? There was little interest there in the fate of Poland and still less of Danzig, but Smuts felt impelled to urge his fellow-countrymen not to stand aside from the conflict. The invasion of Poland by Hitler on 1 September left him with no choice. He must act in accordance with his beliefs. Italy's decision to remain neutral meant that the immediate threat to Egypt and thence to East Africa was removed, but how long would that situation hold?

On 2 September, the day before Britain declared war on Germany in fulfilment of her obligations to Poland, Hertzog summoned a meeting of the cabinet and said he intended to make a statement to the nation and that he assumed the agreement on neutrality taken at the time of Chamberlain's visit to Munich still held good. For Smuts this was the moment of decision. He insisted, therefore, that the annexation of Czechoslovakia had altered the situation. He was supported by seven other cabinet ministers who said that South Africa should stand by the Commonwealth and declare war on Germany. Six others demurred and supported Hertzog. The prime minister then said he would introduce a motion into parliament the following day recommending neutrality. Smuts replied that he would oppose the motion. The same evening Hertzog called on the Governor-General and asked that parliament should be dissolved to seek the views of the electorate if he obtained only a small majority in favour of neutrality. Duncan replied that they must await the outcome of the vote before reaching any decision on further action.[98]

From that moment Duncan's role was decisive. He disagreed strongly with Chamberlain's European policy. His view was that Germany should be left to go her own way in Eastern Europe, but that Britain and France should be prepared to give her a warm reception if she tried to threaten the West.[99] Nevertheless, he was deeply loyal to the Commonwealth and he was not prepared to stand by while South Africa dissociated herself from her Commonwealth obligations. For the moment, however, he must bide his time.

On 4 September Hertzog introduced his motion calling for South African neutrality. He claimed that the Union should not be plunged into war unless her interests were directly threatened. To go to war now would mean that relations between English-speakers and Afrikaners would be irretrievably embittered. In any case, he said, he could sympathise with Germany's desire to rescue herself from the humiliation inflicted on her in 1919. In his reply Smuts knew that he must tread warily. Though he himself was firmly of the opinion that the civilisation which had been built upon Christian foundations over many centuries was now threatened by Germany's actions, he knew full well that many of his countrymen did not share his view. It was essential, therefore, that his main theme should be the danger faced by South Africa herself. He was not anxious, he said, to destroy the co-operation which had existed between Hertzog and himself for the past six years, but it was his duty to challenge the prime minister's statement. Relations with Germany *must* be severed in view of what Hitler had done, but Union troops should not be sent overseas. All South Africa's resources would be needed to protect her own interests. A speech delivered with such caution could not, Smuts feared, carry the day, nor did it necessarily do so. Some members were already committed wholeheartedly to supporting the Commonwealth. Others could well have been converted to Smuts's viewpoint less by his own arguments than by the speeches of Dr D. F. Malan and other Nationalists who defended Hitler without reservation. Whatever the reason, the vote went in Smuts's favour by 80 to 67.[100]

Attention was then focused once more on the Governor-General. Hertzog appealed to Duncan to dissolve parliament to seek the views of the electorate. The Governor-General knew that his constitutional position was a difficult one. He had already sought advice on whether there was any precedent for refusing a dissolution when it was requested by an elected head of government and could find none. He therefore told Hertzog that he must have time to consider the matter but pointed out that a general election in the circumstances of the time was likely to cause bitterness. He added that the present parliament had been elected as recently as May 1938, that at the time of the election considerable prominence had been given to the question of neutrality and that Hertzog and his supporters had consistently said that, if the issue did arise, parliament was the body to take a decision. That being the case, he was not justified in dissolving parliament if Smuts could form a government. Later in the evening Smuts informed Duncan that he intended to try to form a cabinet[101] and the Governor-General then wrote to Hertzog setting down the gist of their previous conversation.[102] The prime minister immediately tendered his resignation, but Duncan could not accept it until he had heard the outcome of Smuts's negotiations.[103]

The drama reached its climax on 6 September when Smuts reported that he had, indeed, succeeded in forming a government. With great relief Duncan was then able to accept Hertzog's resignation. Throughout the exchanges the prime minister, who in parliament could become both irascible and vindictive, had behaved with the consideration and charm which he invariably showed in his personal dealings with others.[104] He took his defeat with dignity, though he was deeply worried by the probable effect of those momentous events on the unity of the party. Smuts, by contrast, was rejuvenated. All his past frustration and weariness left him.[105] Sir William Clark, South African High Commissioner in London, who had agreed to stay in office until November after offering his resignation out of loyalty to Hertzog, said how delighted he was to work with Smuts who seemed to be able to grasp every situation at once and to give a decision instantly.[106]

9

Prime minister again

At the head of government once more, Smuts needed to call upon all his store of mental and physical energy. In March 1939 the Quartermaster-General had admitted that the South African Defence force was administratively ill-prepared to meet an emergency. He doubted whether it would be possible to maintain even one division in the field against a European enemy, and mobilisation would take several months.[1] In spite of that warning, nothing had been done because of Hertzog's refusal to contemplate becoming involved in a war. To add to Smuts's difficulties, his opponents would not accept that their defeat in parliament had finally put an end to neutrality. He was confident that he had the support of the English-speaking population and of a considerable section of the Afrikaners, but that meant little in face of the determination of the opposition.[2] There were those, too, who thought that Hertzog, whatever his shortcomings, could sense the feelings of the Afrikaners more accurately than Smuts ever did.

Events in Europe only increased the doubts of Hertzog's followers about the wisdom of being involved in the war. The Polish army was quickly crushed, and Russia began to occupy those parts of Poland allotted to her by the secret agreement with Germany. Nightly the German radio broadcast an attack on Smuts in Afrikaans.[3] On the credit side, the cabinet, largely composed of Smuts's old and well-tried friends but including some former opponents such as the former Labour Party member, W. B. Madeley, and the erstwhile leader of the pro-Commonwealth Dominion Party, Colonel C. F. Stallard, was a closely knit and loyal group. With their co-operation Smuts began to build up the armed forces, and he invited the minister of commerce and industry, R. Stuttaford, to make a preliminary survey of the Union's agricultural and industrial requirements in the event of a long war and to see what steps should be taken to secure their supply from local sources.[4] But he had to proceed with caution, and, when the British High Commissioner asked him, off the record, whether it would be possible for British air force pilots to be trained in the Union,[5] he felt constrained to reply that South Africa could not help. He added, however, that the Union would have to expand her own airforce to meet a possible attack from the north and that, if the threat did not materialise, South Africa's air power could be a valuable reserve.[6] It was a cryptic but useful hint which the High Commissioner appreciated.

Smuts's programme was a heavy one, yet he found time to walk with members of his family on Saturday afternoons and Sunday mornings. On Sunday afternoons he received company. As always he read. Occasionally the routine was broken by the need to attend public meetings. Early in November he was at a meeting in Bloemfontein to wind up the old United Party. It was sad for Smuts to see his hope of closer co-operation between British and Afrikaners shattered and to feel the bitterness which accompanied the breakup. Nor was there a great deal of consolation to be drawn from the knowledge that his opponents were as divided as only South African – or Irish – politicians could be. The followers of Malan did not sit comfortably with Hertzog's supporters.[7]

On New Year's Eve Smuts broadcast to the nation as he was to do for the rest of the war. There was little he could say, because stagnation seemed to have set in on the Western Front. But he took the opportunity to impress upon his hearers that the decision to go to war was no longer a matter for debate. With the help of letters from Amery, however, he was keeping a close watch on events in Europe and his prognostication regarding future developments was not optimistic. To his friend Florence Lamont, in America, he wrote with astonishing prescience to warn her of the dangers ahead. While Germany held the West, he said, Russia would overrun Europe's eastern flank. Scandinavia was already threatened and Holland and Belgium were in grave danger. In 1940 the Balkans would be in flames. If Germany were successful, Italy would join in and the war would spread to North Africa. The Far East, too, was stirring and America could not escape what would inevitably become a world war.[8]

Though he saw with the utmost clarity the pattern of future events, he admitted he could see no basis for a future settlement. People talked of universal federation, he wrote to Margaret Gillett, but it was a Utopian ideal. The League of Nations had been a heart-breaking disappointment, but he could not think far beyond the League when seeking a way ahead. He could not accept that mere economic reform would achieve the end that was required, and consequently he did not believe that Marxism provided the answer. He himself was fundamentally a Liberal, with a pull towards spiritual and religious values, but it could not be denied that Liberalism had failed. It was a mad world, as Hertzog had just demonstrated by demanding that the Union should make a separate peace with Germany.[9] Once again the former prime minister had brought up the claim that in September 1938 the cabinet had agreed that the

Union should observe strict neutrality in the event of war, but Smuts and other cabinet members strongly denied his statement.[10]

From this turmoil Smuts sought solace in reading again the New Testament in Greek and by glancing at a selection of journals – *Antiquity*, *Mind* and the *Round Table* – sent him by Margaret Gillett. His seventieth birthday was greeted with good wishes from all quarters, but he knew well enough that it was his stand rather than his personality which warmed people's hearts. As he had prophesied, the situation in Europe was deteriorating rapidly as the new year progressed. Norway and Denmark were invaded on 9 April and a British expeditionary force to Norway was heavily defeated. Perversely, these events were of some benefit to Smuts. He was consoled by Chamberlain's resignation because he had never felt the British prime minister possessed the qualities needed by a wartime leader. He would, however, have preferred Lloyd George to have taken charge rather than Winston Churchill, though the latter held him in high regard. Theirs was a strange but none the less deep friendship. They were men of utterly different characters yet they seemed to be drawn together by a powerful attraction.

Of immediate importance was the fact that the violation of Belgium, Holland and Norway gave the lie to Smuts's opponents who had all along claimed that neutrality would be a sure guarantee against German invasion.[11] Though he recognised that there was little prospect of winning over his opponents to his point of view, Smuts decided in June to try to induce them not to work actively against the government. Hertzog, however, remained uncompromising. The Union, he said, must immediately take all steps to withdraw from the war before any *rapprochement* could take place. The war was already lost by the Allies and it was futile to continue the struggle. Smuts would have none of that argument, and on 25 June Hertzog and Malan published a manifesto indicting him for involving the country in war and demanding that parliament be summoned to discuss neutrality. If that were not done, they said, they would hold protest meetings culminating in a vast demonstration and followed by the formation of vigilance committees.

In the face of such hostility Smuts found himself having to organise military aid for Kenya, relying entirely on volunteers so as not to break the commitment made at the outbreak of war. Italy, having entered the war, revived the immediate threat of an attack on British East Africa from Abyssinia. At any moment, too, Smuts expected the German air force to attack Britain.[12] Yet he could not believe Britain would not in the end be victorious. It was an opinion born of faith rather than of evidence, and it sprang from the religious conviction that the evil which Nazism embodied could not triumph in a universe shaped by a divine

providence. To counter some of the gloomy and menacing rumours circulating in South Africa, he took to broadcasting his own views more frequently over the radio and in July he was invited to prepare a similar
broadcast for issue in Britain and America. The extra burden of work
which the request entailed dismayed him, but he felt a thrill of excitement
that at last he was to play a role on the international stage once more.

The fall of France at that time was a disaster, and Smuts freely admitted
its magnitude in correspondence with this friends.[13] Publicly he was
more discreet and his broadcast concentrated on Britain's survival. 'Britain', he said, 'is and remains the inner core of the Allied cause – the
main bastion of the Allied defence – the force with which the Germans
have to deal before a real decision is reached. Until that force is disposed
of it is futile to talk of defeat.' Indicating the shift in his view of the
role of the League of Nations, he went on to say that what must be
aimed at in the post-war world was a society of nations possessing a
central organisation equipped with the necessary authority and powers
to supervise the common concerns of mankind.[14] In the atmosphere
of unrestrained brutality created by Nazism and Bolshevism, the League
as a body of reasonable nations prepared to dispel disagreement by discussion was no longer an adequate concept. In 1919 he had been in
favour of disarmament, but now he no longer was. The rapid recovery
of Germany had taught him a lesson. In any event, there would still
be the problem of a heavily armed Russia or Japan to deal with. The
long-term solution would still require a change of heart among mankind,
but in the meantime an interim organisation, strong enough to maintain
peace, was essential.[15]

Before the broadcast reached the people of Britain, Hitler had launched
his air attack, and Smuts could only admire from afar the staunchness
of the civilian population, especially of London. But in this war he was
compelled to remain at a distance because, as prime minister of the
Union, he could not be spared for lengthy periods, as he had been from
1916 to 1919, and South Africa kept him occupied. A new session of
parliament demonstrated with added force the inconvenience of locating
the legislature in Cape Town while the administration remained in Pretoria. Backwards and forwards he travelled between the two cities, and
Isie had to be satisfied with fleeting encounters with her husband, for
she rarely accompanied him to Cape Town. In any case, she herself
was becoming fully involved in organising a range of activities in support
of the war. Her remark that she hoped to see more of Smuts in the
next life than she had in the present one produced one of Smuts's few
recorded attempts at witticism when he replied that it would depend
on whether they went to the same destination. His repartee when

heckled at public meetings was of a kind to amuse the men of the backveld, but there was little evidence of humour in his letters.

In October Smuts again looked into the future with chilling accuracy. Germany, he wrote to his friend Amery, would next attempt to swallow up Greece and Turkey with a view to attacking Iraq and Syria, thereby reinforcing the Italian attack upon the Middle East and Northern and Eastern Africa.[16] It was, therefore, with a thrill of pleasure that he accepted an invitation to fly to Khartoum in November to discuss with the British foreign secretary, Anthony Eden, plans for a British advance in North Africa to counter the Italian thrust. On the way he observed with interest and indefatigable curiosity the vast craterland on the border between Kenya and Tanganyika, Mount Kilimanjaro and Mount Kenya, the soda lakes, Lakes Nakuru, Naivasha and Elmenteita, and the great desert to the north of Kenya. He also had the excitement of meeting 'his' troops – he always referred to the South African forces as 'his' – on the Abyssinian border, where they were confronting the Italians. Discussing the coming campaign in North Africa with the men who were to command it gave him much-needed stimulus. It may not have been quite like 1917, but it stirred up memories. It was a strenuous journey, but Smuts returned from it optimistic and refreshed.[17]

Already, his prophecies were beginning to materialise. In October German forces had begun to move into Romania and later in the month Italy attacked Greece. The battle for the Balkans had begun. It was reassuring, therefore, to learn that Roosevelt had been returned to office in America for another four years. Roosevelt, Smuts believed, understood the situation, and his help to Britain already went far beyond what was deemed appropriate for a neutral power. Unfortunately, Americans generally were not behind him.[18] Smuts could sympathise with his dilemma. Many Afrikaners were still as strongly opposed to the war as any dyed-in-the-wool neutralists of the Middle West.

Suddenly the situation in the Union took on a new look. The opposition split. Faced by growing criticism of what some saw as his lack of dedication to extreme republicanism, Hertzog relinquished his seat in parliament on 12 December. The apparently callous rejection of their leader by Malan and others grieved some of the older Nationalists. Hertzog's long-time colleague, Havenga, and W. J. C. Brebner who had served in the senate for thirty years, resigned in sympathy with the former prime minister, as did several others members of the party.[19] The Labour leader, Creswell, also gave sympathetic support,[20] and on 30 January 1941 ten of those who had resigned formed the new Afrikaner Party, though two of them later transferred to the United Party. When that happened, the supporters of Malan, who had initially called themselves the *Herenigde Nasionale* Party, reverted to the title of National Party. Within the National Party the *Ossewa Brandwag* continued to exist as a minority group, and because of its association with the party appeared to be stronger and more dangerous than it really was.

Smuts took no pleasure in the manner of Hertzog's overthrow. Although he admitted that the six years during which he had tried to work with the former prime minister had strained his patience to the limit – a feeling which Hertzog would doubtless have warmly reciprocated – he wrote immediately to express his sympathy. Knowing of Hertzog's straitened financial circumstances (for the former prime minister had scrupulously avoided using his office for pecuniary gain), he also offered a pension in recognition of his many years of public service.[21]

Christmas 1940 found Smuts as busy as ever. Though most of his colleagues were able to take a short break, his duties as minister of defence and his sheer delight in being in charge kept him hard at work. As in 1939 he broadcast to the nation on New Year's Eve and once again he was asked to prepare a broadcast to the people of Britain. This time he was able to be more cheerful than he had been the previous year. Though 1940 had begun badly, it had brought many notable triumphs. The Royal Air Force had gallantly withstood and had then defeated the German *Luftwaffe*'s attack on Britain. In December General Wavell had launched a brilliant advance from Egypt which had sent the Italian army scurrying in disarray across the desert. Shortly before that the Greeks had revived memories of their ancient prowess by repelling an Italian attack on their country.

Smuts did not believe Hitler would so easily accept defeat and he was convinced, wrongly as it proved, that he would launch another assault on Britain. Again, therefore, he emphasised the need for American intervention.[22] More acutely he warned that Russia would not be immune from a German attack now that France had fallen.[23] His attitude towards Germany had changed completely since the days when he had preached goodwill and the need to extend the hand of friendship. There were some good German people, he said, but there was much of the devil in the Germans as a whole. They were barbarians who must be tamed before they could be entrusted with leadership.[24]

Once again, In March 1941, the call came to Smuts from the outside world. A brief visit to Cairo enabled him to discuss with Eden and Sir John Dill, Chief of the Imperial General Staff, the plan of campaign in Abyssinia and the Middle East. In the latter some British forces had completed the conquest of Cyrenaica in February, but Hitler had invaded Bulgaria on 28 February and was threatening Greece. The problem for the British strategists was to maintain the impetus in the desert campaign while reinforcing Greece with only limited resources at their disposal. The decision to switch the main effort to the defence of Greece was not necessarily one which Smuts, at that time, would have wholeheartedly endorsed. But pressure from Britain was strong and he accepted that there was little choice. His journey did, however, enable him to renew memories of the First World War when, on the outward flight, the plane in which he was travelling was unable to land in Nairobi and was diverted to Dodoma, in Tanganyika. There he spent a night in the German fort in which he had slept during the East African campaign. When the plane did reach Nairobi it was joined by Lady [Daphne] Moore, wife of Sir Henry Moore, Governor of Kenya, who was to become another of the women upon whom Smuts lavished attention and, in their absence, affectionate letters.

Within a few weeks of Smuts's return to South Africa the war took several sharp turns. British troops entered Addis Ababa, the capital of Abyssinia, on 5 April, and the Abyssinian campaign was quickly wound up. The South African troops in that area were at once released for service in Egypt where their presence was urgently needed. The diversion of British forces to Greece had coincided with the arrival in the desert of German forces under the command of General Erwin Rommel to reinforce the demoralised Italians. Rommel launched a counter-attack on 31 March and by 13 April his troops had recaptured Bardia, near the Egyptian border. Meanwhile, a revolution in Iraq had widened the area of involvement for Britain's hard-pressed Middle East Command. With the signing of a Soviet–Japanese neutrality pact on 13 April, there also seemed to be an imminent possibility that Japan would attack Britain's Far-Eastern dependencies.

So much that Smuts had forecast seemed to be coming true, but he was exhilarated rather than depressed. As he had said in a recent broadcast, 1941 was to be a year of destiny for the democratic world. Under his leadership, South Africa was working hard to support the Allied war effort. Some of his senior officers even warned Smuts that the country might be overstretched. But for Smuts there was no other course. All civilised values were at stake. South Africa herself, he now said, was a particular target of Hitler's expansion policy. He must fight and the Union must fight, whatever the reservations of Malan and his supporters. Increasingly at this time Smuts drew strength from his Christian roots. He may not have abandoned his belief in holism, but, after rereading and reflecting upon Renan's *Life of Jesus*, he wrote to Margaret Gillett that the author had failed to appreciate the deepest insight of all which Jesus unfolded to man – that God so loved the world and that the power of the universe is love.[25] It was a more traditionally Christian view than he had uttered for some time.

In South Africa Smuts received congratulations from two quarters for his policy towards Indians and Africans. The Viceroy, Lord Linlithgow, wrote appreciatively of the measures taken by the Union parliament in April to improve the lot of Indians in the Union,[26] and the four senators elected in 1937 to defend African interests wrote in May to thank Smuts for the sympathetic response he had made in parliament to their questions and complaints. His direct involvement in African affairs had arisen, characteristically, from his having taken responsibility for presenting the estimates for the native affairs department during the illness of the minister, Deneys Reitz. Smuts replied that he had simply expressed views he had long held regarding the need to care for the health of Africans and to ensure that their wages and their conditions of work on the farms were satisfactory. The Whites, he thought, were too grudging in their sympathy for the Africans, whose help was invaluable. There were 30,000 Africans serving in a non-combatant capacity in 'his' army, and more would follow suit. He (that personal pronoun again!) paid them well, and gave them good treatment, and was establishing a standard which would increasingly permeate farming and industry. It was the humane thing to do and – in a rather less idealistic vein – it was sound policy if South Africans did not wish to see the African population falling under the influence of the Nazis or the Communists.[27] It was an indication of white opinion in South Africa that even the senatorial representatives of African interests were well satisfied with such paternalism.

Victory in Abyssinia was soon to be balanced by defeat in Greece. The French government, meanwhile, appeared ready to collaborate with the Germans, and that might bring the French Empire into the conflict. Once again demonstrating his remarkable foresight, Smuts foretold the bitterness France would feel towards those who eventually rescued her from her humiliation. More immediately, in view of Germany's successes in the Balkans, Smuts saw that, if France were to acquiesce, Syria might become Britain's Achilles' heel in the Middle East. Though Britain appeared confident that Egypt would not fall, Smuts was acutely aware that South Africa's war effort was wholly concentrated in Egypt. He had not long to wait for his prognostication to be fulfilled. The French government agreed to allow Germany to use military facilities and air bases in Syria to assist the rising in Iraq and to launch an attack on Egypt. Confident that Hitler would turn his attention fully to the Eastern Mediterranean for his next campaign, Smuts wrote to the British government urging it to send every available aircraft and tank and any other war material to assist General Wavell in Egypt. As a measure of his

215

own concern, he had organised another division of volunteers which was ready to sail immediately for service in Egypt. [28]

On his birthday, Smuts's efforts were rewarded when the King appointed him a field-marshal. It was an honour of which he was intensely proud, yet he still preferred to be addressed as 'General', the rank he had virtually conferred upon himself during the Anglo-Boer War. He often felt nostalgia for those days, as men will when they recall the one time of their life when they were put to the test physically as well as mentally and, often to their surprise, were not found wanting. For Smuts it was the time to which he referred most often when reminiscing with the younger members of his family. Reflecting now upon the problem of maintaining peace after the war, he again rejected flatly all thought of disarmament. The only alternative appeared to be a league of nations strong enough to withstand aggression, and the members would have to be armed all the time. On the other hand, he mused, though nothing less than a coercive union would be strong enough to prevent any one nation posing a threat to peace, the union itself might destroy liberty and national self-determination. His confidence in the power of reason, and particularly of his own intellectual power, was undergoing a severe test.

On 22 June 1941 Germany invaded Russia. Smuts had foreseen that possibility and with a renewed flourish of his self-esteem he at once sat down to draft a letter of advice to General Wavell on how he should conduct the Middle East campaign in the new circumstances. Though he concluded disarmingly enough that Wavell should treat the letter as coming from an armchair strategist and give it only such importance as he might deem fit, it was probably fortunate that it was never sent and Wavell was soon replaced by General Sir Claude Auchinleck. [29] The suggestions Smuts sent to Churchill, on the other hand, on how to handle the strategic and political situation after the fall of Russia, which he believed would take place within a few months, were probably received with interest. In that wider field, Churchill could acknowledge that Smuts was every bit as much of a specialist and every bit as amateurish as he was himself. Being in much closer contact with events than Smuts could be, however, Churchill could appreciate more clearly the nature of the problem, but he could respect Smuts's ideas even if he did not always subscribe to them.

It was well for Smuts, as it was for Churchill, that both men could turn so easily from the stresses of war to seek refreshment in simple things. For Smuts the sight of two barbets playing on his lawn at Doornkloof gave him as much delight as it did to Isie. He enjoyed, too, the sight of his grandchildren playing games together. The news of the flowers blooming in the Cape after heavy rain, which contrasted so sharply with the dusty dryness of the Transvaal, awoke in him feelings of intense pleasure. The difficulty of distinguishing between God and his works brought back thoughts of holism. Yet, when he read Tawney's comment in his *Religion and the Rise of Capitalism* that human nature is too permanent a factor to change in historic time, he recalled immediately that the whole of Jesus' teaching had emphasised the need for a change of heart in the individual, and that by comparison the reform of institutions and society was secondary and consequential.[30]

From this brief respite Smuts was recalled by a powerful letter from Mrs Margaret Ballinger, one of the three Whites elected to the house of assembly to represent African interests. While not unappreciative of the more generous spirit she had noted since Smuts became prime minister, she was incensed by the exclusion of African mineworkers from the benefits of the cost of living allowance recently introduced into the country at large. Even reasonable people, she said, had too easily accepted the mine-owners' claim that their African employees did not need the increase because they were fed and housed. The workers' families, meanwhile, were suffering extreme hardship.[31] Though it was not mentioned in Mrs Ballinger's letter, Africans themselves were beginning to organise more effectively to defend their position, and they had found a new incentive in the Atlantic Charter produced by Churchill and Roosevelt on 14 August 1941.

On 21 January 1942, Smuts delivered what he believed to be an important statement on native policy at a meeting of the Institute of Race Relations in Cape Town. Its significance, in retrospect, lay less in the liberal note which Smuts believed he had sounded than in the friendly reception it had from liberal-minded Europeans who attended the meeting, and in the absence of any fundamental change in Smuts's outlook on the problem during half a century. He made some play with the term 'trusteeship' which, he said, had superseded the arid debate about the superiority of Europeans over Africans. The reality of the situation, though that was something of which he was scarcely aware, was that the Whites, by means of their military and economic strength, had placed themselves in an unassailable position. The concept of trust, he said, instead, placed a heavy obligation upon the Whites to see to the well-being of Africans. It was an ethical question closely related to Christian ideals. 'When people ask me what the population of South Africa is,' he went on, 'I never say it is two millions, I think it is an outrage to say it is two millions. This country has a population of over ten millions, and the outlook which treats the African and Native as not counting, is making the ghastliest mistake possible.' Here at least he appeared

217

to have taken to heart the criticism levelled at him by Merriman over thirty years earlier. But the extent to which Merriman's remark had wrought any conversion in Smuts's attitude to Africans was called in question by Smuts's further statement that 'If he [the African] is not much more, he is the beast of burden; he is the worker and you need him. He is carrying the country on his back.' Apparently there was, after all, some difference between Whites and Africans, even if numerically each person counted as one unit. For Smuts the African was still 'the helpless native' for whom it was important to make adequate provision – for better housing, reasonable wages and fair conditions of labour.

Though his ideas may well have been ahead of those of most of his white compatriots, and this must not be overlooked, Smuts still failed to recognise the existence of educated Africans who might lead their own people by example and precept to the better way of life which he envisaged for them. He never suggested that Africans might be capable of expressing an opinion or of doing anything to better their own status and conditions of life. He may have dispelled the dark future which he had forecast before the Union was established, but he did not see Africans as partners on the brighter road ahead. Only in one area was there any notable development in his thinking, and that was in his recognition of the fact that the drift of Africans to the towns was now irreversible and that his hope of segregating them in rural areas was gone for ever.[32] With that change had also gone all prospect of sustaining traditional ways of life among urban Africans. Yet he still supported the segregation of Africans in urban locations and clung in some undefined way to the idea that Europeans and Africans should retain their own cultures. 'Of course,' he said, 'everybody in this country is agreed that European and African should live apart and preserve their respective cultures.' So, if segregation in the reserves was not enough, it appeared it must be reinforced by segregation in urban locations.

When Smuts spoke of 'everybody' he had probably forgotten again the eight million Africans who went to make up the total population of ten million. Yet, in spite of his confusion, he clearly thought his own ideas an advance on Hertzog's 'segregation policy' which, he said, had 'proved barren'.[33] The difference lay, primarily, in Smuts's genuine concern for the material well-being of the African population. It was an attitude which differed little from that of the more enlightened administrators of Britain's tropical African dependencies. There the theory, if not the practice, of indirect administration still held sway, with the implication that such development as took place should do so on the basis of traditional institutions and through the agency of traditional African leaders. In Tropical Africa as in South Africa Western-educated Africans

were still regarded as something of an aberration – at best an embarrassment, at worst a danger to stable administration. Smuts may have been
more aware than most of his contemporaries in South Africa of the impact
of a Western economy upon traditional African societies, but he was
not ahead of his times in producing ideas to deal with the problem.
He wondered, rather obscurely, whether religion rather than economics
should not now provide the new dynamic for reform, but he could not
establish the link which would enable him to solve the problem of race
relations. The difficulty was that he was captivated by the New Testament
as the new vision of God, but could not wholly reconcile it with his
own philosophical views. It is far from clear whether, at this time, he
believed in the consubstantiality of Jesus. He wrote of him as possessing
the great genuis which has insight into spiritual values and the spiritual
energy which springs from passionate devotion. He also spoke of Jesus'
authority, but it was the humanity of Jesus which he seemed to stress
most heavily. He was deeply conscious of the power of Jesus' message
and of its significance for his own time, but there his reflections halted.[34]

It was much easier, Smuts found, to ponder upon the course of the
war than to find solutions to South Africa's problems, even by invoking
the power of philosophy or religion. The closing months of 1941 and
the opening of 1942 had brought much upon which to ponder, and
not all of it was cheerful. The Japanese attacks on Pearl Harbour and
on British Malaya in early December had been devastatingly successful.
But Smuts took heart from the knowledge that at last America was in
the war and from the stout defence put up by Russia against the Germans.
Auchinleck, too, had had remarkable success in North Africa, though
it had been accompanied by heavy losses among the South African troops
fighting there. In his New Year's Eve broadcast, Smuts appealed for
more volunteers to fill the gaps. They were quickly needed, for early
in 1942 Rommel counter-attacked with immediate success. Japanese
forces were also advancing swiftly to seize many Dutch possessions in
the Pacific and to threaten Singapore.

In South Africa darker moments were relieved by occasional pleasures.
In December 1941 Smuts gave a dinner for the ministers of foreign countries who had taken refuge in the Union and he had an interesting conversation about Plató and Aristotle with Princess Frederica of Greece, who
had taken refuge in South Africa after the invasion of her adopted country
by Germany.[35] Less cheerfully he reported to Margaret Gillett that a
move was afoot to induce Hertzog to return to the political arena to
act as a figurehead to draw together the disunited forces of Afrikanerdom. In fact Hertzog had no intention of rejoining the fray, though
Smuts believed that vanity might induce him to do so. 'The urge to

rule', he wrote, 'seems to grow with age. But in my case the urge seems to be the other way.'[36] It was a clear example of self-deception. The vanity he attributed to Hertzog was his own. He was only really happy in office. Yet, paradoxically, the duties of office irked him. Above all he hated the laborious task of convincing others that his views were sound and deserving of their support. He deemed it enough that he himself believed the views were right. He could not appreciate that there might be sincere differences of opinion. Dissent implied stupidity or deliberate obstruction. This was a far cry from the tentativeness of his early days, the willingness to float a range of alternatives and then to seek the advice of more experienced minds. His years in England during the First World War had changed all that. He was now the man of experience to whom others should turn for advice.

This attitude of mind was reflected in his concern for the physical health of Churchill, who had recently made a great impression in America and who had then had to return to England to take part in a parliamentary debate on a motion of no confidence in his policies – a debate which he won handsomely. 'Democracy does really involve a cruel waste,' Smuts wrote to Margaret Gillett; 'How can a man find time and proper concentration for some of the hardest and most fateful problems of all time when he has continually to pause and prepare for and make speeches which surely involve an immense amount of physical and mental energy. . . . He, being a great orator may not mind it, but *I* do.'[37] In similar vein he wrote to another friend: 'I myself find parliament a sore trial in the midst of all the other far more urgent claims.'[38] Perhaps by this time the jingle referring to Smuts's autocratic outlook, which had been inappropriate when coined many years before, rang true. What was certainly true was that his professed longing for an opportunity to retire to the 'enjoyments of the spirit and the mind' was the product of momentary frustration brought on by having to defend his government's estimates in parliament and did not represent his permanent feelings. It was equally true that he could never seize that opportunity because of a 'bondage to the ideal, to the light one is compelled to follow, whatever the cost',[39] and he would probably have been extremely resentful if the bondage had been forcibly broken.

He would certainly not have wished to leave it to others to take up the challenge thrown down by the enemy's successes in the Far East and in North Africa. Singapore and Rangoon had fallen and Rommel was advancing swiftly. For Smuts the Middle East was still the core of the issue. If the Germans broke through the Caucasus, Iraq and Iran would be at risk, and, with the Japanese advancing through India and dominating the Indian Ocean, the defence of Egypt would become virtually impossible. It was essential, in Smuts's opinion, to concentrate the British and American forces, particularly the naval forces, in the Indian Ocean to keep open the supply line to the Middle East. That view he put to Roosevelt in a letter of 19 May.[40] In South Africa he made sure that every effort was made to give whatever help was possible. In addition to the two divisions fighting in the Middle East, Smuts raised two further divisions for the interior and coastal defence of the Union. He had also enlisted 60,000 non-combatant African troops, whose excellent pay and treatment, together with the wider experience they were getting, must, he hopefully believed, be a powerful instrument of reform and progress. All those troops, Whites or Africans, were 'his' troops. He had become, in his own estimation, the embodiment of South Africa and its spirit too. Even for Jesus the issue had been simplified by the existence of the Roman Empire, he wrote to Margaret Gillett. Jesus had been prepared to leave to Caesar that which belonged to Caesar. But what would Jesus have done if he had been in Caesar's place, for that was where Smuts now found himself. Smuts, like Caesar, was responsible for peace and war, for maintaining the social order against brute violence and aggression. The passive defeatist attitude of Jesus did him scant justice. The true Christians, in Smuts's view, were those who, by prayer and endurance where possible, and by heroic self-sacrifice and battling where necessary, stood up for the right as they saw it.[41] The consciences of Mrs Gillett and her Quaker friends, and even the Sermon on the Mount, it seems, must defer to Smuts's views.

Subsequent events provided some excuse for Smuts's hyperbole. On 18 June he learned that German troops had beseiged Tobruk and that the 2nd South African Division formed part of the beleaguered garrison. Less than a week later the South African High Commissioner in London, S. F. Waterson, telegraphed to say that the defence of Tobruk had collapsed and that the British public could not understand what had taken place.[42] Worse was to follow. It was rumoured that Major-General Klopper, commander of the South African forces, had surrendered unnecessarily. The British deputy prime minister, Clement Attlee, assured Waterson that, although it was too early to give an official verdict on the events in North Africa, he had heard nothing but praise for the conduct of the South African troops.[43] Smuts stoutly defended the reputation of 'his' soldiers. The loss of Tobruk was due to bad planning, he said. The withdrawal of the main body of the Eighth Army eastward had left the South Africans in Tobruk in an impossible position.[44]

Smuts's younger son, Jannie, had avoided the fate of the men of the 2nd Division, but, along with his fellow-members of the 1st Division, had escaped with only the clothes he was wearing in the retreat from

Gazala. 'What an experience!' Smuts wrote to Margaret Gillett. 'I am so glad that he has had this fire baptism and this taste of retreat. It is so different from the victorious advance and bites so much deeper into the soul.'[45] It was an almost boorishly insensitive remark from a man whose son was, for all he knew, still in grave danger, and Mrs Gillett would be unlikely to agree with him. Like many men who have fought in wars or who have experienced great danger, Smuts believed there was merit in the experience and that others would benefit from sharing it. He had never displayed physical fear and now he seemed only to exult in the fact that 'his' South Africans had played the major role in delaying Rommel's advance eastward to El Alamein.

Even more disconcerting than the fall of Tobruk was the rumour that the British forces were to evacuate Egypt and withdraw to Palestine. Smuts could see no justification for such a plan. The British ground forces equalled the armies of Rommel numerically, while in the air British superiority had been firmly established. Even the armoured formations would soon be stronger than those which had brought success for Rommel. But if the plan *were* adopted, it was essential that any German advance southwards through East Africa should be strongly resisted, and the South Africans were the men to do the job. They must, therefore, be detached from the Middle East forces if they were to be free for the task ahead.[46] Fortunately for Smuts's peace of mind, he was summoned to Cairo in August to meet Churchill. There he was informed that withdrawal from Egypt was not contemplated, and he also learned about changes in the higher command of the British forces and of plans for the defence of El Alamein and, subsequently, for a British advance which would turn defeat into victory.

Although in the depressing days of Rommel's advance Smuts had once again talked of resigning office, the stimulus of his discussion in Cairo once again dispelled all signs of weariness. He believed, too, that his presence in South Africa was essential if the critics of the government were to be kept appropriately subdued. It was for that reason, he said, that he had turned down Churchill's invitation to accompany him to Moscow for discussions with Stalin and had also rejected a further invitation to visit London.[47] Even in the dark days of July, however, Smuts had found time to read Raleigh's *Shakespeare*, and T. R. Glover's *The Disciple*, and, during his flight to Cairo, Browning's *The Ring and the Book*. Reflecting upon these differing works, he was moved by the drama of the last days of Jesus. In the midst of the drama, Jesus, transcendent, revealed himself as very God, Smuts concluded – not consubstantial, perhaps, but the nearest to Godlike that mankind could become.[48] This was scarcely holism, but it seemed to go some way to satisfy a spiritual craving which afflicted Smuts so strongly in times of stress, when the mind sought answers but found none from its purely intellectual resources.

The difficulties for Smuts's government were unremitting. The Governor-General, Sir Patrick Duncan, who had been a staunch ally of Smuts, was taken gravely ill. Then, on 16 September, a countrywide congress of the National Party, meeting in Pretoria and attended by 1,100 members, gave a vote of confidence and plenary powers to their leader, Dr Malan. But there were compensations. The daily company of Crown Princess Frederica and other members of the Greek royal family at lunch proved a lively distraction from thoughts of war. The Greek princesses were, Smuts thought, 'great fun and splendid company. They are clever, educated, well-informed women of the world. Princess Katherine a full nurse and the crown princess, Frederica, a thoughtful, well-read woman, very young and good to look at, and as I told you before, a student of holism.'[49] Isie, who accompanied her husband on these occasions, felt less at ease amid the social pleasantries. But, as Smuts readily acknowledged, her popularity in the country at large grew daily as she involved herself more and more, in her determined but unobtrusive way, in a rich variety of activities to assist her people in time of war.[50]

By October Smuts had concluded, erroneously as it proved, that his efforts had left his opponents in such disarray that it was safe for him to go to England. *En route* he had talks with military commanders and learned that the Russians were standing firm against the most powerful attacks that Germany could unleash. In London he discussed the fate of the League of Nations with Lord Cecil and Noel Baker and reassuringly agreed that, although the League had failed to maintain the peace it had been created to ensure, it had formulated a pattern of humanitarian activities which could be regarded as one of humanity's great historic advances. Furthermore, it had underlined the need for more effective machinery to prevent the recurrence of war, and the experience gained through its efforts would benefit the world leaders as they strove to create the new organisation of the United Nations which they now envisaged. Smuts was further reassured by the manner in which the smaller powers of Europe appeared to have recognised the need for such an organisation and of the role the great powers must play in it. In the interests of world security, that role might have to impinge upon the sovereignty of the smaller nations.[51]

More important were Smuts's discussions with Churchill about the new situation created by British and American landings in North Africa early in November. This had led to an agreement being reached between the military commanders of the expedition and Admiral Darlan, the

Vichy-French leader in North Africa. Churchill and Roosevelt had endorsed the arrangement because they considered it essential to the success of the military operations against Germany. The value of it was quickly demonstrated when, on Darlan's orders, the French fleet in Toulon harbour was scuttled to avoid capture by the Germans who had invaded Vichy France in response to the Allied landings in North Africa. But British public opinion had reacted in a hostile fashion to the idea of an accord with a man who, until recently, had been a sworn enemy and who had changed sides on grounds of pure expediency.

Smuts had no doubt about where priorities lay. Strategic necessity must override public opinion. Autocracy came easily to him, and Churchill was glad of his support.[52] Meanwhile, the embarrassment of the Western leaders was lessened when Darlan was assassinated on 24 December 1942. Smuts's stay in England was only brief, but on his return flight to South Africa he was of further assistance to Churchill. Breaking his journey in Algiers, he held discussions with the Allied commanders, General Eisenhower and Admiral Cunningham. In the light of the talks, he wrote to the British prime minister giving his appraisal of the military situation, and he was able to emphasise the importance of curbing any further criticisms of Darlan to avoid unsettling French opinion in North Africa.[53] The flight was also enlivened by the company of Crown Princess Frederica from Cairo onward and by a meeting with Sir Henry Moore, Governor of Kenya, and his wife, Daphne, in Nairobi.

Shortly before Smuts reached South Africa his old rival, Hertzog, died. Smuts was saddened by the news, though he believed the loss of Hertzog would weaken his opponents. Obviously he had little grasp of public opinion, for the Nationalists were, by that time, firmly rallied under the flag of Malan. It was he, they were convinced, who stood wholeheartedly for their ideals of white supremacy within the Union and for South Africa's isolation from the rest of the world.

But it was not the Nationalists who launched the first attack upon Smuts after his return. That came from another quarter. Early in January 1943 he received a letter from a group styling themselves Friends of Africa. The leaders of the group were Margaret Ballinger and Donald Molteno, who represented African voters in the house of assembly and who were less than satisfied with Smuts's native policy. The letter claimed that the government had failed to relieve the African population of the excessive economic burden under which they laboured and had not provided any constitutional channel through which they could make their grievances known. More particularly, African labourers, who were deprived by the Industrial Conciliation Act of 1924 of the machinery for settling industrial disputes provided for members of other races, had recently been forced to accept compulsory arbitration by an emergency regulation which did not apply to Whites.[54] Smuts's performance in the field of native policy had, indeed, been far from impressive, in spite of his speech to the Institute of Race Relations. Native policy was never a matter of prime concern for him and in wartime he simply pushed it into the back of his mind, hoping that events would themselves shape the course which policy should legalise. It was, he thought, a long-term question to which time should be left to find a solution.

Where native policy was concerned, time was not on Smuts's side. After a period of eclipse since the disfranchisement of the Cape Africans, the African National Congress, under the spirited leadership of Dr A. B. Xuma, had begun to show signs of activity. A deputation of Congress leaders had protested so convincingly against the pass laws that Colonel Deneys Reitz, minister for native affairs, had agreed to put their case to the prime minister. Little had come of this, but African hopes were raised when the government appointed an inter-departmental committee of inquiry, under the chairmanship of Douglas Smit, to investigate economic, health and social conditions in urban areas. Xuma gave evidence on behalf of the Congress and the committee duly reported that Africans could not maintain their families on less than £7.50 a month. Since wages in many instances were as low as £3 a month, it was an important admission. Yet, when the wealthy municipality of Johannesburg, which paid its labourers only £5 a month, appealed to the minister of labour to postpone the introduction of new minimum wages, he accepted the plea. He later withdrew the concession after protests had been made against it, but he did so too late to enable other municipalities, who had anticipated similar exemptions, to raise their wages to the required level. The muddle caused considerable disappointment among already disgruntled African employees and a succession of strikes took place along the Witwatersrand and in Natal. In December 1942 rioting broke out in Marabastad, near Pretoria, when the superintendent of the municipal compound was explaining the delay in paying the expected increase in wages. Fourteen Africans and one European were killed and more than one hundred injured before order was restored.

Smuts's response to that pressure was to forbid unauthorised meetings on mine property and to pass wartime measures making all strikes by Africans illegal.[55] He did, it is true, agree to consult the Africans' representatives in parliament, but he had no intention of ameliorating the situation of Africans with a parliamentary election just ahead. When pressed by an influential deputation from the churches he complained to Margaret Gillett that he dare do nothing which might outstrip white opinion. He admitted that the Africans had a case and he said he would do as much as he could, but he would not jeopardise the outcome of the elections. What would it profit the country if justice were done to the underdog and the whole system were then handed over to the wreckers, he asked sententiously. In any case, he went on, reverting to the argument that time would find a solution, the return of thousands of African soldiers to civilian life after the war, men who had enjoyed better pay and conditions, would force a reform in the economic condition of African workers.[56] It was an unconvincing statement, but Smuts was anxious to brush the matter aside, complaining about the time wasted in parliament debating the issue.[57] In a petulant moment he even threatened to prolong the life of parliament, and in any case, he said, he had no intention of announcing the date of the election until absolutely necessary. 'I shall keep the opposition guessing and cursing, and go on with the work of parliament in pure innocence of spirit!' he wrote to Margaret Gillett. 'How angry they will be at such tactics. ... They will howl, let them howl!'[58] They were not the words of a mature parliamentarian.

His temper was not improved when his protégé, J. H. Hofmeyr, again offered to resign from the cabinet in order to explain his opposition to certain sections of the Trade and Occupation of Land (Transvaal and Natal) Restriction Bill which aimed at extending until 1946 restrictions imposed in 1939 upon the purchase of land by Indians in the Transvaal. The extension of the Bill to Natal had been due to fears which had arisen among the Whites after well-to-do Indians had bought land in Durban normally occupied by Europeans. Hofmeyr did not object to this particular aspect of the Bill because it applied equally to Whites and to Indians. His concern was with the Indians in the Transvaal. Smuts urged him not to resign, though he himself was not unsympathetic to the Whites' case. He did not want disunity in the cabinet, however, and he was particularly annoyed by the intervention of the Indian government. Peevishly he wrote to Margaret Gillett: 'What taunts flung at me, what charges of deserting the idealism which I preach . . . and all because some utterly selfish wealthy Indians choose to spend their ill-gotten gains, not by investing in war funds, but in buying up the properties of whites and thus raising the fears of the whites for the future of European civilisation in South Africa.'[59] Nor was it only the Indians who were angered by Smuts's policies. The coloured population also protested when they learned of the appointment of a Coloured Advisory Council, similar to the Native Advisory Council, because they believed the government was trying to cut them off still further from the mainstream of national life.[60]

Smuts was finding South Africa's domestic affairs excessively irksome, so he was glad that, when he eventually decided to announce the date of the forthcoming elections, he was able to do so against a background of military success in North Africa. South African troops had not been involved in the battles which, starting at El Alamein in October 1942, had swept the German and Italian forces westward and had led to the capture of a quarter of a million prisoners, but squadrons of the South African Air Force had played an important role in the victory. Inevitably he was accused by his opponents of rushing into a khaki election in order to take credit for the Allies' successes. But an election was due, and it is of the nature of governments to choose the most favourable time for them. And even amid the turmoil of an election, Smuts found time to share a platform with the Greek Crown Princess at a dinner in Johannesburg to launch an appeal for a relief fund for the people of Greece. 'I have told you', he wrote enthusiastically to Margaret Gillett, 'that she is a remarkable woman, with great gifts of heart and head.'[61] Shortly afterwards the princess joined her husband and father-in-law, King George of Greece, to assist them in their campaign for the restoration of the Greek monarchy.[62]

Smuts appreciated more acutely than the British government did that Britain's efforts to ensure that Greece should not be conquered by the Germans had involved supporting very disparate groups, not all of whom were fighting to restore the Greek monarchy. But it was not until a year later that he wrote to Churchill urging him to make it clear that Britain stood behind King George of Greece, who had been a faithful supporter of the Allied cause. Allied military occupation should continue, Smuts advised, at least until such time as the Greek people, under proper conditions of tranquility, could decide upon the form of government they desired.[63]

After a short holiday, Smuts grew restive as the elections drew near. Once again he affirmed that this must be his last election, and in the same breath went on to discuss the problems of achieving a workable peace settlement as if he alone were responsible for the security of the world.

I failed miserable twenty-four years ago, and fear another and more tragic failure next time [he wrote to Margaret Gillett]. I doubt whether I could have done much more at Paris where I was not in a prominent position and the real reins of power were held by other hands. But since then I have come to be looked upon as one of the elder statesmen and one to expect much from. ... And the question is whether the ordinary methods of political action can be usefully applied in such a case, where really a religious reformation in the human spirit is called for.[64]

The death of the Governor-General, Sir Patrick Duncan, before the election was a sad blow for Smuts who had, with justification, looked upon Duncan as his friend. The results of the election, however, appeared to be a triumph for the government. The United Party won more than twice as many seats as the National Party and had the support of a further sixteen Labour and Dominion Party members as well as the three representatives of the Africans. But the result was deceptive. The United Party's gains had been made at the expense of the minority groups on the Nationalist side. Havenga's Afrikaner Party, the remnant of the Hertzogites, was wiped out. Malan's National Party was now the sole representative of the overwhelming body of Afrikaners, having polled three-quarters of the Afrikaner vote. It had, moreover, increased its share of the votes in the constituencies of the Witwatersrand, and, while the government had won overwhelming majorities in many consti-tuencies, the United Party now held twenty-eight seats with majorities of less than a thousand.[65] These were ominous signs for the future. But if, as hindsight suggests, this was the turning-point in the fortunes of the United Party, Smuts was unaware of it. Already his thoughts were turning to Europe and even further afield. Mussolini had been overthrown and President Roosevelt had invited Smuts to visit America.

But in Europe there were still problems. Smuts was deeply concerned by the great part Russia was playing in the war. He foresaw that she might lay claim to world leadership on the strength of her contribution to the defeat of Germany, and he did not consider she was qualified to take such responsibility. In two telegrams to Churchill he called for the more extensive involvement of Allied ground forces as a counter-balance to the Russians.[66]

Early in October Smuts was able to become involved more directly in European affairs. With the approval of his party caucus, which was confident in its huge parliamentary majority, he accepted Churchill's invitation to visit England. *En route* he had the pleasure of meeting his two sons in Cairo and Crown Princess Frederica and her husband in Alexandria. In Tunis he also met General Klopper, who had escaped from captivity in Italy. He reached London on 5 October to the great delight of Churchill, who hoped he would be able to prolong his visit to the utmost. 'He is a magnificent man', Churchill wrote of Smuts to General Eisenhower, 'and one of my most cherished friends.'[67]

But Smuts did not spend all his time in conversations with Churchill, though he enjoyed his encounters with the prime minister every bit as much as Churchill enjoyed his company. Probably his most important contribution to events in Britain was a speech he made to members of the Empire Parliamentary Association on 25 November, in which he made a number of suggestions for action after peace was restored. To ensure world security called for extremely complex arrangements, he said, a fact which had not been appreciated in 1919. Facile slogans must be avoided. Even democracy was not simply a question of freedom. Leadership was essential. A proper place of leadership must be given to the three great powers, America, Russia and Britain. Britain, however, though standing high in world esteem for the part she had played in the war, had given so much that she would emerge at the end victorious but poor. If she were to play a significant role as the third power, it would be necessary to strengthen the Empire and Commonwealth and also to forge new links with some of the smaller powers of Western Europe. As far as the Empire was concerned – and here Smuts was making a distinction between the dominions with large European populations and the colonies where non-Europeans were administered by a handful of European officials – a possible solution might be found through combining some of the smaller dependencies to form larger, economically viable units. These might then take their place – under white leadership of course – as self-governing dominions alongside the existing members of the Commonwealth. As to links with the Continent, these must be with the Scandinavian countries and other smaller nations because he did not see either Germany or France emerging as significant powers.[68]

Smuts's remarks caused a stir, though he himself insisted that they were of a purely tentative nature. Amery, however, was doubtful about a British link with the smaller powers of Europe which lacked the political outlook of Britain. In any case, the whole of Western and Southern Europe would, he thought, be powerless against a resurgent Germany acting in co-operation with Russia. If democracy were to be defended against Communism, Germany, after due punishment, must be brought back into the European fold.[69] In the event, Amery's plan proved the more workable. Meanwhile Smuts had to return to South Africa, but in April 1944 he was back in London again for a meeting of Commonwealth prime ministers and at once his help was solicited by Amery to combat what he believed to be Churchill's unduly sanguine assessment of the prospects of future co-operation between the three great powers. Once again Amery stressed the need to rehabilitate Germany in order to create a Western bloc strong enough to resist Russia, a view which Smuts himself only accepted some years later. After the other prime ministers returned home, Smuts, to his great pleasure, stayed in England to accompany Churchill on visits to troops embarking for the forthcoming landings in Normandy. Then, on his way back to South Africa, he visited 'his' troops in Italy.

These visits to England were of enormous value in restoring Smuts's morale. He played a relatively insignificant role in determining British strategy because he was unable to be away from South Africa for long enough to become wholly absorbed in European affairs. But the opportunity to touch the fringe of great events, and to be welcomed as warmly as he was by Churchill, meant a lot to him. Compared with that, the problems of South Africa seemed merely irksome. But problems there were, and in every quarter. First, many of the Whites seemed almost to have forgotten the war now that the African continent had been cleared of the enemy and money was plentiful. Africans, too, seemed to be enjoying a period of euphoria. The report of the Smit Commission had encouraged the inhabitants of the township of Alexandra, between Johannesburg and Pretoria, to walk to work rather than pay increased bus fares, and the bus company had given in. That victory, coupled with a government announcement that, in response to the demands of the African Mine Workers Union set up as an offshoot of the African Native Congress in 1941, a commission of inquiry (the Lansdowne Commission) had been appointed to investigate conditions in the mines, created an atmosphere of expectation.

Buoyed up by those hopes, a number of African intellectuals formed themselves into a drafting committee to prepare a Bill of Rights, claiming above all the right of people to choose their own form of government. In the same spirit the 1943 annual conference of the Congress had decided to form a Youth League, manned by students from Fort Hare and the University of the Witwatersrand as well as by young workers from Johannesburg.[70] Next, early in 1944, Donald Molteno, one of the representatives of Africans in the house of assembly, had made an unsuccessful attempt to induce parliament to repeal the pass laws. His failure encouraged the African Youth League to demand more determined action. Land, they said, should be divided between farmers and peasants of all races in proportion to their numbers. Then there should be training in scientific methods of farming for all and the colour bar should be abolished throughout the country. The Congress rejected these ideas as the dreams of young men[71] and in the middle of 1944 launched a campaign to collect a million signatures to a petition demanding the repeal of the pass laws. Its action failed completely to satisfy the urgent needs of the majority of Africans, so thousands of workers living in slums around Johannesburg occupied municipal land where they erected shanty towns. Their example was quickly followed by other Africans along the Witwatersrand. Then, later in the year, the inhabitants of Alexandra staged a second bus boycott.[72]

Smuts's reaction to these various manifestations of African dissatisfaction was unconstructive. When he addressed a congress of the United Party in October he merely reaffirmed 'our well-known standpoint of separateness in social intercourse, housing and field of employment between the colours'.[73] Even the architect of apartheid, H. F. Verwoerd, would not at that stage have differed seriously with Smuts's statement. Nor was Smuts any more successful in appeasing the Indian community. His attempt to replace existing legislation with two ordinances intended to create a joint board to license dwelling areas within boroughs and towns in Natal came up against the opposition of the Natal Indian Congress. After consulting its legal advisers, the central government decided after all that the ordinances were *ultra vires*.[74] Of a different character but nonetheless disheartening was the rejection by his own colleagues of Smuts's proposal to form a Coloureds fighting brigade to make good the casualties suffered by the South African Division in Italy. The cabinet was horrified by the probable reaction to any proposal to go back on government assurances that non-Whites would never be armed except as a final resort in defence of the Union.

With relief Smuts turned from the practical task of dealing personally with what he described as parish pump politics to the greater pleasure of advising others on matters of moment. He was distressed by the way in which the British government seemed to be giving in to the weariness of the public by encouraging hopes of prosperity to come, while still holding out hopes to France that she might again take the lead in European affairs, a role for which Smuts deemed her totally unfitted.[75] He was also able to commiserate with Chaim Weizmann over the failure of the Jews to obtain their homeland, admitting that, while the fault lay with Britain's failure to permit adequate Jewish immigration into Palestine between the wars, the most the Jews could now hope for was a partitioned Palestine because Britain simply had to take into account the opposition of the Arabs,[76] which was little consolation to Weizmann.

Greatly though he longed for peace, the prospect of victory over Germany failed to arouse in Smuts the excitement he had felt at a similar stage of the war twenty-five years earlier. Now he had grave doubts whether purely political methods could deal with the problems created by the religious fervour of the Nazis, Fascists and Communists. Sadly, he saw no corresponding religious strength among the Allies.[77] Russia, he thought, now presented as great a threat as Germany had done. Amery shared his pessimism and for the same reasons. 'It is the height of wishful delusion', he wrote to Smuts, 'to imagine that a system of world peace can be based on Russian participation.'[78] Even the call to attend the peace conference in San Francisco did nothing to stir Smuts's zest for action. He set out with a heavy heart in March 1945, only to learn on 12 April of the death of President Roosevelt. This, in Smuts's view, was a serious blow to whatever prospects of success the conference might have had.

His forebodings were fully borne out when, having been appointed to the chairmanship of the commission appointed to draft the constitution of the General Assembly of the United Nations, he found that other members lacked completely his own burning sense of urgency. What he feared was that, with the surrender of Germany in May, events in Europe rather than the discussions in San Francisco would determine the future of the world. He was disturbed, too, by the growing demand for equal rights for all people, a policy which he was unlikely to be able to promote in South Africa. When the question of the future of the mandates was discussed, he did not hesitate to defend South Africa's claim to South West Africa.[79] The dispute over the right of any one of the great powers to veto decisions of the Security Council – with Russia on the one hand claiming the right to veto any decision and the smaller powers resisting any veto – was eventually settled by a compromise, but Smuts returned to South Africa deeply unhappy about the future of the United Nations Organisation which he had helped to create.

He suffered another blow with the news of Churchill's overwhelming defeat in the elections on 5 July. Though he had nothing against the Labour Party at that time, he feared that the new government lacked both the experience and the understanding of foreign affairs which were so vital if Britain were to play a significant role in Europe. His own role in South Africa he considered even more important than that of Churchill in Britain. 'I have become even more than the government,' he wrote to Margaret Gillett, 'and am like a father to the people and all their complaints and prayers come to me *personally* in the hope or faith that I shall put them all right!'[80] His self-satisfaction was partly redeemed by the exclamation mark. But it was a dangerous opinion to hold, even if it seemed justified by the tumultuous reception accorded him in every large town in South Africa on his return from the peace conference.

The use of the two atomic bombs which put an end to the war with Japan gave him some satisfaction, not because of the havoc it caused but because he believed it provided concrete proof that any future war was unthinkable. Still he continued to have doubts about the Labour leadership in Britain which seemed prepared to rely on trust and understanding in its dealings with Russia to an extent which Smuts believed foolhardy. He was critical, too, both of Russia's political intentions and of America's attempt to dominate the world economy, and sympathised with Amery's view that Western Europe should create a commonwealth along British lines. Meanwhile, the British Commonwealth should retain its imperial preference arrangements in defiance of America's wishes.

Smuts was especially concerned about the future of Italy's colonies lest any decision should adversely affect South Africa's position *vis-à-vis* South West Africa. Why should Britain's hard-earned colonies be surrendered, he asked, while Russia clung to her conquests in Europe and America held on to the bases she had seized in the Pacific.[81] In the despair resulting from all these worries, his philosophy was undergoing a marked change. If human nature alone were not enough to solve the world's problems, then men must hope for divine intervention, he said. The humanity of Jesus no longer satisfied his needs. Reverting to the orthodoxy of his boyhood, he wrote to Margaret Gillett: 'God himself so loved the world that He sent his only son to redeem and save it.'[82] Holism appeared to have taken a back seat.

From these broader issues Smuts was soon recalled to problems at home. The Labour and Dominion Parties had decided to withdraw from the coalition now that the war was over. Though they left without rancour, their departure weakened the Unionists' position. More seriously, relations between Whites and Asians in Natal had deteriorated markedly. A recent commission had recommended that there should be a joint conference between the Indian and South African governments to explore the situation, but Smuts disliked the idea. In his view, South Africa's relations with her Indian population were her own affair, and he knew that any interference by the Indian government would stir up white opposition. Appeals for help to control Indian immigration from white settlers in Kenya[83] only reinforced his belief that Indian political leaders were bringing pressure to bear in every possible way to support Indian expansion into Eastern Africa. He tried to forestall criticism from the Indian community by means of legislation which would give four members to represent them in the house of assembly, elected on a communal roll (three for Natal and one for the Transvaal). In addition, there would be one nominated and one elected member of senate. But he failed to win the Indians' approval because they disliked the idea of a communal roll. Another proposal, that there should be a law which would designate some land in Natal as open to occupancy by all races while in the rest of the province ownership and occupancy should be controlled by a board composed equally of Indian and European representatives, was also attacked by the Indian community.

Deputations were sent by the Indians to Britain, India and America early in 1946. Shortly afterwards, the Indian representative in the United

Nations Organisation pressed the case of the Natal Indians in the General Assembly. Smuts secretly considered that both Whites and Asians in Natal had acted unreasonably, but his sympathies, in the last resort, were with the Whites. He believed that they had brought something of value to Africa which the Indians could never match and which the Indians' claims now threatened.[84] Hofmeyr did not share his view and suggested that the idea of a communal roll should be abandoned in favour of a loaded franchise on a common roll. Smuts, however, would not be moved. He introduced both his bills into parliament in March and they became law in May. The following month the Indian government recalled its High Commissioner and the Indians in South Africa began a campaign of passive resistance which soon spread from Durban to Johannesburg. Several hundred protesters were imprisoned and a conference of Africans in Johannesburg, chaired by Dr Xuma, gave its support to the Indians. Some Africans even joined the passive resistance movement. But African political opinion was not united. The African Youth League looked askance at any action which might threaten its goal of African leadership. It was suspicious of Indians and Communists alike.[85]

The Congress may have been neither active nor single-minded enough to satisfy the Youth League, but since the end of the war it had not been wholly quiescent, though Smuts may have been too busy to notice what it was doing or else considered it to be unrepresentative of the real needs of Africans. In June 1945 the Congress's anti-pass law petition was taken to Cape Town. It did not contain the million signatures for which the organisers had hoped, and Jan Hofmeyr, acting head of the government, refused to meet the deputation. A large demonstration was mounted and several of the leaders were arrested. Meanwhile, two South African delegates attended the Fifth Pan-African Congress in Manchester and met there some of the men, like Kwame Nkrumah and Jomo Kenyatta, who were soon to lead independence movements in their own countries. The congress then supported a resolution in favour of autonomy and independence for Africa. In Cape Town a meeting of several thousand Africans called for the immediate implementation of the Atlantic Charter. Two months later, in December, while the Whites in South Africa were celebrating the Day of the Covenant, a conference of the African Congress adopted a list of claims which included the repeal of the pass laws, freedom of land ownership, one man one vote, equal justice in the courts, freedom of the press, equal opportunity, equal pay, removal of the industrial colour bar and equal educational opportunities.[86]

To all these activities Smuts turned a blind eye. More pressing, in his view, was the need to write to the Anglo-American commission appointed in November 1945 to inquire into Jewish immigration into Palestine. His object was to insist that the Balfour Declaration of 1917 had been a clear statement of long-term policy and that implicit within the declaration was the proposal for a Jewish national home in Palestine.[87] On issues remote from South Africa he still had more generous and often more constructive ideas than on those nearer home. Nevertheless, he was aware that to leave South Africa in April 1946 to attend a conference of Commonwealth prime ministers was inopportune. But the prime ministers' meeting was to be followed by a further peace conference in Paris, and, though he felt he had little to offer there, he could not resist the lure of such an important occasion. In the event he was disappointed. The Paris meeting was postponed because of disagreement among the foreign ministers who were to have prepared the ground for the discussions. But his journey back to South Africa was, as usual, punctuated with useful meetings – in Rome and Cairo with foreign leaders and with the British High Commissioner in Palestine with whom Smuts discussed what he regarded as the disastrous recommendations of the Anglo-American commission.[88] What the commission had recommended was the setting up of a predominantly Arab government in Palestine. Its conclusions had been reached partly through fear of Arab opposition in the Middle East and partly because of resentment at what appeared to be the increasing clamour of Jewish demands and the violence of the extreme Zionists. Another issue of international importance also occupied his thoughts. His first feelings of satisfaction at the news of the atomic bomb had been followed by misgivings and he was relieved to learn that America did not intend to share her knowledge of atomic science with Russia. Such secrets could not suitably be shared with a power as ruthless and immature as Russia, Smuts believed.[89]

South Africa, too, had problems with which to greet his homecoming. African mineworkers, whose wages had fallen to less than half the minimum amount advocated by a government commission a few years earlier, went on strike on 12 August after several attempts to present their grievances had been ignored by the Chamber of Mines. Soon 70,000 miners were on strike, but Smuts was quickly on his way back to Paris to take part in the postponed peace negotiations. Though he may have dismissed the activities of the African National Congress on the ground that they did not truly represent African opinion, the actions of the mineworkers could scarcely have been fitted into the same category. Yet he preferred to attribute the strike to the influence of agitators and, as at the time of the Bulhoek massacre, he chose to regard African problems as the preserve of the native affairs or labour departments. Over minor issues that was a reasonable view. The government alone could handle major problems, but Smuts believed the native problem was simply insoluble in the foreseeable future, and he looked vaguely and without any great confidence for a gradual improvement in race relations. The difficulty was that in his inner heart he still could not reconcile himself to the idea of African equality with the Whites. Meanwhile, the strike was crushed by police intervention.

In Paris he played a more positive role. Sensing the tensions between the various representatives there, he did not become involved in the detail of committee work. Instead, he used his unique position as the one surviving member of the 1919 peace negotiations to hold personal talks with leading representatives from different countries in an attempt to avoid any suggestion that a third world war was already in the offing. During a weekend break he visited the Churchills in Geneva and a fortnight later he spent another weekend as the guest of King George VI at Balmoral. Back in Paris, he was able to discuss with the South African High Commissioner in London the problems posed by the large number of people seeking to immigrate into South Africa, and with Dr Weizmann the role the Jews might play in planning a future for Palestine.[90] Hofmeyr wrote reassuringly about events in South Africa, though he was concerned that the hitherto restrained leaders of the Natives Representative Council, shocked by the authorities' fierce reaction to the miners' strike, had passed a resolution calling upon the government to abolish immediately all discriminatory legislation against non-Whites. They had also adjourned the Council *sine die* in protest against the government's native policy in general. A commission was appointed in August to inquire into the operation of laws affecting Africans, but Hofmeyr was aware that, if he were to give the Africans satisfaction, the Whites would resist strongly.

Smuts reflected upon the dangers to which his absence from South Africa was giving rise as he took his walks in the woods around Paris. But he had no intention of returning home before the meeting of the United Nations in New York.. He knew there would be heavy criticism of South Africa's dealings with her Indian and African communities, and he wished the commission had been able to report before the New York meeting took place. Meanwhile, he replied with some asperity to Hofmeyr's letter, insisting that, although some liberalisation of native policy must take place at a modest rate, it could only occur with the consent of the white population. In any event, he would not submit to dictation from Africans. Once again Smuts was demonstrating his innate ability to look at the native problem through any but Afrikaner eyes. The leaders of the Natives Representative Council in fact had no real wish to confront the government. Their leader, Professor Z. K. Matthews, said he resented Hofmeyr's accusations of extremism and recklessness. The government, he went on, was oblivious to the progressive forces at work in South Africa and in the outside world. It may have defeated the mineworkers by using the harsh intervention of the police and by forbidding their union to operate in future, but by so doing it had turned against itself the educated leaders of the African people.[91] It was here that the confusion in Smuts's thinking was most clearly revealed, for it was the educated Africans whom he rejected who had come so close to adopting the European standards of civilisation which he so fervently wished to preserve. He was not alone in his confusion. Even in those British African dependencies where administrators boasted of their enlightened approach to African affairs, it was the traditional or neo-traditional rulers who were given encouragement and the Western-educated Africans who were regarded as troublemakers. Hofmeyr may not have agreed with Smuts's view, but out of loyalty to his absent leader he could take no other line.

After the Paris conference ended Smuts went to London to try to enlist support for South Africa at the forthcoming United Nations Meeting. While there, a conservative politician, Duncan Sandys, invited him to try to gain the goodwill of the leaders of Western Europe for a plan to form a United Nations of Europe which a British group, under the chairmanship of Churchill, was trying to promote.[92] New York, to which Smuts went next, proved every bit as trying as he had feared. The Indian representative, Mrs Pandit, won considerable applause for her attack on South Africa's discriminatory policies which Smuts thought surprisingly unjust in view of the discrimination and communal disunity in India. To Margaret Gillett he confided that, although he respected the whole human family, in the meeting between East and West he was a westerner. By her invasion and infiltration of Eastern Africa, India was threatening a noble experiment.[93] He seemed puzzled rather than perturbed to meet Dr Xuma in New York. Deeply disturbed by the government's handling of the mineworkers' strike and in view of the resolutions of the Native Representative Council, the African National Congress had sent Xuma to the United Nations to put its case. Smuts met Xuma only briefly and on a social occasion when it was not possible to discuss matters of importance, but it was clear that he could not understand the purpose of Xuma's presence in New York. He found him a totally unexpected phenomenon, even though the Congress had been in existence for over a third of a century. Xuma's visit was not entirely without results, however. The Congress had already been impressed by the Indians' passive resistance policy, and links between Indians and

Africans became stronger after Xuma reported the manner in which Indian representatives in New York had conducted the campaign on behalf of non-Whites in South Africa.[94]

After the traumas of New York, Smuts's return journey to South Africa did much to restore his morale. He visited Holland and Belgium and in both countries was received with acclaim by all except the Communists.[95] In Rome he met the Italian prime minister and in Athens he had a magnificent reception, addressing parliament, the university and the municipal council. He revelled in the adulation given him, happily describing himself to Margaret Gillett as a second Byron, a title, he went on to say, he believed he had fairly earned by the way he had upheld the Greeks, often single-handed.[96]

In retrospect Smuts regarded his mission to the United Nations as a failure. He had won no support for South Africa's policies, while the Indian representatives had even contrived to cast doubt upon the results of a plebiscite taken by the government to test African opinion in South West Africa. The method of consultation through the medium of chiefs denied the people freedom of expression, they argued.[97] 'Colours queer my poor pitch everywhere,' Smuts wrote to Margaret Gillett. 'I quite understand and can look at it all philosophically. But South Africans cannot understand. Colour bars are to them part of the divine order of things. But I sometimes wonder what our position in years to come will be when the whole world is against us.' His own view did not differ as markedly from that of other white South Africans as he would have liked to suggest. Once again, too, he overlooked the opinion of eight million black South Africans as, in his postscript, he went on to say: 'And yet there is much to be said for the South African point of view who fear getting submerged in black Africa.'[98]

Smuts's despondency was in no way dispelled by the situation in the Union. Some Africans, notably the Youth League, were pressing for non-co-operation with the government and, forgetting their earlier reservations, for joint action by all non-Whites. Even more moderate African leaders were looking urgently to the government for some statement that might give them hope.[99] The Indians had rejected his franchise proposals, and even his own supporters were feeling rebuffed by the violence of the attacks on Union policy at the United Nations meeting.

The award of the Order of Merit in the 1947 New Year honours list moved Smuts greatly and for once his modest disavowal of having deserved it contained a ring of truth. From this time there appeared in most of his correspondence an elegaic tone. It was as if, though he continued to meet the day-to-day demands of office, he could reflect like a disembodied spirit upon the tribulations of the world. 'The world does not know or understand us,' he wrote to Margaret Gillett, 'It is a good country, and a good people, but the world sees its mistakes more clearly than its goodness or virtues.'[100] Increasingly South Africa's policy towards its non-white population was holding the centre of the stage, and Smuts had no answer to offer. Nor did he begin to understand the complex issues which Africans were now presenting to the government. He was prepared to behave in a manner which he believed reasonable but that did still not envisage Africans achieving equality with Whites. He admitted that Africans had a genuine grievance, due to the failure of wages to keep pace with rising prices, and he sensed that the debates in the United Nations had had an impact even among humble domestic servants and farm workers. But it was with disbelief that he heard Margaret Ballinger claim that Africans wanted rights, not improvements. Nor, indeed, was she probably right as far as the vast majority of Africans were concerned at that time. But the combination of low living standards and the absence of human rights made it possible for educated Africans to find a ready response from their fellow-Africans when they criticised the government, whether to demand the franchise, or to seek an increase in wages or the abolition of the pass laws. But for Smuts, African opinion, no matter how united, could not be the factor which determined the shape of his country. 'What is the future of South Africa going to be if she can no longer look to European leadership as her bulwark?' he wrote.[101] And again 'I am a South African European proud of our heritage and proud of the clean European society we have built up in South Africa, and which I am determined not to see lost in the black pool of Africa.'[102]

From these troubles Smuts was joyously rescued by the visit to South Africa of King George and Queen Elizabeth and the two royal princesses. His public duties prevented him from accompanying the royal party throughout their tour, but he spent a happy weekend with them in the Natal Drakensburg and they visited his family at Doornkloof. He met them also at the top of Table Mountain up which he had, as always, walked, while they ascended by cable car, and he took part in welcoming ceremonies in Pretoria and Johannesburg. After such exhilaration he felt able to turn his thoughts once again to world affairs. He was delighted by President Truman's offer of financial aid to Greece and Turkey, which suggested that the United States would not now pursue a policy of isolation, but he was shrewd enough to recognise that, if this were so, it might help to divide the world into two camps. If only Western Europe could act as a third force and bring to the world the treasures of European culture and experience, he wrote to Margaret Gillett.[103] He had little confidence in the United Nations. As a body it was trying to set up

239

a form of world government for which it was hopelessly unfitted. It was a democracy without leadership, and consequently a sham. Countries, he wrote, which were unable to govern themselves were sitting in judgement on others who had done their job reasonably well in spite of difficulties.[104] Even at home he was bombarded with correspondence from Jawaharlal Nehru, 'mouthing his broken agreements and human rights. At least we know how to run a country decently and in orderly fashion which Indians have never been able to do without the Raj.'[105] With considerable satisfaction he informed Nehru that a number of Indians in all the provinces had become dissatisfied with the activities of the Communist-led Natal Indian Congress and had formed the Natal Indian Organization. The latter body had already opened fruitful discussions with the government about a wide range of issues and thought it was time for India to send a High Commissioner to South Africa once again.[106]

Towards the spokesmen of the Natives Representative Council Smuts did not show the same peevish spirit. In May he invited a deputation from the Council to meet him and offered what he claimed to be a new deal. The Council members were sceptical, and their suspicions were confirmed when, shortly afterwards, the Industrial Conciliation (Natives) Act became law. Under its terms there were to be no unions for African mineworkers, agricultural labourers or domestic servants, and to organise any union which had not been registered would be a criminal offence. Once again Smuts's actions had not measured up to his promises. In October, however, just before the meeting of the United Nations Organisation, he published a further 'new deal' for Africans which envisaged the increase of the elected members of the Natives Representative Council from twelve to fifty. The Council itself was not enthusiastic about the plan, but the ever conciliatory Congress agreed to give it a trial.[107] It was a relief to Smuts, who could not take time to attend the United Nations meeting himself, and it may have been one of the factors which induced even Mrs Pandit to moderate her attack upon South Africa. More probably it was the problem which India herself was facing which encouraged her to adopt a more reasonable tone in her speeches.

Smuts's reason for staying in South Africa was his concern about the political situation before the elections which were to take place in 1948. He was desperately anxious to win the election because he saw victory for the United Party as the only guarantee that South Africa would remain in the Commonwealth. The republicanism of Malan's National Party was too worrying to contemplate. In addition he feared that the native policy which the Nationalists were formulating would deny Africans any prospect of government support for the improvement of their material condition. He did not have high hopes for the successful handling of the native question even by his own party, but the apartheid proposals which the Nationalists were contemplating seemed to him devoid of all feeling for the well-being of the African people.[108]

Smuts's concern for the future of South Africa was closely linked with his fears for the future of civilisation. The United Nations Organisation he regarded as too grandiose a project to succeed. How far this jaundiced view reflected his distress at the criticisms levelled in the Assembly against South Africa it is difficult to assess, but he noticeably sidestepped the implications of an odd letter which he received in October 1947. The writer was unknown to him – a young man named John Wellington, from the University of the Witwatersrand, who claimed to have been told by God to convey his views to the prime minister. Smuts was wrong, he wrote, to set such store by the Union's links with South West Africa. South Africa's security was in no way bound up with the mandated territory. The greatest security lay in doing what was right, which in this case was to build up the United Nations Organisation into what it should be. If the United Nations were successful, the security of South Africa was assured. Smuts, he believed, knew this in his heart. What was needed now was for him to make the same sort of gesture he had made in taking office under Hertzog, by putting the interests of the United Nations before those of South Africa.[109]

The appeal produced no response. Smuts was more concerned with his conviction that the first task was to hold Russia at bay, and the cold war which was developing in 1947 reinforced his opinion. He did not see America carrying out that task in spite of the benefits likely to accrue from the recently announced Marshall aid plan. Western Europe would, he thought, provide a better counterweight to Communism than American hegemony could. But if that proposal were to be effective, the lead must be taken by Britain, supported by the dominions, and Western Germany must be a member. Though he believed the Labour government was something of a liability in the context, he still thought Britain capable of fulfilling the dual function of heading the Commonwealth and providing the lead in Europe – if the will were there.[110] England's weakness saddened him as much as Russia's strength worried him, but he was delighted that Winston Churchill appeared to be the driving force behind the movement for Western European union.[111] Looking once again to the Commonwealth as his prototype, he was firmly of the opinion that federation was impossible. The most effective form of union would be of that loose variety based upon community of interest which bound the dominions together, but there must be some form of treaty guarantee to ensure that members fulfilled their obligations.

An area in which he believed the British government was still performing less effectively than it should was that of Palestine. He was delighted when the General Assembly of the United Nations agreed to the partitioning of Palestine in November 1947, but he was horrified at the haste with which Britain withdrew from her protective role there. The English, he said, had developed a curious new habit of backing the wrong horse. Their attitude to the Jews and the new state of Israel was a disaster, and he feared that in the end they would be disliked as much by the Arabs as by the Jews in spite of their current policies.[112] He himself had done his best for the Jewish homeland and he wished the state of Israel well.

In February 1948 Smuts received two items of personal news, one of which brought him great pleasure and the other a measure of sadness. The information that he had been elected Chancellor of Cambridge University gave him deepest satisfaction. It meant a visit to England immediately after the rigours of an election campaign. But for Smuts, even at the age of seventy-eight, the joy of having been singled out for the highest honour his old university could bestow was more than adequate compensation for the strain which a visit to England would impose on him. The other news, of the death of his old comrade, Thomas Lamont, moved him deeply, not only because of his own sense of loss but also because he knew how great a blow it would be to his dear friend, Florence Lamont, Thomas's wife. Writing to another close friend, Daphne Moore, about his feelings for Florence, he admitted that he had always found it easier to make closer friendships with women than with men. The friendships were not, he said, of a sexual character but sprang from some inner sense of affinity.[113] Not everyone accepted the innocence of those relationships, but in spite of the intensity of Smuts's attachment to a number of women his claim was probably true. For him the world was divided into two spheres. In one, men shouldered their responsibilities seriously and courageously. In the other, women performed their humane and domestic tasks with warmth and cheerfulness and were ever ready to listen with intelligent solicitude to the problems which men faced in the great battle of life.

The year 1948 was bad for Smuts. Not only did it bring defeat for the United Party but he himself lost his seat in Standerton, though he quickly found another. Many thought the result was largely due to the sympathy felt by Hofmeyr, Smuts's deputy, for the African population.[114] In fact several factors affected the outcome of the elections, not least the desire for a change after nine demanding years of government by one party. There was, too, a strong undercurrent of hostility between those who had volunteered for service overseas during the recent war and those who believed that South Africa should have remained neutral. The red flash the former had been entitled to wear on their uniforms had been a provocation which was not forgotten by those who disagreed with their political outlook. Smuts himself, though a hero to many, seemed aloof and unsympathetic to many others. For the latter his ideas were too rigid or too unconcerned with popular feeling. When he remained steadfast, his critics condemned him as obdurate. When his pronouncements showed greater flexibility, they said he was still the old 'slim Jannie', whose word could not be trusted. Botha might have broken through that wall of hostility. Smuts had not the warmth of character to do it. So, once again he was in opposition, but he had no intention of quitting the political field. He was convinced that South Africa could not yet spare him.

10
Epilogue

After his defeat in the 1948 elections, Smuts's main concern was to protect what he believed he and Botha, and now for many years he alone, had been striving to create – a South Africa in which the white races worked together to establish European civilisation on a firm foundation.[1] Ever since Hertzog broke away from the South African Party more than forty years earlier, Smuts had feared that the exclusiveness of the Nationalists would take the country back to the attitudes of the 1890s and destroy the Union. More recently, as he began to realise that the segregation of Africans in rural areas was no longer a total possibility, he had also come to regard himself as a campaigner for better living and working conditions for Africans in opposition to the Nationalists' apparent desire to banish them to the reserves and forget about them. With these goals before him, a sense of the excitement of battle permeated his letters, almost as if he were glad Hofmeyr was unable to lead the United Party and that the task must fall to him.[2]

Before resuming the political struggle, however, Smuts had the pleasant duty of visiting Cambridge for his installation as chancellor. For once the trepidation he claims to have felt before the event was genuine. He was, indeed, deeply conscious of the honour he had received. But all went well. He was fêted on every hand. In his formal address to congregation he warned his hearers against Russia's policy of peaceful infiltration by means of fifth column activities. The growing power of the USSR was a problem which constantly exercised him, and three months later he was to become so depressed by the overt weakness of Western Europe that he feared Russia might be emboldened to take by force what he had previously thought she was prepared to annex only slowly and by cunning.[3] But for the time being he was in a buoyant mood. On the flight to England he had broken his journey in Athens to be reunited with Queen Frederica and her husband, so that when he was invited to lunch with the British royal family he was able to give Prince Philip news of the prince's own family. The return journey provided further pleasures. He was greeted with acclaim in Holland, where he received the honorary degree of Doctor of Laws at Leiden University. He also stayed in Athens once again and noted with admiration the work the Queen was doing for refugee children.

Back in South Africa Smuts was immediately involved in a parliamentary debate in which he sternly denounced the policies the government proposed to implement for non-Whites. During those opening weeks in opposition he seemed to revel in the sheer pleasure of attacking his opponents. From Professor E. G. Malherbe, Principal of the Natal University College, however, came a warning note. Malherbe considered such enthusiastic demolition of the Nationalists to be unproductive. Instead, he urged Smuts to try to form a coalition with Havenga, Hertzog's old friend, and with some of the more moderate Nationalists; in other words, to create a new United Party. The old party, he thought, lacked youth and imagination, though he absolved Smuts of both those charges in spite of his age. The party needed to broaden its base even if it meant that Smuts must accept Havenga as leader.[4] Smuts attempted to draft a reasoned rebuttal of the proposals, but he did not welcome suggestions from younger and less experienced men and he eventually replied in a dismissive fashion.[5]

In October tragedy struck Smuts and his family. His elder son, Japie, for whom he, and more especially Isie, had had a particular affection, died suddenly of meningitis. Smuts accepted the blow stoically, but it took much of the zest from his life. Isie, less egocentric than her husband, was sorely stricken. Shortly afterwards Smuts suffered another loss when Jan Hofmeyr also died after a brief illness. In spite of his humane views on native policy and the opposition to which they gave rise even in his own party, Hofmeyr had still been expected to be Smuts's successor. His death left the United Party without any obvious leader, so that the need for Smuts to remain involved was even greater. It also meant that considerably more work devolved upon him. Still hoping that the Nationalists would not survive in power for long, he campaigned indefatigably on behalf of members of his own party contesting provincial elections in March 1949. The result was a disappointment and the Unionists lost seats they had fully expected to win. The Nationalists had campaigned on a native policy which aimed to deprive all Africans of the vote and to put coloured voters on to a communal roll. Smuts was profoundly disturbed by the reaction in favour of that policy among both English- and Afrikaans-speakers. He recognised that the Whites were fearful of a future in which Africans would dominate the country, but he believed that to deprive Africans of their constitutional right to elected representation in parliament was a sure way to encourage an upsurge of anger which would threaten the foundations of white civilisation.[6] He set out these views in response to a letter from a United Party supporter who could not understand why the party leaders criticised apartheid when most party members seemed to approve of it. Socially and residentially, Smuts replied, apartheid had always been common policy among South African Whites. But the Nationalists were going far beyond that policy, far beyond the policy even of Hertzog. They were setting aside the South Africa Act in a wild campaign which might well lead to the emergence of African nationalism and a common front against the white minority.[7]

Smuts was also dismayed by the declaration made at the meeting of Commonwealth prime ministers in April 1949 which enabled India to remain within the Commonwealth in spite of becoming a republic. L. S. Amery wrote sympathetically to Smuts, acknowledging his misgivings but suggesting that the repercussions he feared might follow in South Africa could be exaggerated. Malan, Amery said, seemed content with a position which enabled him to leave the Commonwealth if he wished to do so and, having that assurance, he had no desire to go further.[8] Smuts was not convinced, fearing that, whatever Malan might think, other more strongly republican members of the party would not be satisfied with half measures. Nevertheless, he recognised that Britain had been anxious to keep India within the Commonwealth as a means of keeping her out of the hands of the Communists, and for the sake of the future Smuts himself was anxious to preserve the coherence and stability of the Commonwealth.[9]

From these many problems Smuts sought solace in a wide variety of activities which would have taxed the mental and physical powers of a man half his age. He wrote scores of letters – to Winston Churchill, Chaim Weizmann, Queen Frederica and, of course, to Margaret and Arthur Gillett. He wrote to Isie, too, more frequently and more fondly than before. He pursued his interest in botany in the botanical garden at Kirstenbosch outside Cape Town and during the course of a demanding trip to Mozambique with his daughter, Santa, his son, Jannie, and other friends. He still took long walks, not only when he was in Mozambique but also on his farm at Rooikop and on Table Mountain. He read extensively. *Wuthering Heights*, Sir Edmund Taylor Whittaker's recent book, *From Euclid to Eddington* and E. J. Simmons's *Leo Tolstoy* particularly engrossed him and he enjoyed a number of books on Shakespeare – all sent to him by the ever-loyal Margaret Gillett. With his customary generosity to his friends and to opponents who had fallen upon bad times, he took up the causes of Chaim Weizmann and General von Lettow Vorbeck. The latter, Smuts learned, was suffering acute hardship because his pension had been cancelled. At once Smuts got in touch with the head of the South African military mission in Berlin to see what could be done to induce the German authorities to restore the pension.[10]

Four months later, in November 1949, Smuts went to London at the request of some English friends of Weizmann who wanted him to speak at a function which aimed to raise funds to establish a memorial to the Israeli president.[11] He was back in South Africa, however, to attend a United Party congress early in December and on 16 December, the Day of the Covenant, he spoke at the unveiling of the great voortrekker monument, on a hill outside Pretoria, whose foundations had been laid ten years earlier. He took that opportunity to summarise South Africa's heroic past and to call for unity among the white peoples of the Union and for a just rather than a political approach to the problem of relations with the African population.[12] Though the tone of his speech was optimistic, his inner feelings were less so. He did not think the monument would do any good for relations between Whites and Africans. Colour was beginning to dominate the history of the world, he believed, and it boded ill for the Union.[13]

The new year started with mixed fortunes for Smuts. On his arrival in Cape Town for the opening of parliament he was met by his old friends, Arthur and Margaret Gillett, and by Daphne Moore whose husband was in hospital on the Cape Peninsula. Smuts was delighted to see them, but he was suffering acutely from the effects of a displaced vertebra which his doctors seemed unable to deal with quickly. In spite of his pain, however, he delivered a lively attack on the government in a parliamentary debate on 24 January, but he sensed that the Nationalists were secure in office for the time being. He was particularly concerned by the passing of the Population Registration Act. It was intended, he believed, to ensure that the coloured population should register separately for election purposes, thereby depriving them of their equality with the Whites and ensuring that the Nationalists would gain a large number of seats in the Western Cape where coloured voters had formerly supported the United Party.

Outside South Africa Smuts was worried by the defeat of Winston Churchill and the Conservative Party in the elections in England. He sensed, however, that the Labour government would not be able to hold on to office much longer and, for the good of Britain's foreign policy, he hoped they would not do so. He was relieved, on the other hand, that Labour leaders had refused recognition to Seretse Khama, heir to the throne of the Bamangwato tribe in Bechuanaland, who had married an English woman. Feelings among the Whites in South Africa about the marriage were so strong that he was anxious the British government should not change its mind. To do so would strengthen the Nationalists' claim to annex the protectorate, and if that claim were rejected there might well be a move to declare the Union a republic.[14] He was less satisfied with the British foreign secretary, Ernest Bevin's, cold rejection of the suggestion that Germany should play a part in the redevelopment of Western Europe. In Smuts's opinion, the Labour government's handling of the whole question of the future of Western Europe was utterly incompetent.[15] The Commonwealth, too, was weak and confused just when a strong Western Europe was needed in which Britain and the Commonwealth would play a vital role to uphold the fundamental political ideals of Europe against the menace of force and anarchy.[16] Meanwhile, the problem of apartheid and Communism continued to dominate the debates in the Union parliament.

Smuts's eightieth-birthday celebrations swept aside those dark thoughts for a time. Everywhere he was greeted with enthusiasm, in Johannesburg, in Durban and in Cape Town, and, despite the heavy demands imposed upon him by his many public appearances, he fulfilled his engagements meticulously if without real enjoyment. He was far from well and at the age of eighty adulation, if reassuring, had its drawbacks. Shortly afterwards he suffered a heart attack and had to cancel a visit to Cambridge to which he had been looking forward. For a time he was gravely ill, but by early August, though he was still frail, he seemed to be on the road to recovery. A bout of influenza weakened him. On 10 September he played happily with some of his grandchildren in his home at Doornkloof, but the following day he died. The funeral ceremonies were even more impressive than his birthday celebrations. Smuts's critics as well as his supporters recognised that a great force had been taken from South Africa. The United Party was bereft of leadership. In Britain, too, and throughout the Commonwealth and the Western world, there was a profound sense of loss. For half a century Smuts had been in the news and his passing had removed one of the pillars which supported the liberal tradition.

In attempting to reappraise Smuts's career more than a generation after his death, one cannot ignore the changes in attitude which have occurred with regard to those problems which chiefly occupied him in South Africa and those broader questions of world politics to which he also made a contribution. In South Africa his greatest aim was to unite the people of British and Dutch descent in defence of European civilisation, and he failed to achieve that object. Peoples of such differing traditions could not be brought together by cajolery or even by the light of reason. What has united them more recently has been the emergence of what Smuts described as African nationalism but which is in practice a move to rid South Africa of white domination. As Smuts feared, the movement has drawn strength both from the reaction of Africans against the more

extreme policies of the Nationalists and from their response to the encouragement given them by groups outside the Union who are critical of
the apartheid policy practised there.

Smuts's criticism of apartheid does not mean that his own native policy
would necessarily have led to any different outcome. Instinctively he
had recoiled from the measure which might have brought a change.
His acceptance, however reluctant, of the 1936 legislation deprived him
of the support of the one group of Africans who might have assisted
in preserving European standards – the well-educated minority. The
rejection of the principle of the African franchise on a common roll with
the Whites destroyed all hope of reconciling the educated leaders of
African opinion to the continuation, even if only for a time, of a government dominated by Whites. The vast majority of Africans were not,
it is true, seriously concerned about the vote. But Smuts's genuine desire
to give that majority better treatment, coupled with the retention of
social and residential segregation and the development of African culture
along traditional lines, could not be implemented as long as insufficient
land was available for the traditional needs of the African people. Smuts
had no answer to that problem, for white farmers saw no reason to
surrender the land they had gained by conquest or had developed
through years of effort. White industrialists, too, had no desire to lose
their labour force as the result of a drift back to more adequate supplies
of land. Even had Smuts wished to challenge these powerful pressure
groups, and there is no reason to think that he did, he would have
been brought face to face with the fact that land and labour policies
in South Africa are made by the employers. Governments merely put
their seal upon them, which they have been happy to do.

With the well-educated minority of Africans and the less well-educated
majority aggrieved by government policies, elements of both groups
have drawn together in the hope of bringing pressure to bear to bring
about change. This is not African nationalism in the sense of a united
African people. Tribal and ideological as well as temperamental differences are too strong for that, and no one leader has emerged with sufficient authority to focus loyalty upon himself as an alternative to loyalty
to a nation as has occurred in many countries in Tropical Africa. Nevertheless, a more vigorous challenge to white domination has developed,
as Smuts feared it would, and his own policy of segregating Africans
in townships and in the reserves has facilitated the exchange of political
views among Africans while making it easier for the National government
to contain physical opposition.

If it was intellectual conviction which helped to formulate Smuts's
views on the need to unify the Whites of South Africa and instinct which

determined his view on native policy, it was certainly the former which governed his attitude to those international issues to which he contributed so notably. Britain, he considered, had contributed more than any other nation to the civilisation of the world, therefore Britain must be preserved and strengthened. In the First World War his energies were devoted unreservedly to that end and with marked success. Not the least of Britain's gifts to the world was the example of the British Commonwealth, a free association of nations which worked together because they were fully aware both of their common interests and of the quality of life which it was their common aim to uphold. Throughout his career he struggled successfully, and against powerful opposition, to keep South Africa a member of that community of nations. Such a community, in Smuts's opinion, was the ideal model for world unity – not a unity imposed by power nor yet one which demanded total uniformity of behaviour – but a unity based upon freedom and the voluntary principal. That was the image he had in mind for the League of Nations, for which he strove so valiantly. But the voluntary principle leaves room for disagreement, and disagreement leads to conflict, so that his League of Nations, a meeting of men of goodwill, collapsed when the goodwill faded. The lack of that goodwill Smuts saw as the great obstacle to the success of the United Nations. Even the image of the Commonwealth was tarnished when the Republic of India was allowed to remain a member. With that change one recognises that Smuts's dream of a Whole, his philosophy of holism, was really only a philosophy of the part, the white part of society, and even then only that part which adhered to the traditional culture of Western Europe.

Though Smuts never admitted this, towards the end of his life the realisation was being forced upon him. The elegaic tone of much of his later correspondence indicates that he was not unaware of it. He had renounced the simple faith offered him by his forefathers and replaced it by a philosophy claiming to be based upon the sum of human knowledge. But the simple faith tugged at his conscience and to still his doubts he had had to insist more and more firmly upon the power of human intellect – not least his own. The search for the truth which had marked his earlier career had been replaced increasingly by an assertion of it. To be wrong would challenge his whole philosophy. And so he became increasingly didactic, until the events which followed the Second World War gave rise to doubts.

The turning-point in Smuts's career came when he became prime minister on the death of Botha and was forced to reach his own decisions without any effective challenge. He had been at his best acting as the grey eminence to a leader whose ideals he shared and who relished hearing his opinions. In some degree Merriman had played that role, though as mentor rather than as leader. Botha, and Lloyd George during the First World War, had been excellent in that capacity. Each had permitted Smuts to develop his intellectual powers to the maximum while reserving to themselves the task of determining just how far his ideas were practicable, sifting and simplifying them as only great leaders can. Left to himself, Smuts was not afraid of responsibility – indeed, he courted it. But then the perfection which his conscience demanded of him had no one but himself to measure it. His friends lacked the intellectual stature to help him; his critics he despised or simply dismissed. The fear of error took the form of authoritarianism and he repeatedly sought to reassure himself that holism provided the necessary guarantee of his behaviour. But in the end the doubts remained, and by the time of his death he had probably returned to the simple faith in which he had been nurtured.

Notes

Abbreviations

F.P.	A. H. Duminy and W. R. Guest (eds.), *Fitzpatrick, South African Politician, Selected Papers, 1888–1906*.
M.P.	Cecil Headlam (ed.), *The Milner Papers*.
SANA, A1.	South African National Archives, The Smuts Collection.
SANA, A3.	South African National Archives, The Creswell Collection.
S.P.	W. K. Hancock and J. van der Poel (eds.), *Selections from the Smuts Papers*.
UCT, BC294	University of Cape Town Library, The Sir Patrick Duncan Collection.
UCT, BC631	University of Cape Town Library, The S. F. Waterson Collection.

Chapter 1: The student

1. Frank den Berg to the editor, *Cape Argus*, 8 June 1964.
2. *Cape Times*, 29 May 1964.
3. *Cape Times*, 1 June 1964.
4. *Cape Argus*, 8 June 1964.
5. J. C. Smuts, *Jan Christian Smuts*, Cassell, London 1952, 7.
6. S. G. Millin, *General Smuts*, Faber and Faber, London, 1936, I. 23.
7. Smuts to S. M. Krige, 10 Dec. 1887, S.P., I. 6–9.
8. Marais to Smuts, 26 Jan. 1892, S.P., I. 23–5.
9. S.P., I. 35–41.
10. Smuts to M. C. Gillett, 26 Dec. 1942, S.P., VI. 399–401.
11. W. K. Hancock, *Smuts: The Sanguine Years*, Cambridge University Press, 1962, 44.
12. Smuts, 'The Conditions of Future South African Literature', July 1892, S.P., I. 41–8.

Chapter 2: The young lawyer

1. Speech by Smuts reported in the *Diamond Fields Advertiser*, 30 Oct. 1895, S.P., I. 80–100.
2. Smuts to the Council of the South African College, 4 Mar. 1896, S.P., I. 139–40.
3. S.P., I. 103–6.
4. S.P., I. 113–16.
5. J. C. Smuts, *Jan Christian Smuts*, 36.
6. S.P., I. 132–5.
7. *The Critic*, 29 Jan. 1897, quoted in S.P., I. 149–50.

8. S.P., I. 155–85.
9. Ibid.
10. Milner to Chamberlain, 23 Feb. 1898, M.P., I. 220–4.
11. J. C. Smuts, *Jan Christian Smuts*, 38.
12. Smuts to state secretary, 5 Aug. 1898, S.P., I. 194–5.
13. Fitzpatrick to A. Beit, 4 Mar. 1898, F.P., 143–7.
14. Fitzpatrick to A. Beit, 27 Oct. 1898, F.P., 163–5.
15. Fitzpatrick to J. Wernher, 28 Nov. 1898, F.P., 166–9.
16. Ibid., 167.
17. Fitzpatrick to Wernher, Beit and Co., 3 Dec. 1898, F.P., 169–70.
18. Fitzpatrick to Wernher, 30 Jan. 1899, F.P., 172–5.
19. Fitzpatrick to Wernher, 6 and 20 Feb. 1899, F.P., 177–8.
20. Lippert to Merriman, 10 Jan. 1899, Phyllis Lewsen (ed.), *Selections from the Correspondence of J. X. Merriman, 1899–1905*, The Van Riebeeck Society, Cape Town, 1966, 4–11.
21. Fitzpatrick to Wernher, 4 and 6 Mar. 1899, F.P., 183–9.
22. J. S. Marais, *The Fall of Kruger's Republic*, Clarendon Press, Oxford, 1961, 252.
23. Smuts to Leyds, 30 Apr. 1899, S.P., I. 226–9.
24. Milner to Chamberlain, 4 May 1899, M.P., I. 349–53.
25. J. H. Hofmeyr, *The Life of Jan Hendrik Hofmeyr*, Van de Sandt de Villiers Printing Company, Cape Town, 1913, 533–4.
26. E. A. Walker, *W. P. Schreiner*, Oxford University Press, London, 1937, reprinted 1969, 143–4.
27. Hofmeyr to Smuts, 10 May 1899, S.P., I. 230.
28. Smuts to Hofmeyr, 10 May 1899, S.P., I. 233–5.
29. Hofmeyr to Smuts, 15 May 1899, S.P., I. 236–7.
30. Smuts to S. M. Smuts, 1 June 1899, S.P., I. 242.
31. Smuts to Hofmeyr, 10 June 1899, S.P., I. 243.
32. Hofmeyr to Smuts, 7 June 1899, S.P., I. 243.
33. Smuts to Hofmeyr, 13 June 1899, S.P., I. 248–50.
34. Hofmeyr to Smuts, 17 June 1899, S.P., I. 254–6.
35. Merriman to Smuts, 21 June 1899, S.P., I. 259–60.
36. Schreiner to Smuts, 21 June 1899, S.P., I. 262–3, and Malan to Smuts, 21 June 1899, S.P., I. 261–2.
37. Hofmeyr to Smuts, 17 June 1899, S.P., I. 254–6.
38. Chamberlain to Milner, 30 June 1899, M.P., I. 450.
39. Smuts to Hofmeyr, 9 July 1899, S.P., I. 264–5.
40. Te Water to Smuts, 10 July 1899, S.P., I. 266.
41. Smuts to Te Water, 11 July 1899, S.P., I. 266.
42. Te Water to Smuts, 11 July 1899, S.P., I. 267.
43. Smuts to Hofmeyr, 27 July 1899, S.P., I. 272–3.
44. Milner to Chamberlain, 13 July 1899, M.P., I. 459–60.
45. Milner to Chamberlain, 26 July 1899, M.P., I. 471–2.
46. E. R. Groebler to State President, Bloemfontein, 8 Aug. 1899, M.P., I. 483, and Resident Justice of the Peace to President, Bloemfontein, 14 Aug. 1899, M.P., I. 483–4.
47. Milner to Chamberlain, 15 Aug. 1899, M.P., I. 489.
48. Chamberlain to Milner, 16 Aug. 1899, M.P., I. 489–90.
49. Salisbury to Queen Victoria, 16 Aug. 1899, G. E. Buckle (ed.), *The Letters of Queen Victoria, Third Series, 1896–1901*, John Murray, London, 1932, III, 393.
50. Chamberlain to Milner, 23 Aug. 1899, M.P., I. 491.
51. Chamberlain to Milner, 8 Sept. 1899, M.P., I. 534–5.
52. State President, Pretoria, to State President, Bloemfontein, 16 Sept. 1899, M.P., I. 535.

53. Ambassador, Brussels, to Government, Pretoria, 26 Sept. 1899, M.P., I. 535.
54. M.P., I. 542.
55. Ripon to Campbell-Bannermann, 30 Sept. 1899, Campbell-Bannerman Papers, Vol. XIX, British Library Additional MS 41224, 95–9.
56. S.P., I. 322–9.

Chapter 3: The young soldier

1. Smuts to Botha, 2 Apr. 1900, S.P., I. 331–2.
2. S.P., I. 335–6.
3. Smuts to Botha, 22 Sept. 1900, S.P., I. 342–4.
4. Smuts to Reitz, 29 Nov. 1900, S.P., I. 346–7.
5. Smuts to de la Rey, 23 Dec. 1900, S.P., I. 350–1.
6. Smuts to N. J. de Wet, 23 Jan. 1901, S.P., I. 364.
7. Smuts to Botha, 23 Jan. 1901, S.P., I. 360–3.
8. Smuts to de la Rey, 25 Dec. 1900, S.P., I. 354–7.
9. Smuts to Botha, 23 Jan. 1901, S.P., I. 360–3.
10. Smuts to Botha, 3 Feb. 1901, S.P., I. 366–7.
11. Smuts to N. J. de Wet, 28 Feb. 1901, S.P., I. 387–9.
12. Smuts to C. R. de Wet, 10 Feb. 1901, S.P., I. 371–2.
13. Smuts to Botha, 3 Feb. 1901 and Smuts to C. R. de Wet, 10 Feb. 1901, S.P., I. 369–70 and 371–2.
14. Campbell-Bannerman to Ripon, 7 Nov. 1900, Campbell-Bannerman Papers, Vol. XIX, British Library Additional MS 41224, 131.
15. Steyn to Smuts, 15 May 1901, S.P., I. 391–2.
16. Smuts to Botha, 27 Feb. 1901, S.P., I. 382–5.
17. Steyn to Smuts, 15 May 1901, S.P., I. 391–2.
18. Smuts to Kruger, 3 June 1901, S.P., I. 396–7.
19. Kruger to Smuts, 11 June 1901, S.P., I. 399–400.
20. General notice signed by Steyn and Burger, 20 June 1901, S.P., I. 402–3.
21. Smuts to S. M. Smuts, 2 June 1901, S.P., I. 392–5.
22. Report on the position in Cape Colony by Smuts, 16 Dec. 1901, S.P., I. 441–5.
23. Smuts to Stead, 4 Jan. 1902, S.P., I. 464–95.
24. Smuts to S. M. Smuts, 12 May 1902, S.P., I. 511–14.
25. S.P., I. 523.
26. Chamberlain to Milner, 6 Mar. 1901, M.P., II. 212.
27. S.P., I. 529–32.
28. Memorandum by Smuts to the Executive Council, 4 Sept. 1899, S.P., I. 322–9.
29. Milner to Major Hanbury Williams, 27 Dec. 1900, M.P., II. 242–4.
30. M.P., II. 240–1.
31. Kitchener to Milner, 31 May 1901, M.P., II. 251.
32. Smuts to T. Lynedoch Graham, 26 July 1902, S.P., II. 13–16 and Graham to Smuts, 29 July 1902, S.P., II. 19–21.
33. Smuts to Graham, 2 Aug. 1902, S.P., II. 24–6.
34. Smuts to Fischer, 13 Oct. 1902, S.P., II. 37–8.
35. Draft of Smuts's speech to Chamberlain, 8 Jan. 1903, S.P., II. 70–3.
36. Address to Chamberlain, 8 Jan. 1903, S.P., II. 64–7.
37. Botha, de la Rey and Smuts to Milner, 6 Feb. 1903, S.P., II. 80–2.
38. Circular letter from Botha, de la Rey and Smuts to representative Afrikaners in the Transvaal, 7 Feb. 1903, S.P., II. 84–6.
39. Smuts to Kruger, 22 Mar. 1903, S.P., II. 89–90.
40. Memorandum to the Labour Commission (1903), S.P., II. 125–33.

41. Smuts to Emily Hobhouse, 21 Feb. 1904, S.P., II. 147–9.
42. R. V. Kubicek, *Economic Imperialism in Theory and Practice*, Duke University Press, Durham N.C., 1979, 115–40.
43. Smuts to Emily Hobhouse, 19 Mar. 1904, S.P., II. 158–60.
44. Smuts to Merriman, 17 Mar. 1904, S.P., II. 157–8.
45. *Report of the South African Native Affairs Commission* (1905), Cd. 2399.
46. Selborne to Smuts, 13 Jan. 1908, S.P., II. 374–94.
47. Smuts to Steyn, 14 Dec. 1905, S.P., II. 206.
48. Steyn to Merriman, 5 Jan. 1906, Lewsen (ed.), *Selections from Correspondence of J. X. Merriman, 1905–1924*, The Van Riebeeck Society, Cape Town, 1969, 13–14.
49. Merriman to Smuts, 4 Mar. 1906, S.P., II. 238–41.
50. Smuts to Merriman, 11 July 1906, S.P., II. 292–3.
51. Merriman to Smuts, 30 Dec. 1906, S.P., II. 311–14.
52. Smuts to Merriman, 25 Feb. 1907, S.P., II. 323–4.
53. Smuts to Merriman, 4 Mar. 1907, S.P., II. 325–8.
54. Smuts to Merriman, 16 May 1906, SANA, A3, II. 306–9.
55. Smuts to Duncan, 28 Sept. 1907, UCT, BC294, D1.35.1.
56. Smuts to Steyn, 23 Apr. 1907, S.P., II. 340–1.
57. Cf. Correspondence between Patrick Duncan and W. M'Evoy and between Duncan and Smuts, 8–15 Apr. 1908, UCT, BC294, D1.35.2–5.
58. Selborne to Smuts, 30 Nov. 1907, S.P., II. 361–6.
59. Solomon to Smuts, 24 Jan. 1908, S.P., II. 398–401.
60. Merriman to Smuts, 13 Jan. 1908, S.P., II. 394–6.
61. Solomon to F. J. S. Hopwood, Sept. 1908, S.P., II. 518–22.
62. Selborne to Smuts, 9 Jan. 1908, S.P., II. 374–94.
63. Merriman to Smuts, 13 June 1908, S.P., II. 434–5.
64. Smuts to Merriman, 5 Apr. 1908, S.P., II. 429–30.
65. Smuts to Hobson, 13 July 1908, S.P., II. 440–3.
66. Schreiner to Smuts, 2 Aug. 1908, S.P., II. 450–1.
67. Elgin to Crewe, 7 May 1908, quoted in R. Hyam, *Elgin and Churchill at the Colonial Office*, Macmillan, London, 1968, 376–7.
68. Smuts to Merriman, 2 Oct. 1908, S.P., II. 525–6.
69. S.P., II. 457–87.
70. National Convention Papers, SANA, A1, Box 108, No. 2.
71. National Convention Papers, SANA, A1, 108. 8.
72. National Convention Papers, SANA, A1, 108 *passim*.
73. Smuts speaking in the Transvaal Legislative Council, 3 Apr. 1909, S.P., II. 551–62.
74. A. Odendaal, *Vulkani Bantu: The Beginnings of Black Protest Politics in South Africa to 1912*, David Philip, Cape Town and Johannesburg, 1984, 151–227.

Chapter 4: Minister and general

1. C. P. Crewe to Smuts, 30 Jan. 1923, SANA, A1, 210. 62.
2. Botha to Merriman, 29 Dec. 1909, Lewsen (ed.), *Selections from the Correspondence of J. X. Merriman, 1905–1924*, 158–9.
3. Smuts to Merriman, 22 Feb. 1910, S.P., II. 611–2.
4. Merriman to Smuts, 27 Feb. 1910, S.P., II. 621–2, and Merriman to Steyn, 12 Feb. 1910, Lewsen (ed.), *Selections from the Correspondence of J. X. Merriman, 1905–1924*, 165–7.
5. S.P., II. 596–8.
6. Smuts to A. B. Gillett, 19 Sept. 1910, S.P., III. 16.

7. J. C. Smuts, *Jan Christian Smuts*, 119.
8. Botha to Smuts, 26 June 1911, S.P., III. 40–3.
9. Sketch of the proposed South African Defence Bill, SANA, Al, III. 5.
10. Merriman to Smuts, 27 July 1911, S.P., III. 47–8.
11. E. Hobhouse to Smuts, 7 June 1911, S.P., III. 32–3.
12. E. Hobhouse to Smuts, 3 May 1912, S.P., III. 84–5.
13. Wolstenholme to Smuts, 18 Oct. 1912, S.P., III. 116–8.
14. Wolstenholme to Smuts, 24 Oct. 1912, S.P., III. 118.
15. Crewe to Smuts, 17 Aug. 1911, S.P., III. 53–4.
16. Speech by Smuts, 16 Dec. 1913, S.P., III. 143–8.
17. Gladstone to Smuts, 13 Apr. 1911, S.P., III. 25.
18. M. Swan, 'The 1913 Natal Indian Strike', *Journal of Southern African Studies*, 10, 2 (1984), 239–58.
19. J. W. Quinn to Merriman, 8 Jan. 1914, Lewsen (ed.), *Selections from the Correspondence of J. X. Merriman, 1905–1924*, 244.
20. Merriman to Smuts, 10 Jan. 1914, S.P., III. 157.
21. Lady Courtney to Smuts, 19 Jan. 1914, S.P., III. 158.
22. M. C. Gillett to Smuts, 20 Feb. 1914, S.P., III. 164–5.
23. Lewsen (ed.), *Selections from the Correspondence of J. X. Merriman, 1905–1924*, 249–51.
24. S. G. Millin, *Smuts*, I. 286–90.
25. Smuts to Duncan, 22 Oct. 1912, UCT, BC294, A25.4.
26. M. Benson, *The African Patriots*, Faber and Faber, London, 1963, 25–31.
27. Ibid., 33–8.
28. Krause to Smuts, 23 Mar. 1914, S.P., III. 168–72.
29. Creswell to Margaret Creswell, 5 Mar. 1912, SANA, A3, II. 277–305.
30. Smuts to Merriman, 16 May 1906, SANA, A3, II. 306–9.
31. Smuts to Creswell, 25 Feb. 1907, SANA, A3, II. 404–6.
32. E. Hobhouse to Smuts, 8 Aug. 1914, S.P., III. 185–6.
33. A. C. Vlok to Smuts, 8 Feb. 1917, S.P., III. 448–51.
34. Smuts to A. B. Gillett, 27 Sept. 1914, S.P., III. 201–2.
35. R. Jones to Smuts, 26 Sept. 1914, S.P., III. 199.
36. D. Reitz to Smuts, 12 Sept. 1914, S.P., III. 196–7.
37. Botha and Smuts to Steyn, Oct. 1914, S.P., III. 207–8.
38. Merriman to Smuts, 8 Nov. 1914, S.P., III. 209–11.
39. Merriman to Smuts, 29 Nov. 1914, S.P., III. 216–18.
40. Merriman to Smuts, 23 Dec. 1914, S.P., III. 224–7.
41. E. Hobhouse to Smuts, 8 Mar. 1915, S.P., III. 257–60.
42. Smuts to H. C. Hull, 25 Mar. 1915, S.P., III. 262–3.
43. Botha to Smuts, 30 Mar. 1915, S.P., III. 269–71.
44. Smuts to Wolstenholme, 14 May 1915, S.P., III. 273–5, and Merriman to Smuts, 19 May 1915, S.P., III. 275–6.
45. Smuts to Merriman, 28 June 1915, S.P., III. 299.
46. Merriman to Smuts, 2 July 1915, S.P., III. 299–303.
47. Correspondence from Botha to Smuts and others, 5–9 July 1915, SANA, A1, 112. 1–2, 81–7, 87, 90, 92, 95, 97, 101, 103, 105–6, 111–14 and 119.
48. Buxton to Smuts, 9 July 1915, S.P., III. 303.
49. Buxton to ministers, 9 Aug. 1915, SANA, A1, 112, 146.
50. Merriman to Smuts, 30 Sept. 1915, S.P., III. 314–16.
51. Smuts to Merriman, 24 Sept. 1915, S.P., III. 312–13.
52. Smuts to Wolstenholme, 29 Nov. 1915, S.P., III. 324–5.
53. Reitz to Smuts, ? Dec. 1915, S.P., III. 327–8.
54. Smuts to Merriman, 30 Aug. 1915, S.P., III. 310–11.

55. Smuts to M. C. Gillett, 8 Feb. 1916, S.P., III. 334–5.
56. M. C. Gillett to Smuts, 14 Mar. 1916, S.P., III. 337–9.
57. Botha to Smuts, 21 Mar. 1916, S.P., III. 345–9.
58. Statement of Casualties, SANA, A1, 113. 94.
59. Smuts to Botha, 12 May 1916, SANA, A1, 113. 114.
60. Botha to Smuts, 15 May 1916, SANA, A1, 113. 115.
61. Supplement to *London Gazette*, 20 June 1916, SANA, A1, 113. 141.
62. Smuts to Wolstenholme, 21 May 1916, S.P., III. 367–8.
63. Smuts to S. M. Smuts, 3 Sept. 1916, S.P., III. 400.
64. Smuts to Bowyer, 12 Nov. 1934, SANA, A1, 237. 94.
65. H. Burton to Smuts, 12 Sept. 1916, S.P., III. 400–5.
66. Buxton to Smuts, 21 Nov. 1916, S.P., III. 414–15.
67. Laurier to Botha, 1 Dec. 1916, SANA, A1, 114. 98.
68. Smuts to Wolstenholme, 17 Nov. 1916, S.P., III. 410–11.
69. Smuts to S. M. Smuts, 11 Jan. 1917, S.P., III. 438–9.
70. Smuts to Merriman, 15 Feb. 1917, S.P., III. 443–4.
71. Smuts to S. M. Smuts, 15 Feb. 1917, S.P., III. 445–6.
72. A. C. Vlok to Smuts, 8 Feb. 1917, S.P., III. 448–51.
73. Merriman to Smuts, 22 Feb. 1917, S.P., III. 451–3.

Chapter 5: International statesman

1. E. Hobhouse to Smuts, 7 Mar. 1917, S.P., III. 459–60.
2. S.P., III. 505–6.
3. S.P., III. 482–92.
4. S.P., III. 477.
5. Smuts to S. M. Smuts, 5 May 1917, S.P., III. 497–9.
6. Smuts to Botha, 1 May 1917, S.P., III. 495.
7. S.P., III. 506–17.
8. Harcourt to Smuts, 15 May 1917, S.P., III. 518.
9. Speech by Smuts, 22 May 1917, quoted in *Greater South Africa, Plans for a Better World: The Speeches of J. C. Smuts*, Truth Legion, Johannesburg, 1940, 11–21.
10. A. Clark to Smuts, 19 May 1917, S.P., III. 519–20.
11. Smuts to S. M. Smuts, 29 Aug. 1917, S.P., III. 540–2.
12. Smuts to S. M. Smuts, 9 Sept. 1917, S.P., III. 550–1.
13. Buxton to Smuts, with enclosure, 5 Oct. 1917, S.P., III. 558–64.
14. Smuts to S. M. Smuts, 5 Oct. 1917, S.P., III. 556–8.
15. Smuts to Lloyd George, 28 Oct. 1917, S.P., III. 565–6.
16. R. Wherry Anderson, Report on General Smuts's visit to South Wales, 29 Oct. 1917, S.P., III. 566–7.
17. A. Clark to Smuts, 14 Nov. 1917 and undated, S.P., III. 569–71 and 571–2.
18. P. H. Kerr to Smuts, 14 Dec. 1917, S.P., III. 576–7.
19. D. Lloyd George, *War Memoirs*, Ivor Nicholson and Watson, London, Vol. V, 1936, 2460–81.
20. E. von Glaise-Horstenau, *The Collapse of the Austro-Hungarian Empire* (trans. Ian F. D. Morrow), Dent, London and Toronto, 1930, 85–8.
21. Comment by Smuts quoted in diary of C. P. Scott, 5 July 1919, cf. T. Wilson (ed.), *The Political Diaries of C. P. Scott, 1911–1928*, Collins, London, 1970, 375.
22. R. C. Maclaurin to Smuts, 1 May 1918, S.P., III. 628–30.
23. Speech by Smuts, 17 May 1918, S.P., III. 639–54.
24. Smuts to Lloyd George, 8 June 1918, S.P., III. 661–3.
25. Smuts to A. B. Gillett, 10 Nov. 1918, S.P., III. 687–8.

26. S.P., IV. 8–16.
27. Amery to Smuts, 17 Dec. 1918, S.P., IV. 26–7.
28. Smuts to A. B. Gillett, 12 Jan. 1919, S.P., IV. 39–41.
29. Smuts to S. M. Smuts, 15 Jan. 1919, S.P., IV. 45–6.
30. Smuts to M. C. Gillett, 25 Jan. 1919, S.P., IV. 55–6.
31. Smuts to M. C. Gillett, 4 Feb. 1919, S.P., IV. 59–60, and 8 Feb. 1919, S.P., IV. 62–3.
32. Smuts to Lloyd George, 26 Mar. 1919, S.P., IV. 83–7.
33. Smuts to M. C. Gillett, 27 Mar. 1919, S.P., IV. 88–9.
34. SANA, A1, 115. 13.
35. S.P., IV. 93–4.
36. National Congress Memorial to the King, SANA, A1, 115. 4.
37. Botha to Schreiner, 2 Apr. 1919, SANA, A1, 115. 5.
38. SANA, A1, 115.10.
39. Smuts to A. Clark, 1 Apr. 1919, S.P., IV. 99–100.
40. H. H. Fisher, Vice-Chairman of Directors of Hoover War Library, Stanford University, to Smuts, 27 Jan. 1934, enclosing excerpts from Hungarian press of 1919, SANA, A1, 236. 65.
41. Report by Smuts, S.P., IV. 103–5.
42. Smuts to M. C. Gillett, 9 Apr. 1919, S.P., IV. 119–20.
43. Smuts to A. Clark, 23 Apr. 1919, S.P., IV. 125.
44. Smuts to M. C. Gillett, 28 Apr. and 1 May 1919, S.P., IV. 134–7 and 139–40.
45. Smuts to Lloyd George, 5 May 1919, S.P., IV. 148–50.
46. Smuts to Lloyd George and Woodrow Wilson, 14 May 1919, S.P., IV. 157–8.
47. Smuts to A. Clark, 18 May 1919, S.P., IV. 166.
48. Smuts to S. M. Smuts, 20 May 1919, S.P., IV. 176–7.
49. M. C. Gillett to Smuts, 22 May 1919, S.P., IV. 180–1.
50. Smuts to M. C. Gillett, 22 May 1919, S.P., IV. 181–2.
51. Smuts to Lloyd George, 22 May 1919, S.P., IV. 183–9.
52. Smuts to M. C. and A. B. Gillett, 23 May 1919, S.P., IV. 191–2, and to M. C. Gillett, 24 May 1919, S.P., IV. 193–4.
53. Smuts to Lloyd George, 26 May 1919, S.P., IV. 196–7.
54. Lloyd George to Smuts, 26 May 1919, S.P., IV. 197–8.
55. Smuts to S. M. Smuts, 27 May 1919, S.P., IV. 201–2.
56. M. C. Gillett to Smuts, 30 May 1919, S.P., IV. 205–6.
57. Smuts to Wilson, 30 May 1919, S.P., IV. 208–9.
58. A. Lentin, *Lloyd George, Woodrow Wilson and the Guilt of Germany*, Leicester University Press, 1984, 84–5.
59. Smuts to Lloyd George, 2 June 1919, and Lloyd George to Smuts, 3 June 1919, S.P., IV. 215–18.
60. Smuts to Lloyd George, 4 June 1919, S.P., IV. 219–21.
61. Lentin, *Lloyd George, Woodrow Wilson and the Guilt of Germany*, 96–100.
62. Smuts to A. Clark, 16 June 1919, S.P., IV. 231–2.
63. M. C. Gillett to Smuts, 19 June 1919, S.P., IV. 236—8.
64. Smuts to Botha, 21 June 1919, S.P., IV. 240.
65. Smuts to M. C. Gillett, 23 June 1919, S.P., IV. 244–5.
66. M. C. Gillett to Smuts, 23 June 1919, S.P., IV. 245–6.
67. Smuts to M. C. Gillett, 24 June 1919, S.P., IV. 247.
68. Smuts to A. Clark, 25 June 1919, S.P., IV. 250–1.
69. Smuts to C. P. Scott, 26 June 1919, S.P., IV. 252–3.
70. M. C. Gillett to Smuts, 25 June 1919, S.P., IV. 248–9.
71. M. C. Gillett to Smuts, 27 June 1919, S.P., IV. 253–4.
72. Text of statement issued by Smuts to the press, 28 June 1919, S.P., IV. 256–9.

73. Smuts to Keynes, 17 July 1919, S.P., IV. 266.
74. Wilson (ed.), *The Political Diaries of C. P. Scott, 1911–1928*, 375.
75. Statement by Smuts, 18 July 1919, S.P., IV. 268–75.
76. Smuts to M. C. Gillett, 20 July 1919, S.P., IV. 275–6.

Chapter 6: The prime minister

1. Minute from the secretary for mines and industries to the prime minister, 22 Dec. 1919, SANA, A1, 115. 21.
2. Smuts to Merriman, 26 Nov. 1919, SANA, A1, 206. 138.
3. S.P., V. 17–26.
4. Smuts to Alice Clark, 18 Mar. 1920, S.P., V. 37–8.
5. Smuts to Alice Clark, 9 Apr. 1920, S.P., V. 38–9.
6. Smuts's Rhodes Memorial Lecture, Oxford, 1929, *Greater South Africa*, 142–4.
7. Patrick Duncan to Lady Selborne, 1 June 1920, UCT, BC294, D5.14.21.
8. Smuts to Smartt, 30 Sept. 1920, and Smartt to Smuts, 10 Oct. 1920, S.P., V. 44–7.
9. Smuts to J. H. Hofmeyr, 5 Nov. 1920, S.P., V. 54.
10. H. E. Freemantle to Smuts, 7 Nov. 1920, S.P., V. 55–6.
11. Smuts to M. C. Gillett, 26 Dec. 1920, S.P., V. 59–60.
12. Smuts to M. C. Gillett, 3 Jan. 1921, S.P., V. 60–1.
13. Smuts to M. C. Gillett, 1 Nov. 1920, S.P., V. 51–3.
14. Smuts to Creswell, 10 Feb. 1921, SANA, A3, I. 16–17.
15. L. S. Amery to Smuts, 12 Feb. 1921, SANA, A1, 208. 3.
16. Statement in the house of assembly by General Lemmer, member of the Native Affairs Commission, and by F. S. Malan, acting prime minister, cf. *Cape Times* 23 June 1921.
17. Memorandum by Smuts, 1921, S.P., V. 67–77.
18. H. Plunkett to Smuts, 6 June 1921, S.P., V. 85–8.
19. Memorandum of a conversation between the King and Smuts, 7 July 1921, S.P., V. 95–8.
20. Smuts to de Valera, 4 Aug. 1921, S.P., V. 100–5.
21. Press statement sent by Smuts to the *New York World*, 1921, S.P., V. 111.
22. Merriman to Creswell, 27 Nov. 1921, SANA, A3, III. 524–7.
23. Smuts to A. B. Gillett, 18 Oct. 1921, S.P., V. 106–7.
24. Hertzog to Creswell, 26 Oct. 1921, SANA, A3, III. 465–6.
25. Creswell to Hertzog, 14 Oct. 1921, SANA, A3, III. 457–64.
26. Merriman to Creswell, 27 Nov. 1921, SANA, A3, III. 524–7.
27. Smuts to M. C. Gillett, 23 Feb. 1921, S.P., V. 113–14.
28. Smuts to M. C. Gillett, 24 Mar. 1921, S.P., V. 116–17.
29. Secret report, 24 Mar. 1922, SANA, A1, 115. 30.
30. Speech by Smuts in the house of assembly, 31 Mar. 1922, S.P., V. 118–35.
31. Hertzog to Creswell, 1 Feb. 1922, SANA, A3, III. 467.
32. Speech by Smuts in the house of assembly, 31 Mar. 1922, S.P., V. 118–35.
33. Ibid.
34. de Wet to Smuts, 23 Mar. 1922, SANA, A1, 115. 29.
35. Smuts to A. Clark, 24 Mar. 1922, S.P., V. 114–15.
36. Smuts to M. C. Gillett, 20 Dec. 1922, S.P., V. 159–60.
37. Smuts to A. Clark, 24 Mar. 1922, S.P., V. 114–15.
38. Smuts to W. Ormsby-Gore, 19 Jan. 1923, S.P., V. 160–1.
39. Conference Papers, 3–17 Apr. 1922, SANA, A1, 115. 31, and Terms of Admission of Southern Rhodesia into the Union of South Africa, SANA, A1, 115. 32.

40. Hertzog to Creswell, 6 Sept. 1922, SANA, A3, III. 473.
41. Smuts to M. C. Gillett, 31 July 1922, S.P., V. 141–2, and D. Chaplin to Smuts, 30 Oct. 1922, S.P., V. 144–7.
42. Smuts to A. B. Gillett, 27 Apr. 1922, S.P., V. 135–6.
43. Smuts to Bonar Law, 20 Nov. 1922, S.P., V. 149–51, and Smuts to Ormsby-Gore, 21 Nov. 1922, S.P., V. 151–2.
44. Walton to Smuts, 6, 8 and 11 Sept. 1922, SANA, A1, 210. 336.
45. Walton to Smuts, 20 Dec. 1923, SANA, A1, 212. 60.
46. Smuts to Walton, 16 Mar. 1923, SANA, A1, 211. 198.
47. Smuts to Walton, 25 May 1923, SANA, A1, 211. 222.
48. Smuts to Walton, 22 Aug. 1923, SANA, A1, 211. 257.
49. Walton to Smuts, 20 Dec. 1923, SANA, A1, 212. 60.
50. Smuts to Rappard, 4 July 1922, S.P., V. 136–8.
51. Smuts to Hofmeyr, 25 May 1923, S.P., V. 175–7.
52. Smuts to General Lord Rawlinson, 5 July 1923, SANA, A1, 211. 237.
53. Smuts to E. H. Walton, 16 Mar. 1923, S.P., V. 168–71.
54. Smuts to secretary of state for colonies, 16 July 1923, SANA, A1, 116. 9.
55. Smuts to E. H. Walton, 15 Feb. 1923, SANA, A1, 211. 186, and 16 Mar. 1923, S.P., V. 168–71.
56. Smuts to N. Talbot, 5 Dec. 1922, S.P., V. 154–5.
57. Report of Departmental Committee to inquire into and report upon the question of residence of natives in urban areas, 15 Jan. 1936, SANA, A1, 123. 3.
58. Smuts to Crewe, 27 Mar. 1922, S.P., V. 117.
59. Smuts to M. C. Gillett, 24 Mar. 1922, S.P., V. 116–17.
60. Smuts to Lord Robert Cecil, 5 July 1922, S.P., V. 139–41.
61. Smuts to Bonar Law, 20 Nov. 1922, S.P., V. 147–9, and 28 Mar. 1923, SANA, A1, 211. 201.
62. Smuts to M. C. Gillett, 20 Dec. 1922, S.P., V. 159–60.
63. Smuts to Baldwin, 7 July 1923, SANA, A1, 211. 239.
64. Smuts to M. C. Gillett, 15 Mar. 1923, S.P., V. 167–8.
65. Smuts to M. C. Gillett, 14 Aug. 1923, S.P., V. 181–2.
66. Smuts to Keynes, 9 Oct. 1923, S.P., V. 186–7.
67. E. Hobhouse to Smuts, 16 Oct. 1923, S.P., V. 189.
68. Smuts to S. M. Smuts, 11 Oct. 1923, S.P., V. 188.
69. Speech, 1923, S.P., V. 192–205.
70. Keynes to Smuts, 26 Oct. 1923, S.P., V. 207–8.
71. Smuts to the editor of *The Times*, 14 Nov. 1923, S.P., V. 212–15.
72. Creswell to Hertzog, 12 Apr. 1923, and Hertzog to Creswell, 26 Sept. 1923, SANA, A3, III. 474–7 and 485.
73. Creswell to M. Creswell, 10 Feb. 1924, SANA, A3, I. 66–7.
74. *Natal Witness*, 24 Sept. 1923.
75. *Natal Mercury*, 25 Sept. 1923.
76. Hertzog to Creswell, 26 Sept. 1923, SANA, A3, III. 485.
77. Smuts to Alexander, 22 Feb. 1924, SANA, A1, 214. 69.
78. Smuts to C. L. Leipoldt (editor of *De Volkstem*), 24 Feb. 1924, S.P., V. 218–19.
79. Smuts to Sir Henry Strakosch, 7 May 1924, SANA, A1, 214. 104.
80. *Cape Times*, 5 May 1924.
81. Smuts to Alexander, Governor-General's office, Pretoria, 1 May and ? June 1924, SANA, A1, 116. 25 and 26.
82. Violet Carruthers to Smuts, 14 Aug. 1924, SANA, A1, 213. 38.
83. Smuts to M. C. Gillett, 9 July 1924, S.P., V. 234–5.

Chapter 7: Leader of the opposition

1. Smuts to Amery, 25 Nov. 1924, S.P., V. 237–9.
2. Smuts to G. G. A. Murray, 25 Nov. 1924, S.P., V. 239–40, and Smuts to Strakosch, 10 Dec. 1924, SANA, A1, 214. 142.
3. Smuts to E. F. C. Lane, [1] July 1925, S.P., V. 250–1.
4. Smuts to A. Chamberlain, 21 Oct. 1925, S.P., V. 258–9.
5. Smuts to G. G. A. Murray, 8 Apr. 1926, S.P., V. 286–7.
6. *Cape Times*, 11 Nov. 1925.
7. Smuts to T. W. Smartt, 12 Nov. 1925, S.P., V. 263–4.
8. *Cape Times*, 14 Nov. 1925.
9. Hertzog to Smuts, 1 Dec. 1925, and Smuts to Hertzog, 14 Dec. 1925, S.P., V. 266–7.
10. Secretary to government of India to Governor-General, Cape Town, 8 Apr. 1925, and Hertzog, Minute, 13 June 1925, UCT, BC294, A33.12 and A33.13.
11. The Indian Question in the Union of South Africa, UCT, BC294, A33.88.
12. Dr Malan, Opening statement of the Cape Town Agreement on behalf of the Union delegation, UCT, BC294, A33.94.
13. *Cape Times*, 7 May 1926.
14. Ibid., 11 May 1926.
15. D. J. Sioka to Smuts, 17 May 1926, S.P., V. 296.
16. Smuts to C. P. Crewe, 14 May 1926, S.P., V. 294–5.
17. Smuts to M. C. Gillett, 30 June 1926, S.P., V. 302–4.
18. Smuts, Memorandum, 1926, S.P., V. 305–24.
19. Smuts, Speech, 26 Oct. 1926, S.P., V. 327–31.
20. Smuts to Kerr, 10 Nov. 1926, SANA, A1, 289. 308.
21. Amery to Creswell, 9 Oct. 1926, SANA, A3, I. 193–4.
22. Smuts to Duncan, 6 Aug. 1926, UCT, BC294, D15.9.1.
23. G. R. Hofmeyr to Smuts, 6 Dec. 1926, S.P., V. 335–6.
24. Smuts to F. S. Malan, 21 Dec. 1926, S.P., V. 338.
25. Smuts to Duncan, 12 Dec. 1926, UCT, BC294, D1.35.20.
26. Amery to Smuts, 24 Jan. 1927, S.P., V. 342–3.
27. Smuts to Amery, 22 Feb. 1927, S.P., V. 345–7.
28. Smuts to N. Nevi, 21 Feb. 1927, S.P., V. 344–5.
29. Smuts to E. Rooth, 29 Mar. 1927, S.P., V. 350.
30. Smuts to J. Martin, 28 May 1927, S.P., V. 354–5.
31. Smuts to J. H. Hofmeyr, 29 Oct. 1927, S.P., V. 361–2.
32. Smuts to M. C. Gillett, 31 Aug. 1927, S.P., V. 358–9.
33. Smuts to M. C. Gillett, 30 Nov. 1927, S.P., V. 362–3.
34. Notes of conversation with General Hertzog, 15 Feb. 1928, S.P., V. 370–4.
35. Notes of conversation with General Hertzog on native policy, 13 Feb. 1928, S.P., V. 368–9.
36. Notes on conversation with General Hertzog on native policy, 27 Feb. and 12 Mar. 1928, S.P., V. 374–7.
37. Smuts to M. C. Gillett, 18 Feb. 1928, S.P., V. 365–6.
38. Smuts to Amery, 16 Oct. 1928, S.P., V. 383–4.
39. Smuts to Amery, 22 May 1928, S.P., V. 379–82.
40. Smuts to Amery, 16 Oct. 1928, S.P., V. 383–4.
41. Smuts to C. P. Crewe, 15 Feb. 1929, S.P., V. 387.
42. Smuts to H. Mentz, 6 Mar. 1929, S.P., V. 387–8.
43. Smuts to M. C. Gillett, 4 Apr. 1929, S.P., V. 389–90.
44. Smuts to M. C. Gillett, 22 Apr. 1929, S.P., V. 391–3.
45. Speech by Smuts, 30 Apr. 1929, S.P., V. 393–407.

46. Smuts to M. C. Gillett, 11 June 1929, S.P., V. 409–10.
47. Smuts to C. P. Crewe, 19 June 1929, S.P., V. 411–12.
48. Smuts to M. C. Gillett, 19 June 1929, S.P., V. 410–11.
49. Duncan to Smuts, 1 June 1929, UCT, BC294, D15.9.7.
50. Duncan to Smuts, 29 Sept. 1929, UCT, BC294, A18.1.2.
51. Smuts's Rhodes Memorial Lecture, 1929, 'Native Policy in Africa', *Greater South Africa*, 36–56.
52. *Cape Times*, 18 and 25 Nov. 1929.
53. *Cape Times*, 18 Nov. 1929.
54. Smuts to S. M. Smuts, 29 Dec. 1929, S.P., V. 435–7.
55. Lugard to Smuts, 24 Jan. 1930, S.P., V. 439.
56. Weizmann to Smuts, 28 Nov. 1929, S.P., V. 426–31.
57. Smuts to T. W. Lamont, 22 Jan. 1930, S.P., V. 437.
58. Speech by Smuts, 1930, S.P., V. 439–52.
59. Smuts to M. C. Gillett, 28 Feb. 1930, S.P., V. 452–3.
60. Smuts to M. C. Gillett, 7 Mar. 1930, S.P., V. 453–4.
61. M. C. Gillett to Smuts, 26 Mar. 1930, S.P., V. 456–7.
62. Smuts to M. C. Gillett, 8 Apr. 1930, S.P., V. 458.
63. Smuts to M. C. Gillett, 30 Apr. 1930, S.P., V. 459–60.
64. Smuts to J. R. MacDonald, 22 Oct. 1930, S.P., V. 460–1.
65. Smuts to Lloyd George, 22 Oct. 1930, S.P., V. 461.
66. MacDonald to Smuts, 23 Oct. 1930, S.P., V. 461–3.
67. Smuts to MacDonald, 24 Oct. 1930, S.P., V. 463.
68. Smuts to M. C. Gillett, 25 Nov. 1930, S.P., V. 464–6.
69. Smuts to M. C. Gillett, 17 Dec. 1930, S.P., V. 467–9.
70. Smuts to M. C. Gillett, 19 Feb. 1931, S.P., V. 471.
71. Address by Smuts, 23 Sept. 1931, S.P., V. 474–91.
72. Smuts to Duncan, 17 Sept. 1931, UCT, BC294, D1.35.27.
73. Smuts to S. M. Smuts, 6 Oct. 1931, S.P., V. 494–5.
74. Smuts to Duncan, 4 Nov. 1931, UCT, BC294, D1.35.28.
75. Smuts to Philip Kerr, 14 Nov. 1931, SANA, A1, 289. 311.
76. Smuts to Kerr, 14 Dec. 1931, SANA, A1, 289. 312.
77. Smuts to M. C. Gillett, 5 Jan. 1932, S.P., V. 503–4.
78. Smuts to Amery, 3 Feb. 1932, SANA, A1, 234. 177.
79. Duncan to Lady Selborne, 22 Jan. 1932, UCT, BC294, D5.24.3.
80. Duncan to Lady Selborne, 15, 22, 29 Jan. and 4 Feb. 1932, UCT, BC294, D5.24.2–5.
81. Duncan to Lady Selborne, 29 Jan. 1932, UCT, BC294, D5.24.4.
82. Duncan to Lady Selborne, 28 Apr. 1932, UCT, BC294, D5.24.17.
83. Duncan to Lady Selborne, 16 Aug. 1933, UCT, BC294, D5.25.27.
84. Duncan to Lady Selborne, 3 Mar. 1932, UCT, BC294, D5.24.9.
85. Smuts to D. F. Malan, 13 Apr. 1932, SANA, A1, 234. 193.
86. Nicholls to Smuts, 3 and 4 June 1932, SANA, A1, 234.156.
87. Duncan to Smuts, 13 June 1932, S.P., V. 512–13.
88. Duncan to Lady Selborne, 19 Oct. 1932, UCT, BC294, D5.24.24.
89. Smuts to Nicholls, 14 Nov. 1932, S.P., V. 523–4.
90. Smuts to G. B. van Zyl, 15 Nov. 1932, S.P., V. 525.
91. Duncan to Lady Selborne, 25 Oct. 1932, UCT, BC294, D5.24.25.
92. Duncan to Lady Selborne, 14 Dec. 1932, UCT, BC294, D5.24.30.
93. SANA, A1, 108. 1.
94. Smuts to Duncan, 24 Oct. 1932, UCT, BC294, D1.35.31.
95. Duncan to Lady Selborne, 16 Nov. 1932, UCT, BC294, D5.24.38.
96. Smuts to Morris Kentridge, 8 Dec. 1932, SANA, A1, 234. 210A.

97. Duncan to Lady Selborne, 28 Dec. 1932, UCT, BC294, D5.24.31.
98. C. M. van den Heever, *General J. B. M. Hertzog*, A. P. B. Bookstore, Johannesburg, 1946, 236–47.
99. Duncan to Lady Selborne, 8 Mar. 1933, UCT, BC294, D5.25.9.
100. Duncan to Lady Selborne, 17 Feb. 1933, UCT, BC294, D5.25.6.
101. Duncan to Lady Selborne, 15 Mar. 1933, UCT, BC294, D5.25.10.
102. Duncan to Lady Selborne, 29 Mar. 1933, UCT, BC294, D5.25.12.
103. Smuts to M. C. Gillett, 29 Mar. 1933, S.P., V. 551–2.

Chapter 8: The collaborator

1. Smuts to G. G. A. Murray, 20 Apr. 1933, S.P., V. 557–8.
2. SANA, A1, 235. 99, 122, 123, 128 and 131.
3. SANA, A1, 235. 27.
4. Duncan to Lady Selborne, 4 June 1933, UCT, BC294, D5.25.19.
5. Duncan to Lady Selborne, 30 Aug. 1933, UCT, BC294, D5.25.29.
6. Duncan to Lady Selborne, 12 July 1933, UCT, BC294, D5.25.23.
7. Smuts to M. C. Gillett, 5 Sept. 1933, S.P., V. 565–6.
8. van den Heever, *General J. B. M. Hertzog*, 248–67.
9. Duncan to Lady Selborne, 11 Oct. 1933, UCT, BC294, D5.25.34.
10. Smuts to Hertzog, 18 Feb. 1934, S.P., V. 573–5.
11. Hertzog to Smuts, 18 Feb. 1934, S.P., V. 575–6.
12. Duncan to Lady Selborne, 11 Mar. 1934, UCT, BC294, D5.26.5.
13. Duncan to Lady Selborne, 19 Apr. 1934, UCT, BC294, D5.26.10.
14. Duncan to Lady Selborne, 29 Mar. 1934, UCT, BC294, D5.26.7.
15. Smuts to Amery, 1 Feb. 1934, S.P., V, 571–3, and Duncan to Lady Selborne, 13 June 1934, UCT, BC294, D5.26.19.
16. Duncan to Lady Selborne, 15 July 1934, UCT, BC294, D5.26.21.
17. Duncan to Lady Selborne, 25 July 1934, UCT, BC294, D5.26.22.
18. Duncan to Lady Selborne, 1 Aug. and 19 Sept. 1934, UCT, BC294, D5.26.23 and 29.
19. Duncan to Lady Selborne, 10 May and 3 Oct. 1934, UCT, BC294, D5.26.14 and 31.
20. Benson, *The African Patriots*, 68–77.
21. Duncan to Lady Selborne, 6 Dec. 1934, UCT, BC294, D5.26.39.
22. S.P., V. 608–21.
23. Violet Bonham-Carter to Smuts, 29 Oct. 1934, SANA, A1, 236. 34, and Smuts to M. C. Gillett, 14 Dec. 1934, S.P., VI. 5 – 7.
24. Smuts to M. C. Gillett, 10 Dec. 1934, S.P., VI. 4–5.
25. Smuts to M. C. Gillett, 23 Feb. 1935, S.P., VI. 9–12.
26. Jabavu to Smuts, undated, S.P., VI. 12–13.
27. Smuts to M. C. Gillett, 23 Feb. 1935, S.P., VI. 9–12.
28. Duncan's address at a meeting of the standing committee of the Empire Parliamentary Association, 30 May 1935, UCT, BC294, A62.
29. Duncan to Professor R. F. Alfred Hoernlé, 7 Jan. 1936, UCT, BC294, A5.8.8.
30. Duncan's notebook entry for 8 July 1938, UCT, BC294, C15.4.5.
31. R. Stuttaford to Hertzog, 10 July 1935, SANA, A1, 121. 7.
32. SANA, A1, 122. 9.
33. Benson, *The African Patriots*, 78–84.
34. Smuts to M. C. Gillett, 24 Jan. 1936, S.P., VI. 31–2.
35. Smuts to M. C. Gillett, 30 Mar. 1936, S.P., VI. 32–3.
36. Smuts to M. C. Gillett, 6 Dec. 1937, S.P., VI. 107–8.
37. Ibid.
38. John Martin to minister of mines, 8 Jan. 1935, SANA, A1, 120. 1.

39. John Martin to minister of mines, 16 Feb. 1935, SANA, A1, 120. 15.
40. SANA, A1, 123. 3.
41. Smuts to M. C. Gillett, 15 May 1937, S.P., VI. 78.
42. Smuts to M. C. Gillett, 3 Apr. 1937, S.P., VI. 68–71.
43. Smuts to M. C. Gillett, 25 Sept. 1937, S.P., VI. 91–3.
44. Smuts to M. C. Gillett, 23 Oct. 1937, S.P., VI. 99–100.
45. H. C. Lugg, Dept. of Native Affairs, Pietermaritzburg, to D. L. Smit, secretary for native affairs, 19 Nov. 1937, SANA, A1, 125. 44.
46. Smuts to M. C. Gillett, 23 Oct. 1937, S.P., VI. 99–100.
47. Smuts to M. C. Gillett, 14 Dec. 1934, S.P., VI. 5–7.
48. Smuts to Lord Lothian (formerly Philip Kerr), 20 Feb. 1935, S.P., VI. 7–9.
49. Smuts to M. C. Gillett, 23 Feb. 1935, S.P., VI. 9–12.
50. Smuts to Amery, 15 Mar. 1935, S.P., VI. 13–14.
51. Smuts to A. B. Gillett, 23 Mar. 1935, S.P., VI. 14–15.
52. Smuts to M. C. Gillett, 23 Mar. 1935, S.P., VI. 15–16.
53. Smuts to Lothian, 5 July 1935, SANA, A1, 289. 319.
54. Smuts to A. B. and M. C. Gillett, 5 Aug. 1935, S.P., VI. 21–3.
55. Smuts to M. C. Gillett, 10 and 16 Sept. 1935, S.P., VI. 24–6.
56. Smuts to M. C. Gillett, 30 Sept. 1935, S.P., VI. 27–8.
57. Amery to Smuts, 3 Oct. 1935, S.P., VI. 28–9.
58. Smuts to Amery, 2 Dec. 1935, S.P., VI. 29–31.
59. Smuts to Lothian, 24 Mar. 1936, SANA, A1, 289. 320.
60. Smuts to M. C. Gillett, 19 Apr. 1936, S.P., VI. 33–5.
61. Smuts to Lothian, 22 June 1936, SANA, A1, 289. 321.
62. Amery to Smuts, 22 June 1936, S.P., VI. 43–5.
63. U.G. No. 36, 1936, paras. 392–3, SANA, A1, 124. 33.
64. Memorandum by a deputation appointed to wait upon the government of South Africa for the purpose of conveying the resolution of the legislative assembly dated 29 Nov. 1934, and negotiating thereon. 28 July 1936, SANA, A1, 213. 49.
65. Smuts to Lothian, 7 Nov. 1937, SANA, A1, 289. 323.
66. Smuts to S. G. Millin, 12 Nov. 1937, S.P., VI. 101.
67. Jewish Board of Deputies to Hertzog, 1 July 1936, SANA, A1, 123. 44.
68. Duncan to Lady Selborne, 31 Oct. 1933, UCT, BC294, D5.25.37.
69. H. D. J. Bodenstein to Jewish Board of Deputies, 19 Aug. 1936, SANA, A1, 123. 53.
70. Hertzog to Creswell, 17 Aug. 1936, SANA, A3, I. 149–50.
71. Smuts to Amery, 23 July 1936, S.P., VI. 53–5.
72. Smuts to Lloyd George, 23 July 1936, S.P., VI. 55–7.
73. Smuts to M. C. Gillett, 27 July 1936, and Smuts to A. B. Gillett, 7 Sept. 1936, S.P., VI. 57–9 and 63–5.
74. 6 Dec. 1936, SANA, A1, 124. 26.
75. Smuts to Lothian, 7 Apr. 1937, S.P., VI. 71–5.
76. Lothian to Smuts, 14 May 1937, S.P., VI. 77.
77. Smuts to M. C. Gillett, 25 Sept. 1937, S.P., VI. 91–3.
78. Smuts to A. B. Gillett, 2 Oct. 1937, S.P., VI. 93–4.
79. Smuts to T. W. Lamont, 21 Oct. 1937, S.P., VI. 97–9.
80. Smuts to S. G. Millin, 6 Sept. 1937, S.P., VI. 89–90.
81. Smuts to M. C. Gillett, 6 Dec. 1937, S.P., VI. 107–10.
82. Smuts to Amery, 9 Dec. 1937, S.P., VI. 110–13.
83. Smuts to F. Lamont, 13 Mar. 1938, S.P., VI. 116–20.
84. Smuts to Amery, 9 Dec. 1937, S.P., VI. 110–13.
85. Smuts to Lothian, 20 May 1938, S.P., VI. 127–30.

86. Resolution by English-speaking members, 26 July 1938, SANA, A1, 127. 12.
87. Saul Solomon to ?, 12 Oct. 1939, SANA, A1, 246. 18.
88. Smuts to S. G. Millin, 14 Sept. 1938, S.P., VI. 137–8.
89. Smuts to Sir J. Power, hon treasurer, Royal Institute of International Affairs, 15 Sept. 1938, S.P., VI. 139–40.
90. Smuts to Cecil, 6 Dec. 1938, S.P., VI. 144–7.
91. Hankey to Smuts, 29 Dec. 1938, S.P., VI. 147–8.
92. Smuts to A. B. Gillett, 10 Mar. 1939, S.P., VI. 153–4, and Smuts to M. C. Gillett, 17 Mar. 1939, S.P., VI. 154–6.
93. Smuts to M. C. Gillett, 6 Apr. 1939, S.P., VI. 158–60.
94. Smuts to M. C. Gillett, 27 May 1939, S.P., VI. 166–8.
95. Y. M. Dadoo, leader of the Nationalist Group of the Transvaal Indian Congress, to the secretary to the minister of justice, 10 July 1939, SANA, A1, 131. 7.
96. Viceroy to Governor-General, 16 June 1939, SANA, A1, 131. 6.
97. Gandhi to Smuts, 16 July 1939, S.P., VI. 171.
98. Duncan, memorandum, UCT, BC294, A27.1.
99. Saul Solomon to ?, 12 Oct. 1939, SANA, A1, 246. 18.
100. *House of Assembly Debates*, Vol. 36, 17 ff.
101. Duncan, memorandum, 6 Sept. 1939, UCT, BC294, A27.2.
102. Duncan to Hertzog, 5 Sept. 1939, UCT, BC294, A27.3.
103. Hertzog to Duncan, and Duncan to Hertzog, 5 Sept. 1939, UCT, BC294, A27.4 and 5.
104. Duncan to Lady Duncan, 5 Sept. 1939, UCT, BC294, E10.19.5.
105. Saul Solomon to ?, 12 Oct. 1939, SANA, A1, 246. 18.
106. Ibid.

Chapter 9: Prime minister again

1. QMG to CGS, 3 Mar. 1939, SANA, A1, 130. 2.
2. Smuts to M. C. Gillett, 13 Sept. 1939, SANA, A1, 246. 222.
3. Smuts to M. C. Gillett, 21 Sept. 1939, S.P., VI. 192–4.
4. Smuts to Stuttaford, 14 Oct. 1939, S.P., VI. 195–6.
5. British High Commissioner to prime minister, 26 Sept. 1939, SANA, A1, 131. 44.
6. Smuts to British High Commissioner, and Smuts to H. M. Government, 28 Sept. 1939, SANA, A1, 131. 49 and 50.
7. Smuts to J. Martin, 30 Nov. 1939, S.P., VI. 200–1.
8. Smuts to F. Lamont, 22 Dec. 1939, S.P., VI. 205–7.
9. Smuts to M. C. Gillett, 24 Jan. 1940, S.P., VI. 209–12.
10. *House of Assembly Debates*, Vol. 37, 1220 ff., and Vol. 38, 4063 ff.
11. Smuts to M. C. Gillett, 12 May 1940, S.P., VI. 221–4.
12. Smuts to M. C. Gillett, 24 June 1940, S.P., VI. 239–41.
13. Smuts to Lothian, 23 July 1940, SANA, A1, 289. 328.
14. Smuts's broadcast, 21 July 1940, S.P., VI. 244–8.
15. Smuts to Duncan, 16 Sept. 1940, S.P., VI. 251–3.
16. Amery to Smuts, 16 Oct. 1940, S.P., VI. 255–6.
17. Smuts to M. C. Gillett, 5 Nov. 1940, S.P., VI. 257–9.
18. Smuts to T. W. Lamont, 8 Nov. 1940, S.P., VI. 259–60.
19. Brebner to Creswell, 10 Jan. 1941, SANA, A3, I. 153.
20. Brebner to Creswell, 19 Jan. 1945, SANA, A3, I. 154.
21. Smuts to Hertzog, 13 Dec. 1940, S.P., VI. 266.
22. Speech broadcast in Britain, 31 Dec. 1940, S.P., VI. 269–74.
23. Smuts to Cranborne, 2 Jan. 1941, S.P., VI. 274–6.

24. Smuts to M. C. Gillett, 6 Jan. 1941, S.P., VI. 276–9.
25. Smuts to M. C. Gillett, 14 Apr. 1941, S.P., VI. 287–8.
26. Linlithgow to Smuts, 21 Apr. 1941, S.P., VI. 291–2.
27. Smuts to M. C. Gillett, 18 May 1941, S.P., VI. 295–8.
28. Smuts to Wavell, 19 May 1941, S.P., VI. 298–300.
29. Smuts to Wavell, 30 June 1941, S.P., VI. 310–11.
30. Smuts to M. C. Gillett, 23 Sept. 1941, S.P., VI. 320–2.
31. Margaret Ballinger to Smuts, 31 Oct. 1941, S.P., VI. 323–4.
32. Address by Smuts, 21 Jan. 1942, S.P., VI. 331–43.
33. Smuts to M. C. Gillett, 23 Jan. 1942, S.P., VI. 343–6.
34. Smuts to M. C. Gillett, 15 Feb. 1941, S.P., VI. 350–2.
35. Smuts to M. C. Gillett, 13 Dec. 1941, S.P., VI. 327–9.
36. Smuts to M. C. Gillett, 15 Feb. 1942, S.P., VI. 350–2.
37. Smuts to M. C. Gillett, 31 Jan. 1942, S.P., VI. 346–9.
38. Smuts to J. Martin, 26 Feb. 1942, S.P., VI. 354.
39. Smuts to M. C. Gillett, 10 Mar. 1942, S.P., VI. 356–9.
40. Smuts to Roosevelt, 19 May 1942, S.P., VI. 363–5.
41. Smuts to M. C. Gillett, 7 June 1942, S.P., VI. 365–8.
42. Waterson to Smuts, 24 June 1942, UCT, BC631, A3.9.48.
43. Waterson to Smuts, 9 July 1942, UCT, BC631, A3.9.50.
44. Smuts to Waterson, ? July 1942, UCT, BC631, A3.9.51.
45. Smuts to M. C. Gillett, 10 July 1942, S.P., VI. 371–3.
46. Smuts to F. H. Theron, 21 July 1942, S.P., VI. 373–7.
47. Smuts to M. C. Gillett, 10 Aug. 1942, S.P., VI. 377–80.
48. Smuts to M. C. Gillett, 10 July 1942, S.P., VI. 371–3.
49. Smuts to M. C. Gillett, 24 Sept. 1942, S.P., VI. 387–90.
50. Smuts to T. W. Lamont, 14 Aug. 1942, S.P., VI. 380–1.
51. Smuts to Trygve Lie, 12 Nov. 1942, S.P., VI. 392–3.
52. W. S. Churchill, *The Second World War*, Cassell, London, Vol. IV, 1951, 559–69.
53. Smuts to Churchill, 20 Nov. 1942, quoted in Churchill, *The Second World War*, IV. 569–70.
54. Friends of Africa to Smuts, 5 Jan. 1943, S.P., VI. 401–5.
55. Benson, *The African Patriots*, 98–9.
56. Smuts to M. C. Gillett, 13 Jan. 1943, S.P., VI. 407–9.
57. Smuts to M. C. Gillett, 22 Feb. 1943, S.P., VI. 414–7.
58. Smuts to M. C. Gillett, 13 Jan. 1943, S.P., VI. 407–9.
59. Smuts to M. C. Gillett, 15 Apr. 1943, S.P., VI. 424–6.
60. D. M. Buchanan, a Cape lawyer, to Smuts, 9 Apr. 1943, S.P., VI. 424.
61. Smuts to M. C. Gillett, 9 June 1943, S.P., VI. 435–7.
62. Smuts to King George of Greece, 4 June 1943, S.P., VI. 433–5.
63. Smuts to Churchill, 20 Aug. 1944, quoted in Churchill, *The Second World War*, V. 474–5.
64. Smuts to M. C. Gillett, 4 July 1943, S.P., VI. 437–40.
65. H. Kenny, *Architect of Apartheid*, Jonathan Ball, Johannesburg, 1980, 66–8.
66. Smuts to Churchill, 31 Aug. and 3 Sept. 1943, quoted in Churchill, *The Second World War*, VI. 112–4.
67. Churchill to Eisenhower, 21 Sept. 1943, quoted in Churchill, *The Second World War*, VI. 132.
68. S.P., VI. 456–69.
69. Amery to Smuts, 15 Dec. 1943, S.P., VI. 469–72.
70. Benson, *The African Patriots*, 100–1.
71. Ibid., 111–12.
72. Ibid., 113–15.

73. Speech by Smuts, 11 Oct. 1944, S.P., VI. 493–504.
74. Smuts to Amery, 20 Dec. 1944, S.P., VI. 515–16.
75. Smuts to M. C. Gillett, 22 Nov. 1944, S.P., VI. 509–12.
76. Smuts to Weizmann, 14 Nov. 1944, S.P., VI. 507–8.
77. Smuts to T. W. Lamont, 4 Jan. 1945, S.P., VI..518–20.
78. Amery to Smuts, 9 Feb. 1945, S.P., VI. 523–4.
79. Smuts to J. H. Hofmeyr, 6 May 1945, S.P., VI. 533–4.
80. Smuts to M. C. Gillett, 10 Aug. 1945, S.P., VI. 548–50.
81. Smuts to Amery, 27 Sept. 1945, S.P., VII. 9–10.
82. Smuts to M. C. Gillett, 15 Oct. 1945, S.P., VII. 13–15.
83. Scott to Smuts, 19 Feb. 1946, SANA, A1, 270. 9, and Smuts to Scott, 7 Mar. 1946, SANA, A1, 270. 74.
84. Smuts to M. C. Gillett, 9 Mar. 1946, S.P., VII. 46–9.
85. Benson, *The African Patriots*, 121–3.
86. Ibid., 115–18.
87. Statement by Smuts, 1946, S.P., VII. 27–31.
88. Smuts to M. C. Gillett, 23 June 1946, S.P., VII. 59–61.
89. Smuts to M. C. Gillett, 24 July 1946, S.P., VII. 63–4.
90. Smuts to secretary to the prime minister, Pretoria, 18 Sept. 1946, SANA, A1, 270. 121.
91. Benson, *The African Patriots*, 134–7.
92. Duncan Sandys to Smuts, 18 Oct. 1946, SANA, A1, 270. 4.
93. Smuts to M. C. Gillett, 27 Oct. 1946, S.P., VII. 101–3.
94. Benson, *The African Patriots*, 138–41.
95. Lief Egeland, South African ambassador in Brussels, to Smuts, 28 and 31 Oct. 1946, SANA, A1, 268. 131 and 132.
96. Smuts to M. C. Gillett, 26 Dec. 1946, S.P., VII. 112–14.
97. P. R. Digby to Hofmeyr, 15 Nov. 1946, SANA, A1, 268. 124.
98. Smuts to M. C. Gillett, 17 Nov. 1946, S.P., VII. 109–11.
99. Malcomess to Smuts, 16 Dec. 1946, SANA, A1. 269, 128.
100. Smuts to M. C. Gillett, 14 Jan. 1947, S.P., VII. 115–18.
101. Smuts to Sir John Latham, former chief justice of Australia, 12 Feb. 1947, S.P., VII. 124.
102. Smuts to Daphne Moore, 2 Mar. 1947, S.P., VII. 125–6.
103. Smuts to M. C. Gillett, 16 Mar. 1947, S.P., VII. 127–8.
104. Smuts to F. Lamont, 31 Mar. 1947, S.P., VII. 129–31.
105. Smuts to Daphne Moore, 18 May 1947, S.P., VII. 136–7.
106. Smuts to Nehru, 16 June 1947, S.P., VII. 148–50.
107. Benson, *The African Patriots*, 141–5.
108. Smuts to M. C. Gillett, 24 Jan. 1948, S.P., VII. 174–6.
109. Wellington to Smuts, 5 Oct. 1947, SANA, A1, 274. 257.
110. Speech by Smuts, 1948, S.P., VII. 199–203.
111. Smuts to M. C. Gillett, 24 Jan. 1948, S.P., VII. 174–6.
112. Smuts to M. C. Gillett, 26 Aug. 1948, S.P., VII. 225–6.
113. Smuts to Daphne Moore, 8 Apr. 1948, S.P., VII. 193–5.
114. R. E. Bell, United Party member of parliament, to Smuts, 28 May 1948, S.P., VII. 204–5.

Chapter 10: Epilogue

1. Smuts to Daphne Moore, 8 June 1948, S.P., VII. 209–11.
2. Smuts to M. C. Gillett, 28 June 1948, S.P., VII. 212–13.
3. Smuts to Churchill, 27 Sept. 1948, S.P., VII. 248–50.
4. Malherbe to Smuts, 8 Sept. 1948, S.P., VII. 237–45.

5.   Smuts to Malherbe, 13 Sept. 1948, S.P., VII. 246.
6.   Smuts to M. C. Gillett, 22 Mar. 1949, S.P., VII. 286–7.
7.   Smuts to K. Howarde-Browne, 26 Sept. 1949, S.P., VII. 310–11.
8.   Amery to Smuts, 2 May 1949, S.P., VII. 290–1.
9.   Smuts to Churchill, 23 May 1949, S.P., VII. 299–300.
10.   Smuts to Major-General W. H. E. Poole, 26 July 1949, S.P., VII. 303.
11.   Speech by Smuts, 27 Nov. 1949, S.P., VII. 313–21.
12.   Speech by Smuts, 16 Dec. 1949, S.P., VII. 327–32.
13.   Smuts to S. G. Millin, 20 Dec. 1949, S.P., VII. 332–3.
14.   Smuts to Churchill, 16 Mar. 1950, S.P., VII. 348–9.
15.   Smuts to M. C. Gillett, 17 Apr. 1950, S.P., VII. 352–3.
16.   Smuts to M. C. Gillett, 22 Apr. 1950, S.P., VII. 354–5.

Select bibliography

Unpublished sources

South African National Archives, Pretoria
The Smuts Collection. These papers have been recatalogued in a different form
  since Sir Keith Hancock and Dr Jean van der Poel published their excellent
  selection of Smuts's correspondence.
The Creswell Collection. The collection contains a number of letters to and from
  J. B. M. Hertzog.

University of Cape Town Library
The Sir Patrick Duncan Collection
The S. F. Waterson Collection

The British Library
The Campbell-Bannerman Papers

Published sources

Primary works
Brand, R. H., *The Union of South Africa*, Clarendon Press, Oxford, 1909.
Buckle, G. E. (ed.), *The Letters of Queen Victoria, Third Series, 1896–1901*, John
  Murray, London, 1932.
Duminy, A. H. and Guest, W. R. (eds), *Fitzpatrick, South African Politician,
  Selected Papers, 1888–1906*, McGraw Hill, Johannesburg, 1976.
Hancock, W. K. and van der Poel, J. (eds), *Selections from the Smuts Papers*,
  Cambridge University Press, vols 1–4, 1966, vols 5–7 (van der Poel only), 1973.
Headlam, C. (ed.), *The Milner Papers*, Cassell, London, 2 vols. 1931, 1936.
Lewson, P. (ed.), *Selections from the Correspondence of J. X. Merriman*, The Van
  Riebeeck Society, Cape Town, 4 vols., 1960, 1963, 1966, 1969.
Preller, J. F. (ed.), *Die Konvensie-Dagboek van sy edelagbare François Stephanus
  Malan, 1908–1909*, The Van Riebeeck Society, Cape Town, 1951.
Smuts, J. C., *A Century of Wrong*, Review of Reviews Office, London, 1899.
—— *Africa and Some World Problems, including the Rhodes Memorial Lectures 1929*,
  Clarendon Press, Oxford, 1930.
—— *Greater South Africa, Plans for a Better World : The Speeches of J. C. Smuts*,
  Truth Legion, Johannesburg, 1940.
—— *Holism and Evolution*, Macmillan, London, 1926.

—— *Walt Whitman: A Study in the Evolution of Personality*, Wayne State University, 1973.

'Vindex', *Cecil Rhodes, the Political Life and Speeches, 1881–1900*, Chapman and Hall, London, 1900.

Wilson, T. (ed.), *The Political Diaries of C. P. Scott, 1911–1928*, Collins, London, 1970.

Newspapers:
Cape Argus
Cape Times
Natal Mercury
Natal Witness
Observer
The Times

Secondary works

Amery, J., *The Life of Joseph Chamberlain*, Macmillan, London, vol. 4, 1951.

Armstrong, H. C., *Grey Steel: A Study in Arrogance*, A. Barker, London, 1937.

Baker, R. S., *Woodrow Wilson and World Settlement*, Doubleday, Page, New York, 1922.

Baruch, B. M., *The Making of the Reparation and Economic Sections of the Treaty*, Harper, London, 1920.

Beer, G. L., *African Questions at the Paris Peace Conference*, Macmillan, New York, 1923.

Benson, M., *The African Patriots*, Faber and Faber, London, 1963.

Bunting, B., *Moses Katane, A Political Biography*, Inkululeko Publications, London, 1975.

Carsten, F. L. *The Rise of Fascism*, Batsford, London, 1967.

Chanock, M., *Unconsummated Union, Britain, Rhodesia and South Africa, 1900–1945*, Manchester University Press, 1977.

Churchill, W. S., *The Second World War*, Cassell, London, 6 vols, 1948–54.

Coleman, F. (ed.), *Economic History of South Africa*, Haum, Pretoria, 1983.

Crowe, J. H. V., *General Smuts' Campaign in East Africa*, Murray, London, 1918.

Davenport, T. R. H., *South Africa, a Modern History*, Macmillan, London, 1977.

—— *The Afrikaner Bond*, Oxford University Press, Cape Town, 1966.

Dawson, W. H., *Germany under the Treaty*, Allen and Unwin, London, 1933.

Doke, J. K., *M. K. Gandhi: An Indian Patriot in South Africa*, The London Indian Chronicle, London, 1909.

Engelenburg, E. F. V., *General Louis Botha*, Harrap, London, 1929.

Friedman, B., *Smuts, a Reappraisal*, Allen and Unwin, London, 1975.

Gandhi, M. K., *Satyagraha in South Africa*, Navajivan Publishing Company, Ahmedabad, 1928.

Garvin, J. L., *The Life of Joseph Chamberlain*, Macmillan, London, vol. 3, 1934.

Gathorne-Hardy, G. M., *A Short History of International Affairs, 1920–1939*, Oxford University Press, 1950.

Lloyd George, D., *The Truth about Reparations and War-Debts*, Heinemann, London, 1932.

—— *The Truth about the Peace Treaties*, Victor Gollancz, London, 2 vols, 1938.

—— *War Memoirs*, Ivor Nicholson and Watson, London, vols 3–4, 1934, vols 5–6, 1936.

Hancock, W. K., *Smuts: The Sanguine Years*, Cambridge University Press, 1962.

—— *Smuts: The Fields of Force*, Cambridge University Press, 1968.

Hellman, E. and Lever, H. (eds), *Race Relations in South Africa, 1929–1979*, Macmillan, London, 1980.

Hobson, J. A., *The South African War, its Causes and Effects*, Nisbet, London, 1900.

Hofmeyr, J. H., *The Life of Jan Hendrik Hofmeyr*, Van de Sandt de Villiers Printing Company, Cape Town, 1913.

Hutt, W. H., *The Economics of the Colour Bar*, Andre Deutsch, London, 1964.

Huttenback, R. A., *Gandhi in South Africa: British Imperialism and the Indian Question, 1860–1914*, Cornell University Press, 1971.

Hyam, R., *Elgin and Churchill at the Colonial Office*, Macmillan, London, 1968.

—— *The Failure of South African Expansion, 1908–1948*, Macmillan, London, 1972.

Jordan, W. M., *Great Britain, France and the German Problem, 1918–1939*, Frank Cass, London, 1971.

Kenny, H., *Architect of Apartheid*, Jonathan Ball, Johannesburg, 1980.

Keynes, J. M., *The Economic Consequences of the Peace*, Macmillan, London, 1922.

—— *The Revision of the Treaty*, Macmillan, London, 1922.

Krüger, D. W., *The Making of a Nation: A History of the Union of South Africa, 1910–1961*, Macmillan, London, 1969.

Kruger, P., *The Memoirs of Paul Kruger*, T. Fisher Unwin, London, 2 vols, 1902.

Kubicek, R. V., *Economic Imperialism in Theory and Practice*, Duke University Press, Durham N.C., 1979.

Lentin, A., *Lloyd George, Woodrow Wilson and the Guilt of Germany*, Leicester University Press, 1984.

Lewsen, P., *John X. Merriman*, Yale University Press, 1982.

Liska, G., *Russian and World Order: Strategic Choices and the Laws of Power in History*, The Johns Hopkins University Press, 1980.

Lockhart, J. G. and Woodhouse, C. M., *Rhodes*, Hodder and Stoughton, London, 1963.

Marais, J. S., *The Fall of Kruger's Republic*, Clarendon Press, Oxford, 1962.

Marks, S., *Reluctant Rebellion: The 1906–1908 Disturbances in Natal*, Clarendon Press, Oxford, 1970.

Meintjes, J., *President Paul Kruger*, Cassell, London, 1974.

Millin, S. G., *General Smuts*, Faber and Faber, London, 2 vols, 1936.

Neame, L. E., *General Hertzog*, Hurst and Blackett, London, 1930.

Odendaal, A., *Vulkani Bantu: The Beginnings of Black Protest Politics in South Africa to 1912*, David Philip, Cape Town and Johannesburg, 1984.

O'Meara, D., *Volkskapitalisme: Class, Capital and Ideology in the Development of African Nationalism, 1934–1948*, Cambridge University Press, 1983.

Pachai, B., *The South African Indian Question*, C. Struik, Cape Town, 1971.

Pakenham, T., *The Boer War*, Weidenfeld and Nicolson, London, 1979.

Paton, A., *Hofmeyr*, Oxford University Press, Cape Town, 1964.

Pillay, B., *British Indians in the Transvaal: Trade, Politics and Imperial Relations, 1885–1906*, Longman, London, 1976.

Rich, P. B., *White Power and the Liberal Conscience: Racial Segregation and South African Liberalism, 1921–1960*, Manchester University Press, 1984.

Roux, E. and Roux, W., *Rebel Pity: The Life of Eddie Roux*, Rex Collings, London, 1970.

Smuts, J. C., *Jan Christian Smuts*, Cassell, London, 1952.

Swan, M., 'The Natal Indian Strike', *Journal of Southern African Studies*, 10, 2 (1984), 239–58.

Thompson, L. M., *The Unification of South Africa, 1902–1910*, Clarendon Press, Oxford, 1960.

Tillman, S. P., *Anglo-American Relations at the Paris Peace Conference of 1919*, Princeton University Press, 1961.

van den Heever, C. M., *General J. B. M. Hertzog*, A. P. B. Bookstore, Johannesburg, 1946.

van der Poel, J., *The Jameson Raid*, Oxford University Press, London, 1951.

von Glaise-Horstenau, E. (trans. Ian F. D. Morrow), *The Collapse of the Austro-Hungarian Empire*, Dent, London and Toronto, 1930.

von Lettow-Worbeck, P. E., *My Reminiscences of East Africa*, Hurst and Blackett, London, 1920.

Walker, E. A., *W. P. Schreiner*, Oxford University Press, London, 1937, reprinted 1969.

Walsh, P., *The Rise of African Nationalism in South Africa: The African National Congress, 1912–1952*, C. Hurst, London, 1970.

Welsh, D., *The Roots of Segregation; Native Policy in Colonial Natal, 1845–1910*, Oxford University Press, London, 1971.

Wheeler-Bennett, J. W. and Nicholls, A., *The Semblance of Peace: The Political Settlement after the Second World War*, Macmillan, London, 1972.

Willan, B., *Sol. Plaatje, South African Nationalist, 1876–1932*, Heinemann, London, 1984.

Young, F. B., *Marching on Tanga: With Smuts in East Africa*, Collins, London, 1919.

Index